T0385568

Exploring

ECCLESIASTES

THE JOHN PHILLIPS COMMENTARY SERIES

Exploring
ECCLESIASTES

An Expository Commentary

JOHN PHILLIPS

with Jim Hastings

Kregel
Publications

Exploring Ecclesiastes: An Expository Commentary
© 2019 by Betty Phillips

Published by Kregel Publications, a division of Kregel Inc., 2450 Oak Industrial Dr. NE, Grand Rapids, MI 49505.

All Scripture quotations are from the Authorized Version of the Bible (kjv).

ISBN 978-0-8254-2561-5, print
ISBN 978-0-8254-7637-2, epub

Printed in the United States of America
19 20 21 22 23 24 25 26 27 28 / 5 4 3 2 1

Contents

Summary Outline of Ecclesiastes

More detailed outline points can be found in the text.

PART 2: THE PREACHER'S SERMON (1:12–10:20)
  A. Things He Had Sought (1:12–2:26)
    1. His Persistent Search (1:12–2:11)
      a) The World of Thought (1:12–1:18)
      b) The World of Thrills (2:1–3)
      c) The World of Things (2:4–11)
    2. His Pessimistic Summary (2:12–26)
      a) The Barrenness of It All (2:12–16)
      b) The Bitterness of It All (2:17–26)
  B. Things He Had Seen (3:1–6:12)
    1. The Problem of Time Without Eternity (3:1–11)
      a) The Logic of Time (3:1–8)
      b) The Limitations of Time (3:9–11)
    2. The Problem of a New Leaf Without a New Life (3:12–17)
      a) The Works of the Creature (3:12–13)
      b) The Works of the Creator (3:14–17)
    3. The Problem of Mortality Without Immortality (3:18–22)
      a) A Low View of Man's Dignity (3:18–19)
      b) A Low View of Man's Destiny (3:20–21)
      c) A Low View of Man's Duty (3:22)
    4. The Problem of Might Without Right (4:1–3)
      a) A Gloomy Consideration (4:1)
      b) A Gloomy Conclusion (4:2–3)
    5. The Problem of Prosperity Without Posterity (4:4–12)
      a) The Resentful Man (4:4–5)
      b) The Realistic Man (4:6)
      c) The Ridiculous Man (4:7–12)
    6. The Problem of Sovereignty Without Sagacity (4:13–16)
      a) Unsound in His Thoughts (4:13)
      b) Unsuited to His Throne (4:14)
      c) Unsung by the Throng (4:15–16)
    7. The Problem of Religion Without Reality (5:1–7)
      a) The Value of Silence (5:1–3)
      b) The Vow Once Spoken (5:4–7)
    8. The Problem of Wealth Without Health (5:8–20)
      a) Words About the Desire for Riches (5:8–11)
      b) Words About the Deceitfulness of Riches (5:12–20)

2. Look Well to Life's Fleeting Present (11:7–8)
   a) Light Is an Enjoyable Thing (11:7)
   b) Life Is an Enjoyable Thing (11:8)
3. Look Well to Life's Frivolous Past (11:9–10)
   a) A Call to Rejoice (11:9)
   b) A Call to Despond (11:10)

B. He Relates His Conclusions About Life (12:1–14)
1. Man and His Maker (12:1)
   a) Remember Your Creator (12:1a)
   b) Remember Your Condition (12:1b)
2. Man and His Mortality (12:2–8)
   a) The Outward Permanence of the Heavenly Order of Things (12:2)
   b) The Obvious Impermanence of the Human Order of Things (12:3–8)
3. Man and His Mind (12:9–12)
   a) The Preacher's Wisdom (12:9)
   b) The Preacher's Words (12:10)
   c) The Preacher's Worth (12:11)
   d) The Preacher's Work (12:12)
4. Man and His Mission (12:13–14)
   a) Man's Supreme Duty (12:13)
   b) Man's Sobering Destiny (12:14)

Introduction

Solomon, it seems, was growing old when he wrote the book of Ecclesiastes. His wives had already turned away his heart from his earlier commitment to the living God (1 Kings 11:4). He had already faced God's anger because of his compromise with idolatry with the foulest and fiercest king of idolatry, and the sentence of judgment had come—delivered by the prophet Ahijah. He was old, too, when his protégé, the capable and ambitious Jeroboam, began to plot against him. The first snowflake, herald of the coming night.

Solomon hated the very thought of old age. Indeed, toward the end of Ecclesiastes, he graphically describes the aging process (Ecclesiastes 12:1–8). His dismay at the thought that he himself was now numbered among the aged is all the more poignant by the graphic poetry he employs to spread his farce abroad. His old age did one thing for him, it gave force to his determination to salvage something at least from the wreckage of his life. In his old age Solomon's eyes were opened and he became wise again (Ecclesiastes 12:9–10). The book of Ecclesiastes was his offering upon the altar of his repentance and remorse to make whatever amends he could. By and large, it is a wail of despair over his follies and exposure of the emptiness of secular humanism, a warning to all future generations, and an appeal to the young people before whom he had set such a terrible example not to leave God out of their lives.

Solomon might well have borrowed the language of the Gospel hymn writer:

> I tried the broken cisterns, ah!
> But how the waters failed;

> even as I stooped to drink they fled,
> and mocked me as I wailed.

And in his belated restoration to the truth, he would also have endorsed the hymn writer's antidote:

> Now none but Christ can satisfy,
> none other name for me!
> There's love and life and lasting joy,
> Christ Jesus found in thee.[1]

But even in his repentance and inspired one more time by the Holy Spirit, Solomon does not seem to rise much beyond this knowledge of God as Elohim, God of Creation. His tolerance for the pagan gods of his wives, the shrines he had countenanced for such monstrosities as Baal, Ashtoreth, Chemosh, Molech, and the rest, had left its shadow on his soul. Backsliding always leaves its mark.

John Phillips

Tribute to Dr. John Phillips

I had determined in my mind to complete a doctorate. Therefore, in the fall of 1990, I left Houston and made my way to Florida for the first day of my first class of my first semester. I arrived early to find the room lined with six-foot tables so close together that it was almost impossible to maneuver through the chairs to get a seat. Being early, I chose a seat in the front row, just to the right of the teacher's desk. The morning sun was blazing through the window, or I would have taken a chair dead center in front of the desk. The first three hours dragged on; I had been to funerals that were more exciting! Needless to say, I was thrilled when the lunch break came. I remember thinking, "What in the world am I doing here? This is ridiculous!" Most of my classmates went out to eat in groups together, but because I did not know anyone, I remained in the room through the break. To tell the truth, most of my classmates that I did, in fact, know—from a distance at least—were all well on their way to being in the "Who's Who" of the Christian faith—some of them were pastors with their services on nationwide television at the time. I must say, I was a little intimidated by most of them!

As the class began to reassemble, there was an explosion of excitement that I have rarely experienced in a class setting.

"Dr. Phillips is coming. Dr. Phillips is coming!"

I thought, *Who in the world is Dr. Phillips?* I was a musician, a minister of music, not a preacher! A man brought in a tabletop lectern and placed it right in front of me. My stuff began to fall on the floor, and as I was picking it up, the class began to applaud as this short man walked like a soldier around the left side of the room, across the front, and took his place right in front of me. He calmed the room and said, "Please turn to our text for today, Psalm 24." He began to speak. I was amazed! Why? Almost everyone in the class was quoting his message—as he spoke—word for word! I asked a man sitting by me, "Who is this guy?"

He said, "Oh, he is the preacher's preacher! Every preacher worth his salt uses his sermons and books."

Needless to say, by the end of his sermon, I, too, was hooked. I did not care who this man was—I, too, had to have his books! There were about sixteen in print at that time, and I had to own them all! And I did! I devoured them all. Today, I own every book he published, and I have given many sets away to young preachers through the years. In 1994, as I began to write my commentary on the Bible, I decided to mimic the writing style of Dr. Phillips. I figured that if Paul told his listeners to imitate him because he was imitating Christ, Dr. Phillips could be my Paul to imitate Christ.

Speed ahead to March 2017. Almost twenty-seven years had passed, and I was cleaning up my commentary on Ecclesiastes before sending it off to the printer. Years ago, I determined to write commentaries with what I call "low-hanging fruit." I wanted them to be low enough for a child to reach up and grab a piece of juicy fruit but not so low that the mature Christian could not reach down to obtain a piece too. I was struggling with Ecclesiastes 10:1, "Dead flies cause the ointment of the apothecary to send forth a stinking savour." I just wasn't happy with what was on the page. I thought, *I don't remember what Dr. Phillips said about that passage.* I went to my shelf and, to my surprise, my *Exploring Ecclesiastes* was not there! I looked and looked for it and could not find it anywhere. I was so puzzled. I finally decided I would buy another copy—but there was not one to be found. Here is where a strange series of events began in this journey for me.

I found www.drjohnphillips.com and hit the contact button. I put in all my information, and I fired off a note asking where I could find *Exploring Ecclesiastes* for sale. To my surprise, Mrs. Betty Phillips gave me a call. She explained that Ecclesiastes was his only uncompleted manuscript. I was shocked. I knew so much about Ecclesiastes from Dr. Phillips, I thought I could see the book in my mind's eye. It was white with red lettering, in the same binding as the first printing of his *Exploring the Love Song of Solomon.* I was just dumbfounded! A few days later, a handwritten manuscript arrived at my door with the following note.

Dear Jim,
    I have just reread your letter and I am quite excited about the possibility of working with you. Just talked with you. I obviously will not finish my

letter. I dislike the idea intensely of leaving John's book unfinished. My guess is that I came across pretty clearly to you.
Sincerely,
Betty Phillips

First of all, it wasn't my letter! Then, to my amazement, I was holding the original 216-page handwritten manuscript of Dr. Phillips. There are movies made about this kind of stuff, but I never thought it would happen to me. Obviously, I immediately called Mrs. Phillips, and she was very clear that she wanted me to attempt to "finish it."

And so, I began. First, Sam Locatelli typed the manuscript for me. Second, I reread every book of Dr. Phillips word for word and cataloged all mentions of Ecclesiastes. Third, I picked up at Ecclesiastes 5:9 where he had laid down his pen and finished the chapter. Rosemary Rayburn proofed the twenty pages of copy, and I mailed it to Mrs. Phillips for approval. (May I also mention at this point Dr. Kay Hastings, my wife, Tony Minchew, Becky French, Amber McGowen, Donna Manahan, Cookie Gouger, Karen Jones, Sally Hecker, as well as Rosemary Rayburn, who all helped with the proofing of the manuscript.) If Mrs. Phillips and the board thought it was good enough, I would continue; if not, I would stop. Mind you, there were multiple conversations going on all the while—too numerous to record here.

Word came back that I was to complete the manuscript. Then one week later a call came—an unfortunate mistake had been made. I had been confused with another young preacher who was working on the book, the one who had written the letter. To make matters worse, the original manuscript was missing. That problem was an easy fix—I sent it back immediately. The issue of the other writer was a different story.

One of Dr. Phillips' lifelong friends, who had been in contact with Mrs. Phillips, called me. He had arranged with her that his young pastor would complete the manuscript, but his phone call was not intended to bring my journey to an end; rather, his call was to convey that his young pastor friend was overwhelmed by the project and did not feel prepared for the task. By that time, the family had twenty pages of my work, and I had fifty-five pages completed in all. After more conversations, I was granted the privilege of attempting to complete the work.

Dr. Phillips had completed the outline. Without that, I would have been without direction. In one of my classes, Dr. Phillips explained how he always completed the outline before he ever began to write. He taught us how to do what he did. He taught us how to outline based on the text. He was quite concerned that many preachers wrote their sermon first and then came up with a cutesy outline that was forced to fit the message and rarely fit the text. When I saw the outline, I immediately knew what he wanted to say. All I had to do was to turn the outline into sentences and add the illustrations. To do that, I found within the other published works of Dr. Phillips 249 references to Ecclesiastes. In many of those references, he used an Ecclesiastes passage as an illustration to explain the text in the other book. For this work, I reversed the process. For instance, if he used Ecclesiastes as an example of a passage in Psalms, I used that same Psalms passage as an example in Ecclesiastes. With that method, I could be assured that I was presenting the thoughts of Dr. Phillips concerning the text at hand, at least in those passages. Of course, he had his favorite illustrations, and many times the same illustrations were duplicated in his books; thus, the new illustrations are of my choice.

It was not my intent to write like Dr. Phillips. Yet it was my intent that you would not be able to tell where he stopped and I started. Hopefully I have done that. It is not for me to pretend that I am Dr. Phillips. I've done this for the sake of the message when you take it and rework it for your congregation. The big personal illustrations taken from my life are written as if I am speaking of someone else. But then you will notice a footnote that tells you it is from my personal life.

We preachers like to speak of internal and external evidence surrounding a text of Scripture. For me, it was no different. I wanted to know why Dr. Phillips did not finish this book. He published at least thirty books after starting this one. The answer to that question resides in heaven! So I had to be satisfied with asking *when* he stopped writing the book. The specific answer to that question I can reduce to within three years.

By looking at the external evidence within his other published works, I found clues that he was at least working on the outline as early as the mid-1970s. Different portions of this outline can be found in those early works. At the other end, in 1999, he delivered a summary message called "Chasing the Wind" in which he used thirty minutes to communicate what he had completed through chapter 5, and then he spent ten minutes skipping through the rest of the outline to complete his message. That message is transcribed and attached at the end of this commentary. And by the way, I am extremely thankful to Dr. Jerry Vines for leading me to that message.

Internally, in this manuscript, he mentioned having only twenty books in print. That would take the writing to about 1995–96. Also internally, he referenced two recent articles from two magazines, one from June 1997 and the other from July 1997. No other illustration in the manuscript occurred after July of 1997.

That leads us to return to one last external piece of evidence not found in his books. By 1997, Dr. Phillips' first wife was gravely ill, and his attention turned to her. I dare say that hardly any man could pick up the pen and write about the grief of impending death found in Solomon's Ecclesiastes sermon under those same circumstances. Mrs. Jean Phillips died on January 8, 1998. Dr. Phillips would go on to marry Betty, the one who sent me the manuscript. By the way, Jean had suggested to Dr. Phillips that if he ever wanted to marry again, she hoped it would be to Betty.

When I received his handwritten manuscript, I did not change one thing about it. The outline is his, the commentary is his down to chapter 5, verse 8. After that, it has been my privilege to be Dr. Phillips' Joshua, to gather the words to complete this incredible commentary of a book inspired by the Holy Spirit and included in the Holy Writ for one purpose: to record for all generations the hopeless state of a life wasted on the world's wisdom, devoid of God's wisdom. The book of Ecclesiastes is most certainly biblical for it resides in the pages of God's Holy Word, but the majority of what is found within its pages is not Godly, it is not holy, it is not righteous. It is man's way, man's desires, man's nature, all without God. Studies of recent Bible teachers have attempted to find righteous truth in every verse; truth can be found in its words but with only a hint of righteousness scattered here and there throughout the book.

That leads me to this point in the introduction. Dr. Phillips was used by the Lord to reveal to preachers and Bible students the true intent of God. His years of study produced in his sermons inspiring illustrations of the original meaning of the text often lost in the translation from the original language to English. My dear friend Dr. Bailey Smith often invited Dr. Phillips to preach at his Bible conferences. One day the two were sitting together in a car outside a church. It was during a difficult time in Dr. Phillips' life. He was reminiscing over his purpose in the ministry. He said to Bailey something like this: "I just do not understand. I preach my heart out and just a soul or two comes to the Lord. You preach your heart out and hundreds come to know the Lord." Bailey replied, "Oh, but Dr. Phillips, if it wasn't for you, the rest of us preachers wouldn't know what to preach." In many ways, I can give that a hearty amen! God uses Dr. Smith as an evangelist; He used Dr. Phillips as a preacher. Although the two can stand in the same pulpit, the Lord uses one to draw the net, and He uses the other to instruct and mature—the two are different offices in the Church.

There is another difference too; Dr. Phillips wrote his messages with the intent of their being preached long after he joined his Lord in heaven. His words are not recorded in an archive for no purpose at all. "Take them, preach them," he would say, "and let the Lord use them for their intended purposes."

By 2003, Dr. Phillips had more than fifty books in print. Quite an accomplishment. Many of them had been in the works for years. But another thing was going on in his life—his health was beginning to take a turn for the worse. By 2010, he was struggling. A stepdaughter, Dianna Lightfoot, offers the following tribute about her stepfather.

> The last few days of John Phillips' life were spent in hospice. In this intense and sad setting, friends and family came and went throughout the day and night. One night when everyone else had gone, I sat by his bed holding his hand. It was hot from fever; his eyes were closed, and he moaned and writhed as the lack of moisture in his body caused painful leg cramping. He would hold his arms up as though reaching toward heaven, and at one point, I could no longer stand to see the suffering. I began to cry and pray out loud, "God please, please take this away, don't let this go on." Suddenly, the room became very quiet. I opened my eyes, and he was looking at me. He took my hand and placed it on his heart, with a weak smile he shook his head slowly no and said one word, "Submission." I will never forget that word as long as I live. It may have been the most instructive moment of my life.

Several family members were there with him on July 25, 2010. His new wife, Betty Jean Ferrell Phillips, his four children, Joanne Christensen, Marilyn Lobough, Audrey Jose, and John Phillips, and one of his four stepchildren, Dianna Lightfoot.

Dianna continued her story and said, "For many minutes before he died, he reached upward, I believe simply waiting for heavenly hands to take him home."

Jesus promised in John 14:2–3 the following: "I go to prepare a place for you. And if I go and prepare a place for you, I will come again, and receive you unto myself; that where I am, there ye may be also." We have all heard that Scripture, but have we all caught the magnitude of its meaning? For the one who belongs to the Lord, He Himself will come to this place to take us to be with Him. Hallelujah! What a Savior! Selah! What do you think of that (one of Dr. Phillips' favorite questions!)?

Dr. Phillips came into this world on February 11, 1927, in Newport, South Wales, in the United Kingdom. Dr. Phillips served in the British army in Palestine during the closing years of the British Mandate and witnessed the events that led up to the rebirth of the state of Israel. He moved to Canada after World War 2, where he worked for a British bank, married, and in time founded a small church. Later, he joined the staff of Moody Bible Institute in Chicago, where he served as assistant director of its Correspondence School. He also taught in the Evening Extension School and spoke regularly over the Moody Radio Network. In addition, he served as director of the Emmaus Correspondence School, at the time the largest school of its kind in the world. Dr. Phillips held a doctor of ministry degree from Luther Rice Seminary. As you can tell, he taught and wrote about the Bible for just about his entire adult life.

At about 4:00 p.m. on the afternoon of July 25, 2010, Dr. John Phillips made the journey of a lifetime, from the surly bonds of this temporal life on earth to the majestic realm of God. He had preached about it so many times. He knew it well. In submission, he was waiting for it. Not too quick, not too slow, neither to the right, neither to the left. He saw the sweet Lord Jesus coming to take him away, and he reached up to take His hand. Away he went with his Lord. Up, up, up through the atmosphere, leaving behind the old body of clay. Up, up, up to the twelve steps to the city of God, each of a different precious stone. Up, up, up each step they trod to the eastern entrance of the city, right past the pearly gate and onto the golden Hallelujah Boulevard. Down that street they headed west, capturing a glimpse of the river with trees covered in fruit and leaves for healing the nations. He could hear the choir of angels down the road. They would speak lowly and then the chorus would raise in glorious refrain, "Holy, holy, holy is the Lord God Almighty. Blessing and honor and glory forever and ever."

You have heard those words. You know the routine. On down the way, the Lord and John headed toward the sound of the choir. The ground looked like a sea of emerald glass. The Holy City made of gold. On down they went right through Hallelujah Square and on until they reached the throne of the Majesty on High—the one and only God the Father. The Lord Jesus had John by the hand and He said, "Father, this is John Phillips. He belongs to Me, and I belong to him." The Father looked at John and said, "Well done, My child, My good and faithful servant; enter into the joy of your salvation." The crown of life was placed on his head as well as all the rewards that were waiting for him there!

Oh, he had made it! He thanked the Father, he thanked the Son, and he looked around and found all his loved ones that had made the journey before he did. For you see, in that instant, in the blink of an eye, from here on earth to there with the Lord, the fog that blinds us from knowing all there is to know had been removed. Paul said it this way: "For now we see through a glass, darkly; but then face to face: now I know in part; but then shall I know even as also I am known. And now abideth faith, hope, charity, these three; but the greatest of these is charity" (1 Corinthians 13:12–13).

All of a sudden, John knows the answers to all the questions he had from all the years of serving the Lord. Moreover, he knows exactly what the future holds for all those left on earth. He knows when they think of him. He knows about this task to complete his manuscript—he knows, and he understands like no one left behind here on earth can. His title to his eternity was sealed, notarized by the Holy Spirit, delivered to the courthouse by the Son of God, and signed by God the Father Himself! Well done, Dr. John. In some ways we are jealous of the glory that you have experienced, but our time will come and you will be there to welcome us after we have met God face-to-face!

Solomon understood none of that as his days were coming to an end! David, his father, knew all of it. Solomon did not. He had wasted his opportunities, and he could not see past his death to see his beginning. With that all said, whom would you rather be like? Solomon? Dr. John Phillips? Now on to Solomon's sermon that recorded for all time the emptiness, the vanity of vanities, found in the world. Let it stir each heart to move in the right direction away from the monstrosities of the gods of this world that Solomon sought and on to the God of Creation that Dr. John Phillips sought!

Jim Hastings
June 2018

The Preacher's Subject

Ecclesiastes 1:1–11

PART 1: THE PREACHER'S SUBJECT (1:1–11)

    A. The Preacher (1:1)
        1. What He Was (1:1a)
        2. Who He Was (1:1b)
        3. Where He Was (1:1c)
    B. The Problem (1:2–3)
        1. The Great Quotations (1:2)
        2. The Great Question (1:3)
    C. The Process (1:4–11)
        1. A Frustrating Sequence (1:4–10)
            a) Anthropology Does Not Have the Answer (1:4a)
            b) Geology Does Not Have the Answer (1:4b)
            c) Astronomy Does Not Have the Answer (1:5)
            d) Meteorology Does Not Have the Answer (1:6)
            e) Oceanography Does Not Have the Answer (1:7)
            f) Sociology Does Not Have the Answer (1:8a)
            g) Psychology Does Not Have the Answer (1:8b)
            h) Archaeology Does Not Have the Answer (1:9)
            i) Philosophy Does Not Have the Answer (1:10)
        2. A Frustrated Sequel (1:11)
            a) The Frustrating Incompleteness of Our History Books (1:11a)
            b) The Frustrating Inference of Our History Books (1:11b)

———————

PART 1: THE PREACHER'S SUBJECT (1:1–11)

    A. The Preacher (1:1)
        1. What He Was (1:1a)
        2. Who He Was (1:1b)
        3. Where He Was (1:1c)

"*The words of the Preacher . . .*" (1:1a). Kings are rarely noted for being preachers. Warriors, statesmen, law givers, yes! But preachers? No! The Hebrew word Solomon uses to describe himself is *koheleth*, from *kahel*—"to call," "to assemble," "to gather together"—he proclaims himself to be a collector of wisdom to speak to the people.

Solomon had adopted this role at the beginning of his reign (1 Kings 8:1, 2, 5) when he gathered his people together to lead them in a prayer and proclamation at the dedication of the Temple. It was a role to which Solomon now returned at the end of his wilderness wanderings in the pursuit of pleasure, power, and praise.

There can really be no doubt as to who the preacher was, to whom we are introduced at the very beginning of this twelve-chapter sermon. He tells us himself he was *". . . the son of David"* (1:1b). Nor can there be any question as to what he was. He was "king." Furthermore, there can be no doubt as to where he was: *"king in Jerusalem"* (1:1c). True, Solomon did not actually sign this book, but we know that the one who was king in Jerusalem was Solomon.

Long before the time of Christ, this book found its way into the Hebrew Bible. The universal consent of antiquity attributed the authorship to Solomon. The Greek and Latin Fathers agreed. Jewish commentators entertained some doubts concerning the contents but never disputed its authorship. It was Martin Luther who first ridiculed the traditional view and stated it was his opinion that the book was composed by Sirach in the time of the Maccabees. Very little attention was paid to Luther until, at the close of the nineteenth century, his opinion attracted the attention of the German destructive critics. We reject out of hand the idea that some centuries after Solomon an unknown writer impersonated him because of his vast and varied knowledge of human nature, thought, and circumstance in order to secure an audience for his own thoughts and opinions. Such a view is incompatible with the revelation and plenary, verbal inspiration of Scripture, which is the hallmark of all the Bible.

Though Solomon did not actually sign the book, he identified himself plainly enough with his opening verse. Thus, it is that we have in our Bible, a book divinely inspired by the Spirit of God and authored by a man of wide experience of life to show us the folly and futility of worldly-mindedness, living solely "under the sun." This is a book given to us by God to expose once and for all the total inadequacy of the perspectives, plans, and prospects of the unsaved individual and the backslidden believer, as well as such people who have their day and then the end comes as it came to the dismayed and disillusioned Solomon, king in Jerusalem.

The book is of great importance and incalculable value. God allowed Solomon to have everything this world could offer. He had wealth and power. He had a brilliant mind and vast experience. He had a rich spiritual heritage and commanded wide respect and influence. Consider, for instance, the city and country over which he ruled. Jerusalem had a growing population and attracted an ever-flowing stream of talent and enterprise. Solomon's first great undertaking, the building of the Temple, revealed him to be a capable leader and a born administrator. The royal palace he subsequently built covered an area four times that of the Temple.

Solomon fortified the nation he inherited, fully aware that he was not the warrior-king his father, David, had been. Hazor, Megiddo, Gezer, Baalath, Tamar, and Beth-horon were all strategically located. These fortress cities were supplemented by other important cities for his chariots and cavalry. His love of building seemed to grow as time went on. His trading expeditions brought him ever-increasing wealth and ever-increasing oriental luxury in the beginning. It was a development that was not only demoralizing but also dangerous, especially as his polygamy soon knew no bounds.

Before long, strangers, formerly regarded as heathens, poured into Jerusalem. Solomon absorbed their ideas, became familiar with their customs, married hosts of their women, seemed to tolerate their religions, and, eventually, practically turned Jerusalem into Babylon. This was all the more inexcusable because God twice appeared personally to Solomon, something he never did to David.

This was "the preacher." He certainly did not lack for source material for his sermon. Of all the kings of Israel and Judah, only Solomon had the means, the experience, and the motivation to write this book that is supremely concerned with materialism and the high cost of backsliding.

In this sermon, Solomon proves from experience, observation, and deduction that a life lived without God is futile, empty, and pointless. Nothing ever lasts. We become bored with our works. Pleasures satiate. Philosophy raises more questions than it answers. Disappointment comes. Death appears on the horizon. All these somber threads are woven into the tapestry of this preacher's sermon. Gloom and doom lurk everywhere. Nothing "under the sun" satisfies the deepest longings of the human heart.

Solomon would have agreed with the poet Lord Byron. On the day he completed his thirty-sixth year, he cried:

> My days are in the yellow leaf,
> The flowers and fruits of life are gone;
>
> The worm, the canker, and the grief
> Are mine alone.[1]

B. The Problem (1:2–3)
   1. The Great Quotations (1:2)

"Vanity of vanities, saith the Preacher, vanity of vanities; all is vanity" (1:2). The nation of Israel never recovered from the damage Solomon did to it. There was oppression on the one side and abomination on the other.

> For it came to pass, when Solomon was old, that his wives turned away his heart after other gods: and his heart was not perfect with the LORD his God, as was the heart of David his father. For Solomon went after Ashtoreth the goddess of the Zidonians, and after Milcom the abomination of the Ammonites. And Solomon did evil in the sight of the LORD, and went not fully after the LORD, as did David his father. Then did Solomon build an high place for Chemosh, the abomination of Moab, in the hill that is before Jerusalem, and for Molech, the abomination of the children of Ammon. And likewise did he for all his strange wives, which burnt incense and sacrificed unto their gods. (1 Kings 11:4–8)

No wonder God's anger was kindled against the king. He had taken a tour of the city. He had seen these various abominations, dedicated to whoredom and child sacrifice—here, there, and everywhere throughout the city. The worship of Baal and Ashtoreth was consummated with a temple harlot. The worship of Molech climaxed in the placing of a living child on the red-hot lap of the idol while the drummers worked themselves into a frenzy to drown out the screams of the victim. In 1 Kings 11, God is essentially saying, "For David's sake, I'll wait until you're dead. I'm going to tear your kingdom to pieces" (see vv. 11–13).

At first, Solomon was angry. He was astute enough to know where his danger lay. He had an ambitious young administrator, thoroughly capable and influential, by the name of Jeroboam. He was the one to watch. The people, fed up with Solomon's exactions, would turn to open rebellion given the right leader, especially the northern tribes.

Then came word that Ahijah the prophet had graphically conveyed to Jeroboam that he was destined to rule over ten of the tribes. Solomon decided to have Jeroboam put to death. The plan failed, and Jeroboam escaped to Egypt and bided his time (1 Kings 11:40).

In time Solomon resigned himself to the fact he had thrown away an empire, sold his birthright, indeed, for a mess of this world's pottage. It was only a matter of time. He viewed his empty-headed son Rehoboam with a jaundiced eye. Rehoboam was a fool, and Solomon knew it. All of Solomon's proverbs regarding fools are given added potency by the fact that Rehoboam was incapable of learning from any of them. Doubtless Solomon could envision in his mind's eye the kind of idiocy which would pass for statesmanship with Rehoboam once he was on the throne.

We can picture Solomon sitting moodily in his library brooding over his misspent life. Surely, he had built the Temple, but that had been David's vision, not his; even so, it was the Temple written into the archives of heaven. But he had also set in motion the forces which would one day pull it down. Was there nothing he could do? The pangs of remorse and regret gnawed at his heart. Was there nothing he could do to undo the damage he'd done?

We can see him open the scroll. It is a copy of the Hebrew hymnbook. In Solomon's day, almost all the psalms bore David's name. It was the voice of his dead father speaking to him from beyond the grave. We can see him running his eye from psalm to psalm until suddenly it is arrested by the word "vanity!" He found that word in what we know as Psalm 39. The word smote him twice:

> Behold, thou hast made my days as an handbreadth;
> and mine age is as nothing before thee:
> verily every man at his best state is altogether vanity. (v. 5)

To which David added the word "selah," which, translated into our vernacular, simply means, "There, what do you think of it all!" Old age! Vanity! It must have smitten the aging Solomon right between the eyes. Then came the second punch:

> When thou with rebukes dost correct man for iniquity,
> thou makest his beauty to consume away like a moth:
> surely every man is vanity. (v. 11)

And, again, there follows that word "selah." "What do you think of that!" The word "vanity" itself refers to that which soon disappears. It embodies the idea of a vapor, something which appears for a little while and then "vanisheth away" (James 4:14). Someone has suggested paraphrasing the idea behind the word as "chasing the wind."

The word David used for "iniquity" must also have troubled Solomon's thoughts. It suggests perverseness, being bent out of shape, and it, too, must have arrested his attention. Haunted by two words "vanity" and "iniquity," Solomon sat there and pondered.

It was the word "vanity" that finally gripped him the most. It summed up the course of his life. In his pursuit of knowledge and power, pleasure, and happiness, he had ended up chasing the wind. He had squandered the wisdom given him by God. The light that was in him had been turned into darkness, and how great was that darkness (Matthew 6:23). At last there was a gleam of light in the darkness. He could not change the past, but he could lay hold of the future. He could write another book. He could give his testimony. He could warn young people. He could unmask worldliness and carnality. He could preach! But to preach, he needed a text. He found a text. He found that text already in his hand, a one-word text: Vanity! It so gripped the soul of the repentant Solomon, so summed up what he wanted to say, so well stripped the world of its pretentions that, one way or another, he wrote that word "vanity" some thirty-six times into his sermon. It was his predominating text.

Solomon would remember the first time the thought behind the word occurred in the Scriptures. It was immediately after the fall. God had appeared in the garden to pass judgment on Adam, Eve, and the serpent. But judgment was tempered with mercy, for God promised that "the seed of the woman" would one day "bruise the serpent's head." Eve believed God. When her firstborn son arrived she called him Cain, saying, "I have gotten a man from the LORD" or, as some have suggested, "I have gotten a man, even Jehovah" (Genesis 4:1).

The boy began to grow, manifesting the fallen Adamic nature and so much so that by the time Eve's second son was born, she was so disillusioned that she called him "Abel," which means "vanity." So Solomon found his text. He began at once on his topic: man under the sun.

2. The Great Question (1:3)

"What profit hath a man of all his labour which he taketh under the sun?" (1:3). There speaks the businessman. Solomon was a very successful businessman, at least at first. And like all successful businessmen, Solomon kept his eye on his profit and loss statement with special attention directed to what we now call "the bottom line." For years Solomon had been chairman of the board of a number of commercial enterprises. He knew the importance of making sure that every venture turned a profit. And, like so many others engrossed in turning a profit, Solomon lost sight of eternal values. He was the rich fool (Luke 12:16–21) of the

Old Testament, for toward the end Solomon became interested, in ever-increasing absorption, with things "under the sun."

He introduces the expression "under the sun" for the first time. Before he is finished, he will write it into this sermon twenty-nine times. Preoccupation with money makes most men materialists. The love of money becomes the root of all evil (1 Timothy 6:10). Solomon, pen in hand, suddenly sees where it all ends—money in the bank, influence, power, all kinds of material things—but an empty soul.

Solomon, once he was shocked back into sanity by the pronounced judgment of God on his misspent life, would have appreciated the comment of the modern-day successful business executive who declared, "I have spent all my life climbing the corporate ladder, only to find, when I reached the top, that it was leaning against the wrong wall." Thus, too, were the sentiments of Benjamin Disraeli (Lord Beaconsfield), the great Victorian empire builder. He said: "Youth is a blunder; manhood a struggle; old age a regret."

    C. The Process (1:4–11)
        1. A Frustrating Sequence (1:4–10)

No final answers can be found in the sciences of this life:

    a) Anthropology Does Not Have the Answer (1:4a)

"One generation passeth away, and another generation cometh . . ." (1:4a). Solomon now reviews the various sciences in his search for something permanent "under the sun." He begins with what we call anthropology, the study of man. What impresses him at once is man's impermanence. Generation after generation, man's brief tenure on this planet is the most obvious fact of all.

He arrives in successive waves, each wave a generation long but intermingling with the generations immediately behind him. He and his contemporaries have their day. But into the darkness of the tomb they go. Solomon's generation had just about run its course. New generations were on their way to their cradles. His generation was on its way to its grave. If humanity, the crown of creation, was, metaphorically speaking, a river of life, it presented Solomon with many great mysteries. Where are we going? There are no satisfactory answers "under the sun." Human philosophies and man-made religions can only guess at the reason for it all. The Word of God alone has the answers.

All about the preacher was the tramp of feet, people coming and going. He could remember the time when he stood in awe of an older generation, as represented by his parents. Then, all his interests were absorbed by his own generation which had come to prominence and power. Now it was fast becoming the past generation. The new generation came in with the tide. It swirled across the sands of time. It grappled with the rocky headlands of the hour, then hurried back into the ocean of eternity, caught away by the ebb. But what was the point of it all? Some generations lasted longer than others. The generations before the flood had lived for hundreds of years, but it was all the same in the end. They died. And, when all was said and done, what was the life span of a Methuselah who lived for nearly a thousand years compared with time itself? And what was time itself compared with all eternity? So much for anthropology and the science of man. Man ended it all as a fossil.

b) Geology Does Not Have the Answer (1:4b)

"*. . . but the earth abideth for ever*" (1:4b) or so it seems when we compare the geological ages with the life span of even the oldest man. The words Solomon used for the expression "forever" can be translated *ages*—"the earth abideth for ages." And so it does—at least the modern science of geology says it does. Back and back the geologists go.

First is the Quaternary Period which embraces the Glacial Age. Then come the Tertiary Period and the Crustaceous Period. After that the famous Jurassic Period when the dinosaurs are said to have stalked the earth. Back, ever further back, the geologists go—the Permian Age, the Devonian Age, the Silurian and the Ordovician Age, and then the Cambrian Age, the beginning of time of planet earth as conceived by the geologists. Back, in all, some 2,300,000,000 years, they say.

Well, from the standpoint of man "under the sun," the earth does seem to be virtually ageless. But, once we get our sense of direction, age, and distance from above the sun, the age of the earth is but a matter of moments after all. Change and decay are evident everywhere. And there seated on a throne, high and lifted up, is the eternal, uncreated, self-existing God of the universe—well might Isaac Watts declare,

> A thousand ages in thy sight,
> Are as an evening gone;

> Short as the watch that ends the night
> Before the rising sun.[2]

"The earth abideth forever!" Not so. It had a beginning. It will have an ending. Genesis tells about its beginning, and Revelation tells about the ending. And a fiery ending it is to be (Revelation 20:10–13). So Solomon will have to look elsewhere for something permanent "under the sun."

c) Astronomy Does Not Have the Answer (1:5)

"The sun also ariseth, and the sun goeth down, and hasteth to his place where he arose" (1:5). From the standpoint of man on this planet, more restless than anything else, is the sun itself. Day by day it bursts from its bed in the distant east. It climbs to its zenith. It sinks again to rest in the flaming west only to complete the same endless journey day after day, age after age.

The sun so dominated the lives of ancient and primitive people that they worshiped it. All kinds of astronomical data, for instance, were built into the great pyramid of Egypt. The sphinx likewise was made so as to record important astronomical facts. It is oriented perfectly toward due east and is an amazing equinoctial marker. There are four cardinal moments in the year. These are the summer solstice (the longest day in the northern hemisphere), the winter solstice (the shortest day in which the north pole points most directly away from the sun), and the spring and autumn equinoxes (when night and day are of equal length). The sphinx is an equinoctial marker. Its eyes focus on the exact position of sunrise at dawn on the spring equinox.

We cannot wonder that the ancients worshiped the sun. The Egyptian Pharaoh was regarded as the incarnation of Ra, the sun god. In Mexico City today the Metropolitan Cathedral looms over the great central plaza, the Zócalo. A scant block from the cathedral is the site of the Templo Mayor, the main temple and the most important pyramids of the Aztecs, the place where their sanguinary religion reached its grim zenith. The shrines of Tlaloc (god of rain and fertility) and of Huitzilopochtli (god of war) stand side by side. There, too, in front of Huitzilopochtli's shrine, but nearer the edge of the summit, is the sacrificial stone. Here endless streams of victims were laid spread-eagle as their turn came so that the priest could plunge his knife into their chests and tear out their hearts as an offering to the sun. The ancient builders of Stonehenge on the Salisbury Plain in Britain were just as fascinated with the sun, and they marked the summer solstice by placing their gigantic circles and horseshoes of stones so that they were aligned with at least sixteen unique sun and moon positions.

The sun! The solar system! Although just a few specks of cosmic dust in terms of the vastness of space, it is, nevertheless, 50 billion billion times as voluminous as the earth. It is made up of a single star, the sun. It embraces its planets, 181 moons, some 1.1 to 1.9 million asteroids, and about 1 trillion comets. Even so, most of its substance, about 99.86 percent, is located in the sun. The theory is that the sun's gravitational influence reaches to a distance a thousand times farther than the orbit of Pluto, the most distant dwarf planet. The sun's surface is a heavy mass of gases and atomic particles with an average temperature of 10,000 degrees Fahrenheit. At its core, hydrogen atoms are fused into helium at a temperature of 25 million degrees Fahrenheit. It has a diameter of 864,000 miles. It weighs 2 billion billion billion tons, and it is all gas—335 quadrillion cubic miles of it. And with all that, the sun is rated by modern astronomers as a fifth-magnitude star, up to 100,000 times fainter than its brightest neighbor in the galaxy which it orbits about once every 200 trillion years.

It is no wonder the ancients worshiped the sun, though they knew very little about it. We are impressed with it ourselves. What impressed Solomon was its unvarying round, rising in the morning, setting in the evening, ruling all our days. It, too, was restless. No wonder everything "under the sun" was restless. Nor has our vast accumulation of facts about the sun diminished by one iota our own restlessness.

d) Meteorology Does Not Have the Answer (1:6)

"The wind goeth toward the south, and turneth about unto the north; it whirleth about continually, and the wind returneth again according to his circuits" (1:6). The atmosphere broods over all the planet. Like the sea, it has its waves, currents, and tides. The higher we go, the rarer and colder it gets. Ascend three and a half miles, and we leave behind us more than half of the weight of the atmosphere, and the cold is unbearable.

This vast ocean of air has its weight and pressure. At sea level, it presses on us with a force equal to 14.6 pounds per square inch—at 2,000 pounds per square foot and an inconceivable 58,611,548,160 pounds per square mile. On the whole surface of the earth, the air presses on our planet with a weight equal to a lead ball 60 miles in diameter. Or more vividly, the atmospheric pressure on a grown person is no less than 14 tons.

Which brings us to what interested Solomon—the winds. Wind is caused by differences in atmospheric pressure at given places on the globe. When the air in one place is heated by the rays of the sun, it expands and becomes lighter. The surrounding air, which has remained cooler, rushes in, causing the warmer and expanded air to rise. The motion of the colder air is the wind.

All this takes place on a grand scale between the equatorial regions of the planet and those of the poles. The air around the poles is cold and heavy and flows along the earth's surface to the equator. In the torrid zone it becomes heated and ascends to the higher elevations where it flows back over the colder air toward the poles to begin the same cycle over again. Solomon had, at least, a rudimentary knowledge of this.

Of course, many other complicating factors come into play. At certain points in this grand circuit, the air masses are of equal weight and density, and they meet and impede one another. The unequal temperatures of the sea and land, the influence of screening clouds, electrical disturbances, and changes of the seasons produce all kinds of variables.

Along with all this is the wonder of evaporation and condensation. Water in its natural state is 800 times heavier than the atmosphere. Yet, day by day, moisture climbs past the firmament and floats at the rarified altitudes of three to six miles above the land and sea. Water, when it is converted into steam or vapor, occupies a space 1,600 times greater than in its liquid state. It is therefore much lighter than the atmosphere, and so it can soar through the sky.

As water is converted into vapor by heat, by the loss of heat, vapor is reconverted into water and falls back to earth again as precipitation. All this vast machinery functions flawlessly. As great an amount of water daily flows upward by evaporation into the skies as all the rivers of the globe pour into the oceans, a quantity sufficient to cover all the land of the earth to a depth of three feet! This computes to 186,240 cubic miles per annum.

Think of how much heat it takes to boil away a kettle of water, and it will give some idea of the tremendous amount of energy taken up by daily evaporation from the seas.

The science of meteorology is very complex. The television weather channel has made it seem almost humdrum. The weather chart features isobars and barometer readings, centers of high and low pressure, temperatures, fronts, cyclones, anticyclones, and depressions. We know how, where, and why the wind moves. Sophisticated computers assimilate vast amounts of information and give it back in complex weather charts. Solomon would have been fascinated by it all.

However, he grasped the essentials clearly enough. He knew about the major air currents. What depressed him was the fact that it all centered on endless, restless activity which, it seemed to him, illustrated man's own driven movements under the sun. Maybe there was some explanation for all this round of activity. If so, looking at things "under the sun" had eluded him.

e) Oceanography Does Not Have the Answer (1:7)

Solomon turns from the glowing sun and the blowing wind to the flowing sea. *"All the rivers run into the sea; yet the sea is not full; unto the place from whence the rivers come, thither they return again"* (1:7).

The river Solomon knew best was the Jordan. The valley of the Jordan is a rift more than 160 miles long following one of the major fault lines of the Middle East. This volcanic rift is from two to fifteen miles wide. It falls 1,292 feet below sea level, the bottom of the Dead Sea being deeper still—another 1,300 feet. It begins at the foot of Mount Hermon, near the New Testament city of Caesarea Philippi. It gathers within its embrace two lakes, Hula and Galilee, as it twists and turns, like some writhing serpent, through the tangled hills and thickets sprawled across the landscape. Its bed varies in width from one-fourth of a mile to two miles. It pours its waters, finally, into the arid Dead Sea. It has been calculated that 6.5 million tons of water flow into the Dead Sea daily, mostly from the Jordan River.

Solomon, of course, would be familiar with two of the world's greatest rivers, the Nile and the Euphrates, the eastern and western boundaries of the Promised Land (Genesis 15). Solomon's queen was an Egyptian princess. She probably never tired of telling him about the Nile, the world's longest river, flowing 4,135 miles from the mountains near the equator to the Mediterranean.

But it was the Jordan River that he knew best. He must have often pondered the fact that the Jordan pours its water into the Dead Sea and has no outlet. *Where does all that water go?* must have been Solomon's thought. His comment here suggests that he at least guessed at the fact that it evaporated and returned to its headwaters in the form of rain. Indeed, the evaporation process at the Dead Sea is so extraordinary, caused by the intense heat, that the water left in the Dead Sea contains 25 percent solid substances, notably salt, potash, and bromine. By contrast, the water of the ocean contains only from 4 to 6 percent of solids in solution.

Whether or not Solomon was smart enough to realize that the rivers running into the sea do not cause the oceans to overflow because of evaporation, he certainly had the gist of it. But again, it was just another of those ceaseless activities "under the sun" that proved his point. Life was a rat race. It was a merry-go-round. And man was part of it, going round and round in circles, not getting anywhere, simply getting older.

f) Sociology Does Not Have the Answer (1:8a)

"All things are full of labour" (1:8a). Man is just another cog in a vast machine. He is caught up in laborious activity, subject to forces and influences over which he has no control. Constant movement grips the universe. There is no rest. It is Work! Work! Work!

Perhaps Solomon was cynically thinking of all the vast levies of able-bodied men drafted by him to slave at the grandiose buildings. It was accepted with good grace by the people so long as the work levies were for the purpose of building the Temple. The Phoenicians provided Solomon with craftsmen and skilled laborers: carvers, stonemasons, dyers, modelers, and such.

The building of the Temple had commenced in the second month of the fourth year of Solomon's reign. The massive timbers were felled and dressed and conveyed in floats to Joppa on the coast and thence to Jerusalem, forty miles away in the mountains. Similarly, magnificent and enormous hewed stones beveled at the edges (some more than thirty feet long by seven and a half high and weighing over one hundred tons) had to be hauled to the site.

There were no modern mechanical appliances. Vast hordes of workmen had to be employed. They amounted to 160,000 laborers, divided into two classes. There were 30,000 native Israelites raised by a "levy." The Hebrew scholar Alfred Edersheim estimates they comprised 1 out of every 44 able-bodied males. They worked in relays, 10,000 being employed during one month with two months off to pursue their domestic activities. There were an additional draft of 150,000 second-class resident aliens of whom 70,000 were burden bearers and 80,000 "hewers in the mountains" (presumably stonecutters). These men were little more than bond slaves.

It took Solomon seven years to complete the Temple. By then he had cultivated a taste for building. He spent the next thirteen years building his own palace. After that, he turned his workmen to the task of fortifying the nation. It was all done with forced labor, the burden of it falling on the Canaanite inhabitants of his country, his Jewish subjects being chiefly engaged as overseers. But, even so, the division of so much labor and the onerous taxation levied to pay for it all created enormous hardships. The victims of all this viewed it as a "grievous service" and as a "heavy yoke" (1 Kings 12:4). As Edersheim says, "Solomon's love of building and of oriental splendor seems to have grown upon him."[3]

Nor was there any redress. There were no trade unions, no social workers, no power beyond that of the king, and no higher court than his. Solomon must often have visited the sites of his various building activities and congratulated himself that he was a sovereign not a slave.

When I was in the British Army in Palestine, I was stationed on Haifa Docks. I often saw the impoverished Arab laborers working under just such conditions as Solomon's workmen. The poor fellows were dressed in old clothes. Their job was to unload the boxcars full of potash from the Dead Sea. Each man carried a sack of chemicals weighing at least 150 pounds. Their backs were bowed beneath the load. As the work proceeded, they built a vast mountain, with steep slopes up one side, to enable them to reach its summit. When the tower was completed they started on another one. When the cargo ships arrived, all these heavy sacks had to be shouldered again and carried down the steep slope, carried to the vessel, and loaded aboard. The men tried to ease their burdens by keeping up a chant. They were allowed an hour at midday to eat a scanty meal, often a piece of pocket bread and a handful of grapes or a slice of watermelon, and time for a brief rest. Then back into the heat of the sun and the endless round of toil.

Such was life "under the sun" for them. And such was the life of toil of Solomon's workmen. Nor was the lot of the freemen, on their ancestral plots of ground, much lighter labor. It was ceaseless toil in the fields for most of them. Solomon saw it all as part of the inevitable lot of life for the majority "under the sun." There was no relief for most of them. Nobody cared how hard they had to work, nor how long, nor how badly paid they were, nor how dangerous to life and limb it all was. As for Solomon, he did not lift a finger to relieve their burdens. He had too many grandiose plans for which cheap labor was required.

g) Psychology Does Not Have the Answer (1:8b)

"*. . . man cannot utter it: the eye is not satisfied with seeing, nor the ear filled with hearing*" (1:8b). The cause of universal restlessness and dissatisfaction went far deeper than the mere physical. It had its roots in the inner nature of things.

Take the eye, for instance. The eye was made for seeing. Well one would think that when it had seen what it came to see, it would be satisfied. Not a bit of it. It is the inner nature of man which is the trouble. Who, for instance, can be satisfied with a passing glance at Niagara Falls? In the years I traveled as an itinerant preacher, I often found myself in Ontario. I invariably went in and out of Canada by way of Niagara Falls. On the Canadian side there is a restaurant perched almost on the lip of the falls. One can look up the river, watch it come tumbling over the rocks, sweep around the bend, gather force and speed, and then hurl itself into the seething cauldron below. The eye has seen it time and time again and still wants to see it again.

Way out in the American west, across the badlands to the Black Hills of South Dakota and twenty-five miles from Rapid City, is Mount Rushmore National Memorial. The mountain rises 5,725 feet high and there, carved out of a granite cliff, is one of North America's most impressive sights. It shows the faces of four American Presidents: George Washington, Thomas Jefferson, Theodore Roosevelt, and Abraham Lincoln. It is enormous, awesome, unforgettable. The head of George Washington alone is as high as a five-story building (about sixty feet). When one sees it for the first time, the eye wants to gaze and gaze. It never gets enough. I have seen it three times and, even at that, would welcome an opportunity to go and see it again. The eye is not satisfied with seeing.

Nor is the ear filled with hearing. Who, having heard Handel's "Hallelujah Chorus" for the first time, says, "Once is enough"? We never get tired of hearing our favorite tunes. We record them so that we can hear them over and over again. And the more we hear them, the more we want to hear them. They become old, familiar friends, associated with a hundred memories. Whoever says to his eye, "I have seen all I want to see, I would like to become blind"? Whoever says to his ear, "I have heard it all. Now become stone deaf"? No, indeed! We are grateful that we have two eyes and two ears so that should one or other of them fail us we still have another to carry on.

This ceaseless desire to go on seeing and to go on hearing arrested Solomon. He added it, perversely enough, to his overall complaint. It was just another proof that nothing "under the sun" can satisfy. It is in the very nature of things down here, in the very psychology of our souls that we want more and more of the pleasures of life, and this craving pursues us on into old age and down to the grave itself.

h) Archaeology Does Not Have the Answer (1:9)

"The thing that hath been, it is that which shall be; and that which is done is that which shall be done: and there is no new thing under the sun" (1:9).

Archaeology is the science of digging up the past. The past helps us understand the present and prepares us for the future. It sheds light on the rise and fall of former civilizations. It helps us understand history. The chief lesson we learn from history is that people are the same now as they were then. We do not learn from our mistakes, the cynic says. "The only thing we learn from history is that we learn nothing from history."

Solomon himself was a case in point. The book of Judges should have afforded him an eloquent and sufficient example. It covered a period of four hundred years of comparatively recent Hebrew history. It was an endless round of sin followed by servitude, followed by sorrow, followed by salvation—and then the same dismal round all over again. The Mesopotamians, the Moabites, the Midianites, the Ammonites, the Amalekites, and then the oppressive Philistines—all trod the Hebrew people down. Then came the judges Othniel, Ehud, Shamgar, Deborah, Barak, Gideon, Jephthah, and Samson, along with some half dozen known only by name, with Eli and Godly Samuel bringing up the rear. But from servitude to servitude Israel learned nothing. Over and over again, back they went to serving the vile and vicious gods of the surrounding pagan tribes.

They learned nothing from their history. So it was endlessly repeated. Then David came, a man after God's own heart. He had subdued all of Israel's foes. He had established the Hebrew faith and laid up treasure to build its Temple. He had put its archives in order, given it a magnificent hymn book, and founded its Messianic dynasty. He had bequeathed to Solomon an empire which stretched virtually from Egypt to the Euphrates. And what had Solomon learned from all this? Nothing. He himself had groveled at the pagan shrines he had built in Jerusalem for his heathen wives. He had thus paved the way for an eventual return of the nation to the follies of the days of the judges. History had taught him nothing. Or, at least, he had forgotten that history has a way of repeating itself. What had happened before had happened again. Gazing through the mists of the future, Solomon could see the same endless round—sin, servitude, sorrow, salvation— over and over again. Revival, when it came, rarely lasted more than a generation.

It was another discordant note in his dirge of despair with life "under the sun." Indeed, it was only when a prophet, priest, or king came along, with his head above the sun, that history took a positive turn.

i) Philosophy Does Not Have the Answer (1:10)

"Is there any thing whereof it may be said, See, this is new? it hath been already of old time, which was before us" (1:10).

Solomon was bored to tears. We are reminded of the Greeks of Athens, the city of Socrates, of Plato, Demosthenes, Pericles, and Solon, where almost everyone in philosophy worthy of the name was born. Here sculpture had reached the apex of its glory. Here, oratory had surpassed itself. Here flourished a knowledge of everything worth knowing "under the sun." But what struck Paul most about the Athenians was their stupidity. It expressed itself in crass idolatry, in graven images and gods with eyes that could not see and mouths that could not speak. Here stood temples to Apollo, Hercules, Aphrodite, Vulcan, and Mars. The Athenians knew everything about everything, except God. Him they did not know.

These, the Athenians of Paul's day, the philosophers of Mars Hill, lived for one thing only—to find something new under the sun. There before these men stood a nondescript Jew, the greatest intellectual of them all. They called him a "babbler," literally a *seed-picker*, one whose knowledge consisted of odd scraps of information picked up here, there, and everywhere. They wanted to hear "some new thing," and Paul set it before them—Jesus Christ raised from the dead. And, for the most part, they mocked. For Athens had become the home of dilettantism, the shrine of a critical spirit which found all things wanting, the arena where all was looked upon as food for clever argument.[4]

Solomon bestows a similar attitude. He was bored to tears by life "under the sun."

2. A Frustrated Sequel (1:11)
a) The Frustrating Incompleteness of Our History Books (1:11a)

In summing up this opening statement of his, on the pointlessness of life "under the sun," Solomon draws attention to the frustrating incompleteness of our history books: *"There is no remembrance of former things,"* he says (1:11a). There are vast gaps in our knowledge of the past. The sum total of what we know is fragmentary at best. Our knowledge of the past resembles a child's scrapbook in which are preserved bits and pieces of knowledge. This is true not only of history but also of science, even to this day.

Isaac Newton, for instance, worked out the laws of motion and gravity and invented calculus. His findings ruled scientific thought for two centuries. Yet he said of himself, "I do not know what I may appear to the world, but to myself I seem to have been only like a boy playing on the seashore, and diverting myself in now and then finding a smoother pebble or a prettier shell than ordinary, whilst the great ocean of truth lay all undiscovered before me."[5]

But it is in the realm of history that we become most quickly aware of the gaps in our knowledge. Who, for instance, built the pyramids? Who really killed John Kennedy? How advanced was the antediluvian civilization? There are thousands of such questions relating to the larger issues of time. But what about the teeming millions who have peopled the planet and whose names and deeds have been forgotten by one and all? Once in a while a name surfaces in connection with some event or some discovery, but for the most part, people live and die, they are buried, and they are soon forgotten. An afternoon's walk through an old graveyard will soon convince us that Solomon was right. "There is no remembrance of former things."

b) The Frustrating Inference of Our History Books (1:11b)

Based on this observation, Solomon draws attention to another one, to the frustrating inference of our history books: *". . . neither shall there be any remembrance of things that are to come with those that shall come after"* (1:11b). What makes us think that our names will stand the test of time? All too often those who make the headlines today are forgotten as quickly as they rise to prominence. Who, for instance, invented the first practical typewriter or air conditioner or the first electron microscope? Or who, for instance, was Louis W. Parker? Or who won the Nobel Prize for Literature in 1938? Indeed, fame tends to be short lived.

So then, Solomon began his sermon on a sour note. Nothing seemed worth even the strum of a single string. Life kept one on the move. Solomon would have appreciated the complaint of poor Joe in Charles Dickens' *Bleak House*. A policeman had found Joe, the crossing sweeper, loitering, and he ordered him to move on. The following dialogue took place:

> "I'm always a-moving on, sir," cries the boy, wiping away his grimy tears with his arm. "I've always been a-moving and a-moving on, ever since I was born. Where can I possible move to, sir, more nor I do move." . . .
>
> "My instructions don't go to that," replies the constable. "My instructions are that this boy is to move on."[6]

Like the poor crossing sweeper, Solomon, prince of the realm that he was, found that life kept moving him on. It had moved him on at such a pace and with such purpose that he was soon to be ushered out of life altogether. It was one of the things he had against life "under the sun."

He had been kept "a-moving and a-moving on" ever since he was born. And all to very little purpose. Truly life "under the sun," though it offered him what it offered to comparatively few—fame and fortune, pleasure and power—had tricked him in the end. For years, he had been too busy to bother about God. How history and posterity would view him seemed to trouble him most. As for the immediate future, he had a fool for a son, and he knew it. It would not take empty-headed young Rehoboam long to squander the kingdom, the power, and the glory that Solomon would hand on to him. Such a thought might sour any man's soul.

The Preacher's Sermon

Ecclesiastes 1:12–10:20

PART 2: THE PREACHER'S SERMON (1:12–10:20)

    A. Things He Had Sought (1:12–2:26)

        1. His Persistent Search (1:12–2:11)

           a) The World of Thought (1:12–1:18)

               (1) His First Quest: To Exploit His Wisdom (1:12–15)

                   (a) What He Declared (1:12)

                   (b) What He Determined (1:13a)

                   (c) What He Displayed (1:13b)

                   (d) What He Discovered (1:14–15)

                       (i) Man's Works Are Disappointing (1:14)

                       (ii) Man's Ways Are Dismaying (1:15)

                           (a) The Bentness of Things (1:15a)

                           (b) The Bankruptcy of Things (1:15b)

               (2) His Further Quest: To Explore His Wisdom (1:16–18)

                   (a) His Success (1:16)

                   (b) His Search (1:17–18)

                       (i) His Goal (1:17a)

                       (ii) His Gloom (1:17b)

                       (iii) His Grief (1:18)

           b) The World of Thrills (2:1–3)

               (1) Life's Entertaining Thrills (2:1–2)

                   (a) Solomon's Decision (2:1a–b)

                       (i) To Seek Things to Make Him Laugh (2:1a)

                       (ii) To Seek Things to Massage His Lusts (2:1b)

                   (b) His Disappointment (2:1c)

                   (c) His Declaration (2:2)

                     (i) The World of Thrills Is Dangerous (2:2a)

                     (ii) The World of Thrills Is Deceptive (2:2b)

               (2) Life's Enslaving Thrills (2:3)

                   (a) Turning to Wine as an Intended Source of Intoxication (2:3a)

                   (b) Turning to Wine as an Imagined Source of Inspiration (2:3b)

           c) The World of Things (2:4–11)

               (1) What He Accomplished (2:4–6)

                   (a) Magnificent Palaces (2:4a)

                   (b) Magnificent Parklands (2:4b–5)

45

        (c) Magnificent Pools (2:6)
    (2) What He Accumulated (2:7–8)
        (a) All Kinds of People (2:7a)
        (b) All Kinds of Possessions (2:7b–8a)
            (i) Countless Cattle (2:7b)
            (ii) Cold Cash (2:8a)
        (c) All Kinds of Power (2:8b)
        (d) All Kinds of Performers (2:8c)
    (3) What He Avowed (2:9–10)
        (a) That He Retained All His Discretion (2:9)
        (b) That He Realized All His Desires (2:10)
    (4) What He Acknowledged (2:11)
        (a) His Enterprise Considered (2:11a)
        (b) His Emptiness Confessed (2:11b)
2. His Pessimistic Summary (2:12–26)
  a) The Barrenness of It All (2:12–16)
    (1) The Turning Point in His Life (2:12–14)
        (a) Why He Turned (2:12)
            (i) To Make a Comparison (2:12a)
            (ii) To Mature a Conviction (2:12b)
        (b) What He Testified (2:13–14)
            (i) Discretion Is Inestimable (2:13–14a)
            (ii) Death Is Inevitable (2:14b)
    (2) The Turning Point in His Logic (2:15–16)
        (a) Soon Be Finished (2:15)
        (b) Soon Be Forgotten (2:16)
  b) The Bitterness of It All (2:17–26)
    (1) He Hated His Life (2:17)
        (a) Nothing in His Life Was Satisfying (2:17a)
        (b) Nothing in His Life Was Spiritual (2:17b)
    (2) He Hated His Labors (2:18–21)
        (a) Lose Possession of His Things (2:18)
        (b) Lose Power over His Things (2:19)
        (c) Lose Pleasure in His Things (2:20–21a)
            (i) His Gloom (2:20)
            (ii) His Doom (2:21a)
        (d) Lose Purchase of His Legacy (2:21b)

    (3) He Hated His Lot (2:22–26)
        (a) A Question (2:22–23)
           (i) As to an Adequate Reason for Everything (2:22)
           (ii) As to an Adequate Result for Everything (2:23)
        (b) A Quest (2:24–25)
           (i) The Materialist and His Goal (2:24a)
           (ii) The Materialist and His God (2:24b–25)
        (c) A Qualification (2:26)
           (i) God's Gifts (2:26a)
           (ii) God's Government (2:26b)
B. Things He Had Seen (3:1–6:12)
   1. The Problem of Time Without Eternity (3:1–11)
     a) The Logic of Time (3:1–8)
       (1) The Rule Expressed (3:1)
       (2) The Rule Expanded (3:2–8)
          (a) The Parameters of Life (3:2–3a)
             (i) The Providential (3:2a) Born . . . Die
             (ii) The Circumstantial (3:2a) Pluck . . . Plant
             (iii)The Judicial (3:3a) Kill . . . Heal
             (iv) The Pursuits of Life (3:3b) Break . . . Build
          (b) The Pleasures of Life (3:4)
             (i) Personal Emotions (3:4a) Weep . . . Laugh
             (ii) Public Emotions (3:4b) Mourn . . . Dance
          (c) The Pressures of Life (3:5a) Cast Away . . . Gather
          (d) The Proprieties of Life (3:5b)
          (e) The Practicalities of Life (3:6–7a)
             (i) The Merchant (3:6a) Get . . . Lose
             (ii) The Miser (3:6b) Keep . . . Cast
             (iii)The Mother (3:7a) Rend . . . Sew
          (f) The Precautions of Life (3:7b) Silence . . . Speak
          (g) The Passions of Life (3:8a) Love . . . Hate
          (h) The Provocations of Life (3:8b) War . . . Peace
     b) The Limitations of Time (3:9–11)
       (1) What He Discerned (3:9–10)
          (a) The Penetrating Question (3:9)
          (b) The Perpetual Quest (3:10)
       (2) What He Discovered (3:11a)

        (3) What He Decided (3:11b)
2. The Problem of a New Leaf Without a New Life (3:12–17)
    a) The Works of the Creature (3:12–13)
        (1) Man's Limitations (3:12)
            (a) The Realization (3:12a)
            (b) The Resolve (3:12b)
        (2) Man's Labors (3:13)
            (a) His Acceptance of Life's Bounty (3:13a)
            (b) His Acknowledgment of Life's Benefactor (3:13b)
    b) The Works of the Creator (3:14–17)
        (1) In the Material Realm (3:14)
            (a) The Permanence of God's Works (3:14a)
            (b) The Purpose of God's Works (3:14b)
        (2) In the Moral Realm (3:15–17)
            (a) The Past Required (3:15)
            (b) The Present Reviewed (3:16)
                (i) Public Wickedness (3:16a)
                (ii) Personal Wickedness (3:16b)
            (c) The Prospect Revealed (3:17)
                (i) The Truth of Judgment Is Sure (3:17a)
                (ii) The Time of Judgment Is Set (3:17b)
3. The Problem of Mortality Without Immortality (3:18–22)
    a) A Low View of Man's Dignity (3:18–19)
        (1) Man Is a Beast Constitutionally (3:18)
            (a) As to His Being (3:18a)
            (b) As to His Breath (3:18b)
         (2) Man Is a Beast Comparatively (3:19)
    b) A Low View of Man's Destiny (3:20–21)
        (1) A Conclusion (3:20)
        (2) A Complication (3:21)
    c) A Low View of Man's Duty (3:22)
        (1) Investing in the Here and Now (3:22a)
        (2) Ignorance of the Hereafter (3:22b)
4. The Problem of Might Without Right (4:1–3)
    a) A Gloomy Consideration (4:1)
        (1) The Anguish of the Oppressed (4:1a)
        (2) The Arrogance of the Oppressors (4:1b)

     b) A Gloomy Conclusion (4:2–3)
        (1) Praising Those the Tomb Has Received (4:2)
        (2) Praising Those the Womb Has Refused (4:3)
5. The Problem of Prosperity Without Posterity (4:4–12)
     a) The Resentful Man (4:4–5)
        (1) The Lusting Fool (4:4)
        (2) The Lazy Fool (4:5)
     b) The Realistic Man (4:6)
     c) The Ridiculous Man (4:7–12)
        (1) The Situation (4:7–8)
           (a) No Son (4:7–8a)
           (b) No Satisfaction (4:8b)
           (c) No Sense (4:8c)
        (2) The Suggestion (4:9–12)
           (a) Production (4:9)
           (b) Precaution (4:10)
           (c) Preservation (4:11)
           (d) Protection (4:12)
6. The Problem of Sovereignty Without Sagacity (4:13–16)
     a) Unsound in His Thoughts (4:13)
     b) Unsuited to His Throne (4:14)
     c) Unsung by the Throng (4:15–16)
        (1) The Nameless Monarch (4:15)
        (2) The Nebulous Multitude (4:16a)
        (3) The Nagging Misery (4:16b)
7. The Problem of Religion Without Reality (5:1–7)
     a) The Value of Silence (5:1–3)
        (1) Tread Softly in the House of God (5:1a)
        (2) Talk Sparingly in the House of God (5:1b–3)
           (a) The Careless Sacrifice of the Foolish Man (5:1b)
           (b) The Common Sense of the Foresighted Man (5:2)
               (i) The Nature of His Caution (5:2a)
               (ii) The Need for His Caution (5:2b)
           (c) The Continuous Speech of the Foolish Man (5:3)
               (i) How He Dabbles (5:3a)
               (ii) How He Babbles (5:3b)
     b) The Vow Once Spoken (5:4–7)

C. Things He Had Studied (7:1–10:20)
  1. Life's Frustrations (7:1–29)
    a) Cynicism About the Better Things of Life (7:1–14)
      (1) Character Values (7:1a)
      (2) Conventional Values (7:1b–6)
        (a) Life's Sum (7:1b)
        (b) Life's Sorrows (7:2–4)
          (i) The House of Mourning (7:2)
          (ii) The Heart of Man (7:3–4)
            (a) Things We Laugh About (7:3)
            (b) Things We Learn About (7:4)
        (c) Life's Seriousness (7:5–6)
          (i) The Rebuking Comment of the Farsighted Man (7:5)
          (ii) The Ribald Cackling of the Foolish Man (7:6)
      (3) Contemptible Values (7:7)
      (4) Conclusive Values (7:8a)
      (5) Crucial Values (7:8b–9)
        (a) The Principle Expressed (7:8b)
        (b) The Principle Expanded (7:9)
      (6) Comparative Values (7:10)
      (7) Concrete Values (7:11–12)
        (a) Wisdom in the Daily Things of Life (7:11)
        (b) Wisdom in the Deeper Things of Life (7:12)
      (8) Considered Values (7:13–14)
        (a) The Works of God (7:13)
        (b) The Ways of God (7:14)
    b) Cynicism About the Bitter Things of Life (7:15–29)
      (1) Cynicism About the Well Doing (7:15–19)
        (a) What Solomon Saw (7:15)
          (i) Good Behavior Does Not Guarantee a Prolonged Life (7:15a)
          (ii) Bad Behavior Does Not Guarantee a Premature Death (7:15b)
        (b) What Solomon Suggested (7:16–17)
          (i) Be Moderately Religious (7:16)
          (ii) Be Moderately Rebellious (7:17)

(ii) The Respectable Man and the Licentious Man (9:2c)

(iii) The Religious Man and the Lost Man (9:2d)

(iv) The Resolute Man and the Lackadaisical Man (9:2e)

    (3) The Inescapability of Death (9:3)

       (a) The Ghost That Haunts Us All (9:3a)

       (b) The Grave That Hunts Us All (9:3b–c)

          (i) The Follies of Life (9:3b)

          (ii) The Finality of Death (9:3c)

  b) A Callous Declaration (9:4–6)

    (1) A Fatalistic Statement (9:4–5a)

       (a) A Cynical Comparison (9:4)

       (b) A Cynical Comment (9:5a)

    (2) A False Statement (9:5b)

    (3) A Factual Statement (9:6)

       (a) Their Passions Have Faded Away (9:6a)

       (b) Their Persons Have Faded Away (9:6b)

  c) A Carnal Decision (9:7–10)

    (1) Enjoy Your Wine While You Can (9:7)

    (2) Enjoy Your Wealth While You Can (9:8)

    (3) Enjoy Your Wife While You Can (9:9)

    (4) Enjoy Your Work While You Can (9:10)

4. Life's Falseness (9:11–10:15)

  a) The Triumph of Fate (9:11–12)

    (1) The Unattainable (9:11)

       (a) Choice: The Great Inequity of Life (9:11a)

       (b) Chance: The Great Inevitability of Death (9:11b)

    (2) The Unavoidable (9:12)

       (a) Life's Limitations (9:12a–b)

          (i) Indicated (9:12a)

          (ii) Illustrated (9:12b)

       (b) Life's Liabilities (9:12c)

  b) The Triumph of Forgetfulness (9:13–18)

    (1) The City (9:13–15)

       (a) The Size of the City (9:13–14b)

          (i) No Outward Significance (9:13–14a)

          (ii) No Inward Strength (9:14b)

       (b) The Siege of the City (9:14c)

PART 2: THE PREACHER'S SERMON (1:12–10:20)

  A. Things He Had Sought (1:12–2:26)

    1. His Persistent Search (1:12–2:11)

      a) The World of Thought (1:12–1:18)

        (1) His First Quest: To Exploit His Wisdom (1:12–15)

          (a) What He Declared (1:12)

Having told us that he intends to look at life from the standpoint of a man "under the sun" in order to expose the utter vanity and futility of this popular perspective, Solomon gets down to cases. He shows us some of the things he had sought (1:12–2:26), some of the things he had seen (3:1–6:12), and some of the things he had studied (7:1–10:20). He begins with the things he had sought. He had looked for lasting satisfaction in the world of thought (1:12–18), in the world of thrills (2:1–3), and in the world of things (2:4–11), places where people still look in vain for lasting joy. Indeed, most of our education today is in the hands of secular materialists who have nothing else to offer and so train our children and youth to go in for these three empty goals.

Solomon begins with the world of thought. He aimed at becoming the greatest intellectual on earth. We note what he declared: *"I the Preacher was king over Israel in Jerusalem . . ."* (1:12). He had already established that in 1:1. Perhaps he suspected that later generations would try to rob him of his own book. He has only just noted how quickly the past buries even its illustrious dead so that they lie forgotten in their graves. To this day either Shakespeare lies forgotten, robbed of his matchless plays and poetry by a generation which attributes them to Francis Bacon; or, Bacon lies forgotten, his great masterpieces universally attributed to Shakespeare. Solomon gloomily suspected that he would be forgotten or remembered for the wrong things. As Shakespeare declared in *Julius Caesar*, "The evil that men do lives after them; The good is oft interred with their bones."

Solomon, in any case, repeats himself. The man who wrote the book of Ecclesiastes was "the son of David" and he was "King over Israel in Jerusalem." Solomon was the only king of whom this was true. After his death, the kingdom was divided. Ten of the tribes, thereafter, were ruled by various non-Davidic dynasties from various cities and ultimately Samaria. The successors to Solomon, of David's line, ruled from Jerusalem over only the rump kingdom of Judah and Benjamin.

Curiously blind to the obvious, the critics have, indeed, done their worst to rob Solomon of his repentance and of his book. Sad to say, as we have already noted, Martin Luther led the way claiming that the book was written by one Sirach in the days of the Maccabees. Grotius agreed with him, assigning the book to a post-exilic date. By the end of the nineteenth century, a continuous stream of critics was pooh-poohing the authorship of Solomon. Keil, Delitzsch, Hengstenberg, Renan, Ewald, and others wrote Solomon off. In their views, the writer assumed the name and characteristics of Solomon, ascribing to himself, fictitiously, the role of "son of David, king over Israel in Jerusalem." In other words, the man was a pious fraud and the book a forgery. As for the critics, they are at loggerheads among themselves, quite unable to agree as to who this forger was or when he lived. Almost a thousand years separate their various guesses, all the way from 975 to 40 B.C.

(b) What He Determined (1:13a)

We note also what he determined: *"And I gave my heart to seek and search out by wisdom concerning all things that are done under heaven . . ."* (1:13a). Wisdom was God's original gift to Solomon shortly after his accession to the throne when he went to Gibeon, where the Tabernacle was, and celebrated his coronation with a magnanimous offering. That night God appeared to Solomon and asked him to choose a gift. Solomon chose wisdom (an understanding heart) to judge the people. God granted him that which he requested. Shortly afterwards, the people were given such a demonstration of the practical application of Solomon's divinely bestowed astuteness that "they saw that the wisdom of God was in him, to do judgment" (1 Kings 3:28).

The Hebrew word for "wisdom" commonly used in connection with Solomon is *chokmah*. It stands for *common sense*. It means *to be skillful, subtle, wise hearted*. The same word is used when we are told that "Solomon's wisdom excelled the wisdom of all the children of the east country, and all the wisdom of Egypt. For he was wiser than all men; than Ethan the Ezrahite, and Heman, and Chalcol, and Darda, the sons of Mahol: and his fame was in all nations round about. . . . And there came of all people to hear the wisdom of Solomon, from all kings of the earth, which had heard of his wisdom" (1 Kings 4:30–31, 34).

We learn from this same passage that Solomon was learned in natural history, and from the book of Proverbs that he had a thorough understanding of human nature as well. Not least of those who came to sample the fabled wisdom of Solomon was the Queen of Sheba who came all the way up the long reaches of the Nile, across the sands of Sinai, and up into the hill country of Judah just to sit at his feet, listen to his wisdom, and try him with hard questions. And then she said, "Howbeit I believed not the words, until I came, and mine eyes had seen it: and, behold, the half was not told me: thy wisdom and prosperity exceedeth the fame which I heard" (1 Kings 10:7). She then returned, at last, to her own country, awed and overwhelmed. So to begin with, Solomon determined in his heart to become an intellectual, renowned for wisdom.

(c) What He Displayed (1:13b)

We note, next, what he displayed: *". . . this sore travail hath God given to the sons of man to be exercised therewith"* (1:13b). He displayed at once his own discontent with intellectualism. The word for "travail" occurs often in this book, and nowhere else in the Old Testament. Solomon found the pursuit of knowledge, understanding, and wisdom to be a laborious exercise. He had felt himself under a compulsion to make laborious investigations into the nature of things. He displayed dissatisfaction with the results.

The word Solomon used here and throughout the book of Ecclesiastes is *Elohim*. He studiously avoided the covenant name Jehovah. The book refers to mankind in general in relation to his Creator, not to Israel in covenant relation with the Lord. Hence, also, we see the frequent use of the word *adam* for "man" in this book. Solomon had betrayed Jehovah and abused the great gifts given to him. He had lived like a worldling and displays now only a worldling's knowledge of God.

(d) What He Discovered (1:14–15)
(i) Man's Works Are Disappointing (1:14)

We note, further, what he discovered (1:14–15). He discovered first, that man's works were disappointing: *"I have seen all the works that are done under the sun; and, behold, all is vanity and vexation of spirit"* (1:14). The expression "vexation of Spirit" means "feeding on the wind" and it occurs nine times in the book. Of course, Solomon was speaking relatively, not absolutely! We have no record that he ever went to Egypt to view the pyramids, for instance. But he had seen enough to know that feats of mechanical engineering, married to artistic and scientific methods of construction, brought no lasting satisfaction. Tourist attractions soon pale.

In my days as an itinerant preacher, I traveled far and wide throughout the United States and Canada and overseas to some two dozen countries. In time, all cities looked alike and all the fabled sights were just other monuments. I'm glad to have seen Niagara Falls and the Rocky Mountains. I'm glad to have seen Westminster Abbey and the Crown Jewels in the Tower of London. I'm glad to have seen Jerusalem and the crest of Carmel. I'm glad to have been to Egypt and Rome. But the colosseum at Rome after all was but a bigger version of the Roman amphitheater at Caerleon, Wales, only a few miles from where I grew up, and the Eiffel Tower in Paris is not that much more impressive than the towering steel structure known as the Transporter Bridge at the far end of Dock Street in my hometown. I'm glad to have seen the awesome arch which towers over St. Louis and to have seen the Golden Gate Bridge in San Francisco. I'm glad to have stood on the equator in Ecuador and to have been to New Zealand, but now I would just as soon stay at home! Full-color brochures of cruises on the Alaskan waterway or of the changing of the guard at Buckingham Palace now leave me unmoved. If I want to see them I'd just as soon rent a travel video and get the grand tour in my comfortable chair beside the den fire!

Man's works are dazzling. The genius that built the Canadian Pacific Railroad or the Panama Canal or the Great Wall of China or the Taj Mahal cannot fail to impress us. The man-made monuments left behind pay tribute to that genius, but the monuments themselves fail to touch the deepest needs of a hungry heart. To that extent Solomon was right. They are all "vanity and vexation of spirit."

It has often been observed that the local folk, those who grew up within a mile or so of some world-famous site, often never bother their heads to go and see it for themselves. No doubt Solomon could have preached a sermon on that phenomenon alone!

If man's works are disappointing and incapable of satisfying, there is also something else—man's ways are dismaying (1:15).

(ii) Man's Ways Are Dismaying (1:15)
(a) The Bentness of Things (1:15a)

Solomon took note, for instance, of the bentness of things; "*. . . that which is crooked cannot be made straight*" (1:15a). Of all the bent things "under the sun" there is nothing more bent than human nature. There are at least fifteen different Hebrew words for sin in the Old Testament. One of them is *avon* which captures the idea of "perverseness." It stems from a root word which means "to be bent" or "crooked." The word Solomon used for crooked here is *avath* which is similar. It conveys the idea of falsifying something, of dealing perversely or perverting, of turning something upside down—which exactly describes what the fall has done to human nature. Satan himself is bent. He was brilliant. He was the highest of all created intelligences. He functioned as the choir master of heaven (Ezekiel 28:12–15). Then "iniquity was found in him," and the Holy Spirit says that, as a result, he became a fallen creature, warped and bent and twisted and full of guile.

It was thus that he entered Eden and persuaded Eve to eat of the forbidden fruit, deceiving her and bringing about also the fall of Adam through disobedience. As a result of Adam's disobedience, sin entered the world, and death by sin. Adam was created to be inhabited by God. The divine plan was that the human spirit be indwelled by the Holy Spirit and people, made in the image and likeness of God, would walk with God. When sin entered, the Holy Spirit departed, vacating His Temple in man's innermost being.

Man, in sin, is bent and crooked. He has a body and a soul, with intellect, emotions, and will, and since the fall, a conscience as God's vice regent in his heart. He has a spirit, too, but it is the animating energy. As a result, man has no governing principle. Animals are governed by instinct. Man was to be indwelled and governed by God. Instead of being born in the image and likeness of God, Adam's descendants have all been born in the image and likeness of Adam, fallen, bent creatures with natures which are prone to sin.

Solomon's pessimistic comment declares "that which is crooked cannot be made straight." He knew, for instance, from bitter experience that his son and heir, Rehoboam, was a born fool, that it was impossible to teach him wisdom, and that his bent was toward bosom buddies as empty-headed as he. He had himself, early in his reign, executed a man by the name of Shimei, a man with a foul mouth, a black heart, and an incorrigible rebel at that. His bent was toward defiance of authority, and it killed him in the end.

Gloomy as is Solomon's conclusion, there is, in the grace of God, a solution. Tares do not become wheat; whitewashed sows do not become sheep. God does not patch up old garments or put new wine in old wineskins. He does not patch up the apostate Jewish race—He replaces it with the Church until such a time as He can create a new Israel. He does not put the new wine of the Kingdom in the worn-out wineskin of an Adamic nature—He puts the old nature to death in the death of Christ and replaces it with the new nature bestowed upon us through regeneration and the gift of His grace.

(b) The Bankruptcy of Things (1:15b)

Solomon took note not only of the bentness of things but also of the bankruptcy of things: *". . . and that which is wanting cannot be numbered"* (1:15b). A bankrupt businessman can juggle the figures at will but that will not change the fact that he is bankrupt. When I was a boy in school our math teacher once played a trick on us. He liked the challenge of mental arithmetic, and from time to time would challenge the class to work out in their heads sums he set for them. He would call out a string of commands: "Add forty-five to ninety-one. Now multiply that by twelve. Divide by eight. Subtract forty-five. All right, Williams, what's the answer?" I remember on one occasion he threw a particularly difficult string of numbers at us. Something like, "Add two-hundred and ninety-one to one-hundred and ninety-two, multiply by fifteen, add four-hundred and thirty-six. Subtract three-hundred and forty-one. Divide by twenty."

By this time, he'd lost most of us. We hoped, when he called for the answer, the lot would fall on someone else. Then, he threw his curveball. "Multiply your answer by zero," he said. The answer, of course, was zero, for no matter how many zeros you have, you still have nothing! Similarly, "That which is wanting cannot be numbered." A balance sheet which fails to show a profit registers a loss. Nothing multiplied by a million equals nothing—a million nothings, but still nothing.

Many centuries after the days of Solomon, another ruler, a pagan ruler, the last vice regent of the great imperial city of Babylon, was taught the same lesson. The hand of God had come out from the sleeve of the night. It had written upon the wall of the palace these mysterious words: "MENE, MENE, TEKEL, UPHARSIN." Numbered! Numbered! Weighed! Divided! (Daniel 5:25).

It took a prophet of God to translate that into a message of doom. Belshazzar's kingdom was numbered. Its days were done. Already the Persians were at the gates. As for Belshazzar, he was weighed and found wanting. He was bankrupt. He had nothing that could be numbered. When he promised to give Daniel a third of the kingdom if he would read the writing, the prophet rejected the offer. "Thy gifts be to thyself and give thy rewards to another," he said. Belshazzar was bankrupt and as good as dead. He was found wanting and that which is wanting cannot be numbered. That self-same night Belshazzar was slain (Daniel 5:16–30).

To Solomon, it would have been just another proof of the ultimate bankruptcy of life "under the sun." We cannot reckon on that which is not there to count. A bankrupt person cannot solve his problem by juggling with numbers that are not there to count. A man might be considered a very great success as far as this world is concerned and yet be declared bankrupt by God (Luke 12:15–21). That which is wanting cannot be numbered. He was numbering the bags of grain his fields would yield and the number of barns he would need and the banquets he could expect to enjoy. But what he couldn't count, and so therefore ignored, that which was wanting—time! He was the arch materialist of the New Testament, wholly committed to life "under the sun."

(2) His Further Quest: To Explore His Wisdom (1:16–18)
(a) His Success (1:16)

"I communed with mine own heart, saying, Lo, I am come to great estate, and have gotten more wisdom than all they that have been before me in Jerusalem" (1:16). "Yea,

my heart had great experience of wisdom and knowledge," Solomon said. His knowledge was encyclopedic. The trouble with Solomon was that his knowledge and wisdom rarely soared above the clouds and was preeminently wisdom pertaining to things "under the sun." Even the Temple he had built in Jerusalem was really his father's vision, not his, although he had dutifully built it and dedicated it.

In spite of his boast to having unsurpassed wisdom and knowledge, Solomon could not hold a candle to his father. David was far wiser than Solomon, despite his faults and failures, in what really mattered—his knowledge of God. When faced with a choice, Solomon asked God to make him wise. When confronted by sad realities, David asked God to make him good. Solomon for all his heralded wisdom and knowledge, had not the heart that David had to write half the book of Psalms.[1]

Solomon, of course, was not without his more spiritual moments in his early days. His backsliding was a gradual affair. David suffered from a sudden fall into sin. Solomon's condition was much more dangerous. He gradually drifted into a backslidden condition. David knew that he had fallen and could not wait to get right with God once his conscience was awakened. Solomon never did make such a public confession of his sin, and there are those to this day who deny that Solomon ever repented at all.

Solomon's conclusion as a result of his excursion into the world of thought was dismal enough. He had achieved remarkable success. People of high rank came from far-off lands to sit at his feet and listen to his lectures on natural history, psychology, and the art of government. But it left him cold. His success brought him no lasting satisfaction.

(b) His Search (1:17–18)
(i) His Goal (1:17a)

He recapitulates. He describes his goal: *"And I gave my heart to know wisdom, and to know madness and folly"* (1:17a). He did not confine himself to the positive aspects of wisdom but probed just as deeply into the ingrained fallen nature of man and to its dark and bitter fruits of insanity and stupidity. He left no stone unturned in his quest for truth. His research took him into many legitimate realms of thought. He perused the various philosophies of men, explored the religious beliefs of the surrounding nations, and delved into the secrets of nature. He was a man of great catholicity of mind. He could see the other man's point of view and empathize with him even when he did not agree with him.

At the same time, he delved into the knowledge of wickedness and explored what could be called the deep things of Satan. One cannot, however, touch tar and not be contaminated. The knowledge of wickedness is a dangerous knowledge. There are forbidden secrets, especially in the world of the occult, the pornographic, and the erotic. No doubt Solomon justified his exploitations into these realms on the grounds that he needed to know about them if he was to be fully informed and govern well. He needed to know about the criminal mind and the carnal mind and the crafty mind and the cultic mind and the crazy mind.

He wanted to know, for instance, about "madness and folly." The word for "madness" is *holeloth* (an intensive plural). The etymology of the word indicates a "confusion of thought—the madness which deranges all ideas of order and propriety." The word for "folly" is *sickluth*, a word associated with vice and wickedness, the very opposite of goodness.

(ii) His Gloom (1:17b)

He describes also his gloom: *"I perceived that this also is vexation of spirit"* (1:17b). When he had achieved success in the world of thought and had become the greatest intellectual of his day, one whose fame would ring down the centuries, Solomon discovered that it was all just so much "chasing the wind." His success did not make him happy, after all. The world beat a path to his door. His classes were packed. Thunderous applause interrupted and climaxed his lectures. He was world famous. Letters and degrees and honors were bestowed upon him. And it all added up to nothing. Because one can have a dozen Ph.D.'s and be thoroughly miserable. He can end up making the greatest mistake of all—the mistake of leaving God out of things and settling for what is offered "under the sun."

Few men influenced the modern world more than H. G. Wells. His influence on his own age and his legacy to posterity was pernicious, destructive, and malignant. His enormous popularity (his *Outline of History* sold more than three million copies) only increased the damage he was able to do. He spoke blasphemously against Christ, detested the Bible, loathed the Church, and hated Jews. He admired Stalin. His lifestyle was one of promiscuous abuse of women. He postured as a teacher of society. He fancied himself as a revolutionary called to cleanse the world of the Judeo-Christian ethic in favor of his own immoral utopia. He died a disappointed, despairing, and disillusioned man. World War 2 shattered his utopian dreams. He walked increasingly on the edge of despair. One story I've heard is that during the last year of his life he was visited by Rupert

Hart-Davis, a friend and one of his future publishers. Wells was old and ill. He was bedridden and burdened. He remarked that the world was in a terrible mess. "Yes, and it's your fault," replied his visitor.

His last book, little more than a pamphlet, he entitled *Mind at the End of Its Tether* (1946). It was a scream of complete hopelessness and despair. He likened the world to a convoy lost at sea. It was dark. A rocky, unknown coast loomed ahead. Quarreling pirates were in the chart room. Savages were swarming over the ships wreaking mayhem. At the end of the book he summed up (unconsciously describing his own sordid life) by saying, "The old men behave, for the most part, meanly and disgustingly, and the young are spasmodic, foolish, and all too easily misled. . . . Ordinary man is at the end of his tether." We see an old man without faith, without love, and without hope; a man who, like Solomon, lied "under the sun" and having sown the wind reaped the whirlwind of despair.

(iii) His Grief (1:18)

Finally, Solomon describes his grief: *"For in much wisdom is much grief: and he that increaseth knowledge increaseth sorrow"* (1:18). So much for intellectualism. We speak sarcastically of "blissful ignorance." Solomon speaks of bitter knowledge. The more one knows, the more frustrated one becomes at one's inability to correct the unsatisfactory state of affairs at the root of the human condition. Moreover, the more one knows, the more one realizes how little he knows.

We live in an age when knowledge has increased, as the prophet foretold (Daniel 12:4). There is no man living who can know all there is to know about his own particular scientific discipline. It has been said that a doctor, for instance, would need to read the equivalent of one book every hour just to keep up with his specialty. Still less can a person, however brilliant, know everything there is to know. All this knowledge has not made the world a happier or a safer place in which to live. It has only increased the pessimism of men like H. G. Wells.

Or take Albert Einstein, one of the greatest scientists the world has ever known. His genius flowered in the year 1905 when he was working as a patent examiner in Berne, Switzerland, because he was rejected when he applied for academic positions. In that one year, for instance, he came up with his theory of relativity and his quantum theory of light. It says something for the daring of his genius that though the two theories appeared to be contradictory, he proposed both theories at once. (The theory of relativity assumed that light consists of waves, and the quantum theory assumed that light consists of particles.)

Einstein changed the world. The Nazis in Germany officially declared his theories false because Einstein was a Jew. His property was seized, and a reward offered for his capture. When U.S. scientists feared Germany might develop an atomic bomb, they tried to warn the American authorities, but they were ignored. They provided to Einstein a letter addressed to President Roosevelt, who heeded the famous Einstein. As a result, the decision was made to outpace the Germans and build the bomb first. Einstein took no part in the project even though his famous equation $E=mc^2$ had given birth to the atomic age. When he learned what destruction had been wrought at Hiroshima and Nagasaki, he was overwhelmed. His friend and colleague, Banesh Hoffman, in a *Reader's Digest* article, "The Unforgettable Albert Einstein," said the greatest scientist was dismayed beyond measure and from then on there was a look of ineffable sadness in his eyes.[2]

"For in much wisdom is much grief; and he that increaseth knowledge increaseth sorrow." What, we wonder, must have been Einstein's personal sorrow and dismay at the fast-paced developments which followed—the hydrogen bomb, the cobalt bomb, the neutron bomb, the development of intercontinental ballistic missile, the Cold War and the arms race, the stockpiling of nuclear weapons. Science is like that. Particle accelerators and nuclear reactors sprang up in the wake of science. Toxic and deadly wastes were developed, and radioactive by-products posed environmental hazards. Outer space is littered with debris, and men leave trash on the moon. So, there is plenty of sorrow and grief to go around.

> b) The World of Thrills (2:1–3)
>> (1) Life's Entertaining Thrills (2:1–2)
>>> (a) Solomon's Decision (2:1a–b)

Disappointed by the world of thought, Solomon turned next to the world of thrills. As we would say today, he decided to "live it up" or, as the rich fool said in the Lord's parable, he decided to "eat, drink, and be merry" (Luke 12:19). He now becomes the prodigal in the Lord's parable, he "wasted his substance with riotous living" (Luke 15:13). It is of more than passing interest that the word the Lord used, *asotos*, means "to live ruinously."

> (i) To Seek Things to Make Him Laugh (2:1a)

Solomon's decision was twofold. First, he sought out things to make him laugh: *"I said in mine heart, Go to now, I will prove thee with mirth"* (2:1a). Thus, kings of old burdened with the cares and responsibilities of the affairs of state kept court jesters on hand. It was their task to make witty remarks, funny quips, to pillory and lampoon members of the court and make the king laugh.

There can be little doubt that laughter can be therapeutic. For years, *Reader's Digest* has carried a humor page entitled: "Laughter Is the Best Medicine." Indeed, the Bible says, "A merry heart doeth good like a medicine: but a broken spirit drieth the bones" (Proverbs 17:22). It is an observable fact that unhappy people can suffer from psychosomatic disorders for which there is no organic cause.

A number of years ago, *Review Magazine* (April 1980) carried an article about Norman Cousins, onetime owner and editor of *Saturday Review*. He was diagnosed as having collagen disease, a disintegration of the connective tissue between the cells. His symptoms included high fever, heaviness in his legs, and back paralysis.

Mr. Cousins decided to become responsible for his own health. He diagnosed himself as suffering from stress and vitamin C deficiency. He began to take large doses of vitamin C and to watch comedies. The more he laughed, the better he got until at last his symptoms disappeared, and he was able to return to work. In analyzing his recovery, he came to the conclusion that the ascorbic acid possibly helped collagen formation and that hearty laughter helped respiration, oxygenated his blood, and combated levels of carbon dioxide. Even the medical establishment is beginning to believe that attitude and belief are important to recovery from illness. Perhaps eventually, medical science will discover the link between a merry heart and medicine.

Well, maybe Solomon needed a tonic after his depression about the failure of wisdom to satisfy his deepest longings. He decided to laugh off his gloom. Forget the lecture halls of the learned! Life was too short to be spent poring over books and parchments, accumulating an ever-increasing horde of worthless information. It was time to have some fun. He told his soul as much. What he needed was a good laugh. And so, the pendulum swung from logic to laughter. Away with the grey-haired professors and their somber debates! Bring on the clowns! Search the land for comedians! Who has a good joke?

Strong's Concordance gives us the word *simchah* as the Hebrew word for "mirth" which means to be gleeful as at a festival. Gesenius' lexicon suggests "to be very joyful" points us to a joyful banquet. The great banquet of Belshazzar would give us an idea of the kind of thing Solomon pursued at this stage of life. There would be all kinds of gaiety and excess. Wine would flow freely. A dynamic master of ceremonies would be able to command a fortune.

(ii) To Seek Things to Massage His Lusts (2:1b)

One thing leads to another. Solomon now pumps himself up to pursue pleasure, to seek out things to massage his lusts: *"therefore enjoy pleasure"* (2:1b). The primary root for "pleasure" here means "good" but, as the context shows, Solomon made the pursuit of pleasure as an end in itself. There are many good and wholesome pleasures. Solomon, however, was now intent on having what the world would call "a good time" or "a good fling." The word can be rendered "merry," a word we associate in our English Bibles with the prodigal son's older brother. He bitterly complained that no one had ever given him a fatted calf so that he could "make merry" with his friends (Luke 15).

Pleasure has its place. The Bible warns us against "the pleasures of sin" (Hebrews 11). It would seem from the result of his mad indulgence of pleasure that whatever plans Solomon may have had to enjoy legitimate and wholesome pleasures, things soon got completely out of hand. He became, as it were, an Epicurean.

We picture Solomon indulging in every pleasure that came his way. His harem was enormous. His resources were boundless, his revelry was unstinted and unrestrained. Those passing by the palace in those days would hear the beat of the music and the lewd laughter of the revelers on the grounds. There were sights and sounds to shock even the depraved. Drink and drugs were doubtlessly freely available. Unbridled lust reigned in the wild parties thrown by the king. Solomon was determined to seize upon every pleasure available to man "under the sun" until at last he was satiated, soaked, and saturated with the lust of the eye, the lust of the flesh, and the pride of life.

(b) His Disappointment (2:1c)

Solomon's disappointment, *". . . and behold, this also is vanity"* (2:1c). A poet of a later age summed it up in similar words:

> But pleasures are like poppies spread,
> You seize the flower, its bloom is shed;
> Or, like the snow-fall in the river,
> A moment white—then melts forever.[3]

For there is a dark side to pleasure. Not only does it not satisfy, it also enslaves. The cigarette advertisements depict strong, healthy men in the prime of life and beautiful, triumphant women, cigarette in hand. They do not show the man dying of lung cancer or the woman disfigured and marred by cancer of the lip, mouth, and throat. Nor do they focus on the addicted slave trying vainly to quit the habit. The liquor, wine, and beer advertisers never portray the ravished innocence, the broken homes, the squalor, violence, and enslavement which come along with their wares. The young person being introduced to marijuana is not told of its terrible side effects, nor is he shown the steady progression from marijuana to cocaine and heroin and utter, hopeless, devastating total addiction. The young man or woman being tempted to experiment with illicit sex is not shown the potential sorrow, shame, and disgust that follow nor the many varied, horrible and deadly diseases which await the promiscuous.

In his remarkable book *The Screwtape Letters*, C. S. Lewis lets us eavesdrop on the advice given by Screwtape, a senior devil, to Wormwood, a junior devil, as he instructs him in the art of temptation. The subject of pleasure arises. Screwtape concedes at once that their side had won many souls through pleasure. The problem was, however, that pleasure was really God's invention, not theirs. Moreover, Screwtape realized they had not been able to produce so much as a single genuine pleasure. All they could do was tempt humans to the wrongful use of pleasure. Then Screwtape gave Wormwood hell's formula. The idea was to create an ever-gnawing appetite and lust for ever-dwindling enjoyment—to create more and more lust for less and less pleasure.

No wonder Solomon found himself bitterly disappointed by his excursion into the world of thrills.

(c) His Declaration (2:2)
(i) The World of Thrills Is Dangerous (2:2a)

He suddenly realized that the world of thrills was dangerous. *"I said of laughter, It is mad"* (2:2a). Madness is the opposite of wisdom. In a very literal sense, the poppy-strewn path of pleasure often leads to actual insanity. People have "blown their minds" or "fried their brains," to quote popular expressions, in the pursuit of pleasure.

Timothy Leary was king of the mud heap in the cultural revolution of the 1960s. "Tune in, turn on, drop out!" was the battle cry of that generation, and Leary was one of those who led the way. But, like all others, his time came to die. He may not have been insane, but he was bizarre. His home was designed to prop him up in his old age. His bedroom, for instance, was a strange place where the old man still tried in his bed to avoid death, propped up on either side by a large tank of laughing gas and a computer. Leary crowed: "All my life I've hated legal drugs and loved illegal ones." He helped the laughing gas with injections of dilaudid, doses of hallucinogens, assorted other drugs, cigarettes, and a highball. His wish was that when he died his body would be frozen for future resurrection. The vain hope of having his body frozen by a cryogenics lab to give him some sort of a stake in a future resurrection is about all of what man can hope for "under the sun."

Insanity haunts the drug scene. Marijuana, for instance, contains around sixty compounds called cannabinoids. The most psychoactive is delta-9-tetrahydrocannabinol (THC). More than four hundred other chemicals lurk in the plant with many of their effects still unknown. THC and other cannabinoids dissolve and get into the brain and about half a dozen other organs. THC molecules distort the brain's information processing system. It can hamper the user's ability to learn and remember. It contaminates the lungs with three times more tar than tobacco. And, all too often, it becomes the springboard to the use of even worse drugs, cocaine for instance.

In the human brain, there are some ten billion cells called neurons. These take care of our life-support systems and our thoughts and emotions. One of the hundreds of neurotransmitters in the brain is dopamine. Many researchers think that cocaine interferes with the neurochemical processes of the brain. Disturbances in the dopamine supply can lead to serious mental illness such as schizophrenia and Parkinson's disease. Cocaine intoxication can lead to paranoia and to hallucinations. Suicide becomes a risk also.

Then there is the popular drug known as "angel dust," or PCP, which causes bizarre behavioral changes strikingly like those seen in schizophrenia— hallucinations, aggression linked with astonishing physical strength, and catatonic rigidity. Add to this the epidemic of crystal meth and heroin abuse and deaths, and the toll from drug abuse is truly horrendous.

No wonder Solomon, an acute observer with a scientific mind, decided that the world of thrills was fraught with danger. "It is mad!" he said. Did he, perhaps, go right to the brink of insanity in his mad search for pleasure? If so, he was mercifully spared from going over into the abyss.

(ii) The World of Thrills Is Deceptive (2:2b)

He recognized, moreover, that the world of thrills was not only dangerous, it was deceptive: *"I said of laughter, It is mad: and of mirth, What doeth it?"* (2:2). In other words, "What's the point of it?" Solomon searched back through the days of his search for satisfaction in laughter. What had been the end result of it all? What lasting gain had it yielded? What did it accomplish? He could think of all kinds of people who had made him laugh. To what purpose? And to what lasting gain?

There was the scoffer, for instance, the man who made a mockery of sin. He was always ready with a dirty joke. He had developed an obscene laugh and a ready eye for that which was lustful and lewd. All he had done was defile.

Then there was the skeptic, the man who mocked faith in God. He had a fund of supposed errors and contradictions he thought he had found in the Bible. And he was very clever at it. He would mock at belief in God, pointing to countless incidents where faith had seemingly been in vain. His vision never rose higher than things "under the sun." Bunyan's pilgrim met Atheist on his journey from the City of Destruction to the Celestial City. My copy of *Pilgrim's Progress* contains some fine four-color illustrations. One of them depicts Atheist.

He is depicted as an aging well-dressed gentleman. He is standing on the edge of a cliff. He is looking back in the direction of Pilgrim and Hopeful, snapping derisive fingers at them. He has a walking stick in his other hand upon which he is about to lean his weight. The walking stick is poised in space over the abyss.

As Bunyan tells the tale, his pilgrim, Christian by name, sees him coming and draws Hopeful's attention to the man:

> Then said Christian to his fellow, Yonder is a man with his back toward Zion, and he is coming to meet us. . . .
> His name was Atheist, and he asked them, Whither they were going?
> *Chr.* We are going to Mount Zion.
> Then Atheist fell into a very great laughter.
> *Chr.* What's the meaning of your laughter?
> *Ath.* I laugh to see what ignorant persons you are, to take upon you so tedious a journey, and yet are like to have nothing but your travel for your pains.
> *Chr.* Why, man! Do you think we shall not be received?
> *Ath.* Received! There is no such a place as you dream of in all this world.
> *Chr.* But there is in the world to come.[4]

Solomon had met many such people and noticed the pitiful shallowness of their laughter. Then there was the seducer. Solomon, in his prodigal days, had met many such. The abandoned woman and the promiscuous man appear frequently in his book of Proverbs. The seducer ruins a woman and then laughs, jokes, and boasts about it. Solomon, in his book of Proverbs, says that there were some four things which were beyond his comprehension. One of them was "the way of a man with a maid" (Proverbs 30:18, 19). One would have thought he was an expert along those lines! Perhaps the thing that puzzled Solomon was the fine line between love and lust. In his youth, he had seen love turn to lust in the case of one of his older brothers—and seen the terrible results (2 Samuel 13). One thing was certain, there was nothing funny or laughable about seduction.

And so, it went on and on as Solomon tried to find an answer to his question—"Laughter? What doeth it?" How does it help fill the void in the human soul? Most jokes are at someone's expense.

    (2) Life's Enslaving Thrills (2:3)
        (a) Turning to Wine as an Intended Source of Intoxication (2:3a)

Solomon comes back from the philosophical to the practical. He gave himself to wine. He said, *"I sought in mine heart to give myself unto wine"* (2:3a). He sought refuge in drunkenness. The bottle offered him a way of escape from his boredom and bewilderment.[5] He would draw his disgust and dissatisfaction in drink. But to no good end. "Wine is a mocker," he wrote (Proverbs 20:1). Indeed, Solomon had no need to go beyond the pages of his Bible to know the folly of drunkenness. The first drunk man to be shown to us was Noah, of all people (Genesis 9:20–27). There may have been some excuse for him. Certainly, the sequel was of global significance. Doubtless, Solomon had been faced with many incidents involving drunkenness in his court sessions. That he should stoop to follow such people into their folly shows how far he had drifted from God.

We know much more about drunkenness than Solomon knew. Within mere minutes after a person takes a drink, alcohol enters the brain. There it numbs the nerve cells and retards the speed with which they send messages to various parts of the body. As the heart tries to cope with alcohol's depressive effects, the pulse rate increases. As more and more alcohol pours into the system, it causes chaos on the nerve centers which control speech, vision, balance, and judgment. The drunkard's vision is distorted, his speech is slurred, he staggers and reels, he makes rash statements and foolish decisions, and often his lustful desires are increased at the same time his moral judgment is undermined.

By depressing the nervous system, alcohol can produce opposite results in different people. For instance, it can dull the inhibitory neurons, and the drunkard becomes the life of the party. By depressing the excitable neurons, alcohol produces the opposite result—a drunkard who is an obnoxious boor, a brooding recluse, or a belligerent brawler.

If imbibed regularly, alcohol increases the risk of heart disease, organ failure, and cancer. The heart of an alcoholic can swell to twice the normal size.

Alcohol wrecks families and ruins friendships. It fills our prisons, hospital insane asylums, and morgues. It creates havoc on the highways and in the home. In our modern society, it is an expensive commodity. It costs us up to a billion and a half dollars annually along with tens of thousands of deaths. The brewers and distillers have persuaded people that alcoholism is a disease. Then they spend more than two billion dollars a year to help people catch it.[6] So, Solomon gave himself to wine, making him a fool. All wine could do for him was make him drunk.

(b) Turning to Wine as an Imagined Source of Inspiration (2:3b)

"*. . . yet acquainting mine heart with wisdom; and to lay hold on folly, till I might see what was that good for the sons of men, which they should do under the heaven all the days of their life*" (2:3b).

Why do people get drunk anyway? What is the fascination of intoxication? Solomon evidently wanted to find out for himself—presumably by becoming drunk. He persuaded himself that he could experiment with alcohol and still retain his sobriety and sagacity. He rationalized. He wanted to know what was best. He would become a human guinea pig.

Surely, such a course could only end in disaster. Even if he did not find himself trapped and addicted to some sinful and harmful vice, he would nevertheless be stained and contaminated. Ever afterwards, memory and guilt would haunt him. It was the age-old temptation presented by fallen Satan to Eve: "Eat and know" (Genesis 3:4–7). Only in Solomon's case, it was a challenge to drink and know.

Solomon encased himself in the fancied armor of his will and resolve, climbed into his barrel, and committed himself to the turbulent waters of his Niagara. Soon he felt the power of the racing river. There, ahead, was the lip of the falls. Over he went. Down, down into the seething cauldron. And, through no strength or power of his own, but through the grace of God to this royal fool, he was cast up on shore, battered, shaken, and convinced that the world of thrills was no place for a man in his right mind.

Solomon bore the fruits of his folly with him all the days of his life. He acquired a taste for lustful living. Wine? He conquered that snare, but women—well that was a different story. He never could resist women. Because he was rich and royal, he could legitimize his lust by marrying the women he desired. But they reigned over him in the end and cost him his kingdom (1 Kings 11:1–13).

Solomon discovered that the drunkard in his cups may consider himself to be a brilliant wit as a world ruler or a mighty warrior. But, when all is said and done, he is nothing but a drunk.

> c) The World of Things (2:4–11)
>   (1) What He Accomplished (2:4–6)

In the end, Solomon pulled himself together and recognized the fearful dangers that lurk in the world of thrills. He gave himself to yet another venture. He would go into business. He would establish a commercial empire. He would become rich. He would wow the world with his wealth. He was brilliantly successful. The Holy Spirit records three of his enterprises.

First, there were his magnificent palaces: *"I made me great works; I builded me houses"* (2:4a); then there were his magnificent parklands: *"I planted me vineyards; I made me gardens and orchards, and I planted trees in them of all kinds of fruits"* (2:4b–5); and then there were his magnificent pools: *"I made me pools of water, to water therewith the wood that bringeth forth trees"* (2:6).

> (a) Magnificent Palaces (2:4a)

The Holy Spirit records at some length, in both Kings and Chronicles, some of Solomon's building enterprises. It took him nearly twice as long to build his own primary palace than it did to build the Temple—in itself one of the unsung wonders of the world for costliness and magnificence.

His own palace was built nearby, on the eastern terrace of the western hill. Edersheim describes Solomon's palace and some of his other building projects:

> Its site was the eastern terrace of the western hill. . . . It stood right over against the Temple. A descent led from the Palace into the Tyropoeon and thence a special magnificent "ascent" (2 Chron. ix. 4) to the royal entrance

(2 Kings xvi. 18), probably at the southwestern angle of the Temple. The site was happily chosen—protected by Fort Millo, and looking out upon the Temple Mount, while south of it stretched the wealthy quarter of the city. Ascending from the Tyropoeon, one would pass through a kind of ante-building into a porch, and thence into a splendid colonnade. This colonnade connected "the house of the forest of Lebanon," so called from the costly cedars used in its construction with "the porch for the throne," where Solomon pronounced judgement (1 Kings vii. 6, 7). . . . Thus, it really consisted of three separate buildings. Externally it was simply of "costly stones:" (ver. 9), the beauty of its design only appearing in its interior. Here the building extended along three sides. The ground floor consisted of colonnades of costly cedar, the beams being fastened into the outer walls. These colonnades would be hung with tapestry, so as to be capable of being formed into apartments. Above these rose, on each side of the court, three tiers or chambers, fifteen on each tier, with large windows looking out upon each other. Here were the State apartments for court feasts, and in them were kept, among other precious things, the golden targets and shields (1 Kings x. 16, 17). Passing through another colonnade, one would next reach the grand Judgment and Audience—halls, with the magnificent throne of ivory, described in (1 Kings x. 18–20; 2 Chron. ix. 17–19). And lastly, the innermost court contained the royal dwellings themselves.

But this great Palace, the Temple and the enlargement of Millo and of the city wall, were not the only architectural undertakings of King Solomon. Remembering that there were watchful foes on all sides, he either built or repaired a number of strong places. In the North, as defense against Syria, rose the ancient stronghold of Hazor (Joshua xi. 13; Judges iv. 2). The plain of Jezreel, the traditional battlefield of, as well as the highway into Palestine from the west and the north was protected by Megiddo; while the southern approach from Egypt and the Philistine plain was guarded by Gezer, which Pharaoh had before this taken from Canaanites and burnt, but afterwards given to his daughter as dowry on her marriage with Solomon. Not far from Gezer and serving a similar defensive purpose, rose the fortress Baalath in the possession of Daniel (comp. Josephus, Ant. viii. 6, 1). The eastern and north-eastern parts of Solomon's dominions were protected by Tamar or Tadmor, probably the Palmyra of the ancients, and by Hamath-Zobah (2 Chron. viii. 4), while access to Jerusalem and irruptions from the north-western plain were barred by the fortification of Upper and Lower Bethhoron (1 Kings ix. 15–19; 2 Chron. viii. 3–6). Besides these fortresses, the king provided magazine cities and others where his chariots and cavalry were stationed—most of them probably, towards the north.[7]

(b) Magnificent Parklands (2:4b–5)
(c) Magnificent Pools (2:6)

Magnificent, too, were Solomon's parks and pools with their accompanying irrigation systems. Some idea of the splendor of these works can be gathered from the word used for "orchards." It is *pardesim*. It means "paradises, parks, or pleasure grounds." Such paradises were created by eastern monarchs, especially by the Sumerian rulers of Chaldea and by the Assyrian kings. The concept of beautiful gardens of "paradises" paved the way for the use of the word in the New Testament to describe heaven (Revelation 2:7; 22:1–2). The Lord Jesus promised the repentant thief that he would be with Him that day in paradise (Luke 23:43). Solomon's love of gardens is well documented in Scripture. He had a royal garden on the hills south of Jerusalem (2 Kings 25:4) and at Ainkarim about six miles east of the city was "Beth-haccerem, the House of the Vine" (Jeremiah 6:1). There was another extensive vineyard at Baal-hamon (Song of Solomon 8:11).

(2) What He Accumulated (2:7–8)
(a) All Kinds of People (2:7a)

"I got me servants and maidens, and had servants born in my house" (2:7a). Solomon knew the value of people—what we now refer to as human resources. These were the people who got things done. Solomon might have the ideas, but other people did the work and provided the technical skill, did the manual labor, and took care of the management and administration.

Solomon did not rely wholly on Hebrew talent when building the Temple. For instance, he hired Phoenicians who had special skills to execute tasks beyond the ability of his own subjects. Just the same, the design and management were kept strictly in Hebrew hands. Hiram, King of Tyre, was eager to provide such technicians. Phoenicia was largely dependent on Israel for its grain and oil (Ezekiel 27:17). The name of the master craftsman sent to Solomon by Hiram is recorded. His name was Hiram (the same as that of his king), a man of Jewish descent by his mother's side (2 Chronicles 2:13–14; see also 1 Kings 7:14; 2 Chronicles 4:16).

One of Solomon's overseers was Jeroboam, son of Nebat, and a widow named Zeruah. Jeroboam was raised in Zerda within the tribal territory of Ephraim. He was a zealous and capable administrator and Solomon appointed him permanent overseer of the forced labor of his tribe—a position he later exploited to the fullest.

(b) All Kinds of Possessions (2:7b–8a)
(i)   Countless Cattle (2:7b)

Solomon was eminently successful in accumulating things. For instance, he had all kinds of cattle: *". . . also I had great possessions of great and small cattle above all that were in Jerusalem before me"* (2:7b). Solomon's father, David, began life as a shepherd. Solomon had more flocks and herds than he could count. He was far more successful than even Jacob who mastered the genetics of sheep rearing centuries before Solomon's day and who used his knowledge to greatly increase his possessions (Genesis 30).[8]

(ii) Cold Cash (2:8a)

Moreover, he had all kinds of cash: *"I gathered me also silver and gold"* (2:8a). We know from the books of Kings and Chronicles how far reaching were Solomon's commercial ventures. He entered into a mercantile arrangement with Tyre, the Phoenicians being great masters of maritime skills. He had a "navy of Tarshish" (1 Kings 9:27–28) which sailed periodically to the great Phoenician outpost of Tarshish on the Atlantic seaboard of Europe. It was one of the great Phoenician trading centers (1 Kings 10:22). The expression "navy of Tarshish" may also simply mean "Tarshish ships," a name for large ocean-going ships (like English "East Indiamen," a name given by the British to the great sailing vessels which carried on their trade with the Orient in the great days of sail). Solomon had another fleet of ships which sailed to Ophir (1 Kings 9:27–28) from Ezion-gaber at the head of the Gulf of Aqaba in the Red Sea.

The weight of gold which Solomon imported into Israel annually was given by the Holy Spirit as 666 talents, an enormous amount by any standard (1 Kings 10:14). A talent was the equivalent of 3,000 shekels of the sanctuary—about 131 pounds Troy; that is, about 2,096 ounces. Not that all this gold made Solomon any happier. There is something biblically ominous in the actual amount—666 talents. It is the number of the man of sin (Revelation 13:18) and is associated with the final apostasy. The number itself is a trinity. It represents "the perfection of imperfection, the culmination of human pride in independence of God and opposition to His Christ."[9]

In Scripture, the number six is the number of man, doing his own thing and always coming short of the number seven which stands for perfection. The number 666 represents the concentrated expression of man at work, man with God left out of his calculations. In connection with Solomon, the number 666 is symbolic of the very height of his success, but all of it amounting to so much vanity and vexation of spirit, man "under the sun," in all his wealth and power, a moral and spiritual bankrupt just the same—as God reminded the rich fool of the New Testament (Luke 12:15, 20–21).

(c) All Kinds of Power (2:8b)

". . . and the peculiar treasure of kings and of the provinces . . ." (2:8b). This reference, perhaps, refers to the vast extent of Solomon's influence and power. His friendship with the King of Tyre may have had something to do with this. No doubt, Hiram was careful to keep in the good graces with such a sagacious and strong neighbor that he knew Solomon to be. The word for "provinces" here is *hammedinoth*. It possibly has reference to the treasure paid to him by vanquished kings who owed tribute to him and also to the great gifts brought to him voluntarily by such friendly rulers as the Queen of Sheba.

So then, Solomon had the Midas touch. Everything he touched turned to gold. The sacred historian tells us that silver was of no value in Solomon's day. Gold eclipsed it altogether. Solomon, we are told, was so rich that even the pots and pans in his kitchens were made of gold. And in those days, there did not appear to be a cloud in the sky. Even those who would normally be his enemies thought it best to be at peace with him.

(d) All Kinds of Performers (2:8c)

". . . I gat me men singers and women singers, and the delights of the sons of men, as musical instruments, and that of all sorts" (2:8c). We conjure up in our minds the picture of an oriental banquet. As the tables groaned beneath the weight of the various courses presented to the king and his court and guests, the wine began to flow. In the background were the choir and orchestra providing appropriate music.

Then the real entertainment would begin as the musicians stepped up the beat. The singers would perform and then would come the female dancers. The women dancers of the orient would not leave much to the imagination. They were usually an abandoned lot and their dances were provocative and calculated to inflame lust—as at Herod's banquet when Salome danced and Herod lost all control of himself (Matthew 14:6–12). The preacher remembered it all so well. He sums up these wild parties of his by referring to "the delights of the sons of men," evidently a reference to the animal passions aroused and indulged on such occasions. Possibly on such occasions Solomon added another girl or two to his ever-growing harem.

(3) What He Avowed (2:9–10)
(a) That He Retained All His Discretion (2:9)

"So I was great, and increased more than all that were before me in Jerusalem: also my wisdom remained with me" (2:9). This was a somewhat boastful claim. It reminds us of Nebuchadnezzar and his boastful claim, which had such disastrous results, "Is not this great Babylon, that I have built?" (Daniel 4:30). It reminds us, too, of Caesar Augustus who claimed to have found Rome in brick and left it marble. Solomon seems to be taking a similar satisfaction in his achievements.

There has been considerable discussion over his reference to "all that were before me in Jerusalem." Strictly speaking, the only one before him in Jerusalem was David. King Saul was also before him, but he did not reign in Jerusalem. Unless, of course, Solomon is referring to the Jebusite kings. He surely could not be thinking of that majestic and mysterious monarch Melchizedek (Genesis 14:18–20), the latchet of whose shoe Solomon would have been unworthy to unloose.

As for his greatness, what did it amount to? True, he built the Temple, but then he sowed the seeds which led to its destruction by his latter-day idolatries. True, too, he wrote three books which found their way into the Bible. As for the Song of Solomon, God's name does not occur in it at all and its glorious truths had to slumber until such time as Christ came and gave them meaning. Nor does Solomon himself appear to any advantage in the book.[10]

His proverbs are brilliant enough but marred by the fact that Solomon often did not practice what he preached. As for Ecclesiastes, its supreme value lies in warning us not to behave as Solomon behaved. The eternal value of these books lies not in the fact that Solomon wrote them but that the Holy Spirit inspired him to write them and supernaturally so.

"I was great!" Solomon said. "One greater than Solomon is here," Jesus said (see Matthew 12:42).

"My wisdom remained in me," Solomon added. He was proud of his wisdom, or, perhaps, he was relieved he still had it after his days of giddy pleasure seeking, the pursuit of which has led many into abysmal folly.

Nor did Solomon come away unscathed from his profligate and prodigal days. True, he retained sufficient command of himself to be able to look back now, objectively, at the years when he went in for the world of thought, the world of thrills, and the world of things, but his wisdom had become tainted. It was no longer that wisdom "that is from above," which the Holy Spirit describes as "first pure, then peaceable, gentle and easy to be entreated, full of mercy and good fruits, without partiality, and without hypocrisy." It had become both "earthly" and "sensual" if not actually "devilish" (James 3:15–17). It was little more than earthly prudence.

(b) That He Realized All His Desires (2:10)

"And whatsoever mine eyes desired I kept not from them, I withheld not my heart from any joy; for my heart rejoiced in all my labour: and this was my portion of all my labour" (2:10). It would be a foolish person indeed who allowed his eyes to peer at all that is available for them to see. Pornography and perversion are all about us today! Much of our temptation comes through the eyes. Far better to side with Job than with Solomon. Job said that even in the days of his prosperity and power he made a covenant with his eyes that he would not look with lust (Job 31:1). Solomon, by contrast, allowed his eyes to roam at will.

We have an example of it in his own book of Proverbs. He says:

> For at the window of my house
> I looked through my casement,
> and beheld among the simple ones,
> I discerned among the youths, a young man void of understanding,
> passing through the street near her corner. (Proverbs 7:6–8)

Solomon goes on to describe in detail how this simpleton became involved with this immoral woman. He also foretold where it would all end. He seems to have taken a sardonic interest in the whole affair. The least excusable in the whole affair was Solomon, who evidently knew the woman and her wiles very well indeed. To him it was all just an interesting thing to watch and add to his notebook.[11]

While allowing his eyes to wander where they would, prying, peeping, peering here, there, and everywhere, observing the good and the bad, ever watching, ever witnessing, he kept up his pursuit of pleasure. He was ever hopeful that he might unearth some new pleasure even though he was now preoccupied with vast commercial enterprises. We catch a glimpse of this in the Old Testament history book on Solomon's exotic imports such as spices from afar, ivory, apes, and peacocks (1 Kings 10:10, 22).

He could remember, too, the time when he was able to get pleasure from all his various construction projects and commercial enterprises. That, he said, was his share in all the ceaseless activity. He would show the Queen of Sheba his great white throne of ivory. He would take guests on a tour of his zoological garden. He would show them the regal peacocks which graced the grounds of his palace.

And in the acquisition of countless costly, rare, and beautiful things, he spared no cost. If he saw something he wanted he made arrangements to get it. There would be few who could resist pressure from the palace. Even foreign rulers would consider it politics to help the famous Solomon acquire some exotic dancing girl or rare curio.

So, the wealth and wonders of the world flowed into his warehouse. And for a while he was able to gloat over his gains and over his goods. He would go from one building project to another, from one seaport to another when news was received that another of his Tarshish ships had been sighted offshore. He would discuss the voyage with the captain, ask eager questions about the distant markets in far-off lands, inspect the cargo, take his pick of the merchandise, look eagerly for some new thing.

(4) What He Acknowledged (2:11)

(a) His Enterprise Considered (2:11a)

And then the time came to take stock. Had the world of things made him any happier than the world of thought or the world of thrills? We note that he considered his enterprises.

"Then I looked on all the works that my hands had wrought, and on the labour that I had laboured to do" (2:11a). He summoned his managers, his foremen, his architects, his bankers, his custodians, for his daily report on all the

thousand-and-one projects he had in hand. He took a long, cold, hard look at all his "things."

(b) His Emptiness Confessed (2:11b)

Then he confessed his emptiness: *". . . and, behold, all was vanity and vexation of spirit, and there was no profit under the sun"* (2:11b). All his enterprises showed a profit. He added up all the balance sheets and came to the grand total. It all added up to nothing. The final and ultimate bottom line was "no profit!" He had everything. He had nothing. He would have appreciated the confession of Cecil Rhodes. Cecil Rhodes went to South Africa as a young man for the sake of his health and set out to make his fortune. He founded the prestigious De Beers Mining Company and proceeded to seize control of all South Africa's diamond mining industry. Before long he controlled all of South Africa's gold mining industry as well. His legacy to the British Empire at his death was Rhodesia, an enormous tract of territory equal to Germany, France, and Spain all put together. He was probably the richest man in the empire. It so happened he was a personal friend of General William Booth, founder of the Salvation Army and one of the poorest men in the empire. It is said that on one occasion, General Booth asked his multibillionaire friend if he was a happy man. "Happy?" queried Rhodes. "Me, happy? Good heavens, no!" Neither prosperity, nor power, nor position, nor anything else "under the sun" can make a person happy. It was all "vanity and vexation of spirit"; all so much for chasing the wind.

2. His Pessimistic Summary (2:12–26)
a) The Barrenness of It All (2:12–16)
(1) The Turning Point in His Life (2:12–14)
(a) Why He Turned (2:12)
(i) To Make a Comparison (2:12a)

Solomon was not content with a general statement regarding the failure of all the things he had sought to satisfy. He applied his mind, his great intellect, to the problem represented by that failure. Indeed, in viewing the barrenness of things under the sun he seemed to have arrived at some kind of a turning point in his life.

First, he tells us why he turned: *"And I turned myself to behold wisdom, and madness, and folly: for what can the man do that cometh after the king? even that which hath been already done"* (2:12). He pulled himself up short. Madness and folly beckoned to him. He had only to continue the way he was going to become the prime example of both. The path of the sensualist led to satiation and even insanity. The path of materialists was no more satisfactory. Wealth in abundance and public works which awed the beholder soon paled. It was folly to go on building better buildings and bigger bank balances. He turned back to wisdom. True, mere intellectualism, the collection and collation of knowledge for knowledge's sake, was a profitless thing. But true wisdom—well, what else was left? There was nothing else to get, nowhere else to go.

(ii) To Mature a Conviction (2:12b)

So, back to wisdom he went, a sadder and a wiser man. As for his successors, what was left for them to explore? He, the king, had tried it all. All they could do was read his book, so to speak! He had written the last word, or so he thought.

In a sense, he was right. He had already declared there to be nothing new "under the sun" (1:9–10). In her novel about the sinking of the Titanic, Beryl Bainbridge has Morgan tell the tale. Morgan was a nephew of sorts of J. Pierpont Morgan, the U.S. financier, banker, and industrialist. Morgan, the nephew, toured the great liner with a friend soon after the beginning of that fateful voyage. They were awestruck by the might and magnificence of it all. But what gripped them most was the engineering. The opulent and lavish furnishings, the doors inlaid with mother of pearl, the corridors dressed in rich oak and maple did not awe them. Nor did the sparkling candelabra, hung from the high dome above the splendor of the main staircase. These pampered young men moved in the highest social circles. They were surrounded by vast wealth. For them, says the novelist, there was nothing new "under the sun"—that is, when it came to opulence.[12]

Solomon felt that his posterity would have nothing left to explore—he had explored it all, and had nothing new to say. He had said it all. What was new for them to see? What was new for them to savor? He had searched it all. Certainly, his immediate successor whom he seems particularly to have in mind (vv. 18–19) could not hope to fill the shoes of his world-famous sire.

(b) What He Testified (2:13–14)
(i) Discretion Is Inestimable (2:13–14a)

We note, then, not only why he turned, but what he testified (2:13–14). Two things he could see all too clearly, perhaps. First, that discretion is inestimable:

"Then I saw that wisdom excelleth folly, as far as light excelleth darkness. The wise man's eyes are in his head; but the fool walketh in darkness" (2:13–14a). Could there be a greater contrast than between light and darkness? King Solomon would not have to look far for an example of this. He had been preceded on the throne of Israel by David and by Saul. Saul had been a fool. His folly had expressed itself in his fear, jealousy, and persecution of David, who had done him nothing but good. In the end he confessed, "I have played the fool and have erred exceedingly" (1 Samuel 26:21). His folly manifested itself in other crimes, notably the massacre of the priests of God (1 Samuel 22:7–23) and of the Gibeonites (2 Samuel 21:1–2). It came to a head in his last act of lawlessness when he went to Endor to consult a witch because God no longer spoke to him (1 Samuel 28:6–20). All he did had the mark of darkness upon it. He blundered his way through life, exhibiting his folly at every turn, showing how great was the darkness in which he walked and how abysmal was the darkness which led him from Endor to Gilboah and the darkness of death.

By contrast, David behaved himself wisely (1 Samuel 18:14, 15, 30). In the camp and in the court, and in the cave, it made no difference. David's path was illuminated by wisdom from on high. In the camp God displayed His man as with wisdom beyond his years. He laid aside Saul's armor and went forth to fight Goliath in the all victorious name of the Lord. In the court, God defended this man so that David was able to avoid the snares King Saul had set for him. In the cave, God developed this man and brought to him those needy ones whom he transformed and who became his bodyguards and the backbone of his kingdom.

So well might Solomon choose wisdom over folly. The wise man, he said to himself, has eyes in his head. The fool walks around in darkness.

(ii) Death Is Inevitable (2:14b)

Solomon not only testified to the fact that discretion is inestimable, but also to the fact that death is inevitable: *". . . and I myself perceived also that one event happeneth to them all"* (2:14b). If there is one thing we learn about Solomon from the book of Ecclesiastes, it is that, like Cecil Rhodes, Solomon was not a happy man. How could he be when he had lived with such abandon and had been confronted by the active displeasure of God? He was not a happy man, he was a haunted man; and in the book of Ecclesiastes, he introduces us to the ghosts that haunted him. One was old age, already a very present reality. The other was death. Solomon hints at him here. He will come out and name him in a moment. Moreover, as he progresses with his sermon, he will mention this horrifying specter more and more.

(2) The Turning Point in His Logic (2:15–16)
(a) Soon Be Finished (2:15)

Solomon is brought up short by the thought of death. It was an enemy he feared, hated, and sought to flee. Wise or foolish, he says, our lives will soon be finished: *"Then said I in my heart, As it happeneth to the fool, so it happeneth even to me; and why was I then more wise? Then I said in my heart, that this also is vanity"* (2:15).

The first three personal pronouns in this verse are emphatic, as though Solomon is astonished to discover that despite his power, wealth, success, influence, wisdom, and great capacity for pleasure he, too, was mortal. He was on death's list as surely as the lowest scullion in the kitchen or the most desperate criminal in the palace dungeon awaiting execution. Death is no respecter of persons.

(b) Soon Be Forgotten (2:16)

Moreover, our lives will soon be forgotten. He adds: *"For there is no remembrance of the wise more than of the fool for ever; seeing that which now is in the days to come shall all be forgotten. And how dieth the wise man? as the fool"* (2:16). Kings have their counselors. Solomon had his (1 Kings 12:6–11), and prudent men they were. But who were they? What were their names? Nobody knows. Apart from a passing reference to them, they lie forgotten in their graves. The names of Ethan the Ezrahite, Heman, Chalcol, and Darda, the sons of Mahol, are mentioned in the sacred text as having a reputation for wisdom in Solomon's day (1 Kings 4:31), but who were these men? Why were they accounted wise, though not as wise as Solomon? Most people would simply shrug their shoulders if asked who these men were. "Who knows? Who cares?" would be the response. They, like the great heroes of ancient Greece, whose names were hailed and toasted as great and famous athletes, soon passed into oblivion. As the forgotten poet said:

> Proud were those mighty conquerors
> Crowned in Olympic games;
> They thought that deathless honours

> Were entwined around their names;
> But sere was soon the parsley-wreath,
> The olive and the bay;
> But Christian's crown of amaranth
> Will never fade away.[13]

> b) The Bitterness of It All (2:17–26)
> (1) He Hated His Life (2:17)

To think that he, the great Solomon, the world-famous king, renowned for his wisdom, should be destined to die just like some born fool of a fellow with no brain in his head! It soured his very soul. He uttered two bitter complaints. Nothing in his life was satisfying anymore: *"Therefore I hated life; because the work that is wrought under the sun is grievous unto me."* Nothing in his life was spiritual anymore: *". . . for all is vanity and vexation of spirit"* (2:17).

Solomon sat back upon his great throne of ivory and ran his mind's eye over all his remarkable accomplishments. He had been so eager and optimistic when, soured on the mere gathering of information and satiated with lustful living, he had turned his attention to big business. For a while it held his interest. There were new buildings springing up everywhere. There were cities to be made impregnable all across his wide domain. There were ships to be built. There were caravans to be organized. There were treaties to be drafted, contracts to be signed. He was kept happily busy morning, noon, and night.

> (a) Nothing in His Life Was Satisfying (2:17a)

And then it had crested, and he lost interest. He plunged into a deep depression. *"Therefore I hated life . . ."* (2:17a), he said. We can't be sure, but had he contemplated committing suicide, out of sheer boredom? Wise man and fool alike died sooner or later. So, why not sooner? Nothing in his life was satisfying anymore.

> (b) Nothing in His Life Was Spiritual (2:17b)

". . . for all is vanity and vexation of spirit" (2:17b). There is an old Scandinavian fable which tells of a spider who descended on a single thread from the lofty rafters of a barn. He anchored the thread to a corner of the window and, using the thread as his main support, proceeded to weave his web. He had chosen a busy

corner of the barn and he waxed fat and prospered. One day in his prosperity, he was walking across his web when he noticed the strand which led up into the unseen. He had long since forgotten its significance. He thought it but a stray thread and reached up and snapped it. And instantly his whole world caved in.

That is what Solomon did. In his early days, he established diplomatic relations with heaven. There was a strand in his life which reached up and up to the unseen. Then he waxed prosperous and careless, and he broke his tie with heaven and his whole world caved in. Gone forever were the Temple building days. (He now built shrines for idols.) Gone were the days when he led his people in prayer and entertained great and costly thoughts of God and the covenant. Now, he was a worldly, sin-stained, materialistic philosopher, and everything was "vanity and vexation of spirit."

(2) He Hated His Labors (2:18–21)

Because he was going to:

(a) Lose Possession of His Things (2:18)

"Yea, I hated all my labour which I had taken under the sun: because I should leave it unto the man that shall be after me" (2:18). It was his way of saying, "You can't take it with you." That may be so. But you can send it on ahead. A preacher friend of mine used to say, "If you want to have treasure in heaven you had better give some money to someone who is going there." Solomon found the thought of leaving all that he had accumulated to someone else to be profoundly depressing. He had seen too much of what took place when that happened. History gives us scores of illustrations.

If ever a man was born to glittering prospects it was Edward VIII, son and heir of King George V of England. The British Empire had reached its high-water mark. After the end of World War 1, Edward, as Prince of Wales and heir to the throne, visited British domains in Canada, New Zealand, Australia, India, the Far East, and Africa. He was handsome and popular. He became king on January 20, 1936. The world was at his feet. Some idea of the wealth, pomp, and magnificence which surround the British throne must surely impress everyone who visits the Jewel House beneath the Waterloo Barracks in the ancient Tower of London on the River Thames. There are displayed orbs, swords, and other regalia, ablaze with diamonds and rubies and other gems.

Edward the Confessor's crown is a Saxon diadem which some think dates back to Alfred the Great (A.D. 849–899) who saved England from the Vikings and laid the foundations for the unification of the country. Its name and traditions survive in the great golden crown made for Charles II's coronation. It contains some 440 precious and semiprecious stones.

Along with this priceless diadem is the Imperial State Crown, which contains jewels of great antiquity and historical significance. It is worn by the Sovereign as he leaves Westminster Abbey after the coronation ceremony and on all subsequent State occasions. It was made for the coronation of Queen Victoria and contains gems of awesome magnificence. There is, for instance, Edward the Black Prince's ruby, said to have been given to him by Pedro the Cruel of Castile. Far older is Edward the Confessor's sapphire. Below the Black Prince's ruby is the second Star of Africa cut from the famous Cullinan diamond. There is also the Stuart sapphire which likewise has a long and colorful history. The Imperial State Crown is resplendent with rubies, emeralds, and sapphires, 277 pearls and over 3,000 diamonds.

There are other crowns and regalia in the collection. There is a scepter, for instance, which contains a superb amethyst and also the largest cut diamond in the world, the pear-shaped Star of Africa found in 1905 by the manager of the De Beers Premier mine in South Africa. When found, it was an astonishing 3,106 carats. It was presented to Edward VII on his birthday by the Transvaal Government with the request it should be set in the crown of England. It had to be cut, however, and eventually it yielded four gems, the largest being the Star of Africa, 530 carats.

To come back to Edward VIII, he was crowned king and reigned from January 20 to December 11, 1936. He then abdicated the throne, throwing away a crown and an empire in order to marry Wallis Simpson, a divorced and remarried American woman he had met in June 1931. On October 27, 1936, Mrs. Simpson obtained a divorce from her second husband, and on November 13 the king told Prime Minister Stanley Baldwin that he intended to marry the woman, even if he had to abdicate to do so. His younger brother was crowned in his place as George VI. The new king created his older brother Duke of Windsor. On June 3, 1937, the Duke married his American divorcee. If she had hoped to partake of the glamour of royalty, she was soon disillusioned. The king decreed that only the Duke could be styled "royal highness" and forbade his subjects to curtsey to the Duke's wife as they would to the royal family.

Edward VIII had thrown away everything for a shallow and short-tempered woman. She became "queen of the jet set." She had a passion for things. The Duke and his Duchess went from night club to night club, living lives of extravagant and monumental uselessness. The risqué nature of Wallis' humor was well known. The Duke dreaded her bullying. When once the Duke asked her if she would consider adopting a British war orphan as a gesture to lessen adverse publicity, she retorted that the idea was silly. At one time, the Duke was distraught because his wife was running around with Jimmy Donahue, a disgusting rake who had a scandalous reputation, a man who was completely vile.

Solomon would have said to the father, "I told you so, George V!" Edward had handed an empire to his brother. He may have had insight enough into the boy's character to have secret doubts about him. After all, when he was still the Prince of Wales he had kept a married woman, Freda Dudley Ward, as his mistress and only abandoned her when he met Wallis Simpson.

So, Solomon lamented the fact that he was going to lose possession of all the countless things he had collected to his son, Rehoboam. There was more.

(b) Lose Power over His Things (2:19)

"And who knoweth whether he [his successor] shall be a wise man or a fool? yet shall he have rule over all my labour wherein I have laboured, and wherein I have shewed myself wise under the sun. This is also vanity" (2:19).

This was the worst part of it. He, Solomon, was going to die. He ruled an empire which reached from the Egyptian border to the Euphrates (1 Kings 4:21) and his son and heir was a fool, as he knew only too well. He really had no need to speculate. He only had to listen in on the conversations of the nitwits Rehoboam chose for his friends. Probably the proverbs which Solomon wrote regarding fools were written with Rehoboam in mind, as were the Proverbs he wrote on good government.

There would be a much more orderly transfer of power to Rehoboam than there had been to him. Just the same, there was Jeroboam to contend with, a dangerous man, a man he had tried to have killed, a man even now ingratiating himself with Pharaoh in Egypt and in touch with restive elements in the northern tribes of Israel. King Hezekiah, many years later, would weep because he had to die, he had no son and heir (2 Kings 20). King Solomon wept because he had to die, but he had a son and heir and wished ever so much that he had a second chance.

(c) Lose Pleasure in His Things (2:20–21a)
(i) His Gloom (2:20)

He mentions, for instance, his gloom: *"Therefore I went about to cause my heart to despair of all the labour which I took under the sun"* (2:20). In other words, he gave himself up to despair. To think that he had to leave it all! And to a fool no less. It drove him to distraction.

Some years ago, I realized that many people, to a greater or lesser degree, had to face Solomon's problem when making their wills. The factor which complicated mine was my book royalties. With more than two dozen books in print and the prospect of continuing royalties coming due year after year, I had a problem to face. Though not that large, the royalties will keep on coming so long as the books remain in print. Normally after an author's death, royalties would be paid into his estate for distribution to his heirs. I had no problem with the royalties going to my children, but what about their children and then their children, and so on for possible generations yet to come? Maybe such distant heirs would be most undesirable and undeserving people. Maybe they would be godless individuals involved in a wicked lifestyle or God-haters and the like. I certainly would not want my royalties, derived from books which exalted the Lord Jesus, and which had been written with such toil and spiritual exercise over more than half a lifetime, to go to support the lifestyles of people like that. In my case, I was able to devise a will which was fair to my children yet safeguarded royalties from falling into the wrong hands. Solomon had no such leeway. Upon his death, all that he had so painstakingly accumulated would fall into the foolish hands of Rehoboam. And, we know how soon he lost it all (2 Chronicles 12:1–11). No wonder Solomon mentions his gloom and despair.

(ii) His Doom (2:21a)

He mentions also his doom: *"For there is a man whose labour is in wisdom, and in knowledge, and in equity; yet to a man that hath not laboured therein shall he leave it for his portion"* (2:21a). He was going to leave. The thought was hateful to him. His body would leave his soul. His life would be over. He would leave his palace. He would vacate his throne. He would leave forever the wondrous works on which he had labored so lovingly and for so long. He would leave his robes and regalia. He would leave his family and friends. He would leave earth for an uncertain destination. Nor could all the wisdom he had labored to obtain stave off the fatal moment.

(d) Lose Purchase of His Legacy (2:21b)

"This also is vanity and a great evil" (2:21b). What galled Solomon, particularly at this point in his musings, was the fact that he was not only going to leave his things, it was to whom he was going to leave them. Nor was it that alone. It was not so much that the beneficiary might squander the fortune, he had already faced that (v. 9). What galled Solomon now was the fact that he had labored and worked and slaved to amass wealth beyond the dreams of avarice, and the man who was going to fall heir to it all had bestowed neither skill nor toil on it at all.

Thus, it was with Barbara Hutton, who died at the age of sixty-six. She was the granddaughter of the founder of the Woolworth's five-and-dime store chain. She inherited about $25 million at the age of twelve. She was attractive. She was rich. But the media called her "the poor little rich girl." Her seven husbands included a Laotian, a Lithuanian, a Russian prince, a Prussian count, and actor Cary Grant. She was long plagued by illnesses that ranged from kidney disease to cataracts. She spent her last years as a recluse, often bedridden. She died of a heart attack in Los Angeles. At the time of her death, she weighed only eighty pounds (*Time*, May 21, 1979). Inherited wealth is often more of a curse than a blessing.

It was how Solomon felt as he looked at his son and heir, soon to inherit vast wealth. And to think he had never so much as lifted a finger to accumulate it. It added another flavor of bitterness to Solomon's acid thoughts.

(3) He Hated His Lot (2:22–26)
(a) A Question (2:22–23)
(i) As to an Adequate Reason for Everything (2:22)

He wondered, first, if there was an adequate reason for everything: *"For what hath man of all his labour, and of the vexation of his heart, wherein he hath laboured under the sun?"* (2:22). What's the point of it all? What's the good of it all? All this work and planning, all this striving to be rich and successful? All this toil! To what end?

Alexander the Great felt much the same way. He had come storming out of

Greece, driven by a fierce determination to make an end of the Persian Empire once and for all. He succeeded. He was probably the greatest general the world has ever seen. His sole business was war; his supreme goal, personal glory. He carried war and slaughter for some twenty thousand miles and then wept because there were no more worlds to conquer. Drinking heavily and suffering from a fever, he took to his bed, seriously ill. He had gained the whole world and lost his own soul. What was the point of it all, now that death haunted his bedroom? What was the point of it all? To whom now must he bequeath it all? Certainly not to some idler. Not even to the son of Roxana, whom he had married some years before. He was only a boy. Of what use was an empire to a boy? How could a boy tame his generals? No, that was no way to leave an empire. It was his empire. He had won it by his genius and with his sword and by the force of his will. He had the same "vexation of his heart" as Solomon had known. The thought of leaving it all to someone who had not fought and struggled and toiled for it was too much. His Macedonian subjects clamored outside his palace. They were allowed to file past his bed. The dying Alexander viewed them with a jaundiced eye. At last his leading generals demanded an answer. To whom did he leave it all? "To the strongest," he said.

<h3 style="text-align:center">(ii) As to an Adequate Result for Everything (2:23)</h3>

Solomon wondered, moreover, if there was an adequate result for everything: *"For all his days are sorrows, and his travail grief; yea, his heart taketh not rest in the night. This is also vanity"* (2:23).

It seemed to Solomon now that all his days had been a weariness and all his nights plagued by sleeplessness. He would lie awake at night wrapped with splendor. All the appointments in his royal quarters were rare, beautiful, and costly. He had skilled servants to hang upon his words and rush to do his bidding. He had beautiful women within call. Exotic fruits from a score of lands were within reach. Books and parchments on every conceivable subject were waiting to be read or had been read heavily underlined. Rare perfumes procured at infinite cost added their fragrance to satisfy his senses. He would lie awake and think, and think, until he was weary of thinking. He was bored. He longed for the day. But the day, when it came, soon turned to boredom as well. His days were freighted with emptiness and sorrow. His enterprises soured on him. He longed for the night. Such was life "under the sun," even the most brilliant and successful life. Where would it end?

(b) A Quest (2:24–25)
(i)   The Materialist and His Goal (2:24a)

He had become a materialist. He thinks of the materialist and his goal: *"There is nothing better for a man, than that he should eat and drink, and that he should make his soul enjoy good in his labour"* (2:24a). It would be hard to imagine a lower philosophy of life. It is the view of a man both morally and spiritually bankrupt. Solomon had already explored the world of thrills and found it empty. He had, however, acquired a taste for it. He came hankering back to it. The pleasures of the table and of well-produced entertainment took a fresh hold on his heart. He was like the children of Israel in the wilderness who, once the novelty of their redemption wore off, began to lust after the onions, leeks, cucumbers, and garlic provided for them, in their unregenerate days, by their Egyptian task masters (Numbers 11:5). They had forgotten the terrible bondage that went with it. Once we create an appetite for something, it is hard to give it up. Solomon glamorizes pleasure, having already forgotten its chains. But then, Solomon was a lustful man.

The view he espouses here is the view of many. Materialism has nothing to offer but the things of time and sense. Indeed, those are the very words Solomon uses, "nothing better." A man might just as well get what pleasure he can out of life, since this is the only life there is. What a goal!

(ii) The Materialist and His God (2:24b–25)

Solomon thinks next of the materialist and his God. *"This also I saw, that it was from the hand of God. For who can eat, or who else can hasten hereunto, more than I?"* (2:24b–25). Man cannot escape God, even the fanatical materialist. Nobody had lived high, wide, and handsome more than Solomon. He had lived as though there were no God in heaven and no one to be pleased but himself, just as the humanistic materialist lives. Perhaps he did not go quite so far as the materialist, who is really a practicing atheist, in ignoring God altogether. But he went far enough. He woke up to the realization, in the end, that it was God who had given him soul and senses, body and mind, appetite and desire. It was God, too, who allowed him to go his own, careless way. There is no escape from God. Apart from God, a man cannot either eat or enjoy himself. He may choose to throw away his life in the pursuit of pleasure but, at last, he will have to face God. And God will require an accounting of what has been done with his life.

So my lifelong friend Stephen Olford discovered, as I have related in his biography. He was raised by missionary parents in Angola where he saw the miracles of grace wrought and accepted Christ as Savior. As a young man, he returned to England to further his education and became interested in motorcycle racing. He drifted away from God, becoming more and more involved in worldly things. Then came an accident in which he nearly lost his life. He was lying in a hospital bed, hovering between life and death, when he received a letter from his father living in Africa. The letter had been written some months before and had taken that long to reach him. His father, when he wrote that letter, had no idea of the life-and-death struggle going on in that hospital room when the letter arrived. Stephen read what his father had to say, and one sentence stood out: "Only one life t'will soon be past, only what's done for Christ will last." All of a sudden, the young Olford realized what a mistake he was making, throwing away the life God had given, for some worthless worldly prize. He was on the wrong quest. He committed his life unreservedly to Christ.[14]

> (c) A Qualification (2:26)
> (i) God's Gifts (2:26a)

In closing this section of his sermon Solomon acknowledges God's gifts. *"For God giveth to a man that is good in his sight wisdom, and knowledge, and joy"* (2:26a). Suddenly humbled, Solomon came down off his materialistic high horse. He was not captain of his own soul and master of his own destiny. His successes in life were not the result of his own skills. He was, after all, a creature of clay, not the potter, just a vessel. Every good and perfect gift he had came from God. Apart from God he would not even have been born. Indeed, the circumstances of his birth were portentous enough and should have predisposed him toward humility and a fear of sin and self-will (2 Samuel 12:15–25). His wisdom and his knowledge were God-given (1 Kings 3:5–15), a fact he seemed to have conveniently forgotten. Gifts are bestowed on men by God, their Creator (James 1:17), they are not inherent in matter or the "fortuitous concourse of atoms." It was not merely a matter of IQ, though doubtless Solomon's IQ would have registered him as a genius. His IQ was a gift. We have nothing except what we receive from above, as the Lord reminded Pilate (John 19:11).

As for joy, well, the world does not have it. It is a far superior quality than mere happiness, which depends on what happens. Even at its best, happiness consists more in liking what we have rather than in having what we like, a lesson

Solomon learned the hard way. Joy is an exotic plant, not native to a sin-cursed world. It is a heavenly bloom (Luke 15:10), and it is one of the cardinal fruits of the Spirit (Galatians 5:22).

Solomon seems to have belatedly come to the realization that the world of thought and the world of thrills and the world of things, and all three together, cannot provide a single spark of pure joy. Joy is a gift from God. At the end of this vain quest for something "under the sun" to really satisfy, the preacher comes back to God. He acknowledges God's gifts.

(ii) God's Government (2:26b)

Moreover, in finally concluding the first major part of his sermon, Solomon acknowledges God's government: *". . . but to the sinner he giveth travail, to gather and to heap up, that he may give to him that is good before God. This also is vanity and vexation of spirit"* (2:26b). The sinner! The Hebrew word is *chata*. It means "to miss the mark." It conveys the idea of coming up short. His aim is not high enough. His targets are set up "under the sun" and so are inadequate. He reckons without God, but God is sovereign anyway, regardless of whether or not the sinner recognizes that. So, he goes about his business. He takes endless pains, expands endless labor to amass wealth—and God lets him do it. More! He sets him to the task of doing it, but only so that he can leave it to somebody else, hopefully someone more worthy of it. For God is on the throne whether the sinner pays heed to that or not.

Thus it was with Henry Grattan Guinness, one of the heirs to a family fortune built on beer. The Benjamin Lee Brewing business was founded in 1759 when Arthur Guinness bought a small brewery in Dublin. The business so prospered that Guinness beer virtually became the national drink of Ireland. Benjamin Lee catapulted it on its way to becoming one of the largest breweries in the world.

Tragedy dogged the family. And no wonder. The curse of God rests on those who put a bottle to their neighbor's lips (Habakkuk 2:15–16). The first Arthur Guinness did not live long enough to see it. The boomerang came back to smite his grandchildren. Three of them became drunkards. Two of them spent time in mental institutions. Several more were reduced to beggary. It fell to his son, the second Arthur Guinness, to cope with his insolvent and debauched nephews and nieces.

There was one grand exception. Henry Grattan Guinness (1835–1910), grandson of the first Arthur, became a believer and served as an elder in the Marion Hall (Plymouth Brethren) in Dublin. He gave away his inheritance, threw himself into evangelism and world missions. He lived by choice on the edge of poverty. He and his wife, Fanny, lived in a large house in a dilapidated district, barely able to pay their rent. Yet he was spiritually rich, and great was his inheritance in the Kingdom of God. Some of the peers, who now sit in heaven, sat at his table—Dr. Barnardo, for instance, who became almost as famous as George Mueller for his ministry to homeless children, and Hudson Taylor, who founded the China Inland Mission, and Henry Morehouse, a former pickpocket who became an evangelist of such gift and grace that he revolutionized D. L. Moody. Thus, the Lord, in the person of Henry Grattan Guinness, diverted some of the blood money earned by the brewery to nobler ends and destined his devoted servant to a great reward in heaven.

Solomon became a mercantile prince. He built a great commercial empire. His camel caravans went right across the Fertile Crescent down into the exotic markets of the distant east and his great Tarshish ships plowed the seas to bring the wealth of the world to his warehouse. And he had the Midas touch—everything he touched turned to gold—and he was extremely successful in business. He had everything that money could buy. He had ten of everything. He had a hundred of everything. He had warehouses filled with stuff. And when he succeeded in the realm of things, he said, "I hated life" (2:17). I think that you can read into that that he had actually contemplated whether or not it would be just as well that he should commit suicide. These were the things that he had sought but he had not been willing to divert some of the blood money, earned by his businesses, to nobler ends and devote himself to a great reward in heaven.

Thus, Solomon brings to an end the first major subject of his sermon. The things he had sought in the world of thought, the world of thrills, and the world of things all proved to be totally inadequate. There was nothing "under the sun" big enough to fill the God-shaped vacuum in the human heart. Yet these are the goals toward which, to this very day, our secular schools and universities are pointing those who come to them for guidance and education. Our educational system in this great country is dedicated to getting young people to achieve in three things: in the world of thought, in the world of thrills, or in the world of things. But when you've got it all, all you've got is nothing. You've just been chasing the wind.

B.   Things He Had Seen (3:1–6:12)

When I first came to North America I was with a very large Canadian bank. They sent me clear across the country to British Columbia, then to the interior.

And there in the interior of the great heart of the lumber business in Canada, we met some folks who were in the lumber business. One of these men became a friend of ours, and he invited us to his home one day for a meal, and we went. He had a lovely log cabin on the edge of the bush. We went in and sat down. I was sitting on the couch and right in front of the wall opposite me there was a picture. It was a picture of a grinning human skull. It was a horrible thing. It didn't matter where you looked, your eye went right back to it. It just hung there and seemed to jibber at you across the room, you know. I thought to myself, *What would ever possess a man in his right mind to put a picture of a grinning human skull on his living room wall?*

By and by the man's wife said supper was ready, and everyone trouped off into the dining room, and I made a detour by way of the picture. When I got up close to it, it wasn't a picture of a skull at all. It was a black-and-white pen and ink drawing done by an artist. It depicted a beautiful woman sitting in front of a vanity mirror—an old-fashioned vanity mirror, kind of a circle. In front of her she had an array of jars and bottles and things. And she'd obviously been spending her time on nature because she was admiring the end result. She had done a pretty incredible job on herself. She had piled all her hair up on top of her head somehow and she had, well, just done a nice job. She looked pretty nice. Well, it satisfied my curiosity, and I stepped back from the picture. And as I stepped back farther and farther from the picture all the different parts began to come together again. The round mirror became the dome of the skull, the woman's black hair and the reflection of it became the empty eye sockets and the jars and bottles she had were the grinning teeth. By the time I got back across the room all the different parts had blended back into one, and there it was, the skull grinning at me across the length of the living room. Underneath, the artist, Charles Allan Gilbert, had written this one word—"Vanity." It is this concept of death, writing the word "vanity" across everything under the sun, that takes prominence in this second part of Solomon's sermon.

1. The Problem of Time Without Eternity (3:1–11)
   a) The Logic of Time (3:1–8)
      (1) The Rule Expressed (3:1)

"To every thing there is a season, and a time to every purpose under the heaven" (3:1). Solomon had not found any lasting or satisfying joy in the things he had sought. But maybe someone else had discovered the elusive elixir of life, some pot of gold

at the foot of the rainbow. So, he kept his eyes open. He became a great observer of life. He hoped, perchance, he might find answers to his questions somewhere if only he looked carefully enough and long enough.

We live in a time universe. God invented time. It is a period of undetermined length, cut out of the immeasurable vastness of eternity. It is marked by both a beginning and an end. It is both finite and measurable and both absolute and relative. It can be expressed in vast epochs or in micro flashes. We express it in light-years, for instance, when studying the stars. Light travels at 186,000 miles a second, yet, even at that speed light requires a measurable amount of time to get from here to there. Sunlight reflected off the moon requires a second to reach earth. On the other hand, when we consider the atom, time takes on another face. Electrons, which whirl around the nucleus of an atom, complete billions of trips in a millionth of a second.

When God created the sun and the moon, He established units of measure for us so that we can regulate our lives in meaningful units of time. The sun enables us to divide time into days, seasons, and solar years. The moon gives us our months and lunar (biblical) years. The concept of a week likewise comes from God and is related both to God's "days" of creative activity and to His Sabbath "rest."

"Everything has its appointed hour," observed Solomon. "There is a time for all things under heaven." Throughout Scripture, we find God working to a timetable, one infinitely greater than ours, but one which touches human life at every twist and turn. Much of Bible prophecy highlights God's forecasting of times and seasons, appointed days and hours. The ritual law of the Old Testament was regulated by clock and calendar. Take, for instance, the prophetic typology of the annual Hebrew Passover. D. M. Panton says:

> The identification of the Lamb is revealed in a type perhaps more detailed and more astounding in its fulfilment than any in the whole range of Scripture. For the Paschal Lamb is explicitly stated by the Holy Spirit to be Christ—"Our Passover hath been sacrificed, EVEN CHRIST" (1 Corinthians v. 7); it is stated of our Lord at the crucifixion (John xix. 36); and the Holy Spirit, descending upon Jesus, so unveiled the unknown Victim to John that the Baptist cried, "Behold, THE LAMB!" Throughout the Bible no one is ever called the Lamb of God except Christ. Nor had God ever had in mind any but one Lamb; of the hundreds of thousands slain at every Passover—for to every household there was a lamb—Jehovah never says, "Kill them," but always, "Kill it"

(Exodus xii. 5, 6); all Divine sacrifice embodied only "the Lamb slain from the foundation of the world" (Revelation xiii. 8). So, in Calvary, as we now proceed to see, culminates down to the minutest detail, the converging slaughter of a myriad of lambs.

1.– The lamb of the Passover had to be taken up on the tenth day of the first month. "In the tenth day of the (first) month they shall take to them every man a lamb" (Exodus xii. 3). In that month Jesus was crucified; and John tells us the day on which He entered Jerusalem. "Jesus therefore six days before the Passover came to Bethany;" and "on the morrow"—that is, five days before the Passover—"Jesus was coming to Jerusalem" (John xii. I, 12). Now the Passover feast was on the fifteenth; therefore—five from fifteen—our Lord arrived in Jerusalem on the very day the lamb was to be taken, the tenth of Nisan.

2.– The lamb was to be bought on the day that it was tethered. Every householder was to "take" a lamb, by purchase, if not already possessed (Exodus xii. 3). As soon as the supper at Bethany was over, "then Judas went unto the chief priests, and said, "What are ye willing to give me, and I will deliver him unto you?" (Matthew xxvi. 14). At six o'clock that evening the ninth day had already closed; Jesus was bought on the tenth. He was bought for exactly the predicted amount. "They weighed for my hire thirty pieces of silver" (Zechariah xi. 12). And the money was ultimately paid to the right persons. "The money for the guilt offerings, and the money for the sin offerings, was not brought into the house of the Lord; it was the priests'" (2 Kings xii. 16); so, Judas "brought back the thirty pieces of silver, . . . and the chief priests took (them), and said, it is not lawful to put them into the treasury" (Matthew xxvii. 3).

3.– The lamb was to be kept tethered for four days within reach of the place of slaughter. "Ye shall keep it up until the fourteenth day of the same month" (Exodus xii. 6). From the tenth to the fourteenth Judas kept watch over the bought Lamb, with a view to its sacrifice; "They weighed unto him thirty pieces of silver. And from that time, he sought opportunity to deliver Him unto them." Each day (which seems to have included a Sabbath) was spent in Jerusalem, and—a Sabbath day's journey off (Luke xxiv. 50; Acts

i. 12)—each night in Bethany, and from the tenth day Jesus was marked, at the Bethany supper, for slaughter. "She hath anointed my body aforehand for the burying" (Mark xiv. 8);—not for coronation, but for sacrifice.

4.– The lamb must be of special birth, character, and behaviour. (1) It must be a firstborn (Exodus xiii. 2); Jesus could not have been the Lamb if we did not read,—"she brought forth her firstborn son: (Luke ii. 7). (2) It must be without any evil-favouredness (Deuteronomy xvii. 1); "your lamb shall be without blemish" (Exodus xii. 5); so, Pilate pronounced, I find no fault in Him at all" (John xviii. 38); and Caiaphas, the priestly examiner of lambs, pronounced the witnesses against Him false. (3) The prophets foretold Messiah as standing on His death-day as a dumb lamb (Isaiah Liii. 7); "and He gave him no answer, not even one word" (Matthew xxvii. 14).

5.– The lamb must be killed on a specific date, and by the whole assembly of the congregation. "They killed"—not ate—"the Passover on the fourteenth day of the first month" (2 Chronicles xxxv. 1); "the whole congregation of Israel shall kill it between the two evenings" (Exodus xii. 6). . . . Between the two evenings, says Josephus, was from the sixth hour until the ninth hour. "Now from the sixth hour there was darkness over all the land"—a more dreadful going down of the sun than the world had ever known—"until the ninth hour. And about the ninth hour . . . Jesus yielded up His spirit" (Matthew xvii. 45, 50). To the month, to the day, to the hour, God's Lamb was slain: "our Passover hath been sacrificed, even Christ" (1 Corinthians v. 7).[15]

(2) The Rule Expanded (3:2–8)

He looks at:

(a) The Parameters of Life (3:2–3a)
     (i) The Providential (3:2a) Born . . . Die

The rule is expanded by Solomon. He looked at the parameters of life. There are three of these mentioned here. First, there is the providential: *"a time to be born, and a time to die"* (3:2a). God is sovereign in the matter of people's birthdays. This is one area of life over which we have no control. Nobody asked me, for instance, if I should like to be born into a rich family or a poor family, born black or white, born gifted or unintelligent, born in the United Kingdom or the United States, born in this century or some other century. All these things were beyond our control.

In one of his books, F. W. Boreham draws attention to the year 1809, midway between the battle of Trafalgar, which put an end to Napoleon's naval prowess, and the battle of Waterloo, which put an end to Napoleon's military power. "All the world," he said, "was thinking of battles, momentous battles," indeed, which changed history. God was thinking of babies! For in that very year William Gladstone, who became prime minister of Britain in the heyday of its power, was born. So was Alfred Lord Tennyson, bard of an empire; Oliver Wendell Holmes, the Harvard physician who became one of America's foremost essayists; Charles Darwin, whose claim to fame is undisputed based on dubious propositions; Abraham Lincoln, one of America's greatest presidents; and Frederick Chopin and Felix Mendelsohn, who filled the world with song. For a baby is usually God's answer to man's dilemmas. Thus, it was, says Boreham, that two thousand years ago God sent a little Babe into this world. It was, indeed, a time to be born!

And just as sovereignly, there is a time to die, as King Hezekiah learned. He had been one of Judah's greatest and Godliest kings. He had brought the nation back to God. He had restored the Temple worship and cleansed the land of idolatry. He had labored on the canon of Scripture and had done what he could to prepare his people to resist a threatening Assyria. Then he fell sick. God sent the prophet Isaiah to tell him it was his time to die. He must put his house in order. Hezekiah wept. He did not think for one moment it was time to die. His reforms were in their infancy. The Assyrian threat continued to overshadow all meetings of his cabinet. Above all, he had no heir. He prayed that he might not die. God granted him a fifteen-year life extension (2 Kings 20:1–11). Three years later Manasseh was born. He ascended the throne at the age of twelve, the most dangerous period of awakening manhood. He cancelled all the reforms instituted by Hezekiah. He plunged Judah into utter apostasy, including the Assyria-Chaldean worship of the stars and the fierce Canaanite worship of Molech. He is even reputed to have sawn the prophet Isaiah asunder in a hollow cedar tree. Add to all that was the extraordinary length of his reign. Judah never recovered from the damage he did. Truly, there was a time to die, and Hezekiah should have accepted it.

(ii) The Circumstantial (3:2a) Pluck . . . Plant

Next comes the circumstantial: *". . . a time to plant, and a time to pluck up that which is planted"* (3:2b). We see this principle illustrated in the history of Israel. God had promised Abraham, the founding father of the Hebrew people, that he would give him a land that would reach from the Nile to the Euphrates (Genesis 5:9–21) but that it would take time, some four hundred years, when the iniquity of the Amorites "was full." His descendants, in the meantime, would be enslaved by one of the world powers (Egypt). They would be emancipated, however, "in the fourth generation."

And so it was. The first generation to go down to Egypt with Jacob, when Joseph controlled the country, was Levi. Then came Kohath, then Amram, then Moses, in the fourth generation. A biblically literate Hebrew could have figured it out. When Moses was born, God's great clock struck the hour. It was a time to plant. The power of Pharaoh was broken. Israel was emancipated and settled in the Promised Land—planted indeed (Exodus 15:17; Isaiah 5:1–2).

There was also a time to "pluck up that which is planted," illustrated in the deportation of Israel by the Assyrians and of Judah by the Babylonians. History gives us countless examples of God uprooting nations great and small when the proper time comes. One of the prime biblical examples is summed up in the significant statement: "That night was Belshazzar the king of the Chaldeans slain. And Darius the Median took the kingdom" (Daniel 5:30–31).

Back in the days of Noah, when the spirit of prophecy fell upon the old patriarch he made a threefold prophecy. The Messiah would come from the descendants of Shem, his youngest son. The descendants of Japheth, his oldest son, would be "enlarged." He passed his middle son, Ham, over in total silence, ignoring him altogether and cursed Canaan, Ham's youngest son, whose descendants became the utterly vile Canaanites (Genesis 9:20–27). This prophecy must have been ridiculed by the agnostics of old. World superpower was seized not by Japheth but by the Semitic and Hametic nations. The great Egyptian Empire was Hametic. Nimrod, Ham's grandson, founded both Babel and Nineveh (Genesis 10:6–12). The Assyrian and Babylonian empires were Hametic-Semitic empires. But when Belshazzar was slain, the time to pluck up that which was planted had come. The world empire passed forever out of the hands of Shem and Ham and into the hands of Japheth. It has remained there from that day to this. It will remain there until the last Japhetic emperor comes, the Roman Antichrist of the Apocalypse (Leviticus 13). In all this circumstantial ebb and flow of events, the hand of God can be seen, planting and uprooting according to His own will.

(iii) The Judicial (3:3a) Kill . . . Heal

There is also the judicial: *"A time to kill, and a time to heal"* (3:3a). God reserves to Himself the right to terminate life. Thus, He upholds both the Noahic and Mosaic covenants (Genesis 9:6; Leviticus 20:2–27) and the principle of judicial execution of criminals. The same principle is carried over into the New Testament era as well (Romans 13:4). On a larger scale, war, which is essentially built around the killing of people, is often ordained of God to carry out His disciplinary actions on a national and global scale.

It was a time to kill when the iniquity of the Amorites was full at last. Then God unleashed Joshua and the conquering Israelites on the accursed Canaanites. There was to be no mercy. The evil breed was to be exterminated. Their religion was both fascinating and foul. Doubtless evil diseases, the constant companion of promiscuity, held sway over the condemned people. Joshua's failure to obey his orders to the letter sowed the seed of the apostasies and immoralities which marked the days of the judges. It was a time to kill when God commanded King Saul to "slay utterly" the Amalekites (1 Samuel 15:1–23). Saul's failure to do what he was told cost him his kingdom. It was a time to kill when Elijah put to the sword the false prophets of Baal (1 Kings 18:40).

There is a time, likewise, to heal. It was a time to heal when the Son of the living God came to earth. It was a time to heal when the early Church was launched upon the stormy seas of a pagan world. It was surely a time to heal when Charles Wesley was born. He was destined to travel 250,000 miles on horseback in the cause of Christ, preach 40,000 sermons, and bring revival to the Church. He hardly made it alive. The world into which he was born was utterly vile. The stage was decadent, the court was corrupt. Hume, Gibbon, Voltaire, and Rousseau ruled men's minds. There was soon infidelity. The Church and religion were blatantly scorned. Drunkenness was widespread. Every sixth house in London was a gin mill. Thugs sallied forth from the taverns in gangs to wreak mayhem on peaceful citizens. A converted minister, in the established Church, was as rare as a comet.

God sent a baby into the world to do something about it, Charles Wesley by name, one of nineteen children. It was a time to heal when he was born. His biographer says:

There was an element of the miraculous about the birth of Charles Wesley. His mother was delivered of him before the appointed time, and he appeared to be dead; he neither opened his eyes nor cried. For some time, there were no signs of life, but at length Mrs. Wesley detected a faint heart-beat. She resolved to try to save the infant, and he was accordingly wrapped in soft wool and laid aside, with neither food nor drink. He thus remained apparently lifeless for several days, until the moment came when he should have been born according to due process of nature. He then opened his eyes and cried and behaved in every respect like a new-born babe. He was immediately given nourishment, and thereafter lived a normal and rational life until he went to Oxford University and was converted, at which time the Lord appeared to him in a vision, a phenomenon not unusual in the spiritual rebirth of a Methodist.[16]

(iv) The Pursuits of Life (3:3b) Break . . . Build

". . . a time to break down, and a time to build up . . ." (3:3b). In 1961, the Communists decided it was a time to build. They built the infamous Berlin Wall. After World War 2, Germany and its capital city, Berlin, were divided between the Western powers and Russia. Berlin itself, though divided into East-West zones, was deep within East Germany, the Communist puppet state. The Communists built the wall to separate East Berlin from West Berlin in order to prevent the constant flight of East Germans to the West. The Russians had already tried other methods. In 1948, for instance, they began to block the highway, rail, and water routes connecting Berlin with the Western zones. The Western allies broke the blockade by airlifting some eight thousand tons of supplies daily into the city. The wall went up, and it became the symbol of tyranny. Frustrated, East Germans tried to get over, under, and around the wall. Those caught trying to escape were shot. For the Russians, it was a time to build. They hoped their infamous wall would put a stop to the hopes and aspirations of East Germans for freedom.

Slogans appeared all over the wall. These slogans were dubbed "the handwriting on the wall." One of them read: "Socialist Paradise: 100 m," with an arrow pointing to East Berlin. Another read: "Jump Over and Join the Party."

Then came the time to break it down. That wall, twenty-seven miles long, had stood as the symbol of the division of Europe and the world and of Communist suppression for twenty-eight years. At the stroke of midnight, on November 9, 1989, thousands who had gathered on both sides of the wall let out a roar and surged over that wall. Only nine months before, Erich Honecker, the East German Communist boss, had vowed that the wall would remain for a hundred years. But he was wrong. It was a time to break it down. And, not long afterwards, the wall was swept away.

(b) The Pleasures of Life (3:4)
(i) Personal Emotions (3:4a) Weep . . . Laugh

There are our personal emotions: *"A time to weep, and a time to laugh"* (3:4a). The Lord entered this vale of tears we call planet earth knowing that it was a time to weep. He sojourned here as "a man of sorrows and acquainted with grief." He had known all about the sadness and sorrows of the sons of men, known about it as the eternal God wrapped in omniscience, knowing all things. But, with the incarnation, He entered into suffering, tasted pain, and tasted death. It is recorded in the Bible that on three notable occasions, He wept. He wept at the tomb of Lazarus for one dead man. He wept on the heights over Jerusalem for the impending doom of Jerusalem. He wept with "strong crying and tears" in Gethsemane for a lost world. It was a time to weep. The cost of our salvation was to be so great that the very thought of it broke Him. As the old hymn puts it:

> For me it was in the Garden,
> He prayed, 'Not My will, but Thine';
> He shed no tears for His own griefs,
> But sweat drops of blood for mine.

How else could He have become our Great High Priest, "touched with the feeling of our infirmities" (Hebrews 4:15)?

"A time to laugh!" There is very little humor in the Bible. The Bible deals with sin, and there is nothing funny about sin as God sees it. Just the same, the Bible records occasions when it was "a time to laugh." Both Sarah and Abraham laughed when the Lord announced that they were to have a son, that Sarah would be his mother, and that all God's promises would be "yea and amen" in that child. Sarah laughed in unbelief (Genesis 18:12–15), and Abraham in faith—he called the son "Isaac" which means "laughter" (Genesis 21:3; comp. Romans 4:3, 18–22). In the same context we have the mocking laughter of Ishmael which brought immediate judgment (Genesis 21:9–11).

Then we have the terrible laughter of God about which David wrote in one of his psalms. The psalm is prophetic and anticipates end-time events. David sees the nations of the earth in battle array, mobilized against the Lord and His Anointed. They confer together. They came to a decision. They will wage war against God. They will grapple with the Lord God and get rid of Him forever. Russian Communism gave voice to the same blatant atheism in its heyday.

"He that sitteth in the heavens shall laugh," the Holy Spirit says (Psalm 2:4). "The Lord shall have them in derision." Down through the ages men have mocked their Maker. Now it is God's turn. He sees men massed by the million at Megiddo. The Antichrist is there. The False Prophet is there. Satan is there. The hosts of hell are there. The world is there. And God is there. He sees their puny little nuclear warheads, their man-made weapons of war. He sees fallen Satan and his lost legions. He sits back upon His great white throne and laughs. The terrible sound fills the universe. It echoes across the everlasting hills. It rolls like thunder over the Esdraelon plain. It is a time to laugh, for God to laugh. And that spine-chilling, soul-shattering sound, that personal laughter of God the omnipotent rings out men's doom. God has waited a long time for that time to laugh to arrive. His purposes in grace have kept Him from laughing at the sheer idiocy of puny men with their big mouths and their scornful words and their paraded insolence. Now He takes up His purposes in government. And He laughs. And all heaven laughs with Him (Revelation 19:1–7).

(ii) Public Emotions (3:4b) Mourn . . . Dance

There are our public emotions: *". . . a time to mourn, and a time to dance"* (3:4b). Latin and Eastern peoples wear their emotions on their sleeve far more so than Nordic and Anglo-Saxon peoples. We see public displays of emotion very often in the Bible. At funerals, for instance, it was customary to carry public grief to the point of hiring paid mourners to weep and wail. It was, thus, a time to mourn when Jairus' daughter died. The hired mourners scoffed at Christ when He defined the young child's death as "sleep" and He, in turn, wasted no time in turning them out before performing one of His greatest miracles.

It was a time to mourn when Moses died. "The children of Israel wept for Moses in the plains of Moab thirty days," we read (Deuteronomy 34:8). We, too, mourn our illustrious dead and bury them with pomp and pageantry in our national shrines, and it is fitting to do so.

If ever there was a time to mourn it was when the Lord of Glory died on Calvary's tree. A handful of disciples wept. As for the world at large, it wagged on its way as though Joseph's tomb contained nothing but an ordinary corpse. Not so! The Holy One who knew no sin lay there, untouched by change or decay while angels hovered by. That silent tomb held heaven and hell enthralled. Men in their blindness might go about their petty affairs as though nothing of a great moment had transpired. The angels from on high hushed their songs and counted the hours until the third day dawned. The dark angels of Satan licked their wounds (Colossians 1:1–15) and counted down the hours with trembling trepidation to that same third day.

It was likewise "a time to dance" when the third day dawned. The tomb burst open. An angel came to sit upon its stone. The Roman guards fled, their yells of terror matched only by the speed of their feet. When David danced before the Lord with all his might, when he brought back the ark from exile and placed it on Mount Zion, it was joy in motion and a fitting tribute to the gladness of that day (2 Samuel 6:16), though Michal failed to see it. David wrote at least four psalms to commemorate the day (Psalms 24, 68, 87, and 132). The disciples, surely, ought to have danced for joy around the supper table in the upper room when the risen Christ came in through the solid stone wall holding the keys of death and hell as His forevermore (Revelation 1:18).

(c)   The Pressures of Life (3:5a) Cast Away . . . Gather

"A time to cast away stones, and a time to gather stones together . . ." (3:5a). We are reminded of Jesus and Jerusalem. He had been rejected by officialdom. Scribes and Pharisees, Zealots and Herodians, elders and priests had but one thing in common at that time. It was their rejection of Christ. They had rejected Him. He had rejected them and handed the nation over to judgment (Matthew 23) in a series of reverberating woes. The disciples, dull of understanding, took Him aside to show Him the magnificent buildings of the Temple. The Lord was not impressed. All He could see was the coming day, well within the span of a generation, when it would be a time to cast away stones: "Verily I say unto you, There shall not be left here one stone upon another, that shall not be thrown down" (Matthew 24:2).

And so it came to pass. The Roman conquest of Jerusalem in A.D. 70 was one of the most terrible in history with both the Romans and the Jews being fired up by the utmost courage and determination. When the Romans at last succeeded in scaling the Tower of Antonia, the end was but a matter of time. The Jewish defenders of Jerusalem fled to the Temple.

The Romans passed through the new deserted Antonia and made a furious attack on the Temple, where they met an equally furious resistance. The warring factions in the city laid aside their animosities and united to face the common foe. Titus gave orders that the magnificent tower be razed to the ground and its stones used to make an easy ascent for his whole army to march up the hill on which it was built.

The troops advanced now to the Temple. The deluded Jews still cherished a vain notion that God would not allow the holy Temple to fall into pagan hands. The relentless Roman advance continued. First the cloisters that ran along the inside of the western wall were destroyed and the entire outer court, the court of the Gentiles, fell to the Romans. The Romans then brought up their battering rams and assailed the north gallery of the Temple. Orders followed to set fire to the gates. Soon, a circle of fire enshrouded much of the Temple.

Titus was disturbed that so much splendor and beauty should be reduced to ruins. He ordered his troops to try to extinguish the flames. A greater voice than that of a Roman general, however, had already decreed the total destruction of the Temple. It was a time to cast away stones. A flaming board was thrown into the Temple itself by an enraged Roman. Soon the whole Temple was ablaze. When the fires died down, the victorious Romans plundered it of its gold, prying its very stones apart to get at the molten gold which had run between them.

It was "a time to gather stones" when Khufu (Cheops) came to power in Egypt. He was the second king of the fourth dynasty. He built the great pyramid at Giza. His reign and that of his son Khafre (Chephren) were described by Herodotus as 106 years of oppression and misery. To begin with, he wanted stones, and he wanted them at his building site. He harnessed his people to do his will. Some had to drag blocks of stone from the quarries in the Arabian hills to the Nile where they were handed over to others who had to drag them to the Libyan hills. The men were organized in three monthly shifts, one hundred thousand men to a shift. It took ten years just to build the road along which the stones were hauled. To build the pyramid took twenty years. It is a square at its base 756 feet along each side. Originally, it stood 481 feet high. It has been compared in height with the Washington Monument which is 555 feet high. It is estimated that the builders of the Great Pyramid needed some two and one-half million blocks of limestone of an average size of four feet by four feet by two and one-half feet and weighing about two and one-half tons, though some blocks weighed up to fifteen tons. When it was finished, it contained ninety million cubic feet of stone. The pyramid was covered over on all sides (some 925,000 square feet of it) with polished limestone. Truly, it was "a time to gather stones together," at enormous cost in lives and treasure.

(d) The Proprieties of Life (3:5b)

"*. . . a time to embrace, and a time to refrain from embracing . . .*" (3:5b). Solomon must have been one of the world's experts on the subject! He married at least a thousand women. He reigned for forty years. If he began his marital career when he came to the throne, then some simple arithmetic gives us an interesting picture. We can picture him marrying some twenty-five women a year (one thousand wives divided by forty years)—unless, of course, he married them in batches. So, we can picture him proposing to a new wife-to-be this week, taking her on his honeymoon the next week, and proposing again to someone else the week after that! We wonder (tongue in cheek) when, with Solomon, there was ever a time to refrain from embracing!

"A time to embrace," says Solomon. What a scene it was in Egypt when Joseph, at long last, made himself known to his brethren. They had despised and rejected him because he did always those things that pleased their father. They hated him for the life that he lived, the truth that he told, and the future he foresaw. They conspired against him and sold him for the price of a slave and handed him over to the Gentiles. He was made to suffer for sins not his own and was put in the place of death. Soon, however, he had the keys of that place. He came forth "a mighty victor o'er the dark domain" and was exalted at the right hand of the majesty of the Pharaoh. He was given a name above all names and every knee to him was made to bow. He then received a Gentile bride and began to deal in judgment with the children of Israel, his kinsmen according to the flesh, until they were convicted of their long-standing rejection of him. They said, "We are verily guilty concerning our brother," though blindness in part had happened to them and they still did not know him for who he was.

Then came "a time to embrace." He revealed himself to them. "I am Joseph, your brother," he said. And they knew him and remembered and were sore afraid. "Ye sold me!" he said. "God did send me!" (Genesis 45:5). "And he fell upon his brother Benjamin's neck, and wept; and Benjamin wept upon his neck. Moreover he kissed all his brethren, and wept upon them: and after that his brethren talked with him" (Genesis 45:14–15).

"A time to refrain from embracing," the wise man declared. There was a time when David imagined he had found a vehicle capable of transporting him on the winds of the morning to dwell in the uttermost parts of the sea, to take him soaring ever upward into heaven or down, down to make his bed in hell (Psalm 139:8–10). Could we but borrow some such extraterrestrial time and space anni-hilating conveyance and transport ourselves to the uttermost reaches of hell's darkest domain, there we should find a man who never heeded Solomon's wise words—there is "a time to refrain from embracing." And that man's name is Judas. It is a name well known on earth, and a well-known name in hell. He is in the hands of the tormentors. He has gone "to his own place," Jesus said. His eyes fixed in his head, all tears long since spent on futile remorse. His cries are enough to stir pity to the very demons themselves who know not pity. His lips burn with fire. His memory is a worm that never dies, gnawing at him as the endless ages roll. He betrayed the Son of Man with a kiss. He embraced Him in order to betray Him. If ever there was a time and place and occasion to refrain from embracing, that was it. Had he pointed out the Christ to the Romans, the rabbis, and the rabble, that would have been hell-brand enough. But to say, "Hail Master!" and kiss Him, having agreed with Satan's agents to betray Him with an embrace, the very symbol of warmth and love, why, as Shakespeare would have put it, "That was the most unkindest cut of all." Solomon was right. There is a time when an embrace ought to be the furthest thing from one's mind.

(e) The Practicalities of Life (3:6–7a)
(i) The Merchant (3:6a) Get . . . Lose

Solomon turned to the practicalities of life. There is, for instance, the case of the merchant: *"A time to get, and a time to lose"* (3:6a). Perhaps Solomon was thinking of his days as a merchant prince, though he was careful enough, when venturing his capital, to make sure it was "a time to get" far more often than "a time to lose." But doubtless, even so canny, Solomon, an investor, had some deals that went sour.

There was a time to get, as Israel learned in her onward march from Egypt to Canaan. A month and a half had elapsed since the triumphant tribes marched out of Egypt. They had come to Elim with its twelve wells of water and its seventy palms. But now they had moved into the forbidding wilderness of Sinai. There were no wells and no water. There were no palm trees and nothing to eat. They had nostalgia for the bread baskets of Egypt and accused Moses of bringing them into this wasteland, howling wilderness, to kill them all with hunger. Then, God gave them the manna, bread from heaven, "angel's food."

But this bountiful supply came with instructions. There was bread enough and to spare. But it must not be hoarded. They were to get each man an omer. That would suffice for the day. There was to be none left over. Each day would bring its own supply. Those who tried to hoard it discovered it bred worms and stank if kept overnight. God would have us live our lives a day at a time. He will take care of us day by day.

It was different on the sixth day. On that day, they were to get a double ration. For the manna did not fall on the Sabbath. The Sabbath was to be a day of rest. There was a time to get (Exodus 16:4–31). There was also an omer of manna put in a pot and treasured generation after generation in the Holy of Holies. It retained its freshness year after year, a reminder of God's faithful supply.

There is "a time to lose," Solomon added. For life is not all a matter of getting. We have to give and take, as the saying goes. As a general rule, we learn deeper and greater lessons in those times when things go wrong than we do in those times when everything is going our way. The question is, have we learned to be good losers? Job learned how to be a loser. Like Solomon, he ruled as a merchant prince. He had vast possessions and extensive commercial interests. Then, one disastrous day, loss after loss overwhelmed him, and he was left both beggared and bereaved.

First, Job lost his fortune. He had hardly sat down at his desk on this particular day when the first piece of bad news arrived. He learned that his five hundred prize female donkeys and his five hundred yoke of oxen had been swept away. A roving band of Sabeans had seized them, massacred their keepers, and made off into the blue. Sadly, Job wrote them off. It was a serious loss, but it barely made a dent in his fortune.

However, he had barely blotted the journal entry which wrote off this loss when more bad news came. His enormous flock of seven thousand sheep had been destroyed by a bolt of lightning. Job made another journal entry, visibly shaken, but still calm. He had three thousand camels. They formed great caravans, trading to the distant east, to the very borders of Babylon. Those caravans alone could help him rebuild his liquid assets. But then came the final blow. Some Chaldean marauders had fallen upon his camels, slaughtered their drivers, and made off with the lot. Job was bankrupt.

Still, he had seven sons and three daughters. It would still be possible to recover. He could marry off his daughters for rich dowries. He could put his sons to work. All he had lost, so far, as material possessions, they could be replaced in time. Then came the worst news of all. A hurricane had killed his beloved children, all ten of them. Job was utterly bereft and bereaved.

The disasters followed hard on each other's heels. "While he was yet speaking," records the Holy Spirit. It was a time to lose. Job did not know the reason, but he was a magnificent loser. All heaven rejoiced to hear his first recorded words: "The LORD gave, the LORD hath taken away; blessed be the name of the LORD" (Job 1:21).

Nor was that by any means the end of his losses. He lost his health. He lost the goodwill of his wife. He lost the regard of his friends. His life became a veritable storm of controversy and conflict, until, at last, purified by the furnace of afflictions, he emerged more than a conqueror and blessed with twice as much as he had before.

(ii) The Miser (3:6b) Keep . . . Cast

There is, then, the case of the merchant. Next, there is the case of the miser: *". . . a time to keep, and a time to cast away"* (3:6b). There are numerous instances in the Bible when it is a time to keep. One of the most famous that comes to mind is recorded in connection with the Exodus of Israel from Egypt. God told the Hebrew people to "borrow" from the Egyptians "jewels of silver and jewels of gold and raiment" and to "spoil the Egyptians" (Exodus 3:22). Normally when people borrow it is with the understanding that the items be returned. The Israelites had no such intention. Truly, the word used for "borrow" is *sha'al*, which means "to ask," "to beg," or "to require." But even if we let the word "borrow" stand unchallenged (Exodus 11:2), there is no real problem. Hannah called her little boy Samuel, meaning "asked of God," because, she said, "I have asked him of the LORD" (1 Samuel 1:20). As soon as the child was old enough to leave home she brought the child to the sanctuary to be raised for God by the high priest. "For this child I prayed," she said, ". . . therefore also I have lent him to the LORD; as long as he liveth he shall be lent to the LORD" (1 Samuel 1:27–28). She borrowed the child from God, so to speak, and God borrowed the child back from her—forever.

For Israel, it was "a time to keep." They had been forced into slavery by the Egyptians. What they "borrowed" back was rightfully theirs—on two counts. It represented back payment for years of forced labor. It was the legitimate "spoil" of war. Later on they used the vast amount of treasure which, in the end, the Egyptians lavished upon them to speed them out of their country (Exodus 12:35–36), to make the Tabernacle (Exodus 35:1–9).

It was "a time to cast away" in two cities beside the Bay of Naples in the sunny, fertile Italian province of Campagna, when, with a roar to awaken the dead, on August 24 in A.D. 79, Mount Vesuvius awoke to terrible life. There had been a warning. A devastating earthquake had shaken the area in A.D. 62.

A vivid description of the eruption of Vesuvius has been left by Pliny the Younger, who was visiting in the area when Pompeii and Herculaneum were destroyed. It was not until 1750 that Pompeii was disinterred. Since then, the story has been told and retold by historians, novelists, and movie playwrights. One of the most famous offerings is Lord Lytton's *The Last Days of Pompeii*. In one of his footnotes he tells us that his primary characters are drawn from life, or rather from death, being based on actual skeletons found as described in the text.

The fatal plume of ash and pumice, water, and fragments of burning stone held the doomed cities in a vice. Those who escaped the accompanying earthquake fell victim to the smothering ash. Those who escaped the deadly ash were overwhelmed by the crash of rocks falling from the sky. Those who escaped the ruckus faced the boiling stream of lava. Those who escaped the lava were parboiled by a scorching rainstorm.

It was "a time to cast away." Those who kept their wits about them fled. The foolish went back to gather up their treasures or saw an opportunity to enrich themselves with loot. Many were overwhelmed in the darkness as the tremendous showers of fire and brimstone and smothering ash overwhelmed them.

Thus it has been time after time in the onward march of time, "a time to cast away." Thus, the Lord warned the Jews of the impending disasters soon to come upon Jerusalem: "When ye see Jerusalem compassed with armies, then know that the desolation thereof is nigh. Then let them which are in Judaea flee . . ." (Luke 21:20–21). And, by extension, He warned a future generation of the peril when the Antichrist comes to power: "When ye therefore shall see the abomination of desolation . . . stand in the holy place . . . Then let them . . . flee into the mountains: Let him which is on the housetop not come down to take any thing out of his house; neither let him which is in the field return back to take his clothes" (Matthew 24:15–18). A time to cast away. Hard advice for the miser who finds himself bound hand and foot to his treasures.

(iii) The Mother (3:7a) Rend . . . Sew

Then too, there is the case of the mother: *"A time to rend, and a time to sew"* (3:7a). For centuries God had held His hand. He said so in His message to the exiled elders of Israel (Ezekiel 20:22). The Jews had come back from their captivity cured of idolatry but a prey to other things: formalism, hypocrisy, legalism, ritualism, skepticism, and complacency. The enthronement of such things as these led them to reject and crucify the Son of God when He appeared in their midst. His life exposed their lives. His teachings exposed their teachings. His power exposed their total lack of power. His goodness exposed their badness, His love exposed their hardness. So, they arranged with the Romans to have Him crucified. Rulers, rabble, and rabbis alike met at the cross to mock and jeer as He died. Yet, Solomon knew nothing of these things. Nevertheless, the things he had done in his day were not so different from those of his nation's descendants.

It was a time to rend. Matthew tells us what happened: "And, behold, the veil of the temple was rent in twain from the top to the bottom; and the earth did quake, and the rocks rent; and the graves were opened . . ." (Matthew 27:51–52). The sanctuary! The stones! The sepulchers! Even the soldiers were rent and torn by inner terror and dawning comprehension. It was a time to rend.

Take, for instance, the rending of the veil. The veil was key to the Old Testament Jewish religion. It was a wide, thick, colorful curtain which divided the inner Tabernacle (and Temple) into two parts. It hung between the Holy Place and the Holy of Holies as an impassable barrier. Beyond the veil, in the innermost sanctuary, God sat enthroned in the Shekinah glory cloud upon the mercy seat which covered the sacred ark of the covenant. Once a year, after the most elaborate ritual precautions, the high priest was allowed to venture beyond the veil into the Holy of Holies. The complex ritual of the Day of Atonement was related to this once-a-year passage of the veil. The Day of Atonement, like the Passover and the Feast of Tabernacles, was a Jewish religious highlight. The rending of the veil signified two things: the fact that Judaism was now obsolete and that it had been replaced by "a new and living way" (Hebrews 10:20). It was "a time to rend." The Old Testament way of rites and rituals, sacrifices and offerings, visible Temples and Tabernacles, elaborate priesthoods and Levitical services were over. Calvary had made it all null and void. The New Testament way gives us instant access to the presence of God. It emphasizes faith rather than works, grace rather than law, the spiritual and the eternal rather than the material and the temporal. A time to rend indeed! Calvary had changed it all.

There is "a time to sew." The first mention of sewing in the Bible is in connection with Adam and Eve. They had listened to the voice of the serpent. Their eyes were immediately opened, but not to the contemplation of amazing mysteries suddenly revealed or to glorious glimpses of heaven above or to deep understanding of the potentials of the earth. They saw, to their horror, that they were naked.

Their shimmering robe of light which had clothed them in their unfallen state was gone. They were unclothed, naked. It was "a time to sew." And sew they did. "They sewed fig leaves together," the Holy Spirit declares, "and made themselves aprons" (Genesis 3:7). It was a human expedient to cover the first, shocking, shameful display of their new, lost estate. Later on, they stood in the presence of God aware that their self-effort to cover the consequences of sin were wholly inadequate. He Himself graciously provided covering on a sound basis, "coats of skins" indeed, which were provided by the sacrifice of substitutionary, innocent victims, and which pointed a way to Calvary.

It was "a time to sew" for Godly Hannah after she presented her beloved little Samuel to Eli at the door of the Tabernacle to be raised for God. Year after year, she watched from afar as her child grew up before God and treasured His words in his heart. Year after year, she and her husband came to the Tabernacle "to offer the yearly sacrifice." Year after year, she took last year's pattern and cut out a bigger coat. It was "a time to sew." Year after year now she had a personal stake in the Tabernacle. Her Samuel was there! And as the appointed day drew near, out came her needle (1 Samuel 2:19)!

It is "a time to sew" for us as well, as we learn from the psalmist. He has been describing the King in His beauty, His grace, His goodness, His government. Then he turns to the Queen arrayed in garments of gold. "The King's daughter," he says, indicating her royal parentage, "is all glorious within: her clothing is of wrought gold. She shall be brought unto the king in raiment of needlework" (Psalm 45:13–14). It is a planned picture, of course, of Christ and His Church and a prophetic foreview of the marriage supper of the Lamb. We are presented by our Beloved with a robe of righteousness, procured for us with the cost of Calvary. We are arrayed in His righteousness. Just the same, we are to do our own needlework, adding "the righteousness of the Saints" (Revelation 19:8) to bring out the individual and unique glories of Christ as wrought out in us by the Spirit of God.

(f)   The Precautions of Life (3:7b) Silence . . . Speak

". . . a time to keep silence, and a time to speak . . ." (3:7b). Well did our Lord know when it was a time to keep silent. He was standing before Herod. He knew all about Herod Antipas, about his savage father, a man who tried to murder Him when He was born, and about his Samaritan mother. He knew about his education at Rome, about his rivalry with his full brother Archelaus. He knew about his tetrarchy over Galilee and Perea and about his palace at Sepphoris. He knew about his marriage to the daughter of Aretas, King of the Nabataean Arales whose capital was Petra. He knew all about his sordid affair with Theodias, his brother Philip's wife. He knew about the war Aretas waged against him when he cast off his lawful wife to take Herodias instead. He knew how the man had murdered his conscience. The time before, Jesus had called the man a fox because of his wiles. He knew all about the banquet, the dance of Salome, the rash promise, the murderous hatred of Herodias toward John the Baptist, and how that witch's brew resulted in the cold-blooded murder of John by Herod.

And now Jesus stood before this evil man, sent to him by Pilate who hoped, thus, to avoid having to deal with Jesus. John had boldly denounced Herod. Herod had brutally decapitated John. His conscience had been awakened. He superstitiously imagined that Jesus could perform miracles because He was, in Herod's opinion, John the Baptist raised from the dead.

He was delighted when Pilate deferred the case of Jesus to him. He had always wanted to see a miracle. He, no doubt, thought Jesus would perform a miracle for him, to satisfy his curiosity and to buy his goodwill. He plied Jesus with questions. But it was "a time to keep silence." The Lord refused to perform a miracle and refused to answer Herod's questions. Between him and Christ there stood "a great gulf fixed"—the murder of John, the divinely appointed forerunner of Jesus, the "man sent from God" to preach repentance to the nation in view of the coming of Christ. No John! No Jesus! The man who rejected John would equally reject Jesus. So the Lord retreated into silence. And Herod revealed his own wickedness. The man who murdered John went on to mock Jesus. Jesus read the man like a book. His silence goaded Herod into revealing himself—godless to the core of his being. To the man who had murdered his conscience by murdering John, Jesus had nothing to say. A time to keep silent! It was a silence more eloquent than speech.

Then, too, there is "a time to speak." It was "a time to speak" for the Lord Jesus when the high priest put Him under oath. It had been His settled policy to ignore the lying accusations which were hurled at Him. He answered His accusers with silence, simply allowing those godless men to perjure themselves and contradict one another until the whole plan to employ false witnesses fell apart. At last, however, the wily high priest thought of a way to make Him speak. ". . . I adjure thee by the living God" [I put you on your oath], he said, "that thou tell us whether thou be the Christ, the Son of God" (Matthew 26:63). Then Jesus spoke. It was "a time to speak." Boldly, He affirmed that He was in truth exactly that and one day they would see Him "sitting on the right hand of power, and coming in the clouds of heaven" (v. 64).

It was similar when Jesus stood before Pilate although He had more to say to him than He had to say to His nation's priests. It is a wise man who knows when to speak and when to be silent.

(g) The Passions of Life (3:8a) Love . . . Hate

"A time to love, and a time to hate . . ." (3:8a). Esau and Jacob were twins. Never were twin boys more unalike. They were dissimilar in physical appearance, in temperament and character, in their occupations, and in their spiritual discernment. Esau was hairy, Jacob was smooth. Esau was a hunter, Jacob was a shepherd. Esau scorned both birthright and blessing, Jacob prized both. Jacob, for all his craftiness, backsliding, and failure, loved God. Esau, for all his power and charm, never did.

Thus, at the very end of the Old Testament, God drew a terrible line between these two boys. With the light of half a millennium of history to go, God declared, "Was not Esau Jacob's brother? saith the LORD: yet I loved Jacob, and I hated Esau" (Malachi 1:2–3).

It was "a time to love." Jacob found God at Bethel when running away from home with Esau's threats ringing in his ears (Genesis 28). There he learned that there was a way back to God from the dark paths of sin. He enthroned God in his life at the Jabbok, some twenty years later, when, weary of his life in far-off Padan-aram, he found his way back to the Promised Land. There, by the Jabbok River, Jacob became Israel (Genesis 32). Here, too, he began to grow in grace, increasing in the knowledge of God until, at last, we find him, father of the tribes, prophetically blessing his boys and the nation which would spring from them. A nation intended to be a blessing and schoolmaster to all nations, and into which nation, and of Jacob's seed, Christ Himself would be born. "A time to love," indeed!

Esau, born in the same hour, with Isaac his father and Abraham his grandfather, placed no value on these things. He sold his birthright to Jacob for a bowl of stew and consequently lost the blessing as well (Genesis 25:29–34). That birthright was of incalculable value. It carried with it the right to a double portion of the family inheritance, the right to be the family priest, and, in Jacob's family, the right to be the progenitor of Christ. All this Esau threw away for something to eat. "Thus, Esau despised his birthright," is the Holy Spirit's cutting comment on the affair.

In the same spirit of utter disregard for God and His revelation, Esau married a number of pagan women, went off to Edom where he became great and powerful in this world, and founded the Edomite nation. This nation hated the Hebrew people. The two countries were constantly at war. They cheered the Babylonians on their way to complete the destruction of Jerusalem and the deportation of the Jewish people. They sang the praises of the Babylonians and even went so far as to capture Jews, fleeing from stricken Jerusalem, and handed them over to their Babylonian tormentors. Haman, who, during the days of the Persians, instigated an attempt to exterminate the Jews throughout all the empire's vast domains, was descended from Esau. So was Herod who tried to murder the infant Christ. Indeed, the whole evil Herodian brood sprang from Esau. No wonder God said, "Esau have I hated." The time to love and the time to hate were simultaneous, growing to their appointed harvests side by side.

(h) The Provocations of Life (3:8b) War . . . Peace

"*. . . a time of war, and a time of peace*" (3:8b). It was a time of war for Abraham when word was brought to him of Lot's capture by the invading army from the east (Genesis 14). It was a time for war when the Philistine champion, the mighty Goliath of Gath, led his army into Israel (1 Samuel 17). Many times, in the Old Testament, it was a time for war. The Bible rings with the din and noise of war. God Himself is described as "a man of war" by Moses after the final overthrow of the Egyptian army at the Red Sea (Exodus 15:3).

The pacifist wants peace—at any price. He will accept any compromise, appease the most vicious aggressor. Thus, the Aztec Empire was destroyed. Montezuma was overawed by the Spanish conquistadors. They were clothed in metal. They rode upon fierce beasts. They had weapons which made a noise like thunder and which slew from afar. They carried weapons of shining metal in their hands. He could see no possible defense. He believed they were the children of the pagan god Quetzal come back to take the land. He spurned the advice given to him, that the invading Teules, as the Aztec called the Spaniards, were few; that Montezuma could muster a thousand soldiers for everyone who followed Cortez, the Spanish conqueror; that he should fall upon them and crush them before they could find allies among Indian tribes hostile to the Aztec power.

"No!" he said, "I will not fight them, but meet them with gifts and fair words." Thus, with vast treasures of gold and gems, he sought to buy off the Spaniards, not realizing in his folly and policy of appeasement that the more he fed the Spaniards' craving for gold, the more their appetite grew and the more determined they became to seize Tenochtitlan, the Mexican capital, plunder it of its treasures, and enslave the Indians to dig for more.

Too late, the Aztecs awoke. Too late, Montezuma realized his folly in not understanding it was "a time for war." Fallen from his throne, hated by his subjects, a prisoner of the Spaniards, he tore the bandages from his wounds and courted death.

It was the same when Neville Chamberlain came back from Munich waving a worthless piece of paper and proclaiming, "Peace with honor, I believe it is peace in our time." The rape of Czechoslovakia by Hitler made World War 2 inevitable. It was the final capitulation, in a long policy of appeasement, which guaranteed that Hitler would soon engulf the globe in a horrendous war. It is a wise man who knows how and when to draw the line between war and peace.

It was a time of peace when the Son of God stepped off the throne of the universe, entered these scenes of time, and condescended to be born on this planet of Adam's ruined race. The angels came from the high halls of heaven to awaken the echoes of the old Judean hills with song: "Glory to God in the highest, and on earth peace, good will toward men" (Luke 2:14).

He had come at last, the One Isaiah had heralded as "The Prince of Peace" (Isaiah 9:6). Man's answer was the cross. God's reply is a risen Christ and a renewed offer to individuals to make "peace through the blood of his cross" (Colossians 1:20). Happy are they who recognize that this is a time of peace. For God, in sovereign grace, makes peace that the blood of that cross will one day make war over that blood. That is what the book of Revelation is all about.

That is Solomon's logic of time. Time is what we have, given to one and all, absolutely impartially, for us to waste or save, squander or invest.

"Don't waste it!" That was Solomon's logic about time.

> b) The Limitations of Time (3:9–11)
> > (1) What He Discerned (3:9–10)
> > > (a) The Penetrating Question (3:9)

"What profit hath he that worketh in that wherein he laboureth?" (3:9). Each day brings us its quota of time, just 24 hours, 1,440 minutes, 86,400 seconds. These fleeting moments come our way in a seemingly endless stream. They touch our lives for a fleeting instant. Then, carrying a record for better or for worse, they pour into the past where they are kept in custody to the day of judgment. Then, suddenly, there are no more of them. The sandglass of our days pours its last

moments our way, and our days on earth are done. We cannot lengthen our allotment by so much as a moment. Solomon organized his time, with a time and a place for this, and for that, and for the other. He had so many interests. He begrudged each passing moment with its hasty departure into the past. He was determined that each moment of time should contribute something to his life. It was to that end he organized his time into so many categories. Each day was to add some new pleasure, some new enterprise, some new idea, some new experience.

But it all added up to nothing. Recently I read John Dickson Carr's biography of Sir Arthur Conan Doyle, who began life as the youngest son of a famous family. His mother never tired of reminding her son that she could trace her lineage back for six hundred years to the marriage of Barrow Percy to a niece of King Henry III. She sprinkled her lectures with references to Sir Denis Pack charging the French at Waterloo and to Admiral Foley in action at the battle of the Nile. As the creator of Sherlock Holmes, he rose to fame and fortune. He had everything: good looks, polish, a commanding physique, a brilliant mind, a rich heritage, countless friends in high places, wealth. Educated by the Jesuits, he became a medical doctor and turned his back on the Roman Church. He became an agnostic. Book after book poured from his pen. He was in demand around the world as a speaker. Men of rank, influence, and prestige sought his company. He had a devoted family. Honor and integrity were his watchwords. Old fashioned chivalry marked his conduct. Yet for all that, he could have echoed Solomon's lament here. Yes! There was a time and place for everything. No! With all his achievements and successes, he had not found peace. "What profit hath he that worketh in that wherein he laboureth?" Solomon turned at last to the pagan gods of his heathen wives. Sir Arthur Conan Doyle turned to spiritualism.

More and more, he became a missionary for that evil cause. He wrote articles. He attended séances. He, for all the brilliance of his mind, was duped by demons masquerading as the departed loved ones of those sitting in the dark of the medium's parlor waiting for some voice or vision from the dead.

Time, and all that time has to offer, is, after all, only time. We were created for something much bigger than time. Sir Arthur Conan Doyle thought he'd found it in the séance. Solomon found it in a belated return to God.

(b) The Perpetual Quest (3:10)

"I have seen the travail, which God hath given to the sons of men to be exercised in it" (3:10). The expression "seen the travail" can be rendered "seen the business."

The word for "travail" indicates "toil that brings about fatigue." It occurs only in Ecclesiastes (1:13; 2:26; 3:10; 4:8; 5:15). All of Solomon's splendid organization of his time wore him out. Moreover, it left him drained and dissatisfied, and full of weariness and emptiness. Life had become a perpetual quest for something more, something bigger, something better. Work was all well and good. Indeed, work can be therapeutic. But work left one tired—and there was still so much more to see, so much more to do, so many more places to go, so many more people to meet, so much more to learn. He was tired of it all. Bored to tears, indeed. Surely there was more to life than a crowded calendar!

(2) What He Discovered (3:11a)

"He hath made every thing beautiful in his [its] time [proper season]: also he hath set the world in their heart, . . ." (3:11a). The word for "the world" here is *'olam.* It means "the ages," or the world as it relates to time. Here is a figure of speech, metonymy, where an attribute of a thing is used for the thing itself. "The world" set in the heart is that which is beyond human scrutiny. It reminds us of man's inability to know all about the past, and his even greater inability to know all that the future holds. As a result, he cannot even begin to comprehend the full scope of the plans and purposes of God. Some have rendered the statement: "God hath set eternity in their hearts."

Solomon, in all his preoccupation with time, was aware that there was beauty and order in creation. He had explored the wonders of the natural world. His book of Proverbs, for instance, abounds in references to ants and other creatures, the ways of which he had evidently explored and admired. Even the most cloddish individual must at times admire the rugged grandeur of a mountain range, the majestic splendor of a stormy sunset, the restless surging of an angry sea marching its white-capped waves against a rocky shore.

None of that satisfied the royal preacher. He wanted more, much more. Everything was beautiful in its time. The sea was beautiful when hushed to rest, and it was beautiful when its surging billows dashed themselves to pieces on the ramparts of the cliffs. The sky was beautiful when the westering sun sank slowly beneath the circle of the earth bathing all in glowing reds. It was just as beautiful when the billowing thunderheads heralded the coming storm. Solomon had seen it all time after time. And yet he remained restless and unsatisfied.

"He hath set the world in their heart" was his final cry. What was the good of time, time with all its treasures, when the human heart hungered for something much vaster than time—eternity!

The tragedy with Solomon was that he realized it too late. He had been engineered by an infinite God for eternity. And he had become preoccupied with time.

One of Scotland's greatest ministers was Thomas Chalmers of Kilmany. He was called to the ministry in 1799 and served a church in a half-hearted way. Ordained, but still not saved, his real ambition was to occupy the chair of mathematics at the University of Edinburgh. In those days, he wrote a pamphlet in which he expressed the opinion that a person could discharge all his pastoral obligations in three or four days, leaving the rest of the week free to follow any avocation upon which he set his heart. His desire was to teach mathematics. Then came his conversion in 1811, followed by his triumphant ministry. He was considered by some to be one of the greatest preachers of the age.

In his later years, Chalmers attended a meeting where other ministers of his denomination were present. One of them, motivated by jealousy, stood up and read to the Synod from the pamphlet Chalmers had written in his unconverted days and made much of the low views of the ministry it espoused. Then he turned on Chalmers and demanded if he recognized the sentiments. Chalmers jumped to his feet. "Yes," he said, "I wrote those words, strangely blinded as I was. In those days, sir," he thundered, "I aspired to be a professor of mathematics in the University of Edinburgh. But what, sir, is mathematics? It is magnitude and the proportion of magnitude. And in those days, I had forgotten two magnitudes. I had forgotten the shortness of time; and I had forgotten the length of eternity."[17]

That is what Solomon had done. He had been preoccupied with time. Now he had to face eternity. He had found time for everything—even the fierce, foul, and false gods of his pagan wives. Now God had awakened him to the looming prospect of an endless eternity. He discovered, almost too late, indeed, that time, however well organized, was no substitute for eternity.

(3) What He Decided (3:11b)

"*. . . so that no man can find out the work that God maketh from the beginning to the end*" (3:11b). Nowhere is that more evident in our world than in human philosophy, secular materialism, and mechanistic evolution. God's ways reach back beyond the beginning of time. They continue into eternities yet unborn. They are inscrutable and infinite. When we explore the wonders of His ways in creation and redemption in grace and in government, we cry out with the great Apostle: "O the depth of the riches both of the wisdom and knowledge of God! how unsearchable are his judgments, and his ways past finding out! For who hath known the mind of the Lord? or who hath been his counsellor? Or who hath first given to him, and it shall be recompensed unto him again? For of him, and through him, and to him, are all things: to whom be glory forever. Amen" (Romans 11:33–36).

We learn so much and know so little. So, indeed, Isaac Newton felt toward the end of his life. When he was attending Cambridge University, the Great Plague broke out in Britain (1665–66). A tenth of the population died in three months. The university was closed. Newton returned home and gave himself to meditation. He had enormous powers of concentration and an ability to come to the very crux of a matter. He had solved the laws of motion and universal gravity by the time he was twenty-four. He had also invented calculus! He discovered the laws of the tides and proved that light is composed of all the colors of the spectrum. He put into our hands the mechanics of the universe. For some two hundred years his *Principia*, made up mostly of mathematical formulas and equations, controlled scientific thought. He was the first scientist ever to be knighted by the crown.

Newton had discovered but "the edges of His ways." There was always more and more to discover and explore. And so, it will always be. When we have been in heaven ten thousand times ten thousand years, we shall still have touched the fringe of the garment of God's ways.

As for the unregenerate, and the thoughtless unbelieving, they never do understand God's ways. David declared that God "made known his ways unto Moses, his acts unto the children of Israel" (Psalm 103:7). The children of Israel saw only His outward acts. Moses was permitted to see the reasons for those acts. Very few penetrate beyond the veil into that hidden place where God makes known the secrets of His ways as Job discovered. It was not until after his period of tribulation had come and gone that he was let into the secret of God's ways. If this be true of the saint, how much more so of the sinner. In their quest for knowledge people wander far away from the truth. They substitute false religions for the Gospel. They banish the Bible and replace it with behavioral psychology. They ignore the evidence of a creator and replace it with the blind workings of chance bolstered by the false theory of evolution. Or, like Pilate, they throw up their hands and say, "What is Truth?" even when it is staring them in the face (John 18:37–38).

That, then, was Solomon's first problem, the problem of time without eternity. Now came his next one.

> 2. The Problem of a New Leaf Without a New Life (3:12–17)
>   a) The Works of the Creature (3:12–13)
>   (1) Man's Limitations (3:12)
>   (a) The Realization (3:12a)

"I know that there is no good in them, but for a man to rejoice, and to do good in his life" (3:12a). Solomon looks now at the works of man himself. He comes to the conclusion that, since man cannot fathom God's ways in the world, he might just as well accept his limitations and make the best of things by enjoying the good things of life so long as they last. This is utter materialism.

> (b) The Resolve (3:12b)

Still, he urges his readers to *"do good"* in their lives (3:12b). This is sometimes taken to mean that they should "do good" to themselves. Enjoy to the fullest what we call "the good life." "Live it up," as we would say. This was the philosophy of the rich man with his bursting barns: "Eat, drink, and be merry" (Luke 12:19). On the other hand, the expression may reflect a moral scene and be a reminder that goodness is essential to happiness. In any case, man is limited. He is limited by his means, his motives, and his mortality.

> (2) Man's Labors (3:13)
>   (a) His Acceptance of Life's Bounty (3:13a)
>   (b) His Acknowledgment of Life's Benefactor (3:13b)

Solomon continues his theme. We should accept life's bounties: *". . . every man should eat and drink, and enjoy the good of all his labour, . . ."* (3:13a). And he should acknowledge life's Benefactor: *". . . it is the gift of God"* (3:13b).

For that is the danger of materialism. It causes people to forget God. The rich man, in the Lord's parable, forgot God. He can be seen sitting up in bed, gloating over his balance sheet, rubbing his hands, making far-reaching plans for business expansion, and totally occupied with the things of time and sense. Little does he realize that he has run out of time. God, too, was keeping a balance sheet of this man's life. He called him a fool (literally, "a senseless one"). He was rich, but he was not rich toward God. God had written the word "bankrupt!" across His balance sheet of this man's life. He was going to call in all this man's accounts. His soul was to be required of him. He would be found dead in bed the next morning, surrounded by financial statements, sketchy blueprints for bigger and better barns, and notes on the best way to get top dollar for his bumper crops. Life's bounties are not given to us to keep to ourselves. Even the power to make money comes from God, and He refuses to be left out of the equation of our lives. The rich farmer's fields, bursting with crops, were proof of God's bountiful goodness to him. Were it not for God, every seed sown would die. But that was not the way the rich man saw it. He saw those far-flung fields of golden grain as a tribute to his own skills as a farmer.

> b) The Works of the Creator (3:14–17)
>> (1) In the Material Realm (3:14)
>>> (a) The Permanence of God's Works (3:14a)
>>> (b) The Purpose of God's Works (3:14b)

Solomon comes back to God. He mentions the permanence of God's works: *"I know that, whatsoever God doeth, it shall be for ever: nothing can be put to it, nor any thing taken from it"* (3:14a), and he mentions the purpose of God's works: *". . . and God doeth it, that men should fear before him"* (3:14b).

There is a pitiful impermanence about man's works. We build bridges, and they are attacked by rust. We clear away the forest and build great cities and at once the forest plans a comeback. The city is an aberration. It must be fought. The wind and the rain come to tear and rot. The frost and the ice join forces to explore and exploit any crack or opening where they can get in and tear and split. Fire awaits its turn. Where today is mighty Nineveh, a city on the Tigris which once terrorized the Middle East? Gone! Where is Nebuchadnezzar's boasted Babylon or Xerxes' great Persepolis? Gone. If we did not constantly renew and repair them, where would our great cities be? Tornado and hurricane, earthquake and volcanic fire, thunderbolt and raging flood would soon make short work of them.

But these very forces of nature we so much dread are mere tools in the hand of God to build and rebuild His works. These vast forces raise up continents and create mountains. They gouge out gorges and make paths to the sea. Forest fires clear the way for new growth and future trees. We call these things "Nature." But Nature is just another name for God.

Worlds that Solomon never knew are now an open book to us, from the nucleus of the atom to remote galaxies in space. In comparison with our works, God's works are ancient, vast, and carried out on such gigantic scales as to be virtually akin to eternal. He has taken enormous galaxies of countless billions of stars and tossed them into prodigious orbits, traveling at inconceivable velocities with such mathematical precision that we can foretell the occasion of an eclipse or the visit of a comet years in advance. Such are the works of the Creator. Well might Solomon have recommended reverential awe. We can put a man on the moon, indeed, but we would do well to recall that God put the moon in place. We can manufacture artificial protein and tinker with DNA, but God creates life—and can create it out of nothing. We can split the atom, but God can make black holes. Men can put up structures, such as the ancient pyramids, which appear virtually immune to the gnawing tooth of time. But what are three score thousand years compared with the billions of years astronomers demand for an expanding universe?

Solomon, however, was not only taken up with the permanence of God's works, as compared with man's. He was compelled to consider the purpose for God's works: "And God doeth it, that men should fear before him" (3:14b). "The fear of the LORD is the beginning of knowledge" (Proverbs 1:7). Part of God's overwhelming indictment of the human race is that "there is no fear of God before their eyes" (Romans 3:18; Psalm 36:1). It explained all the rest. That appalling catalog of crime which made up God's case against heathen, hypocrite, and Hebrew alike (Romans 1–3), all stemmed from that. The blasphemies and obscenities, the toleration of pornography and perversion, the wholesale rapes and murders which plague our country, wickedness, graft, and corruption in high places are all signs of the same thing. Man no longer fears God. Moreover, the vastness of His work in creation intended to fill people with reverential awe of God's wisdom, love, and power is shrugged off. Evolution is supposed to explain it all, the blind working of chance. Evolution, the most popular false religion on the planet, backed up and bolstered by pseudoscience, is the average man's working hypothesis for atheism. So, men do not fear God, and the floodgate is opened for every conceivable form of wickedness.

G. K. Chesterton is reported to have said: "When a man stops believing in God he doesn't then believe in nothing, he believes in anything." The fact that millions of people believe in evolution and have no fear of God proves nothing. Anatole France declared, "If fifty million people say a foolish thing, it is still a foolish thing." "One can't believe impossible things," protested Alice. "I daresay you haven't had much practice," said the Queen of Wonderland. "Why sometimes, I've believed as many as six impossible things before breakfast."

When translated from the realm of pseudoscience to the moral realm, the theory of evolution, which robs men of their fear of God, stands exposed as a destroyer. "It is the moral standard of the jungle, and its motivation is only self-ishness. It is the law that might is right. Cruelty, deceit, cowardice, and whatever will enable the individual to survive immediately become virtues if judiciously exercised. The acceptance of such a code of ethics would involve the abandonment of all that is noble and good and right and would destroy all that is beautiful and worthy in human nature."[18] Evolutionary theory lay at the roots of Communism. Hitler saw the whole of nature as a continuous struggle between strength and weakness and an eternal victory of the strong over the weak. Two world wars have already resulted from this kind of belief.

Solomon himself drifted away from God. It was because there was no fear of God in his heart anymore that he groped his way around the idolatrous groves, groveling before the gruesome gods of his pagan wives. Once he regained his sanity, he again looked at God's awesome witness to Himself in His creational work and acknowledged, "God doeth it, that men should fear before him" (3:14b). Those who fear God face their inescapable accountability to an omnipotent, omniscient, and omnipresent God.

(2) In the Moral Realm (3:15–17)

(a) The Past Required (3:15)

Solomon passes inevitably from a contemplation of God's works in the material realm to a consideration of His works in the moral realm. He looks at the past, the present, and the future. He says, *"That which hath been is now; and that which is to be hath already been; and God requireth that which is past"* (3:15). The past and the future are ever present before a God who transcends time. We express our mode of being in three tenses: "I was, I am, I will be." God does not do that. He simply says, "I AM" (Exodus 3:14). Nothing takes God by surprise. The past, the present, and the future are all an open book to Him. "That which hath been is now," He can say with reference to the past. "That which is to be hath already been," He declares with regard to the future.

With reference to the future, He can foretell it in all its details. He alone can do that. Thus, for instance, His prophets, inspired and enlightened by His Holy Spirit, could add detail after detail to distant events regarding the first coming of Christ, describing His virgin birth; His human lineage; the place where He would be born; His sojourn in Egypt; His forerunner; His unique anointing; His miraculous life; the time, place, and manner of His death; His burial and accompanying incorruption; His resurrection and His ascension; and the subsequent coming of His Holy Spirit. Similarly, His Apostles and prophets were subsequently able to add detail after detail to scores of Old Testament prophecies regarding the Lord's coming again. Many of these prophesies have slumbered for centuries in the womb of time but are now, in our own day, travailing for birth.[19]

The future holds no secrets from God. Nor does the past. With a belatedly quickened conscience gnawing at his memory, Solomon wrote, "And God requireth that which is past." There are few statements in the Bible more disquieting than that one. As memory of our sins and transgressions recede further and further into the past, we tend to dilute them, rationalize them, and, all too often, forget them altogether. But they are still there, locked permanently into sealed chambers of the past. We may forget them but those against whom we have transgressed do not forget the injuries done, the lies told, the betrayals and treacheries wrought. Nor does God.

It does no good to turn over a new leaf and try to reform our behavior; commendable though it may be, it does not erase the past. Suppose a businessman for example, were to find himself unable to pay debts he had accumulated over a period of time. One day he summons his accountant and says to him: "Write a letter to all our creditors. Tell them we are unable to meet our obligations. Tell them that, as from today, we are turning over a new leaf in our ledgers and starting afresh. Tell them that from now on we intend to live up to the highest standards of business integrity." Do you think the man's creditors would be satisfied with that? Of course not! They would, and rightly so, require that which is past. No good resolutions for future impeccable business conduct wipes out the past.

Just so with God: no good resolutions, even present exemplary conduct, will wipe out the past. God requires a complete accounting for the past. Just the other day there was a news story on the local television channel about a man who had committed murder seventeen years ago. All that time he had eluded the officers of the law. He had provided himself with a new identity. He had settled in a small town, gone into business, and became an exemplary citizen. He had gone on to become the pastor of a local church, much loved and respected by his congregation. But, in time, his past caught up with him. The FBI tracked him down. He was arrested in his home and led away in handcuffs to face his past.

"God requireth that which is past." All of it. All of which He knows. Thank

God for Calvary and the substitutionary death of the Lord Jesus, who there took my place so that I might go free.

(b) The Present Reviewed (3:16)
(i) Public Wickedness (3:16a)

"And moreover I saw under the sun the place of judgment, that wickedness was there; and the place of righteousness, that iniquity was there" (3:16a). The word for "wickedness" and "iniquity" is the same word in the Hebrew. It means "lawlessness." It speaks of the restless activity of fallen nature and to the impious activity of the godless.

The picture Solomon paints is a gloomy one. He looked in "the place of judgment, the law courts," and saw wickedness entrenched there. He looked in "the place of righteousness," what we would call today the Church, and saw wickedness entrenched there. Wickedness everywhere, even in the two places where least expected. What a description of our modern society where God and His Book and His Son are ruled out of court and insulted even in His courts.

The worst forms of decadence are now countenanced by our courts and even by the Supreme Court. Many years ago Senator Daniel Patrick Moynihan acknowledged that the courts of the United States have lowered the standard of acceptable behavior by "defining deviancy down." *Insight* magazine says that we have "normalized" all kinds of deviant behavior. As a result, the level of violent crimes, for instance, which would have shocked us a few decades ago, is now considered the average. The numbers no longer have shock appeal. Nor do the statistics on pornography, perversion, rape, child molestation, divorce, free love, AIDS, and the like (see *Insight*, June 2, 1997, p. 48).

Sodomy is now virtually accepted at all levels of society as an alternate lifestyle. Once a criminal offence, it is now condoned by courts and country alike.

In the same edition, *Insight* magazine reported, in a matter-of-fact way, that a new doll was now on the market for children to play with. It was manufactured by *The Pride Factory* in Fort Lauderdale, Florida. It was called *Billy the Gay Doll* and was touted as "everyone's little dream guy." More than 25,000 were sold in four months—at a price of nearly $50 each.

And the Supreme Court smiles. When President Clinton, a friend of "gay rights" and late-term abortion, signed into laws the Communications Decency Act, designed to protect children by prohibiting "indecent" speech or images from being sent through cyberspace, the bill was immediately attacked by the free speech advocates as "an unacceptable infringement of the First Amendment." The Supreme Court agreed unanimously that it was unconstitutional to reduce online communication to a "safe-for-kids" standard. The right to freely express pornography was more important in the Court's eyes than safeguarding the nation's children. The Court's eyes were dazzled by the fact that the Internet had some fifty million users at the time. The Communications Decency Act was struck down. After all, who in their right mind would want to "touch a large segment of the Internet community"? Indiana Senator Daniel Coats, coauthor of the CDA, protested: "The court has ignored the clear will of the Executive Branch, and the Congress, and the clear will of the American people" (*Time*, July 7, 1997, p. 28).

(ii) Personal Wickedness (3:16b)

So, we have wickedness endorsed in *"the place of righteousness"* (3:16b), one far greater than any Supreme Court judge long ago warned the world about doing or supporting anything which might damage the innocence of a child. Across the portals of the Supreme Court should be written these words of the Lord Jesus: "Whoso shall offend [from Gr. *scandalon*, 'a snare' or a 'stumbling block in the way'] one of these little ones which believe in me, it were better for him that a millstone were hanged about his neck, and that he were drowned in the depth of the sea" (Matthew 18:6).

Moreover, we have wickedness endorsed in the place of judgment in the courts, and wickedness endorsed in the place of righteousness, in the sanctuary. "Iniquity was there" (3:16b), Solomon said. If it was there, he was responsible for it, for one thing is certain, David, for all his faults and failings, was no man to stand idly by while God's house was being polluted. In this he was like his greater Son, the Lord Jesus, who took a whip of cords to scourge those out of the Temple courts in His day, those who had turned it into a den of thieves (John 2:13–16). As for the Church, its history has been one of constant defilement crowned, in our day, by gay congregations and sodomizing clergy.

(c) The Prospect Revealed (3:17)
(i) The Truth of Judgment Is Sure (3:17a)

There can only be one end when a country's highest and holiest institutions tolerate and even endorse wickedness—judgment. Solomon recognized that. *"I said in mine heart, God shall judge the righteous and the wicked"* (3:17a).

What Solomon has in mind here is the certainty of future judgment. It is not so much God's periodic judgment of offending nations that Solomon has in view, though history affords us many examples of that. God allows national wickedness to rise and rise until it overflows all its banks. Then He acts decisively and catastrophically. The enemy comes in like a flood and the Spirit of God raises up a standard against him (Isaiah 28:2). The Flood, the overthrow of Sodom, the fall of Nineveh, the overthrow of Babylon, the downfall of Persia, the disintegration of Alexander's empire, and the fall of Rome furnish us with abundant instances. Other examples would include the downfall of Hitler's Germany, the demise of the British Empire, and the collapse of the Soviet Union.

(ii) The Time of Judgment Is Set (3:17b)

". . . for there is a time there for every purpose and for every work" (3:17b). Here, however, Solomon's thoughts seem to be taken up with end-time apocalyptic judgment. In his day, of course, predictive prophecy had barely begun. It would be centuries before Isaiah, Daniel, Ezekiel, and Zechariah would bring prophecy to a fine art, and longer still before the Lord and His Apostles added their views of end-time events to the ever-growing panorama of prophetic truth. Still, Solomon was son enough of his father, David, a prophet of no small stature, to be able to see where present trends would inevitably end. Psalm 2, alone, would give him at least a basic working knowledge of things to come.

3. The Problem of Mortality Without Immortality (3:18–22)
   a) A Low View of Man's Dignity (3:18–19)
     (1) Man Is a Beast Constitutionally (3:18)
       (a) As to His Being (3:18a)

"I said in mine heart concerning the estate of the sons of men, that God might manifest them, . . ." (3:18a). Man is no better than the beasts. Such is Solomon's pessimistic and humanistic assessment of the human race. It is indeed a view much endorsed in our humanistic society brainwashed by the theory of evolution. Countless billions of dollars have been spent, incalculable millions of research hours have been invested, to propagate the theory that man is simply a beast. Then our generation wonders why man behaves in a beastly way. It is no wonder that in biblical apocalyptical prophecy, Daniel saw world empires, and especially the end-time empire of the Antichrist, as beastly (Daniel 7:1–28; 13:1–18). When

moral standards are undermined, and all the old landmarks swept away, men behave in a beastly fashion. They behave worse than beasts. Animals, after all, only follow their instincts. Fallen man, free from the restraints imposed by a healthy society, and from the hindering work of the Holy Spirit (2 Thessalonians 2:7), exhibits all forms of decadence and depravity and indulges in every form of vice and violence.

(b) As to His Breath (3:18b)

". . . and that they might see that they themselves are beasts" (3:18b). Solomon's gloomy view that men are beasts ignores the creation teaching of Genesis and the creation teaching of Psalms (Psalms 8, 104). Man is not just an efficient animal. Man was made to be inhabited by God. What we see today is not proof of the false theory of evolution but evidence of the fall (Genesis 3). Man in sin has lost the governing principle of the indwelling Holy Spirit in his life. He needs to be born again. When a person is regenerated by God, the Holy Spirit again takes up residence in his spirit, producing a change in his behavior. Solomon, with a third of the Old Testament in his hands, should have been wise enough to see through the materialistic view that man is simply a beast and no better than a beast.

(2) Man Is a Beast Comparatively (3:19)

"For that which befalleth the sons of men befalleth beasts; even one thing befalleth them: as the one dieth, so dieth the other; yea, they have all one breath; so that a man hath no preeminence above a beast: for all is vanity" (3:19). Men and animals share a common fate. They are born to die. That is a grossly materialistic concept of life. It is true that death reigns. It is not true that men and the brute creation share a common experience when life's short span is over. There is a whole subdivision of biblical eschatology that deals with man's destiny beyond the grave. Solomon's own father knew full well that there was life after death (2 Samuel 12:15–32). When God spoke to Moses regarding Abraham, Isaac, and Jacob, His words were interpreted by the Lord Jesus as teaching the survival of the soul after death (Exodus 3:6; Matthew 22:23). Solomon was certainly familiar with the Spirit-inspired answer David received to his question: "What is man?" The answer ranked men as being "a little lower than the angels" and, therefore, considerably higher than the animals (Psalm 8:4–5). Solomon, probably, did not know how

the incarnation of Christ would radically change all that for the child of God. The eighth psalm is made to apply not just to men in general but to the Lord Jesus in particular. He is the One who, in condescending grace, stepped from the throne of the universe to be "made a little lower than the angels" and under whose feet all the created universe is one day to be placed (Hebrews 2:7–11). But there is far more to it than that. The redeemed, in Christ, are seated in Christ "far above all principality, and power, and might, and dominion, and every name that is named, not only in this world, but also in that which is to come" (Ephesians 1:21; see also Ephesians 2:4–7).

Solomon, grubbing in the garbage pails of materialism, reminds us of the man with the muckrake in his hand in *Pilgrim's Progress*. The poor fellow could look no way but downward. One offered him a crown in exchange for his muckrake, "but the man did neither look up nor regard, but raked to himself the straws, the small sticks, and the dust on the floor." Of this wretched man someone has said:

> Could'st thou in vision see
> The man God meant,
> Thou never more could'st be
> The man thou art, content.[20]

But such a man was Solomon in his muckraking days when he turned his back on his Scripture and groveled in the groves of the gods of his pagan wives and opened his mind to all the false philosophies of his day.

b) A Low View of Man's Destiny (3:20–21)
(1) A Conclusion (3:20)

First there is a conclusion: *"All go unto one place; all are of the dust, and all turn to dust again"* (3:20). But it is not that simple, as Solomon immediately admits. There is a complication: "Who knoweth the spirit of man that goeth upward, and the spirit of the beast that goeth downward to the earth?" (3:21).

Dust! That is the lowest common denominator of all living things. They are all made of dust. "Dust thou art, to dust thou shalt return." The words are often recited at the graveside of a departed loved one.

The statement was much misunderstood by the little boy who asked his Sunday school teacher the question: "Where did I come from?" "Dust," replied the teacher. "Where am I going?" he asked. "Dust," replied the teacher. The next day the little boy called to his mother, "Mom," he said, "come upstairs quickly. Somebody is under my bed, either coming or going!"

Dust! Solomon's philosophy has some roots in Scripture. In the Genesis account of the creation of man we read: "And the LORD God formed man of the dust of the ground" (Genesis 2:7). And He didn't use gold dust! He used calcium, carbon, chlorine, phosphorus, potassium, iron, sulphur, and glycerin—all combined, in exact sequence and proportions into a total chemical formula which staggers the imagination. Some "dust"!

It is true that "all go to one place," if Solomon has the grave in mind. "All turn to dust again" is true enough if we are concerned solely with the physical. The moment we rise beyond that we are faced with a complication. What happens to the spirit? Whether it be that of a beast or that of a boy? Solomon, confining himself to the materialistic view of life, can only guess. Man's spirit goes upward. The animal's goes downward. Apart from divine revelation, nobody can prove any such contention. It is quite beyond experience.

If Solomon had paid attention to his Bible, he would have remembered the case of King Saul and the witch of Endor. She was requested by the king to produce the spirit of the dead prophet Samuel. "Whom shall I bring up unto thee?" the woman asked. Saul did not know enough to know what he was asking for. He called it a "spirit" rather than a "soul." The medium was evidently expecting that her familiar spirit, her earthly comrade in demon deception who impersonated the dead people in her séances, would appear in the guise of the prophet. Instead, and to her surprise, the prophet himself appeared. "I saw gods [a spirit manifestation . . . *elshim*] ascending out of the earth," she said. "An old man cometh up," she continued (see 1 Samuel 28:8, 11, 13–14).

(2) A Complication (3:21)

"Who knoweth the spirit of man that goeth upward, and the spirit of the beast that goeth downward to the earth?" (3:21). So Solomon was wrong. In his day, to the best of his knowledge, the spirit of a dead man went down, not up. All that has been changed now by virtue of Christ's conquest of death (Ephesians 4:8; Revelation 1:18).

We know so little about what happens at death whether to a beast or a human being. We can only speculate in cases where the Bible is silent. Preachers are often asked if their loved household pets will be in heaven. It is a natural question. Who knows?

In his memoirs of hunting man-eating tigers in India, Jim Corbett tells the story of a dog called Robin. He bought him for fifteen rupees. When he died at the age of fifteen, not all the gold in Indian could have bought him. All Corbett knew of the pup's ancestry was that his father was a keen gun dog. He became the hunter's constant companion on the trail. The dog and its master became partners. When they picked up the tracks of a leopard or a tiger, they would follow them. When the foot marks could be seen, Corbett did the tracking, but when the quarry took to the jungle, Robin took the lead. Adventure followed adventure. The two became one, deeply attached one to the other, thinking alike, working in harmony, closer than brothers.

Jim Corbett, in one of his stories, tells how once and once only, in a tight corner, Robin parted company with his master. He came back later, when the danger was past, with downcast eyes and dejected ears. He licked his master's face and made little sounds in his throat to say he was sorry and that he was glad to find his master unhurt and how ashamed he was. All was soon forgiven.

Jim Corbett, with Robin's permission no doubt, told the story. He records the death of his dog, from old age, lying on a bed he would never leave again, his wise, old eyes lovingly fixed on his master. The hunter describes him as "the biggest-hearted and the most faithful friend man ever had." "He has gone to the Happy Hunting Grounds," he remarked, "where I know I shall find him waiting for me."[21]

And why not? The Bible remains silent on the subject. Certainly, we shall remember such loyal animal friends when we get home, for memory survives death (Luke 16:25). Who is to say that a creature, which has become the loyal friend of a human being, will not be there, in the presence of a God with whom all things are possible?

Along the same line is a story told me by Robert Little when he was Radio Pastor of the Moody Bible Institute radio network. He was one of the busiest men I knew. He not only carried a full load of broadcasts but also a voluminous correspondence. We were chatting together during our coffee break one day. "Been out, Bob?" I said, noting he had his hat and coat with him.

"Yes," he said," I've been to a funeral."

"Friend of yours?"

"No. As a matter of fact, it was the funeral of a dog."

"A dog? You're kidding."

He was serious. A man had called him up that morning, a complete stranger, a member of his vast listening audience.

"Pastor Little?"

"Yes."

"I want you to come and bury my dog. He's just died. I'm alone in the world. No relatives, no friends, just my dog. Now I've got nobody. And I want my dog to have a Christian burial. You are the only other person I know. I listen to you all the time. Will you come and bury my dog?"

He went out to one of the Chicago suburbs. He found the house and met the man. They put the little dog in a carton. They went out to a shady corner of the garden. They dug a hole and Robert committed the dog's remains to the ground and prayed for that lonely man, commending him to that Friend that sticketh closer than a brother.

In concluding the story, Robert Little said, "I may never see that man again, down here. But I am certain of this, he will always listen to me on the radio. One day I hope to meet that man in heaven."

And who's to say that he will not meet the dog, who was given "a Christian funeral" in heaven, too? Solomon was just as wrong when he said that the spirit of a man goeth upward. He might just as well be wrong in implying that a man and his dog are parted forever because the spirit of man goes up and the spirit of a dog goes down. Certainly, we cannot dogmatize but wouldn't that be just like Jesus, to give us back our faithful, humble friends in that land of fadeless day?

c) A Low View of Man's Duty (3:22)
(1) Investing in the Here and Now (3:22a)

Solomon concludes this paragraph, dealing with the problem of mortality without immortality, by relating it to our daily concerns. He mentions investing in the here and now: *"Wherefore I perceive that there is nothing better, than that a man should rejoice in his own works; for that is his portion"* (3:22a), and he mentions ignorance of the hereafter: *"for who shall bring him to see what shall be after him?"* (3:22b). "Make the best of things. They will not last. Even if they do, we won't be here and so will know nothing of the onward march of events. A most unsatisfactory state of affairs." Truly the materialist, the atheist, the secular humanist must be, of all people, the most miserable.

So, Solomon comes back to the bitter realization that life on this earth is brief and the future, even here, "under the sun," is a largely closed book to us. Don't worry about the future! That seems to be Solomon's theme. What will be will be. Our hopes, our fears, our labors for the future may well be all in vain. Our precautions and preparations may be for contingencies which may never arise and, in any case, may be totally inadequate if they do. For all we know the pains we take to anticipate future events may be completely wasted. We cannot control or change the long-term course of events on earth. So, make the most of the present.

(2) Ignorance of the Hereafter (3:22b)

We need to constantly remind ourselves that Solomon wrote Ecclesiastes under the inspiration of the Holy Spirit, to expound the perspectives and prospects of man "under the sun." He tells us what the worldly person thinks, the person whose horizons are dominated by the things of time and sense. Solomon himself had been a materialist for years (setting his heart on wealth, works, and women). Doubtless he had engaged in conversation with countless people more worldly, more wedded to stoicism, Epicureanism, and materialism than he. He knew how these people thought. He wrote their conclusions about life into his book. He himself had recovered from the worst of his past worldliness. He tells us what such people think. Their conclusions about life are wrong. Solomon knew them to be wrong. But he recorded them anyway, often without editorial comment. It is up to us, Bible in hand, to expose the error of their false opinions about life and death. Perhaps the shadow of his backsliding days still clouded his mind. He wrote no great psalms as David, his father, did, penitential psalms for instance, such as Psalms 6, 32, 38, 51, 102, 130, and 143; or devotional psalms, such as Psalms 3, 16, 28, 41, 59, 61, 67, 70, 86, 122, 144, and 145; or prophetic psalms, such as Psalms 2, 16, 22, 24, 40, 68, 69, 72, and 110. His thoughts of God in Ecclesiastes, the book of his old age, do not soar much higher than to view God as Creator.

It is up to us to recognize the fact that when Solomon wrote down such low views of man's duty, espousing investing in the here and now and confessing ignorance of things to come, he was simply recording the spiritual blindness of the natural man (1 Corinthians 2:14). We ought to have no difficulty in seeing through that.

4. The Problem of Might Without Right (4:1–3)
a) A Gloomy Consideration (4:1)
(1) The Anguish of the Oppressed (4:1a)
(2) The Arrogance of the Oppressors (4:1b)

Solomon now looks at another aspect of life on this little planet in space. It is full of injustice. Solomon mentions the anguish of the oppressed: *"So I returned, and considered all the oppressions that are done under the sun: and behold the tears of such as were oppressed, and they had no comforter . . ."* (4:1a). Then he mentions likewise the arrogance of the oppressors: *"and on the side of their oppressors there was power; but they had no comforter"* (4:1b).

Human history since the fall of man is but the record of such things. Every page is soaked with tears and stained with blood. Libraries could be filled with books documenting the terrible tales that could be told. The history of Israel, even in Solomon's day, had its record of persecution and oppression. That Pharaoh who "knew not Joseph" had plans for the long-term extermination of all Hebrew males and for the assimilation of the women. The cry of their torment reached to heaven (Exodus 3:7–8). The Assyrians, in their turn, filled the Middle East with terror. Graham Scroggie says:

> These people ruled with hideous tyranny and violence from the Caucasus and the Caspian to the Persian Gulf, and from beyond the Tigris to Asia Minor and Egypt. The Assyrian kings literally tormented the world. They flung away the bodies of soldiers like so much clay; they made pyramids of human heads; they sacrificed holocausts of the sons and daughters of their enemies; they burned cities; they filled populous lands with death and devastation; they reddened broad deserts with carnage of warriors; they scattered whole countries with the corpses of their defenders as with chaff; they impaled "heaps of men" on stakes, and strewed the mountains and choked the rivers with dead bones; they cut off the hands of kings, and nailed them on the walls, and left their bodies to rot with bears and dogs on the entrance gates of cities; they cut down warriors like weeds, or smote them like wild beasts in the forests, and covered pillars with the flayed skins of rival monarchs (Farrar); and these things they did without sentiment or compunction.[22]

More! They gloried in their atrocities and boasted of them in their monuments.

Or take the case of Shaka, the Zulu Napoleon who rose to power from next to nothing and whose shadow lay dark and grim upon that part of Africa for years after his death. He was a military genius and his Zulu warriors went forth to battle, to conquer or to die. Tribe after tribe was either exterminated or absorbed into the Zulu nation. When he fell beneath the aegis of his brothers, all southeastern Africa was at his feet, and in his march to power, he had slaughtered more than a million people.

Shaka ruled with hideous cruelty. It was the rule of Shaka's life to have no children though he had many wives. Every child born to him was instantly put to death. He murdered his mother, Unandi, because he thought she had conspired with one of his wives to preserve him a son, alive. He would have no son lest that son grow up to murder him.

During the early part of his reign of terror the whole country cowered before the witch doctors. No man might sleep safe. No one knew when the wand of an Isanusi would fall upon him, and he be led away to his death. Shaka connived at this so long as the witch doctors hunted down people he wanted out of the way. However, when they were no longer useful to him, he massacred them.

After the murder of his mother, Shaka's moods became even more terrible, oppressive, and vindictive. He slept little and what sleep he had was haunted by dreams, and all Shaka's dreams led to the same end—death for those it pleased his fancy to kill. Nor did his murder ease the lot of his subjects. His brother, Dingaan, oppressed them just as Shaka had oppressed them. But at least Shaka had made the Zulu people great. Dingaan had all of Shaka's cruelty without Shaka's genius.

"What mind," asks Sir Robert Anderson, "is competent to grasp the sum of all this world's misery, heaped up day after day, year after year, century after century?" He gives just one example culled from the *Contemporary Review* (Jan. 1896), describing the Turkish massacre of Armenians in 1895:

> Over sixty thousand Armenians have been butchered. In Trebizond, Erzeroum, Erzinghian, Hassankaleh, and numberless other places the Christians were crushed like grapes during the vintage. The frantic mob, seething and surging in the streets of the cities, swept down upon the defenseless Armenians, plundered their shops, gutted their houses, then joked and jested with the terrified victims, as cats play with mice. The rivulets were choked up with corpses; the streams ran red with human blood; the forest glades and rocky caves were peopled with the dead and dying; among the black ruins of once prosperous villages lay roasted infants by their mangled mothers' corpses; pits were dug at night by the wretches destined to fill them, many of whom, flung in when but lightly wounded, awoke underneath a mountain of clammy corpses, and vainly wrestled with death and with the dead, who shut them out from light and life forever.
>
> A man in Erzeroum, hearing a tumult, and fearing for his children,

who were playing in the street, went out to seek and save them. He was borne down upon by the mob. He pleaded for his life, protesting that he had always lived in peace with his Muslim neighbors, and sincerely loved them. The statement may have represented a fact, or it may have been but a plea for pity. The ringleader, however, told that that was the proper spirit, and would be rewarded. The man was then stripped, and a chunk of his flesh cut out of his body, and jestingly offered for sale: "Good fresh meat, and dirt cheap," exclaimed some of the crowd. "Who'll buy fine dog's meat?" echoed the amused bystanders. The writing wretch uttered piercing screams as some of the mob, and who had just come from rifling the shops, opened a bottle and poured vinegar or some acid into the gaping wound. He called on God and man to end his agonies, but they had only begun. Soon afterwards two little boys came up, the elder crying, "Hairik, Hairik (Father, father), save me! See what they've done to me!" and pointed to his head, from which the blood was streaming over his handsome face, and down his neck. The younger brother—a child of about three—was playing with a wooden toy. The agonizing man was silent for a second and, glancing at these his children, made a frantic but vain effort to snatch a dagger from a Turk by his side. This was the signal for the renewal of his torments. The bleeding boy was finally dashed with violence against the dying father, who began to lose strength and consciousness, and the two were then pounded to death where they lay. The younger child sat near, dabbling his wooden toy in the blood of his father and brother, and looking up, now through smiles at the prettily dressed Kurds and now through tears at the dust-begrimed thing that had lately been his father. A slash of a sabre wound up his short experience of God's world, and the crowd turned its attention to others. These are but isolated scenes revealed for a brief second by the light, as it were, of a momentary lightning-flash. The worst cannot be described.

Time would fail to tell of the oppressive regimes of our own days, of the millions upon millions slaughtered by Communist regimes to further their wicked agenda, or of the millions slaughtered by the Nazis to rid Europe of Jews, Gypsies, Slavs, and other detested groups.

"And on the side of their oppressors there was power," Solomon mused, "but they had no comforter."

b) A Gloomy Conclusion (4:2–3)
(1) Praising Those the Tomb Has Received (4:2)

Solomon eulogizes those the tomb has received. *"Wherefore I praised the dead which are already dead more than the living which are yet alive"* (4:2). One is better off dead, he decides. He cannot see that life is worth a candle if it has to be lived out under conditions of oppression. He conveniently ignores the fact that he himself was an oppressor. The vast building projects he carried out all over Jerusalem were largely carried out by forced labor. Upon his death, the tribes promptly demanded of his son and heir a prompt redress of their grievances—onerous taxation and virtual slavery (1 Kings 12:3–4).

(2) Praising Those the Womb Has Refused (4:3)

He eulogizes also those the womb has refused: *"Yea, better is he than both they, which hath not yet been, who hath not seen the evil work that is done under the sun"* (4:3). It is best not to be born at all, he decides, than to be born into a land where oppression sits enthroned.

Again, he seems to have forgotten that "the powers that be are ordained of God," as a later saint would put it (Romans 13:1). And, over it all, God reigns supreme. He had forgotten, too, the history of his own people. When God promised to give to Abraham a promised land, ultimately to stretch from the Nile to the Euphrates, built in was not only a long, four-century delay, but a period of oppression as well (Genesis 15). It was not that God was indifferent to their sufferings. But He had other purposes in hand. "The iniquity of the Amorites" was not yet full. Nor would the oppressor escape his punishment when the time was ripe. Moreover, the intervening period was used to multiply the Hebrews from a family to a populous nation. And when the judgment did fall on Egypt and the oppressing Pharaoh, it was thorough, deserved, and widely publicized. Indeed, it struck terror in the hearts of the Canaanite kings, who usurped the land deeded by God to Abraham, and facilitated the conquest of Canaan (Joshua 2:9–11).

Solomon would have been better off studying his Scripture and drawing scriptural maxims from the fact of oppression instead of echoing the gloomy conclusions of materialistic philosophers. It would have helped Solomon, too, if, instead of embracing such a myopic and pessimistic view of the sad fact of oppression in the world, he had studied the cycles of oppression recorded in the book of Judges. They were always connected with God's discipline of His people.

In understanding those times, it would have lifted his thoughts above the sun and helped him understand God's ways "under the sun."

> 5. The Problem of Prosperity Without Posterity (4:4–12)
>   a) The Resentful Man (4:4–5)
>   (1) The Lusting Fool (4:4)

Two fools loom up, new, before the wise man's eyes. First, there was the lusting fool, the man who covets his neighbor's lot in life: *"Again, I considered all travail, and every right work, that for this a man is envied of his neighbour"* (4:4a). The expression "every right work" can be rendered "all dexterity in work." The word "this" is emphatic. Solomon has in view the man who rolls up his shirtsleeves and goes about his business. He makes full use of his skills and opportunities. He gets ahead. And for this he is envied by his lazy, careless, and slipshod neighbor. *"This is also vanity and vexation of spirit"* (4:4b), Solomon adds.

> (2) The Lazy Fool (4:5)

Solomon reinforces this statement by drawing further attention to the lusting fool. He is also a lazy fool: *"The fool foldeth his hands together, and eateth his own flesh"* (4:5). The word for "fool" here literally means "fat" or "dense," even "stupid," his folly showing itself, finally, in impiety. Solomon uses the word forty-nine times in Proverbs.

In her classic novel *The Good Earth*, author Pearl Buck traces the fortunes of a Chinese peasant named Wang Lung. Lung owned a piece of land which he cultivated with loving, hardworking devotion. It supported him and his family well. He not only provided a comfortable living for his family, but was also able to save the occasional piece of silver as well.

But Wang Lung had an uncle, the younger brother of Lung's father. He was a lazy, good-for-nothing, leech of a man. He scratched at his land, barely eking out enough to feed himself, his wife, and his seven children. His wife, too, was lazy, too idle to sweep the floor of their hovel.

Lung's uncle envied his hardworking nephew's successes. He blamed his own poverty on his bad luck. Other people's fields were fruitful, his yielded weeds. Other people's houses were stoutly built, his trembled on its foundation. Other men were blessed with sons, he was cursed with daughters.

But Wang Lung's uncle had a card up his sleeve. Since he was Lung's uncle, by all the sacred ties of relationship, he could demand his share of his nephew's prosperity. Custom decreed he could put his hand in Lung's pocket and take his share of the wealth. "You are rich! You are rich!" he screamed at Wang Lung. "If you don't support me, you will dishonor your father, my elder brother. I will tell everyone of your shame." Lung protested in vain, "I am not rich! I work! My wife works! My children work! You are lazy. You waste your money gambling and gossiping."[23]

And so it went on. Solomon had seen it all before. On the one hand, hardworking and successful people. On the other hand, indolent wasters, too lazy to work, content to allow their affairs to fall into ruin all about them and consumed with envy at their neighbors' prosperity and eager to get what they consider to be their share of it.

The Mosaic law made provision for the poor and the unfortunate. It was a welfare system based on hard work (Exodus 23:11; Leviticus 19:9–10; 23:22). As for the lazy, the biblical principle is that "if any would not work, neither should he eat" (2 Thessalonians 3:10). It is unlikely, deep thinker that he was, that Solomon thought his way through to the modern welfare state where the government picks the pockets of the successful to redistribute the proceeds to the poor and indolent alike. Even if he did, it is not likely he would have approved of it.

b) The Realistic Man (4:6)

"Better is an handful with quietness, than both the hands full with travail and vexation of spirit" (4:6). Better to be content with one handful, with the power to enjoy it, than to seize two handfuls at the cost of toil and futile effort. The realistic man comes to grips with life as it is. Better half a loaf than no loaf at all. Better to settle for less and be content with what one has than to get in over one's head and have to contend with constant worry and woe. Making money is not all there is to life.

We have the Lord's famous parable to cast light on that. It is introduced by a passing incident. A man in the crowd called aloud the Lord, asking Him to speak to his brother that he would divide an inheritance with him. The Lord refused to get involved in any such matter. The law of Moses was already in place to take care of such worldly issues (Deuteronomy 21:15–17). Instead, Jesus told a story. "Take heed," He said, by way of introduction, "and beware of covetousness: for a man's life consisteth not in the abundance of the things which he possesseth" (Luke 12:15).

Then came the parable of the rich fool, the man who vowed to build bigger and better barns and to have more and more fun, only to wake up in the darkness to a sudden realization that his days on earth were done. "Thou fool, this night," rang the voice of God, "thy soul shall be required of thee: then whose shall those things be, which thou hast provided?" (Luke 12:20).

This man was not content with his handful. He wanted both hands full, and his belly, and his barns too. Much joy it brought him when it was all his. It was all purchased at the price of his soul.

Solomon would have appreciated the story—unless, indeed, with the parable recounted to him, had come the Lord's words: "Thou art the man!" For Solomon himself liked to have both hands full. The Lord's parable is a classic for all time of the folly of living for the wrong world, something of which Solomon himself, for all his philosophizing, was verily guilty.

> c) The Ridiculous Man (4:7–12)
>   (1) The Situation (4:7–8)
>   (a) No Son (4:7–8a)

The first thing Solomon tells us about the third man in this series is that he had no son: *"Then I returned, and I saw vanity under the sun. There is one alone, and there is not a second; yea, he hath neither child nor brother"* (4:7–8a). The thing which struck Solomon was the utter loneliness of this man. He was wholly without next of kin. His estate would pass into the hands of others. We know how bitterly Abraham felt when he himself was childless. God had already promised him a son and heir, but time passed, and no son had been born. Then, after the thrilling rescue of Lot, his nephew, from capture by the kings of the east, Abraham's depression deepened for a short while. His tents and encampment had rung with the voices of Lot's children. But now they were all gone, back to Sodom, and Abraham's heart was heavy. Then God appeared. He said, "Fear not, Abram. I am thy shield and thy exceeding great reward."

>   (b) No Satisfaction (4:8b)

Somehow that did not cheer up the grieving patriarch. "Lord God," he said, "what wilt thou give me, seeing I go childless, and the steward of my house is this Eliezer of Damascus?" (Genesis 15:2).

The man Solomon saw was in the same sad state. But, then, Solomon tells us something else about him. He had no satisfaction: *"Yet is there no end of all his labour; neither is his eye satisfied with riches"* (4:8b). He was wedded to his work. It was all he had. It never occurred to him to go out and make friends of the poor and needy, to seek out widows and orphans and enlarge his heart with kindness and compassion, or to lay up treasure in heaven by helping impoverished believers. No! He narrowed his interests and isolated himself more and more by throwing himself more and more into his work.

A vicious old man had a son, Edward Cossey, but he watched him like a hawk, ready to cut him out of his will at an instant, should he show any sign of not following zealously in his father's footsteps. Cossey & Son was the name of the firm, a London banking concern. William Quest was the company lawyer and man of business in the country branch. Squire De la Molle was the country gentleman whose ancient estate was mortgaged up to the hilt to the avaricious old banker.

The old man Cossey had just suffered a stroke. Nevertheless, when Quest called on him in his palatial home, he was sitting up in bed while his oldest daughter read to him from the financial page of the newspapers. The consuming passion was strong in him in spite of the shadow of death which was on him.

The novelist Sir Henry Rider Haggard records the conversation that followed:

"How do you do, Mr. Quest!" he said; "sorry that I can't shake hands with you, but you see I have been stricken down, though my brain is clear enough, clearer than ever it was, I think. And I ain't going to die yet—don't think that I am, because I ain't. I may live two years more— the doctor says that I am sure to live one at least.

"A lot of money can be made in a year if you keep your eyes open. Once I made a hundred and twenty thousand for Cossey & Son in one year; and I may do it again before I die. I may make a lot of money, ah, a lot of money!" and his voice went off into a kind of thin scream that was not pleasant to listen to.

"I am sure I hope you will, sir," said Mr. Quest, politely.

"Thank you; take that for good luck, you know. Well, well, Mr. Quest, things haven't done so bad down in your part of the world; not at all bad considering the times. I thought we should have had to sell that old De la Molle up, but I hear that he is going to pay us off. Can't imagine who has been fool enough to lend him the money. A client of yours, eh? Well, he'll lose it, I expect, and serve him right for his pains.

But I am not sorry, for it is unpleasant for a house like ours to have to sell an old client up. Not that his account is worth much, nothing at all—more trouble than profit—or we should not have done it. He's no better than a bankrupt, and the insolvency court is the best place for him. The world is to the rich and the fullness thereof. There's an insolvency court specially provided for De la Molle and his like—empty old windbags with long-sounding names; let him go there and make room for the men who have made money—hee! hee! hee!" And once more his voice went off into a sort of scream.

Here Mr. Quest, who had had about enough of this sort of thing, changed the conversation by commencing to comment on various business transactions which he had been conducting on behalf of the house. The old man listened with the greatest interest, his keen black eyes attentively fixed upon the speaker's face. . . .

"Now good-by, Mr. Quest; they'll give you a bit of dinner downstairs," he said at length. "I'm getting tired, and I want to hear the rest of that money article. You've done very well for Cossey & Son, and Cossey & Son will do well for you, for we always pay by results; that's the way to get good work and make a lot of money. Mind, Edward, if ever you get a chance don't forget to pay that blackguard Quaritch out pound for pound, and twice as much again for compound interest—hee! hee! hee!"

"The old gentleman keeps his head for business pretty well," said Mr. Quest to Edward Cossey as soon as they were well outside the door.

"Keeps his head?" answered Edward; "I should just think he did. He's a regular shark now, that's what he is. I really believe that if he knew I had found that thirty thousand for old De la Molle he would cut me off with a shilling." Here Mr. Quest pricked up his ears. "And he's close, too," he went on, "so close that it is almost impossible to get anything out of him. I am not particular, but upon my word I think that it is rather disgusting to see an old man with one foot in the grave hanging on to his moneybags as though he expected to float to heaven on them."[24]

(c) No Sense (4:8c)

The man Solomon had in mind not only had no son and no satisfaction, he also had no sense: *"Neither saith he, For whom do I labour, and bereave my soul of good? This is also vanity, yea, it is a sore travail"* (4:8c). It was all toil and labor to no end. What was the point of it, except as a means of passing the time, and of exerting power and influence, and of securing ease and things and creature comforts. But a man can wear only one suit of clothes at a time and live in one house at a time.

Jeffery Farnol catches the tragedy of such an aimless life in one of his books. His character Geoffrey Ravenslee was a multimillionaire. He was thirty-five years of age. He had been everywhere and done everything and was bored with life to the point of contemplating suicide. His butler tried to distract him from such gloomy thoughts, but with little success because all he had to offer was more of the same kind of thing. Ravenslee, the young millionaire, began the conversation:

"Now, Brimberly, as a hard-headed, matter-of-fact, common-sense being, what would you suggest for a poor fellow who is sick and tired of everything and most of all—of himself?"

"Why, sir, I should prescribe for that man change of air, sir—travel, sir. There's your yacht a-laying in the river, sir—"

His master leant his square chin and still frowning at the fire, gently shook his head.

"My good Brimberly," he sighed, "haven't I travelled in most parts of the world?"

"Why, yes, sir, you've travelled, sir, very much so indeed, sir."

"Next, sir—in Italy, we find your ancient Roman villa, sir—alabaster pillows and columns, sir—very historical though a trifle wore with wars and centuries of centurions, sir, wherefore I would humbly suggest a coat or two of paint, sir, applied beneath your very own eye, sir—"

"No, Brimberly," murmured young R., "paint might have attractions—Italy none!"

"Certingly not, sir, cer-tingly not! Which brings us to your schools in Germany, sir—"

"Nor Germany! Lord, Brimberly, are there many more?"

"Ho, yes, sir, plenty!" nodded Mr. Brimberly, "your late honored and respected father, sir, were a rare at buying palaces, sir; 'em collected 'em, as you might say, like some folks collects postage stamps, sir!"

"And a collection of the one is about as useless as a collection of the other, Brimberly!"

"Why, true, sir, one man can't live in a dozen places all at once, but why not work round 'em in turn, beginning, say, at your imposing Venetian palazzo—canals, sir, gondoliers—picturesque though dampish? Or your shally in the Tyro-leen Halps, sir, or—"

"Brimberly, have the goodness to—er—shut up!"

"Certingly, sir."

Later in the conversation when Ravenslee complained that he had never accomplished anything worthwhile in life Mr. Brimberly expressed his surprise:

"But, sir," he said, "you are one as don't have to do nothing—you're rich."

Ravenslee replied: "Rich? I'm so rich that my friends are all acquaintances—so rich that I might buy anything in the world except what I most desire—so rich that I am tired of life, the world, and everything in the world, and have been seriously considering a—er—a radical change. It is a comfort to know that we may all of us find oblivion when we so desire."

In the end, Ravenslee challenged his butler to come up with some worthwhile goal, to suggest something worth living for. The butler asked for some hints. Should the object be animal, mineral, or neuter? The youthful millionaire opted for "animal."

"As to gender, sir?" Mr. Brimberly inquired.

"Feminine," decided Ravenslee, "and singular number," he added.

The butler retired, and the stage was set for the story—feminine gender, singular number, objective case, governed by the verb "to love."[25]

The man Solomon had in mind had no goals at all, at least no goals of any value. He was interested in making money just for the sake of making money. He was all alone in this world. He had no family, no friends, no next of kin. He had no one with whom he could share his wealth. Yet on and on he went, on the great treadmill of his ceaseless activity, getting more and more of the world's goods and piling up wealth he did not need to leave to those he did not even know. He needed "a definite object" animal, singular number or plural, male or female, someone to give focus and purpose to his ceaseless round of activity. Beyond that, he needed God. But he recognized no such need. For all his business acumen, he was silly. Jesus called a similar successful materialist in his day a fool. The word he used was *aphron*, literally, a "senseless one."

(2) The Suggestion (4:9–12)

Having a partner is good by way of:

(a) Production (4:9)

The man needed a partner, he needed another person in his life. Solomon backs the suggestion with four considerations which ought to appeal to even this trapped and senseless individual. Having a partner would be good for production: *"Two are better than one; because they have a good reward for their labour"* (4:9).

The fellow who "goes it alone" misses a great deal in life. Man was created by God for fellowship. After the creation of Adam, God gave him a space in the Garden to come to the realization that there was a lack in his life. He needed a "helpmeet." Then God met that need, saying, "It is not good that the man should be alone" (Genesis 2:18). The ideal life was one with an ideal wife.

The businessman who caught Solomon's eye had no wife or family or friends. Putting things on the lowest level, Solomon advised him to get a partner. A partner helps share burdens and responsibilities. He halves the load and doubles the output. The loner is cast back always on his own resources.

Ebenezer Scrooge was a loner. He once had a partner, but he was long since dead. Later on, in one of the best-known hauntings in literature, Jacob Marley appeared in Scrooge's miserly apartment and gave the miserable old man the best advice he ever had. It was the beginning of Scrooge's redemption.

One important station along the way was when the ghost of Christmas Past made Scrooge relive the scene in his former life when he lost the young woman he had once wanted for his wife. "She left him, and they parted," says Dickens. This time there was no rebellious "humbug" from the old miser. "No more!" he cried. "No more! I don't wish to see it. Show me no more." But he did. The ghost gave Scrooge a glimpse of a happy home, filled with children and laughter. He saw the same young woman, older now and happy. Her husband came in. ". . . I saw an old friend of yours this afternoon. . . . Mr. Scrooge, it was. I passed his office window. . . . His partner lies upon the point of death, I hear; and there he sat alone. Quite alone in the world, I do believe." The scene broke the miser. It brought home to him how bitter his life had become, how empty, how lonely.

Indeed, Dickens is our best commentary on the man Solomon had in mind. "A tight-fisted hand at the grindstone, Scrooge! A squeezing, wrenching, grasping, scraping, clutching, covetous old sinner." Cruel as the grave to Bob Cratchit, his clerk! Colder than the winter's frost on his nephew. Hard as steel to those who tried to solicit a donation to charity. Hard as nails to those he did business with.[26]

Solomon hoped an acquaintance would do better than that. "Get a partner," he advised. "Two is better than one." Even when it comes down to just making money.

(b) Precaution (4:10)

Moreover, having a partner would be good for precaution: *"For if they fall, the one will lift up his fellow: but woe to him that is alone when he falleth; for he hath not another to help him up"* (4:10). It is this principle which underlies all mountaineering, especially on the world's highest peaks. Before Sir Edmund Hilary and his companion, the Sherpa Tenzing, finally stood on the summit of Mount Everest, 29,029 feet above sea level, Annapurna was the highest peak attained (26,545 feet). Maurice Herzog, a French mountaineer, led the assault and tells the tale.

He tells not only of the difficulties of the ascent but also the trials and testings of the descent. In particular, he records the frightening ordeal of an avalanche. He himself was the victim. Head over heels he went. His head hit the ice. A violent blow to his left thigh stabbed him with pain. Round and round he went, at the end of his rope, his one hope of getting out alive. The rope joined him to two Sherpas, Sarki and Aila. The snow crushed him. He fainted and came to to discover his desperate situation. He was hanging downward "in a sort of hatchway of blue ice," the rope around his neck and left leg. He blessed the rope, however. It was his one hope of life.[27]

Truly it was a case of two being better than one—three, indeed, in this case, being better than two. Woe would it have been to him when he fell had he been alone with not another to help him. The loner in life may enjoy his self-reliance so long as all goes well but there are those tides in the affairs of men which ought not to be ignored. John Donne said it well, "No man is an island." We need each other.

(c) Preservation (4:11)

Then too, a partner is good by way of preservation. *"Again, if two lie together, then they have heat: but how can one be warm alone?"* (4:11). We smile at such a truism, perhaps, in our comfortable, centrally heated and air-conditioned homes, surrounded as we are by every creature comfort. But life is not always lived in such luxury.

At the age of eighteen I was drafted into the British Army. I entered a strange new world. My pleasant job with a large British bank was changed for a parade ground. My supervisor at the bank, a gentlemanly, helpful individual, was changed for a blustering drill sergeant. My family home gave way to a barracks room. My well-fitting business suit was surrendered for an ill-fitting uniform. My circle of old familiar friends was replaced by a battalion of raw recruits, drawn from all walks of life, some as green as I, some very worldly-wise indeed.

Before long, we sorted ourselves out. I made friends with the two fellows next to me in the barracks hut. We helped each other, sharing strengths and weaknesses and doing things together. This new comradeship helped us over many a hurdle on our way from being new recruits to becoming soldiers.

Solomon's observation, here, reminded me of an incident in those far-off boot camp days. We were on a route march, a particularly arduous and long one, designed to test our newfound toughness. We were to camp overnight in the wilds. If nothing else, that campout taught us how good it was to have friends.

Night was approaching when we were commanded to halt and make camp. It was already getting dark. It was drizzling rain with the promise of a downpour before morning. It was cold. We were miles from any town or village. No one gave us any advice. We were on our own.

When we were inducted into the army, we were issued our gear. It included a ground sheet to keep us from the damp ground when lying down, and a shapeless, billowy, camouflaged coverall, to put over our packs and uniforms when marching in the rain. Little did we know how useful these things would turn out to be!

We three pooled our resources. We used our rifles and bayonets as tent posts. We arranged our waterproof coveralls to make a small shelter from the rain. We put our ground sheets side by side on the ground. We hauled out our topcoats and made a communal bed. Then, carefully, we crawled gratefully into our makeshift tent, fully dressed, and huddled together for warmth.

"If two lie together," said Solomon, "then they have heat; but how can one be warm alone?" Ask these fellows on that route march who had no close friends! Those who had tried to "go it alone" were a bedraggled and haggard sight when the bugle next morning summoned us from our beds.

(d) Protection (4:12)

Moreover, a partner is good by way of protection: *"And if one prevail against him, two shall withstand him; and a threefold cord is not quickly broken"* (4:12).

Numbers are used with remarkable precision in the Bible. The number one denotes unity. The first time a subject is introduced in Scripture is always of special significance. It invariably denotes the place that item has in the mind and heart of God. Similarly, words that occur only once are emphatic and important in the original texts. The number is associated with the unity of the Godhead, as we see from Genesis 1. "In the beginning God" (*Elohim*, plural) "created" (singular) "the heaven and the earth" (Genesis 1:1). The unity of the Godhead is emphasized in the Hebrew text. There is an accent used to emphasize and give pause on the word "God." This is the first occurrence of this important name for God.

By contrast, the number two denotes difference—not necessarily bad. The first vessel made by the potter was "marred," the second was perfect to the mind of the maker (Jeremiah 18:1–4). The second person of the Godhead partook of two natures—perfect Deity and perfect humanity. The believer has two natures, one good and one bad, the first taking precedence over the second. Ishmael came first by grace, but Isaac, who came second, took precedence. The same is true of Adam and Christ, Esau and Jacob.

The number three signifies that which is solid and substantial and complete. It takes three straight lines to complete a geometric figure, and thus create a solid. The universe is twined together in character, consisting of matter, space, and time. Space is expressed in three dimensions—latitude, longitude, altitude; time is divided into past, present, and future; matter is expressed in terms of energy, motion, and phenomena. There are three kingdoms—animal, vegetable, and mineral. Man consists of body, soul, and spirit.

The number three is associated with the Deity—in the number one we see the sovereignty of the one God; in the number two, the second person is revealed; and in the number three the Holy Spirit comes into view. Thus, the Godhead is a mystical three in one, harmonious and complete in all their fullness. Incidentally, the word "fullness" is itself remarkable in that it occurs only three times in the Bible (Ephesians 3:19; 4:13; Colossians 2:9).[28]

Truly, "a threefold cord is not quickly broken." The words express, as Solomon no doubt knew, the underlying essential of Hebrew jurisprudence as expressed in the Mosaic law. There had to be two or three agreeing witnesses before judgment could be made (Deuteronomy 17:6; 19:15; 2 Corinthians 13:1).

6. The Problem of Sovereignty Without Sagacity (4:13–16)

The foolish king is:

a) Unsound in His Thoughts (4:13)

"Better is a poor and a wise child than an old and foolish king, who will no more be admonished" (4:13).

The old, foolish king was Solomon himself, though, truly, the pages of history are filled with examples. Solomon had been told by God Himself that his son and heir would lose ten of the twelve tribes to Jeroboam, one of Solomon's own officers. Instead of bowing to the divine sentence passed upon him for his own wickedness and backsliding, he tried to murder Jeroboam. The astute young man fled to Egypt where he was able to enlist the interest of the reigning Pharaoh in Hebrew affairs. Later on, the Egyptians sent an army to do battle with the kingdom of Judah over which Rehoboam, Solomon's heir, ruled with such ignominy.

The "poor and wise" child was Jesus, rightful heir to the throne of David. The only glimpse we have of Him between His birth and His baptism shows Him to full advantage, filling the learned doctors of the law with amazement not only at the questions He answered, but, equally, at the questions He asked (Luke 2:46–47).

A similar comparison could be made to an earlier time in Solomon's life and to recent history of which he had full cognizance. There was King Saul, already so deeply compromised by disobedience as to have been disinherited from the kingdom by God. And there was young David, the giant killer, so rich in wisdom that Saul was not only deathly afraid of this teenage lad, but the Holy Spirit, who, in the space of a few short verses, names and bears testimony to David's wisdom (1 Samuel 18:5, 14, 15, 30). Moreover, King Saul became increasingly obsessed with jealous rage that David was God's own choice to be Israel's next king, that his whole life degenerated into one continuous crusade to catch and kill God's true anointed. Truly, a foolish king is unsound in his thoughts.

b) Unsuited to His Throne (4:14)

"For out of prison he cometh to reign; whereas also he that is born in his kingdom becometh poor" (4:14). The "he" here evidently refers to that poor, wise child of the previous verse. He leaped from obscurity to power. He replaced, perhaps by a palace coup or maybe by virtue of overriding circumstances, the decrepit and degenerate king, who, though born to the throne, was now covered with disgrace.

The obvious Bible parallel is Joseph who, in one bound, was taken from Pharaoh's prison to be seated as grand vizier of Egypt, in the highest office in the land.

Another view of this verse is that the "he" refers to the king. In that case the reference is to the king's personal history. He was a nobody to start with and, in his old age, he fulfilled the promise of his ignoble birth.

Such a man was Felix, who began life as a slave. For some unknown reason, he was manipulated by the Emperor Claudius who advanced him and made him procurator of Judea in A.D. 53. Tacitus said he was cruel, lustful, and exercised power with the disposition of a slave. He says, further, that Felix considered himself authorized to commit any crime, relying on his influence in Rome. He encouraged the Sicarii (a band of assassins) in their lawless activities. He entered into an adulterous relationship with Drusilla, a daughter of King Herod Agrippa. He trembled before the preaching of Paul but kept on deferring the just release of his prisoner because he wanted to squeeze a bribe out of the Apostle. In the meantime, his rule in Judea got increasingly out of hand until, at length, the corrupt governor was summoned to Rome. The Jews, still a power to be reckoned with, followed him to the capital. The only thing that saved his neck was the fact that his brother was Pallas, the infamous favorite of Claudius.

     c) Unsung by the Throng (4:15–16)
        (1) The Nameless Monarch (4:15)

"I considered all the living which walk under the sun, with the second child that shall stand up in his stead" (4:15). Solomon still appears to be considering the uncertain fortunes of the throne. Normally the heir to the throne is the reigning king's firstborn son. It is not at all uncommon, however, that the kingdom falls into the hands of a secondary son, one more fitting to fill the throne than the constitutional heir. Solomon must have wished for any other son than the one he had, the one who would take his throne, the one he knew was unfit to reign. But he did not have another son.

        (2) The Nebulous Multitude (4:16a)

"There is no end of all the people, even of all that have been before them: they also that come after shall not rejoice in him" (4:16a).
    The king, swept away from the seat and center of power, despite all his advantages and breeding, proved himself to be of very common clay indeed. He failed to rise above the common herd. Looking back to the distant ages of the past, the observer cannot see anything of distinctive, distinguishing value about this unworthy king. Instead of towering above his fellows, like some spreading tree in the midst of a prairie of tossing grain, he simply merged into the landscape. Indeed, any initial promise of greatness, which might once have been hopefully attributed to him, soon proved to be illusionary after all.

Thus, it was with the son of Kish. Solomon would be fully alive to his story. When Israel demanded that they be given a king, so that they could be like the nations all about them, God gave them Saul. He stood head and shoulders above all the people, the sacred historian notes (1 Samuel 9:2). The people, choosing by outward appearance, hailed him with joy. Saul soon revealed himself to be big of body and small of soul, and he had to be deposed by God (1 Samuel 16) even though he continued to disgrace the throne for several decades.

Samuel almost made the same mistake as the common people when sent by God to find a replacement for Saul among the sons of Jesse. Jesse was rich in tall, handsome, impressive-looking sons. Samuel was about to anoint the magnificently endowed Eliab when God stopped him: "Look not on his countenance, or on the height of his stature; because I have refused him: for the LORD seeth not as man seeth; for man looketh on the outward appearance; but the LORD looketh on the heart" (1 Samuel 16:7). Eliab, and his equally attractive brothers, Abinadab and Shammah, were of no more use in the valley of Elah when Goliath showed up than was King Saul (1 Samuel 17:13–29). What a different story it was with David, a man Saul first despised (1 Samuel 17:33) and then feared because of his wisdom and evident fitness to rule (1 Samuel 18:15).

Many a time history tells of those born to high office who soon proved themselves to be nobodies after all. By the time of Solomon, just two generations later, Saul was but a dismal memory, remembered only because his story had been woven into the tapestry of Holy Writ because of the many negative lessons it could still teach. Perhaps Solomon was afraid that his memory might be equally tarnished. His concluding lament suggests it.

(3) The Nagging Misery (4:16b)

"Surely this also is vanity and vexation of spirit" (4:16b). It was just another example, this chasing after greatness by those unequipped for greatness or balked of greatness by stronger circumstances, of chasing the wind. Solomon had secured for himself a place among the great ones of the world. Had he asked God to make him good, instead of asking God to make him wise, he might have been a truly great man. As it was, his greatness was tarnished and his wisdom all too often mixed with folly. There was a nagging misery which dogged his days now that he was old and unable to change things much. He knew, too late, that he himself had sovereignty without sagacity. It was a bitter pill to swallow. The doleful

note which predominates in Ecclesiastes, Solomon's last word to the world, well illustrates that.

    7. The Problem of Religion Without Reality (5:1–7)
        a) The Value of Silence (5:1–3)
            (1) Tread Softly in the House of God (5:1a)

"Keep thy foot when thou goest to the house of God" (5:1a). In other words, "Watch your step!" Or, "Don't enter God's house carelessly." Solomon had discovered that the secular side of life could not secure happiness. What about the spiritual side? At once he reminds us that, in this sphere, we are up against strict restraint, something people are all too inclined to forget. So, he begins with a warning. Reverence is essential in God's house, be it the Tabernacle and Temple of Old Testament worship, or the meeting place of believers in New Testament times. Our irreverent age needs to heed Solomon's cautionary words.

The first mention of the house of God is an oblique one. Abram had come at last to Bethel (the house of God) and it proved to be the high point, so far, in his pilgrimage. He stood there on that rising elevation, gazing up to heaven, with nothing between his soul and the Savior. There he "called upon the name of the Lord" (Genesis 12:8).

The question now arose as to what he would do with his feet. The question was quickly answered. Abram "journeyed, going on still toward the south" (Genesis 12:9). At once threatening circumstances began to cloud his way (Genesis 12:10). His move away from the house of God developed into outright backsliding as he gathered momentum and headed for Egypt, where he lost his testimony completely and fell into terrible disgrace. He was rescued by God before Sarah could be hopelessly compromised! He wasted no time in getting back to Bethel. There he renewed his commitment to God (Genesis 13:1–4).

It was the same with Jacob. His flight from the fury of Esau brought him to his first encampment away from home. There he had a vision of God, which made a lasting impression on him. He called the place "Beth-el" because it was, indeed, the house of God (Genesis 28:17, 19). But he did not "keep his feet." He moved away, far, far away. Years later on his way back to the Promised Land, he remembered Bethel and the deep impression the place had made upon him (Genesis 28:20–22). Now God specifically told Jacob, "Arise, go up to Beth-el, and dwell there" (Genesis 35:1). Jacob put his house in order (Genesis 35:2–6) and moved his family to the place where he had once met God. There he built an altar and there God again revealed Himself.

Alas! Jacob did not "keep his feet" when he came again to the house of God. No sooner had he acknowledged the significance of Bethel in his spiritual pilgrimage (Genesis 35:14–15) than, sad to say, he took his journey away from there (v. 16). It was a fatal move and one emphasized by the use of the polysyndeton "and . . . and . . . and" (nine times repeated) (vv. 16–20). As a direct result of this failure to "keep his feet," Rachel died.

Well should we watch our feet where the house of God is concerned. It is no coincidence that the Holy Spirit, having urged us not to forsake the Lord's house, the place where His people meet, follows up His admonition with one of the most terrible warnings in the Bible (Hebrew 10:25–39).

> (2) Talk Sparingly in the House of God (5:1b–3)
>   (a) The Careless Sacrifice of the Foolish Man (5:1b)

"And be more ready to hear, than to give the sacrifice of fools: for they consider not that they do evil" (5:1b).

We must beware of making rash promises to God when in His house. The Holy Spirit labels this as "evil." The Hebrew word is arresting. It is *ra'a'*. It is a very strong word. It comes from a root which suggests the breaking up of all that is good and desirable. It implies injury to others. The corresponding Greek word is *poneros* ("evil") or *kakos* ("bad"). It is especially used of moral depravity, corruption, and lewdness. "Good for nothing" is an appropriate English expression. The "sacrifice of fools," making commitments we do not mean or do not keep is indeed "good for nothing." Far better to stand still, and to say nothing than to promise sacrifices which come to nothing and which God views as "evil" in consequence.

> (b) The Common Sense of the Foresighted Man (5:2)
>   (i) The Nature of His Caution (5:2a)
>   (ii) The Need for His Caution (5:2b)

Caution! That's the word. Solomon underlines the nature of that caution. *"Be not rash with thy mouth, and let not thine heart be hasty to utter any thing before God"* (5:2a), and the need for that caution: *"for God is in heaven, and thou upon earth: therefore let thy words be few"* (5:2b). The book of Job supplies us with all kinds of illustrations. Job, for instance, spoke at much greater length than his companions. His last speech of self-justification (Job 29:1–31:40) reeked with self-righteousness. He used the personal pronouns, I, me, and my, sometimes. Elihu, the self-appointed mediator, went on and on through six chapters of opinionated monologue. Nobody bothered to answer him. As soon as the recital ended God answered Job, not Elihu, who was completely ignored (Job 38:1).

Now Job, technically, was not in the house of God but he was certainly in the presence of God. God, moreover, had been listening to all this lengthy argument and debate. "Who is this that darkeneth counsel by words without knowledge?" (Job 38:2), God demanded. Before long Job was on his face before God, overwhelmed with a sense of sin (Job 40:5), and confessing his self-abhorrence and repentance (Job 42:6). As for Job's three loquacious friends, God's answer was kindled against them for the folly of their accusations and arguments.

So, let us beware. The Lord Jesus Himself has warned us that we are going to be held accountable for "every idle word" on the day of judgment (Matthew 12:36–37).

Solomon had doubtlessly heard people taking God's name in vain, accusing Him of injustice and indifference, and using profane, abusive, and obscene language. People who spoke in this way had lost all sense of proportion. Solomon restored it. God is in heaven, he said. We are on earth, creatures of time and space confined to a remote planet in the sky. People should muzzle themselves rather than give utterance to "hard speeches" (Jude 15) against God.

(c) The Continuous Speech of the Foolish Man (5:3)
    (i) How He Dabbles (5:3a)
    (ii) How He Babbles (5:3b)

We know how the foolish man dabbles, *"For a dream cometh through the multitude of business"* (5:3a), and how he babbles, *"and a fool's voice is known by multitude of words"* (5:3b). A man dabbles all day in a multitude of business cares and worries and, as a result, cannot sleep at night or tosses and turns in his bed haunted by fevered dreams. A fool occupies himself all day with a multitude of words. He goes to bed at night and, like the fool he is, goes off to sleep careless that he has proved himself a fool by his babble. Solomon treats both men with cynical disdain. He puts them in bed together by tucking them into the same verse, the one to go on dabbling in his business in his dreams, the other to go on babbling, more likely than not about everyone else's business, in his sleep. Having recommended the value of silence, Solomon moves on, still in the same vein.

b) The Vow Once Spoken (5:4–7)
  (1) What Must Be Paid (5:4)
    (a) The Requirement (5:4a)
    (b) The Reason (5:4b)

"When thou vowest a vow unto God, defer not to pay it; for he hath no pleasure in fools: pay that which thou hast vowed" (5:4).

The classic New Testament example is found in the story of Ananias and Sapphira. They seem to have been moved by the example of Barnabas, a recently saved Cypriot Levite. He sold property he owned on the island and laid the proceeds at the Apostles' feet (Acts 4:36–37). The deed seems to have been a conspicuous one (perhaps because of the generosity of the gift), because Luke, years later, deemed it worthy of note. It certainly seems to have caught the attention of Ananias and Sapphira. They eyed with envy the attention bestowed on Barnabas though it seemed rather to embarrass the Godly Levite.

The upshot was that Ananias and Sapphira sold some of their property. They pledged the whole amount to the Lord's work, but gave a fraudulent price to the gift, pretending they were giving the whole amount whereas, by mutual agreement, they had skimmed off a percentage for themselves.

"When thou vowest a vow unto God, defer not to pay it." It was written large as life in their Hebrew Old Testament. "God hath no pleasure in fools." And what fools! To imagine for one moment they could fool God! "Pay that which thou hast vowed"—every last penny of it. The Holy Spirit smote twice. Before the day was out the pair of them were in their graves. The omniscient Spirit of God has been the silent listener to their whispered agreement in their bedroom. He had been present when the bill of sale was signed in the marketplace, there when the proceeds were put in the bank, there when they wrote the check, there when they handed the money to the Apostles with the plain intent to deceive and defraud, there when first Ananias and then Sapphira lied to the Church and thus lied to Him, the Holy Spirit of God. Thus, He set up this conniving couple as an example for all time of not living up to commitments made to God.

(2) What Might Be Preferred (5:5)

"Better is it that thou shouldest not vow, than that thou shouldest vow and not pay" (5:5). It would certainly have been better for Jephthah never to have vowed than to vow as he did and have to pay the price that he did. It would most certainly

have been better for his daughter. It was a rash vow and when delivered for payment, called for a price above and beyond anything he had intended to pay.

The nation of Israel was in a state of complete disarray. There was no king, no judge, no prophet, and no priests. Jephthah himself was the son of a harlot, ostracized by his father's regular sons. Cast out, he collected about himself an outlaw band of freebooters. The country, invaded by the Ammonites, turned to Jephthah. He agreed to go to war with Ammon and made clear his terms.

Then he made his vow. If God would deliver the Ammonites into his hands then "whatsoever cometh forth of the doors of my house to meet me, when I return in peace from the children of Ammon, surely shall be the Lord's, and I will offer it up for a burnt offering." Such was the vow (Judges 11:30–31). It was rash and foolish to make any such vow. Suppose it had been an unclean animal to God? As it turned out the price was immeasurable. It was his beloved daughter who met him. It would have been better if he had not vowed. His daughter had to pay a high price for her father's folly.

God does not need our vows or our sworn oaths. Jesus said, "Swear not at all" (Matthew 5:33–37). James says the same thing (James 5:12). Paul took a vow at Anchrea (the port city for Corinth), from where Paul would sail to the Holy Land, toward the end of his second missionary journey (Acts 18:18). We have no information as to the details. Later on, James involved Paul with some vows others had made. The outcome was disastrous (Acts 21:20–31).

Making vows, then, is a tricky business. They can take us much further than we intended to go, and cost more than we ever intended to pay. Solomon was right. His next words add weight to what he has already said.

> (3) What Must Be Perceived (5:6)
>   (a) The Kind of Vow Indicated (5:6a)
>   (b) The Kind of Vengeance Indicated (5:6b)

"Suffer not thy mouth to cause thy flesh to sin; neither say thou before the angel, that it was an error: wherefore should God be angry at thy voice, and destroy the work of thine hands?" (5:6).

The angel! Paul says something similar to the Corinthians when calling them to order as regards to God's will concerning headship in the local church. When commanding sisters in the fellowship to put a covering on their heads when taking a leading role—to advertise their subjection to the man—he says, "because of the angels" (1 Corinthians 11:10).

There are different orders of angelic beings, both in the ranks of the sinless sons of light who stand before God's throne and in the company of the fallen angels who serve Satan as lord. Solomon seems concerned here about God's angels.

There are the martial angels, led by Michael the Archangel who does battle with Satan's angelic princes who lord it over the nations of mankind. The special province is the nation of Israel, a nation marked out for God and surrounded by a sea of hostile Gentile nations. Michael is called their Prince (Daniel 10:20–21). There are also messenger angels, headed by Gabriel, angels which stand before God's throne, hang upon His words, and rush to do His bidding. We find them in both Testaments conveying messages to men—to Gideon, to Samson's parents, to Elijah and Daniel, to Zacharias the priest, to Mary, and to Joseph. They appeared on various occasions to the Apostle John. There are also the ministering angels. We see them active on behalf of children and churches. We see them on various occasions in connection with the ministries of Peter and of Paul. They minister to believers, as David well knew, and are keenly interested in the outworking of God's purposes in grace, in this age, desiring to look into them. Then too, there are the managing angels, the "watchers" who keep an eye on events passing on earth. One of them, for instance, smote Nebuchadnezzar when his pride overtook him. One of them, for instance, was commanded to set free four powerful and malignant angels of Satan presently incarcerated at the Euphrates River. They used their freedom to visit the earth with a devastating war. The subject is vast and of endless fascination.

Solomon warns his readers not to provoke "the angel." God is not amused when we break our solemn promises to Him. The angels would willingly visit instant judgment upon such fools, no doubt, but God often holds them back. At times, however, He responds, and answers fools according to their folly.

D. L. Moody told of a man he knew who made a vow to God. Moody had often tried to lead this man to Christ but always the man procrastinated. Then he was taken seriously ill. Moody went to see him in the hospital. "I'll tell you what, Mr. Moody," he said. "If I get better, I promise I'll get saved." It was a vow. Well, the man recovered, and the evangelist went to see him in his home. He again explained the Gospel and called on the man to redeem his vow and accept the Lord, but once again the man prevaricated. Moody left him, the man still promising to get saved "one of these days."

Not long afterwards Moody heard that the man was back in the hospital. He went to see him again to urge him one more time to pay heed to his soul. "It's too late, Mr. Moody," he said. "My heart is as cold as the grave." "I'll pray for you,"

Mr. Moody said. "It's no use," the man replied. The evangelist tried to pray. The prayers would not come. He tried again and then gave up. He knew his prayers did not so much as reach the ceiling. It was indeed too late. The man had gone back on his vow. He had provoked the angel. He had angered God with his voice. All that remained was destruction.

"He died," said Mr. Moody, "and we buried him in a Christless grave. How dark!" It is a serious thing when our vows, and our failure to redeem them, provoke God.

> (4) What Might Be Prevented (5:7)
>> (a) The Cause of Much Folly (5:7a–b)
>>> (i) Beware of Too Many Visions (5:7a)

"For in the multitude of dreams and many words . . ." (5:7a). The wise man warns against too many visions and too much verbosity. These things can become the cause of much folly. Too many visions are as treacherous as too many vows. Besides, visions can emanate from Satan as well as from God. The problem with Job's critical friend Eliphaz lay in his fascination with ghosts and visions and extrabiblical revelations. He certainly did not impress Job who was too wise to be taken in by this kind of thing, and he was certainly as unable to comfort, convince, or correct Job as any of the others.

> (ii) Beware of Too Much Verbosity (5:7b)

". . . there are also divers vanities . . ." (5:7b). Visions are at the core of divers varieties of many false cults. Joseph Smith was addicted to them, and his gullible followers accepted them without question. His alleged "first vision" saw him "seized upon by some power" which entirely overcame him. He saw a pillar of light exactly over his head which gradually descended upon him. The Mormons accept all this as Gospel truth. They have accepted "the totally unsupported testimony of a fifteen-year-old boy that nobody ever preached Jesus Christ's Gospel from the close of the apostolic age until the 'restoration' through Joseph Smith, Jr., beginning in 1820."[29]

Then came the alleged second vision at which time the angel Moroni is supposed to have given him a message concerning some golden plates—what was to become the *Book of Mormon*. The angel is said to have appeared to Joseph Smith at his home and told him to dig in a nearby hill. He would find a record relating to the Bible. The subsequent excavation unearthed some "Golden Plates." They were covered with writings in "reformed Egyptian hieroglyphics." Fortunately for the would-be prophet, the plates were accompanied by the Urim and Thummim, a couple of miraculous stones. When he looked at the writing through these stones, the "Egyptian hieroglyphics" were magically transformed into modern King James English.[30] Thus was born the Mormon heresy.

(b) The Cure of Much Folly (5:7c)

Solomon concludes all this discussion about voices and visions by stating the cure for much folly: *". . . but fear thou God"* (5:7c). While it is true that God has spoken "in divers manners" (Hebrews 1:1), it is His practice to write things down. The result is the Bible, "a more sure word of prophecy," so Peter thought, than even the things he experienced by voice and vision on "the holy mount" (2 Peter 1:18–19).

8. The Problem of Wealth Without Health (5:8–20)
a) Words About the Desire for Riches (5:8–11)
(1) Wealth Acquired (5:8–9)
(a) By Injustice (5:8)

Solomon was an old hand at collecting wealth. He spoke first of those who acquire wealth by injustice: *"If thou seest the oppression of the poor, and violent perverting of judgment and justice in a province, marvel not at the matter: for he that is higher than the highest regardeth; and there be higher than they"* (5:8). Oppression! Perversion! The one is a total disregard of justice, the other is a total distortion of justice. The one sets before us a picture of heartless cruelty, the other a picture of heedless crookedness. Both crimes exploit the helpless.

(i) The Woe (5:8a)

The classic biblical example is found in the story of Naboth's vineyard. Naboth had a vineyard in Jezreel, the fertile plain of Esdraelon. It was near a delightful summer palace belonging to King Ahab. But a palace without a garden is just a big house, and Ahab coveted Naboth's vineyard. He made him a fair offer for it and was turned down. Naboth was within his rights according to the land laws of Israel (Leviticus 25:23; Numbers 36:7; Ezekiel 46:18). Ahab went home to pout.

Then Jezebel took over. She wrote letters in Ahab's name and sealed them with his seal ordering the judicial murder of Naboth. He was to be accused of blasphemy and treason, publicly and on a festive occasion. A couple of false witnesses were to swear to his guilt. He and his heirs were to be executed.

(ii) The Warning (5:8b)

That very evening Jezebel received news that Naboth and his sons were dead. The land was seized by the crown, and Ahab went to Naboth's vineyard to gloat over his acquisition. His joy was short-lived. The prophet Elijah was waiting for him to pronounce God's judgment on both Ahab and Jezebel (1 Kings 21).

Truly Solomon spoke the truth when he said of the oppressor and of the unjust judge, "There is One higher than they."

(b) By Integrity (5:9)

He speaks next of those who acquire wealth by integrity. *"Moreover the profit of the earth is for all: the king himself is served by the field"* (5:9). More than four hundred years before Solomon's investigation, the Lord's laws concerning the Promised Land were given to the Israelites directly after the Ten Commandments (Exodus 20–23). During all the time in Egypt, the Israelites owned no land; they were originally guests of the Pharaoh and then became enslaved with the takeover of the dynasty and the new Pharaoh who knew not Joseph (Exodus 1). Strictly speaking, the heirs of Jacob still owned Abraham's well at Beersheba, the burial cave of Abraham, Sarah, Isaac, and Jacob at the Oaks of Mamre in Hebron, as well as the plot purchased by Jacob in Shechem. But with the passing of four centuries of bondage in Egypt, the Canaanites had surely forgotten who owned the title deeds to those parts and parcels of the Promised Land.

(i) The Principle Inculcated (5:9a)

Coming out of Egyptian bondage, the Israelites were under the Lord's judgments that any debt could take no longer than six years to repay in any circumstance and that included becoming a voluntary slave of a lender to pay off the debt (Exodus 21). In the seventh year, the debt was paid in every circumstance and the voluntary slave could leave the master owing him nothing. That judgment came when the Israelites were just a little over ninety days out of Egypt while camped at the foot of Mount Sinai. There, Moses was given all the Lord's instructions to be held as absolute when the Israelites settled in the Promised Land (Exodus 19:1). Just about anything could be used as collateral against a loan, including a cloak used for cover and warmth each night, but not the land that was properly acquired from the Lord during the conquest.

Under the capable leadership of Joshua, the Promised Land was acquired and then divided into tribal areas. Then the land of each tribal area was divided among the family clans with permanent deeds issued with boundaries. During the forty years in the wilderness, the Lord provided for all the needs of the people making ownership of the land they were sojourning on of little concern. Once in the Promised Land, each family would need a tract of land to produce crops or provide a place for livestock that could be bartered or sold for other family needs. The original family deeds were extremely important in the Lord's plan. The land was never to be used as collateral for a debt; rather, a family member would pledge service as a slave to pay the debt. The land, therefore, provided the perpetual livelihood of each family. In some cases, for instance, the land might be sold but the Lord ordered that the land had to be returned to its original family clan every fifty years in a celebration called the Year of Jubilee (Leviticus 25). The purpose of this law was to stabilize the economy of the nation of Israel and return it to its original state every fifty years. When a man decided to purchase the property of another family, the Year of Jubilee would need to be considered to determine if the gain from the investment would be great enough before the land would legally be required to be returned to the original family clan at no cost.

By the time of this message from Solomon, he had seen in the Israelite records that the Year of Jubilee had reset the economy no fewer than ten times. The land rightfully belonged to each family clan, given permanently by the Lord. Therefore, "the profit of the earth is for all."

(ii) The Prince Included (5:9b)

About four hundred years after all the family clans had received their original title land deeds in the Promised Land, the people began to grumble to the prophet Samuel for a king. Although they were warned that a king would impose a tax on the people, they were not deterred by the counsel and pressed Samuel to anoint a king to rule over them and their land. A Benjamite by the name of Saul was selected and anointed. His capital for thirty-eight years was more or less a military campsite on a hill called Gibeah in his own tribal area (1 Samuel 8–31). More than likely, Gibeah was on the land of his own family clan bequeathed to him from his father, Kish, brought down through his ancestors.

No more than eighteen years into the reign of Saul, Samuel anointed David as the future king just days before he would kill Goliath with the sling of a stone and the slice of a sword (1 Samuel 15–17). From his disobedience, which precipitated the revelation and anointing of David as the future king, Saul's reign was fraught with turmoil, much of which was because of David's popularity among the people of Israel. Yet, in God's divine providence, Saul was allowed at least twenty-two more years of service as king. Meeting David for the first time at the death of Goliath, Saul's son, Jonathan, took to David and they became the dearest of friends.

When Saul and Jonathan died in battle, David was immediately crowned king in the tribal area of Judah, the tribe of David's ancestry. He made Hebron the capital of his kingdom. The rest of the tribes crowned Saul's son Ishbosheth as their king. Israel was thus divided for the first time. After the death of Ishbosheth, his kingdom recognized David as king, and Israel was once again whole as a nation (2 Samuel 3–4).

At least three years before Solomon's birth, David moved his capital from Hebron to the city of the great Jebusite citadel and named it Jerusalem (2 Samuel 5). Once there, David set about defending his nation from the Canaanite enemies and moving the Tabernacle and all its contents to his new capital. He developed plans to build a permanent Temple for the Lord's house, but the Lord would have none of that; David had spilt too much blood in his life. So David created the plans that Solomon would use to build the Temple, and David would have to be satisfied with just that and nothing more (2 Samuel 8).

Then, in a special moment shortly before his sin with Bathsheba, David thought of King Saul, and he wondered if any of his descendants were still alive to whom he could show kindness. Word came that a son of his dearest friend Jonathan was living with a family in Lo-debar, a village on the east side of the Jordan River far from the land that was originally deeded to his family. His name was Mephibosheth, and he was only five years old when Saul and Jonathan died. He was crippled in the rush to flee during the battle that killed his father and grandfather as his nurse fell while carrying him and both his feet were broken. Here was an heir of Jonathan who needed David's kindness.

David wasted no time in bringing Mephibosheth to his home, embracing him because of his great love for his father and his wanting to bring honor to his grandfather. At their meeting, David decreed that Mephibosheth would eat at his table for the rest of his life. In that same meeting, David restored to Mephibosheth the original land deeded to King Saul's family more than four hundred years before, and he assigned a servant named Ziba with his fifteen sons to manage that land for Mephibosheth, so he could have a livelihood. Only in his mid-teens at the time, Mephibosheth would go on to have a son and a family that would live on the land grant, but Mephibosheth would eat at David's table in Jerusalem. Solomon had seen this because Mephibosheth was dining at David's table well before Solomon's birth and for as long as David lived (2 Samuel 9).

Mephibosheth was not the only heir of King Saul who survived the battle which killed him. Mephibosheth had a brother and five male cousins whom Jonathan's sister had borne (2 Samuel 21). They would live with their families on the land rightfully granted back to Mephibosheth by David. It was not stolen land; it lawfully belonged to them; it was given to them by the Lord and from its bounty the descendants of the king were "served by the field."

(2) Wealth Accumulated (5:10–11)
(a) The Limitation of Wealth (5:10)

Solomon had seen the limitation of wealth as he stated, *"He that loveth silver shall not be satisfied with silver; nor he that loveth abundance with increase: this is also vanity"* (5:10). Three times previously Solomon had addressed this topic (1:8; 2:10–11; 4:8). First, the man was not satisfied with what he could see, and he wanted to see more but he never could see enough to be satisfied. Second, the man was not satisfied with the reward of his labor and thus worked more in search of satisfaction that never came. Third, the man sought no end to his labor, gaining and gaining beyond measure with no heir to pass it on to when he died, which did not satisfy him.

Here, Solomon sees the man under the sun who loves the abundance of money and yet, once acquired, finds that it is not enough and hastens to want more. More of the same will never satisfy when what already obtained does not satiate. Even the sheer abundance, the height of his heap, never gratifies the uneasy desire for more; nothing fulfills his longing, nothing quenches his thirst for more. Even so, there is a great limitation of wealth without health; wealth cannot be taken with one after death.[31] Thus, vanity results in stockpiling riches upon riches when riches are not enough; the soul remains empty—dry to the bone—empty and worthless.

(b) The Liability of Wealth (5:11a)

Solomon then speaks of the reality of the liability of acquired wealth. *"When goods increase, they are increased that eat them"* (5:11a), and that imposes the liability of an attraction of people with certain characteristics who are known by many names in this world under the sun, but we shall kindly call them takers as opposed to givers.

In many places in the United States mega lottery games are now weekly events with Saturday night drawings offering multimillion-dollar jackpots. On a fairly regular basis new millionaires are instantly made once the last of a series of numbers is selected. In many cases, a person who has always lived paycheck to paycheck instantly has more money available to him than he ever dreamed possible. What could be more satisfying? What could be more exciting? What could be more of a blessing? Or, is it a curse?

In Edward Ugel's 2006 book, *Money for Nothing: One Man's Journey Through the Dark Side of Lottery Millions*, he reveals that of the thousands of lottery winners, few are happy and most wish they had never won. Why? Because now that they are "rich," friends and family hound them for money. Others pretend to want to protect them from greedy people while attempting to profit under the pretense of friendship. Furthermore, those who were prone to drug or alcohol addiction heightened their use until every cent was gone or the money outlived them! Others who longed for companions purchased extravagant gifts to garner alleged friends. And the examples of the liability of wealth go on and on.

A major problem with the liability of wealth stems from the problem of the limitation of wealth previously addressed by Solomon. The wealthy person has his own problems to deal with as to what he does with his money but those who latch on to him are never satisfied with the amount of money they have received from him; a little or a lot, given by the wealthy man, is never enough for the taker. He always wants more; he finds reasons why he needs more; he lusts for more; he covets more; he may even do anything for more, not limited to stealing and killing.

Solomon knew all too well the liability of newfound wealth. At the moment of his father's death, all of King David's wealth transferred to him; all wives, concubines, siblings, children, grandchildren, servants, slaves, and livestock instantly belonged to him, and were included in his newfound wealth. Within days, his mother came to ask him to give one of David's wives to a brother to become his wife. First, this action would have violated the Israelite law; secondly, the brother wanted part of Solomon's wealth; surely with all of Solomon's wives he would not have missed one that actually belonged to his father (1 Kings 2).

Lotteries to the extent offered in our day were not common in Solomon's; yet, the lure of wealth was readily used for evil purposes. The classic example can be found in the story we have already discussed of Jezebel's unjust acquisition of Naboth's vineyard.[32]

By the time of Ahab and Jezebel, a strong tradition existed in the Northern Kingdom of Israel concerning days of fasting. A careful study of God's Word reveals that the concept of fasting was not included in the first five books of the Bible. It will not appear in Scripture until Joshua 20.[33] Two things must be noticed about the placement of this occurrence. Israel's first recorded fast occurred approximately three thousand years after Adam's creation, near the halfway mark between the creation and today. Why did it take so long? Did people fast prior to this occasion? What does fasting mean? Fasting simply means *abstaining from food*. It leads us to the next important thing we need to notice about this occurrence. In the context of this story, eleven tribes of Israel were attempting to correct the actions of their brother Benjamin's tribe which had committed a grievous sin. In the morning of the battle, the tribe of Benjamin killed 18,000 men from the other eleven tribes. In despair, the people of the eleven tribes gathered at Bethel, weeping and mourning late into the afternoon. During those hours, they did not eat anything; rather, they cried, they howled, they wailed, and they sobbed for their dead. Before sundown, they offered burnt and peace offerings to the Lord; both included the consumption of certain parts of the offerings by the people and the priests. Therefore, the current concept of fasting does not fit this example or any others within Scripture.

Had any such mourning occurred during the history recorded in the first five books of Scripture? Surely it had; however, fasting was not a requirement of the Lord for the nation of Israel.

How then did Israel begin to celebrate days of fasting? For that, the answer in Scripture is unclear; however, what is clear is that in Israel's tradition, fasting was associated with periods of mourning a tragedy or a need for repentance of sin. As time progressed after the conquest of the Promised Land, the nation began, on its own, to memorialize days of great tragedy in their history with fasting. On those days, the nation would share from its abundance with the poor of the land—both poor Israelites and non-Israelites. As such, fasting days would bring the beggars and takers into the villages for the gifts of food and alms. By the time of Jezebel, all she had to do was write a letter instructing the elders to proclaim a fast in the name of Ahab, stamped with his seal, and on that appointed day, the city would be filled with unscrupulous people willing to do or say anything for a dollar. In her attempt to steal the vineyard of Naboth, two worthless men fit the bill and accused Naboth of cursing God and the king. Naboth was found guilty by all the alien undesirables in the city, and that day he was stoned. Ahab then seized his vineyard (1 Kings 21).

Jezebel had used the increase of wealth in the nation of Israel for evil purposes as a liability against Naboth to tempt those who would flock to the city in droves in desire for even the smallest of a token gift. Her task was easy because "when goods increase, they are increased that eat them."

Wealth in the Bible days was not based on the amount of gold and silver acquired; rather, it was determined by the amount of mouths one was able to feed including wives, concubines, siblings, children, grandchildren, servants, slaves, and livestock such as mentioned before. Abram was a wealthy man when he left Haran with Sarai and journeyed down to Bethel and then on to Egypt. The famine was great in the land and Abram, new in Canaan land, felt that his only option to feed his house was to seek help in Egypt. The debacle with Pharaoh is recorded in Genesis 11, but the point for our study here is that Pharaoh added to Abram's wealth when he sent him away. The text states that Pharaoh made Abram exceedingly wealthy. Pharaoh gave to Abram what he needed to survive in Canaan. It is not until we delve further into the story where we find Lot and the villages associated with him captured by the great kings of the Babylonian area. Notwithstanding, these were kings who surely knew Abram for he, too, was from Ur of Chaldees in the Babylonian area; and according to the distribution of languages after the Tower of Babel, these too were close cousins of Abram.

When Abram heard of the calamity involving his nephew Lot, Abram gathered three hundred men able to fight with the sword and chased the kings down, rescued the prisoners, and returned them to their villages. Where did Abram gather three hundred men of his house who were prepared to fight? He had only one biological son at that time, Ishmael, and he was far too young to fight. No other direct descendants of Abram were there, yet because a man's wealth was determined by the number of mouths he fed each day, Abram was exceedingly wealthy. Every mouth required a daily ration of food, whether human or beast. To provide for these meals, produce was required. When he hired one man to work the fields or the flocks, a wife and children would follow, if not already there, providing more mouths to feed than just the one who was hired. Three hundred men, able to use the sword, would have parents, wives, siblings, and children all hungry for a meal each day. At some point, the wealthy man had to wonder if less wealth with fewer humans to feed might be easier to manage. One famine might devastate the house of Abram just as one famine devastated the house of Jacob and Egypt was the only place to find food. Many may look wealthy, but no one understands the true wealth of a man until the financial books are opened.

(c) The Hurt of Wealth (5:11b)

". . . and what good is there to the owners thereof, saving the beholding of them with their eyes?" (5:11b). Solomon may have had more wives than any other man in all of humanity and the liability of feeding their families fell to him alone. He also had laborers and their families who had to be fed who were hired, albeit by force, to build the Temple, the palace, and other buildings. Surely, he felt the hurt of wealth and could ask, "And what good is there to the owners thereof, saving the beholding of them with their eyes?" The nation of Israel was wealthy under Solomon but even that nation could withstand only a finite budget of expenses each year and Solomon understood the liability of the appearance of wealth. Everyone wanted to trade with Solomon; everyone wanted a daughter to become one of Solomon's wives; everyone wanted to be part of the national wealth system Solomon had developed. But only Solomon knew how dangerously close to the brink of bankruptcy his nation as well as his personal wealth were; from the perception of all standing at a distance, both were wealthy beyond imagination; up close, within the accounting offices of his administration, Solomon must have wondered a few times if his resources would hold out until the next influx of tax at the appropriate time in the appropriate season when taxes were due "under the sun." A plea for the collection of more taxes out of season would have reverberated through the surrounding nations as a sign of internal financial trouble and that would destroy the perception Solomon wanted. Wealth is pretty to look at while it is there, but its upkeep too often becomes its downfall. When it falls, it never falls alone. The tentacles of collapse are always far greater than the eye can see, or the accounting system can justify or predict.

b) Words About the Deceitfulness of Riches (5:12–20)
(1) How Wealth Disturbs (5:12)

The wealthy have employees working for them. In most cases, those employees do not know or understand the details of the business. They are just thankful for their jobs. They go to work, clock in, do the job, clock out, go home, and sleep, not worried about their work in particular as to whether or not it will be there in the morning. That is not to say employment does not come with its struggles, but when the job pays the bills and the climate in the office is pleasant, the job is good. Little does the employee know of the struggles the owner is experiencing, a personal daily battle that is a robber of his sleep at night. It is in that context that Solomon is correct when he says, *"The sleep of a labouring man is sweet, whether he eat little or much: but the abundance of the rich will not suffer him to sleep"* (5:12).

In 1985 a corporation was formed and relocated to Houston, Texas, that was a conglomeration of the merger of other energy businesses, some of which began as far back as 1925. It was known as Enron, and by 2001 it claimed to have yearly revenues of over twenty billion dollars. In that year, it employed more than twenty thousand people directly, all with families that were relying on the wealth of the corporation for their livelihood and future retirement. Most of those employees had every penny of their life savings in the company stock. It was a giant machine that, in the minds of most of the employees and Wall Street investors, was too big and too wealthy to ever fail or falter. But in 2001, the CEO of the corporation took to the media outlets to declare Enron was stable and to give confidence to the everyday investor in its stock, a public attempt to fix the crumbling underlying foundation of the company. The financial professionals who owned the stock were nervous and began pulling out. The CEO could not sleep at night for he did not want a mass sell-off of the stock. He was well aware of the fraud allegations that had been disseminated concerning the true condition of the company, and he was without excuse. He had every right to be worried, for some of his upper management as well as some of those who had left the company had cashed out their paper wealth in the company to capture their real wealth to work and invest in other places. They knew! They led the people down the rat hole and left them there. They protected their own wealth at the cost of those who worked for them.

Within a few days after the CEO's announcement, the company could not pay its bills and filed for bankruptcy. The value of the stock in the retirement funds of all the employees was gone. The jobs of Enron's employees were gone. In the downfall, a major prestigious accounting firm would not bear up under the loss of the client nor survive the perception of criminality that went along with the company's collapse. Besides the accounting firm, other businesses which held contracts with Enron were devastated, the mom-and-pop services that were contracted to handle the maintenance, cleaning, grounds, elevators, copiers, storage, Internet, telecommunications, electricity, gas, water, insurance, transportation, food, furnishings, and so on. All were left holding the bag, all were left with bills on their desks for products used to support Enron but had no chance of an invoice being paid. The offices were adorned with custom furniture, nothing but the best of the best for Enron. On the morning that the bankruptcy was filed, the furniture maker received a check for the payment of an invoice he had presented for $350,000. He rushed to the bank, but it was too late, the check was no good. He had other invoices sitting on some desk at Enron amounting to ten times that amount, and they were never paid. His product was gone, his raw materials were gone, the reimbursement for wages he had paid and the utilities he had used were gone; within a few months, his business was gone.

Solomon had seen enough in his life "under the sun" to know that wealth comes with disturbing consequences often hidden from those who are part of the wealth system.

(2) How Wealth Disappears (5:13–14)
(a) The Reasons (5:13)

"There is a sore evil which I have seen under the sun, namely, riches kept for the own-ers thereof to their hurt" (5:13).

Solomon uses the word *holah* which is translated "sore" here but would be bet-ter translated *sick* for our day. The word "evil" is *raah*, and it too would be better translated *disaster* or *misfortune*. So, Solomon is declaring that "under the sun" wealth often disappears in some calamity of *sick misfortune*.

Solomon was well aware of the fragility of a man's wealth and the reason for which it might disappear in a time of "sore" disaster. It can come in any form at any time in any way. Perhaps the best illustration that Solomon was surely aware of and which ultimately shaped how he knew wealth could disappear occurred in his father's life about three years before his birth.

Just after moving to Jerusalem, Amnon, one of David's adult sons, raped David's daughter Tamar. The detestable act infuriated Absalom, another son of David. Absalom was frustrated by Amnon's sin, but he was even more infuriated that David did not quickly bring punishment upon Amnon. Absalom took matters into his own hands and killed his brother. David's sick family calamity turned into a national disaster, putting David's wealth in jeopardy as well as the wealth of the nation of Israel. Absalom attempted to seize the throne of David, and David had to flee the city. The nation convulsed in divided loyalty between David and Absalom. Even Ziba, the caretaker of Mephibosheth, turned on David, expecting

Mephibosheth to emerge as the new king. Mephibosheth remained loyal to David as he sank into deep depression, failing to take care of his hygiene (2 Samuel 9–11).

(b) The Result (5:14)

As a result, in the end, Absalom was killed by David's men but without his permission and ten of the tribes of Israel were greatly offended by the way David returned to Jerusalem. Much of the wealth of David was lost; much of the wealth of Israel was lost.

"But those riches perish by evil travail: and he begetteth a son, and there is nothing in his hand" (5:14). David could never have planned for the family disaster that travailed his family and his nation. The wealth of David in the lives of two of his sons was gone; the wealth of the life of David's daughter was forever damaged.

Upon the death of David, his wealth immediately transferred to Solomon. No sooner had Solomon taken the throne when another family disaster occurred that could have divided the family and nation again. Adonijah asked Solomon's mother if he could have the Shulamite wife of David as a bride. Had David consummated the marriage with this woman, at his death, she would have been free to marry, and Adonijah's request would have been perfectly legal under the Israelite law. But she was a wife who acted as a nurse to David, and the marriage was never consummated. Because of that, under the law, she could never be given in marriage to another; therefore, to Solomon, the request was an abomination. Had Solomon thought otherwise, the nation would have rebelled against him. He was not willing to make the same mistake with Adonijah that his father had made with Absalom. Absalom had brought dishonor to his father, and the penalty was death (Exodus 21:15). Adonijah had also brought dishonor to his mother and dead father. Solomon handled the request quickly, once and for all, by executing his brother Adonijah, as was consistent with the ordinance set in place by the Lord when He had given the Ten Commandments to the children of Israel at the foot of the mountain of Sinai. For Solomon, another mouth was gone from the wealth of his house (1 Kings 2).

(3) How Wealth Derides (5:15–16)
(a) What Does the Rich Man Leave? (5:15)

"As he came forth of his mother's womb, naked shall he return to go as he came, and shall take nothing of his labour, which he may carry away in his hand" (5:15).

Solomon was no stranger to death. By the end of his life he had seen many die and as his father recorded in Psalm 49:6–13:

> They that trust in their wealth,
> and boast themselves in the multitude of their riches;
> none of them can by any means redeem his brother,
> nor give to God a ransom for him:
> (for the redemption of their soul is precious,
> and it ceaseth for ever:)
> that he should still live for ever,
> and not see corruption.
> For he seeth that wise men die,
> likewise the fool and the brutish person perish,
> and leave their wealth to others.
> Their inward thought is, that their houses shall continue for ever,
> and their dwelling places to all generations;
> they call their lands after their own names.
> Nevertheless man being in honour abideth not:
> he is like the beasts that perish.
> This their way is their folly:
> yet their posterity approve their sayings. Selah.

There, what do you think of that?

And so it was with the story of the man who had a gold-plated Rolls-Royce. It was his prize possession which he never drove but kept safe in his garage. Upon his death, it was his desire to be embalmed, set behind the wheel, and buried in the car in the grave. One onlooker thought, "Man, that is living!" Another brought him back to reality by saying, "No, that is dying."[34]

(b) Why Does the Rich Man Labor? (5:16)

"And this also is a sore evil, that in all points as he came, so shall he go: and what profit hath he that hath laboured for the wind?" (5:16). If a man comes into this world as a babe with nothing and if a man leaves this world with nothing, what in the world is the purpose of laboring "under the sun" to gain wealth that a man cannot take with him in death, the same wealth that cannot satisfy while he is alive? What a depressing misfortune for every human born into this world!

Why does the rich man labor for wealth that cannot be his forever? He does it because it is a psychological illness. More, more, more, he must have more while he is in this world. Hoarded in heaps beneath the shelters, hoarded in tons grazing in the fields, hoarded in bags hidden under the saddles, hoarded everywhere "under the sun." It is an illness!

Trying to capture the wind is ludicrous. I heard a story of a child who tried, before the days of air conditioning, to capture the wind. Sweltering in the classroom of his elementary school, he longed to go outside where the wind was blowing and he could find a shady spot to be refreshed as the wind blew across his clothing filled with perspiration. The breeze brought chills and, as a young man, he thought he could capture the wind for a moment of coolness when he returned to the class. A quart Mason Jar had held his lunch, and by recess it was empty and clean. He held it into the strong blowing cool air and quickly replaced the lid tightly on the jar so not one BTU would escape. At just the right moment, when the heat in the class was especially high, he slipped the jar from his satchel, pointed it toward his face and quickly removed the lid, expecting a quart's worth of breeze. To his dismay, nothing!

In Solomon's investigation, he had seen the problem of wealth without health here on earth. He understood how we are derided by wealth. Chasing after wealth "under the sun" is like working to capture the wind in a jar. When the health is gone, the wealth is gone from you! Nothing! How empty, how hopeless, how discouraging, how devastating, how dark!

(4) How Wealth Darkens (5:17–20)
(a) The Misery It Brings (5:17)

And so it is that wealth darkens the soul and brings misery. *"All his days also he eateth in darkness, and he hath much sorrow and wrath with his sickness"* (5:17). We would expect Solomon to say, "All his days also he walketh in darkness," but that is not his point at all. Solomon uses the word "eateth" and that is precisely what he means. Eating should be associated with joy, but here, eating is associated with gloom. In Solomon's own words, the man who chases after wealth is sick; his sickness brings both "sorrow and wrath." Misery! In both cases! Eaten up!

"Darkness" is the word *choshek*, and it properly means *to obscure*. Wealth obscures reality. Gorging on wealth does just that! It obscures! While healthy, the wealthy can buy what they want, sell what they wish, and hide what they will. In their sickness, the hustle and bustle of constant buying, selling, and hiding acts as a front to cover the misery of reality that death lingers near at any moment "under the sun" for everyone. And so, James agrees with Solomon when he says,

> Go to now, ye rich men, weep and howl for your miseries that shall come upon you. Your riches are corrupted, and your garments are motheaten. Your gold and silver is cankered; and the rust of them shall be a witness against you, and shall eat your flesh as it were fire. Ye have heaped treasure together for the last days. Behold, the hire of the labourers who have reaped down your fields, which is of you kept back by fraud, crieth: and the cries of them which have reaped are entered into the ears of the Lord of sabaoth. Ye have lived in pleasure on the earth, and been wanton. (James 5:1–5)[35]

(b) The Materialism It Breeds (5:18–20)
(i) The Materialist's Narrow Views (5:18)

Being keenly aware, we must remember that Solomon is preaching about the life of a man devoid of God in every way. He was that man for most of his life, and he could look back and say, *"Behold that which I have seen: it is good and comely for one to eat and to drink, and to enjoy the good of all his labour that he taketh under the sun all the days of his life, which God giveth him: for it is his portion"* (5:18). Lest we forget, even the most heathen of this world will mention the name of God when it suits his situation. And just as bad, the name of God is often tagged at the end of some saying to lend credence and justification to the sad life of a person. Solomon fell into the same trap during his life, ever seeking wealth and acting as if it was "good and comely" to do so; and therefore, Solomon had convinced himself that his actions were God ordained and that he should enjoy the journey with feasting and drinking. It was his attempt to satisfy his longing deep within his soul. His deep desire to increase his wealth is called *materialism*, in which physical possessions and comfort are more important than spiritual values.

In the bookkeeping of the world of Solomon, "under the sun," wealth was determined by the human lives who were considered physical possessions under one's control. Solomon was not quite wealthy beyond imagination in those terms. And so, he had a nagging problem that affected his happiness and pressed him to desperately seek what he truly wanted in a materialistic rather than spiritual way.

Perhaps the greatest single illustration of Solomon's thought in this passage is found in the desperate life of one king of England, Henry VIII, twenty-five hundred years after these words were written.

The young King Henry took the throne at the age of eighteen. It wasn't his place to be king, for he was the second son in lineage, but his brother's, Arthur, who was raised to be the king of England. Arthur was married to Catherine of Aragon who was three years his senior. Married for only five months, Arthur died suddenly at the age of fifteen. Young Henry was thrust onto the political scene as the heir apparent of the throne, the next male in line, even though he was only ten years of age. When his father died, he became the king at the age of eighteen. With that kingship, he was required to have a queen. His deceased brother's wife became his wife even though she was eight years older than he.

Three years into his reign and his marriage, a son was born, and the nation erupted with joy! But in just fifty-two days, the son was found dead in his bed. The nation mourned, and the king was devastated. What started as the exuberant reign of a young, tall, handsome, educated, popular, public king who sought to correct the wrongs of his father, began to decline over his reign to become an old, fat, ugly, stubborn, paranoid, and secretive king whose orders had spilt the blood of many of his closest and most loyal English men and women.

After the death of her first son, and over the next twenty-three years, Catherine could not give Henry another male heir, and he became obsessed with having one. Ten years before the end of that marriage with Catherine, Henry began investigating other women, even the maid of his wife, Catherine, in search of a suitable replacement queen who could bear a son.

Ultimately, King Henry asked the Church in Rome, of which he was a faithful and astute member, for a divorce solely for the purpose of taking a wife who could give him a son. The Church refused, and the enraged King Henry severed ties with the Catholic Church and placed himself as the head of the new Church in England. Henry may have been a political leader, but he was in no way suitable to be the religious leader of England—but that he was according to his own decree. Catherine was removed from being queen, the twenty-six-year marriage was annulled, and Henry immediately married Anne Boleyn. Henry's action brought pain to the nation that was shocked and to Catherine's family that was demoralized, and his new marriage placed a whole cadre of souls in jeopardy.

Ten years earlier, Anne had been engaged, which was not made common knowledge in England. Her sister was Mary, who had become Henry's mistress, during his marriage to Catherine. Mary had accepted Henry's invitations to decorate his bed, but Anne had refused. Eventually, Anne was chosen over

Mary, and she married Henry the year he annulled his marriage to Catherine. Anne gave Henry a child, a daughter, Elizabeth. When Anne was unable to bear a son, Henry was in a pickle because he soon wanted another wife who could give him a son. Henry trumped up charges that Anne had committed high treason against the crown by not revealing to him her past sexual history. The charges stuck, and her head was separated from her body. But she was not the only victim; many of her family members as well as associates were put to death also, including her father and her former fiancé. Henry's narrow, focused desire had destroyed the lineage of another family in England in order to pursue his own lineage.

Henry immediately took another wife, Jane. Within one year she was successful in giving Henry a son, a sickly son, Edward VI; however, she died shortly after childbirth. As expected, Henry gave her a queen's funeral in England, the only wife of Henry to receive such honor.

Henry then reluctantly agreed to marry Anne of Cleves, but he could not bring himself to consummate the marriage. He had no attraction to her at all. After just a few months of marriage an agreement was made, and the marriage was annulled, but not without Anne's receiving a healthy gift and the homestead of Henry's second wife who had lost her head.

He then married a woman he had been seeing while married to Anne of Cleves. Her name was Catherine Howard, and she was just seventeen years old. She was youthful and beautiful in all her ways and pleased Henry; however, during the plague of 1540 and the relocating from the home in the London castle during that sickness, circumstances presented themselves for Catherine to begin a romantic relationship with one of Henry's servants. The two were found out; she was convicted of treason, and she lost her head as did several family members, politicians, clergy, and Henry's servants. The actions of Henry vomited again against his home and nation because of his materialistic narrow desire, and the Howard family line was nearly destroyed. Worldly in his will and ways, Henry was devoid of a spiritual will and ways.

Henry found a third Catherine to wed; she was fortunate in that she outlived him. As such, England bestowed upon her the title "Queen Dowager" upon Henry's death. Kindly, before he died, and in spite of their short marriage, Henry provided a generous salary from the royal treasury for her until her death. Within eighteen months after Henry's death, Catherine had secretly remarried, had a child by the new husband, and died.

Edward VI, Henry's only son, took the throne at the age of nine in 1547. He was too young to lead the kingdom of England effectively. Just six years later, Edward fell sick and died at the age of fifteen, and was buried.

Henry VIII, although highly educated in religious matters as a child, lived his life in rebellion to God and sought such a narrow path in life with one underlying goal in view—his heirs.

Solomon had to have understood the same in his time "under the sun." How in the world did Solomon marry seven hundred wives and engage the services of three hundred concubines and arrive at the end of life with only one son? Rehoboam! And no record of a daughter? In all the years of his reign, one thousand women were not the only souls spoiled by his materialistic desire. For each woman, there was the potential of a living father, mother, siblings, children, and cousins galore, all victims of Solomon's materialistic obsession to move on to another in search of a male heir, the most valuable possession of a man's wealth. His sole son was not prepared to carry on the kingdom, a son who would divide Solomon's kingdom within the year after he took the throne. And why? It began with Solomon's unhinged narrow lust for wealth, centered on a quiver full of sons which he never received. Solomon may have been wealthy beyond all others, but in sons, he was extremely poor.

(ii) The Materialist's Neglected Values (5:19–20)
(a) What He Forgets (5:19)

Ever so quickly, Solomon needed a jolt of eternal spiritual reality infused into the discussion. To accomplish that he says, *"Every man also to whom God hath given riches and wealth, and hath given him power to eat thereof, and to take his portion, and to rejoice in his labour; this is the gift of God"* (5:19). Solomon had lived most of his reign as king as a prime example of a misspent life, chasing material things, neglecting the truly important and highest spiritual aspect by forgetting that it was by the divine providence of God that he was the king. He had forgotten that God was in control of the nation of Israel, the chosen nation of the Lord, one that had its own angel assigned to guide and guard it from those who would seek to destroy it. Pitiful Solomon, in his wisdom, thought it was his responsibility to provide the next heir to the throne. What about Rehoboam? Rather, what if Rehoboam died? What would be the case then? How would Solomon be able to control the next king if his son did not survive? How foolish this wise king was to think it was his choice and the Lord had no control. How many lives attached to his wives and concubines were affected negatively by his forgetting that it was the Lord who gave life, and no human, not even a king, can change that important spiritual fact.

Shall we forget the outcome of Henry VIII's life and the longest reigning ruler of the Tudor line after him? Dare we analyze the fact and bear under the weight of the heavy truth? In his life as king he ruined the lives of many families trying to perpetuate his own posterity with male heirs after his first male heir had died when he was fifty-two days old. Along the way he had a son, Edward VI, but he was sickly. A backup of at least one or two sons was needed in Henry's opinion and his obsession. Henry, too, had forgotten that he held the position as king by the gift and grace of the Lord God. He was part of God's plan, and although Henry seemed to be religious, God was not truly in the center of Henry's heart.

When it was all said and done, Edward VI took the throne after his father's death but lived as king for only six years. Under the guidance of the young king's counselors, a decree was put in place that made his cousin, Lady Jane Grey, the next ruling Queen of England. She was crowned but her reign lasted only nine days.

Mary, Henry's first daughter, then took the throne nine days after her brother's death and reigned for five years. At her death, Elizabeth, the only daughter of Henry's second wife, took the throne and reigned for forty-five years.

With all his human manipulation in pursuit of children, Henry's three children successfully carried on his immediate legacy for fifty-six years. Elizabeth never married and thus Henry's Tudor line came to an end. A cousin took her place on the English throne; James Stuart was his name, a name used for centuries to come in English-speaking churches across the world for he was used by the Lord to produce the Authorized Version (KJV) of the Bible.

Likewise, Solomon, twenty-five hundred years before Henry, had forgotten who truly controlled the throne and who would sit upon it. Solomon and Henry were both rulers under God's heavens and ministers of the people. How dare they forget that they were both wealthy beyond normal human imagination, yet placed on their thrones by the Lord? But in their materialistic states of mind, they forgot the most important values of their lives. God, the Giver of life!

(b) What He Faces (5:20)

All, pray tell, was vanity for Solomon "under the sun." Solomon speaks, *"For he shall not much remember the days of his life; because God answereth him in the joy of his heart"* (5:20). The days of a man's life are but a vapor—one follows another all too quickly until all certain memories of daily events run into a blur in time. Everyone must face that as reality when facing life and the end of days. A time will come too quickly for all when the joy of life is immediate and momentary, found in the laughter of a child, the holding of a loved one's hand, the breeze on the bench in the park, the ice cream on Sunday afternoon, the chicken for Sunday lunch, the piece of hard candy to sooth a dry throat, the buttermilk and cornbread, the favorite pie, or the kids coming home for Christmas. Memories that God allows to bring joy to the heart! Dare one neglect to grant the joy of all of that to the Lord, the rightful owner?

  9. The Problem of Treasure Without Pleasure (6:1–6)
   a) Take a Good Look at the Gift (6:1–2)
    (1) The Evil Seen (6:1)

Under the sun, Solomon had seen the problem of the lost opportunity to enjoy the pleasure that he thought should accompany treasure. The problem he identifies as he speaks, *"There is an evil which I have seen under the sun, and it is common among men"* (6:1).

 Evil! Solomon was no stranger to evil. For almost forty years of his reign as king of the mighty Israel, evil could have been his middle name. His collection of one thousand women, for instance, was nothing short of his lust of the eye, his lust of the flesh, and his pride of life, the three prime evil roots of sin. By the time he wrote the Song of Solomon, his play was one of more than a thousand plays he had written. At that time, he had collected sixty wives, eighty concubines, and virgins beyond number (Song of Solomon 6:8). Surely, some of the wives were a result of contractual agreements with neighboring nations, and some of them might be explained away as only ceremonial in nature; but each marriage required a consummation to be called a marriage. We cannot find a ceremonial reason for his eighty concubines. Nothing can explain away his evil purpose with them. Concubines were collected for one purpose, the bearing of children. And Solomon's harem was still filled with virgins without number, all awaiting their turn with the king. Once they spent the night with him, they would not return to the virgin harem but join the harem of those he had enjoyed, as would be the case with Esther's story many years after Solomon's.

 Why? The virgins were there to provide him more women for service in his evil desire for more. The virgin in the Song of Solomon was just one more from his perverted harem, but this one was different. His words, which increasingly became more sensual and seductive through the course of the play, seeking to lure her to his bed, were futile. She refused. What? A simple, solitary virgin, one of the thousands, denied the most powerful king in the world at the time of his fancy. Why? She belonged to another! She had already found her beloved. He had gone away but promised to return. Solomon had her in his bedroom, the table was set, but she was gazing out the window, casting her eyes off to the hills of Jerusalem, watching intently for her beloved to return. Solomon had offered her food, but her beloved had offered her love. Solomon was stunned. Could he have finally found a wife instead of just another woman in his life? Another female? Another try? This one would not turn her eyes to him. Her eyes were eternally focused on her future with her true love. Out she looked, through the window to the hills of Zion. Because she would not look at him in the room, Solomon formed a parade of all he had to offer, marching down the roads in those hills outside that window but nothing caught her eye that could change her mind. To be his wife, he offered. She turned him down flat.

Rejected, Solomon would go on to collect seven hundred wives and three hundred consummated concubines from his harem in his evil pursuit. What was he wanting? More women? No! He was pursuing this evil path with woman after woman in his desire to acquire children. With all these women from all the surrounding nations came their worship of false gods. But Solomon was willing to turn his head from their evil, blinded by his personal evil. With all those consummated relationships, a thousand at least, Solomon had but one child, a blabbering foolish idiot who would divide the nation of Israel into two kingdoms within a year after Solomon's death. The only reason the Lord did not divide Solomon's kingdom during his life was because of his father, David.

Solomon had tried to warn his idiot son of the troubles that accompany fools. He wrote a personal letter to him found in the first nine chapters of the book of Proverbs. Poignant, purposeful, and pragmatic are his words, but young Rehoboam will ignore every bit of it when he takes the throne. Be assured, Solomon had seen evil. His wives were evil, his son was evil, he was evil.

Solomon's wives, concubines, and son embodied just one facet of all of Solomon's treasure that brought him no pleasure. Under the sun, Solomon's evil acquisitions were no different in nature from the common man. This king of the Israelites, son of David, of the tribe of Judah, had conveniently ignored the Lord's warning of making any kind of covenant with anyone of any nation except Israel and that included the covenant of marriage (Exodus 34; Deuteronomy 7). Solomon was in rebellion against the Lord with all his foreign women and their gods. For "Solomon did evil in the sight of the LORD, and went not fully after the LORD, as did David his father" (1 Kings 11:6). He was just in a position where his evil could be exploited without fear, in plain sight of the nation, instead of hidden in the closet of a house as with most common men.

> (2) The Evil Stated (6:2)
>   (a) Great Gifts Bestowed (6:2a)

Solomon had seen evil and assuredly he was a participant in it. But what evil had caught his eye to say, "*. . . a man to whom God hath given riches, wealth, and honour, so that he wanteth nothing for his soul of all that he desireth, . . .*" (6:2a)?

And what may be defined as "riches, wealth, and honour" under the sun? Solomon knew well what they were firsthand! He had riches, and he had wealth. The Hebrew word for "riches" is *osher*, which can refer to any commodity of value such as silver, gold, flocks, herds, houses, land, wives, and the greatest riches under the sun, children. The Hebrew word for "wealth" is *nekes*, and it refers to the accumulation of any commodity. Solomon had seen the ability of man to have great riches flow through his hands, but holding on to those riches was a different story altogether. The working man must figure a way under the sun to accumulate a little of the riches that passes his way each day until he can call himself a wealthy man. To the riches and wealth, Solomon adds the word "honour." The Hebrew word is *kabod*, and in this context it means the splendor that accompanies the weight of wealth and riches. What the rich, self-made man Solomon had seen, was that he was known because of his wealth, loved because of his prosperity, esteemed because of his treasures, revered because of his resources. It was a worldly glory based on worldly possessions. But what would the worldly people think of the same wealthy man if he suddenly had nothing? Vanity might be the appropriate word from Solomon.

But did Solomon address the self-made man in this passage? Not so! Here he plainly states that the "riches, wealth, and honour" are great gifts bestowed from God. The man had the gifts regardless of his work. Inherited they may be! The luck of one draw from the hat. The turn of one card. The retrieval of one diamond. The selection of one bride. Solomon would have known the words of Job, "The LORD giveth and the LORD taketh away, blessed be the name of the LORD." Worldly admiration would still accompany the man made wealthy by the Lord, that is the very nature of the world, but it is a different story from that of the self-made man. Is wealth evil? No. But a man made wealthy by the Lord does not know how to make that wealth again if he squanders it. The self-made man can retrace his track and start again. He knows the road; he knows the formula; he knows the pitfalls; he knows the perils; he knows the goal. Rarely does the self-made man realize that it was the Lord who created him with the ability to be wealthy! Solomon surely knew that too.

(b) Great Grief Bestowed (6:2b)

Solomon was not addressing wealth as being evil. If he were, he would be at the head of the class. The evil about which Solomon speaks was of wealth when, *". . . yet God giveth him not power to eat thereof, but a stranger eateth it: this is vanity, and it is an evil disease"* (6:2b). The grief of stolen wealth!

Lo, how wealthy is wealthy? Who is the arbitrator of wealthy versus poor? Perhaps it is the man himself who decides if he is wealthy enough though his means be meager and his possessions few. Perhaps Solomon has heard of the poor man filled with joy because of his new young, beautiful wife, his job in the king's army, his personal integrity in all his actions, and his loyal service to his country. Would that not be a wealthy man? Who would dare disagree?

Had Solomon ever seen such grief in the life of a rich poor man? Maybe, maybe not. Had he heard of such a story? Yes, for it was written into the king's record of his father and mother, David and Bathsheba.

More than seventy years before Solomon regained his Godly wits and penned this sermon, at least four years before his birth, an evil event occurred in the life of his father and mother, one often quickly skimmed over when reading the Holy Writ of God because it is an embarrassing debacle in David's life, one difficult to explain, one no one's parents would openly want to repeat.

King David was approximately forty-seven when he captured the great Jebusite fortress in the city of Zion and made it his capital. He had ruled as king of Israel in the city of Hebron for seven years and six months when this great conquest and victory occurred. From the time David was about seventeen until he was forty-seven, David had collected seven wives and at least ten concubines. His first wife was the daughter of King Saul, Michal. Like Saul, she was a Benjamite and perfectly legal to marry under the law of the Lord. She was young and in love with the handsome David, the mighty warrior in battle, the killer of the Philistine giant. Saul had offered his oldest daughter to him first, but she was in love with another man and did not want David. When Saul discovered that his youngest daughter adored David, she was offered. David already knew the trouble he was having with King Saul's anger, and David married her to be part of the king's family, a tactic that did not work. She grew to hate David and bore him no children. Six more wives were taken, and a son was born to each along David's journey, most of them born before he became king. Daughters are rarely mentioned in the Bible record; however, because of a disgusting, evil event which occurred among three of the siblings in David's family, the record shows that David had at least one daughter named Tamar by his fourth wife, who was also the mother of Absalom. With seven wives and most of his children nearing adulthood, he moved his family and his capital to Zion, the city of Peace, Jerusalem.

Through his adult life, David had also gathered a band of mighty warriors, a troop of special forces of at least thirty-three men. They were loyal to him in every way, bodyguards of the king! He could trust them with his life, and they thought they could trust him.

As spring arrived in David's new capital city, so, too, it was time for the men to go out to make war against the many enemies of Israel. For whatever reason, David did not join his mighty men in this endeavor but tarried behind in Jerusalem. One evening, after resting for a while on his bed, David strolled onto the roof and saw the beautiful Bathsheba. That night he lusted for her with his eyes, he lusted for her flesh upon his bed, and he sent for her—the wife of one of his finest men, Uriah, the Hittite. That night, David stole this man's wife!

First of all, as a Hittite, Uriah was a descendant of the Canaanite tribes. He was not Jewish by birth although he may have been Jewish by faith. In his early years of running from King Saul, David made close friends of many Canaanites, and Uriah was one that stuck with him for life. Second of all, as a Canaanite living in an Israelite realm, Uriah had attained just about all that he could in life: a beautiful young wife, a job in the king's personal army of bodyguards, a reputation for his personal integrity, and a fierce loyalty to his adopted kingdom. By all means, by every calculation, by the subjective and objective agreement of all reasonable minds in David's day, Uriah had accumulated great riches, wealth, and honor by any standard as an alien in David's kingdom. But he was robbed!

Second Samuel 11 tells that on the night David stole Bathsheba, she was past her days of a woman's uncleanness and ready for the conception of a child, and that she did. She did not stay long with David, she returned to her house, and the days passed. A month passed, and she realized something was different. Another month and she knew for sure! She sent a message to the king: "I'm pregnant."

The king would not admit his sin. The pride of life gets to him. He called for Uriah to come home from the battlefield. He tried to make him spend the night with his wife in the hopes that the pregnancy would be considered Uriah's. But the loyal soldier would not do so. He would not enjoy the pleasures of his wife when his comrades were still in the field. He had his integrity, he had his loyalty, he had his standards; David did not. The evil lust of the eye made him a thief, the lust of his flesh made him an adulterer, the pride of his life made him a conspirator of murder. David was trapped. David ordered that Uriah be put in the heat of the battle, and he died.

When the appropriate time of mourning had passed, David lovingly took Bathsheba, a widow with child, into his palace to care for her, to make her his wife, to give honor and integrity to his faithful fallen soldier. His kingdom would love him; his kingdom would adore him. What a great king in the public eye! What an evil king in God's eye!

The ninth month arrived; the child was born. All was well, David knew. Bathsheba knew. The kingdom knew nothing except that the child was born. But God knew! And God had a prophet. Nathan was his name. This man of God entered David's court and told him the story of a thief. David, enraged in anger, decreed that the thief must die. The finger of the prophet pointed to the face of the king, and he said, "Thou art the man" (2 Samuel 12:7). That moment, the baby became sick, and David would mourn for his child, but it died.

Of all the actions of David in his life, this one even the Lord took notice of for its evil. Scripture tells us that David "did that which was right in the eyes of the LORD, and turned not aside from any thing that he commanded him all the days of his life, save only in the matter of Uriah the Hittite" (1 Kings 15:5). Bathsheba gave him four more children, and so did several more concubines. Nineteen children lived at least to early adulthood. At least one, Bathsheba's first, died as an infant. David continued in life, but Uriah could not. He went to the grave, as wealthy as he could possibly have been without the gift of having time to enjoy the pleasure of his treasure.

b) Take a Good Look at the Grave (6:3–5)
(1) A Comfortable Journey (6:3a–b)
(a) A Large and Living Legacy (6:3a)

"If a man beget an hundred children . . ." (6:3a). Rightfully, Solomon should have spoken these words of despair. He should have been concerned about the problem of wealth in life without pleasure. This old man's kingdom was coming apart. The prophet Ahijah had already anointed the next king of Israel who

would control 83 percent of Solomon's kingdom soon. All Solomon had built, all the souls he had led, all the land he had acquired, all the cities and fortresses he had established will be reduced to two small tribes in the southern part of the kingdom, and there was nothing in this world that he could do to change the future course of his life's work. Jeroboam was the man chosen to rule the lion's share of Solomon's dynasty, and he was safe and secure across the Wadi of Egypt where Solomon, with all his political connections and consummated contacts, could not reach him. Rightfully, Solomon had a dose of reality under the sun. Rightfully, Solomon's reign, with all its toils and labors, building projects and acquisitions, was about to end in failure. For all the wealth he had acquired, he had no pleasure in the legacy he would leave.

What had changed? What clenched his attention? What strangled his godless life? Like an Australian boomerang that, if it does not hit its intended target, will return to injure its thrower if he is not paying attention, Solomon had not paid attention to the thing most important—the Lord.

Just about forty years before, Solomon had cast his life on a thwarted journey that had returned to him in his old age. He had lived for the day with no thought of eternity. He had continued to wallow in his old life instead of embracing a new life. Immorality surged. Wrong took precedence over right. No posterity existed. His renowned wisdom blighted his sagacity. His royal fantasy ignored reality. And now, now that his health was gone, he found no pleasure in his journey. Solomon had to face his next step. He had to take a good look at the grave.

Shouldn't this wise preacher have known that the past cannot be changed? Old and decrepit, he looked back in despair and played the what-if game. What if this had been different? What if that was changed? What if another road had been taken? What if a different choice was made? What if, what if, what if?

What could have made Solomon's life better? He daydreams and says, "If a man beget an hundred children," that might provide a comfortable journey and a large and living legacy.

I once heard a preacher, who was considered by his congregation to be the wisest man on earth, a master of all trades, a man's man, a Bible scholar, a walking encyclopedia, lament, "If I had known my child was going to turn out so good, I would have had a dozen." How foolish the wise man was! Even the simplest minded person can testify that no two children are ever the same. Perhaps Solomon had ignored the diversity of his own nineteen siblings. Just look at three that we know a great deal about, Amnon, Absalom, and Adonijah. Solomon should have known better. A hundred children would not guarantee his desire.

(b) A Long and Lengthy Life (6:3b)

"... *and live many years, so that the days of his years be many* ..." (6:3b). But a hundred children would require time, lots of time. If that man bears a hundred children "and live many years, so that the days of his years be many," would that guarantee a comfortable journey? Here Solomon added the one facet he possessed. He would reach his seventieth year although his father's life was ten years longer. His life would be lengthy and long, but he was near its end as he penned this sermon. If Solomon had rested his quill at this point, his mental game would have been but one disappointment and one joy. Thankfully, he did not stop the flow of the ink.

(2) A Coming Judgment (6:3c–5)
(a) A Blighted Soul (6:3c)

"... *and his soul be not filled with good, and also that he have no burial* ..." (6:3c). Solomon could not resist returning to his empty and vain conclusion of his own destiny and his own blighted soul.

Half of his life was steeped in pursuit of that which he could not obtain. More than a thousand women were in the path of his determined goal. Now he sees his own coming judgment. He knows he soon will die, but it has not arrived. The tomb built. The monument etched. The funeral garb sewn. The sepulcher open. The incense stored. The embalming spices ready. The ceremony planned. The caisson drawn. The horses groomed. The harnesses checked. The physicians notified. The mourners hired. The musicians tuned. The dirge selected. The only thing that is missing is the king's death—Solomon's death.

Solomon was not different from most sickly elders; he, too, was wasting the last days and hours of his life retracing the memories, lamenting many moments, languishing over many choices of his misspent life under the sun, all vanity.

(b) A Barren Sepulcher (6:3d)

Look! Perhaps Solomon is casting his stare into the casket that will store the dust of his body for far more days than he ever will live. He speaks, "*I say, that an untimely birth is better than he*" (6:3d). Than who? Solomon!

Had Solomon never been born, his journey would never have existed. The brother killed by him might still have breathed. The barren concubines might have husbands and children. The forced laborers, injured and lamed in his projects, might have been whole and healthy. The kingdom of his father might be in the hands of a sibling and therefore, whole, Godly, sacred, esteemed, faithful, and loyal to the Lord. Solomon's soul is rightfully blighted.

(c) A Burning Sorrow (6:4–5)
(i) What Is So Bitter (6:4)

Clearly taunted by the record of his misspent life, Solomon's burning sorrow engulfs him. He murmurs, *"For he cometh in with vanity, and departeth in darkness, and his name shall be covered with darkness"* (6:4). What is so bitter? Solomon concludes that had he died at birth, none of this would matter, none would be his fault, none would even be known.

(ii) What Is Much Better (6:5)

Solomon further concludes that had he never lived, that would have been much better. He speaks, *"Moreover he hath not seen the sun, nor known any thing: this hath more rest than the other"* (6:5).

In his despair of the moment, knowing his days ahead are few, Solomon cannot escape his coming judgment. The flesh of all shall die and this king, in all his earthly splendor, cannot change the course of his life. Upon his last breath, all his deeds will be sealed in the record book of his life. His world will judge him. His people will judge him. His Lord will judge him. He cannot run from it! Perhaps, he thinks, it would have been better had he never lived. He has lost sight of the purpose of life and here he is taking a long look at the grave.

c) Take a Good Look at the Ghost (6:6)
(1) Death Postponed at Length (6:6a)

Deeper and deeper, Solomon sinks as he takes a good look at the ghost—the ghost of death, postponed at length. He cannot run from it. *"Yea, though he live a thousand years twice told, . . ."* (6:6a). Solomon will have seventy years, far short of the two thousand years. Where can a man travel in two millennia that will take him far enough away from the ghost that lurks near every life? Nowhere! Wishful thinking on Solomon's part for an extended life far beyond the years of anyone who had ever lived.

But Solomon is wise enough to know his health is failing, his days are tallied. But how many remain? A thousand? Six hundred? Three hundred? The one thing that affects Solomon at this point, the catalyst that causes his thoughts, is that he is too sick to do anything to change his past, and he is too healthy not to care. If he were only a little sicker, a little nearer to the ghost of death, then, as with all aged people near death, he would feel so bad that he would not care.

(2) Death Prevailing at Last (6:6b)

More time cannot help Solomon as he looks back at his past and says, *"yet hath he seen no good: do not all go to one place?"* (6:6b). He is so blinded at this point that he questions all that he did in his life. "No good" are the words he uses. It would seem that he would have considered his thoughts and actions as not good long before now. Perhaps during his negotiations with Hiram. Perhaps with the Queen of Sheba. Perhaps with the Hittites, Amorites, Perizzites, Hivites, and Jebusites. Perhaps with the deal for Pharaoh's daughter. Perhaps his plays that have not survived the test of time. Perhaps with his appetite for gifts from other nations. Did he really find "no good" in all of that?

And then the clincher, his conclusion to all that has been for him and will be: "Do not all go to one place?" What a question! How wrong could he be! He has mentioned this before in this sermon when he said, "For that which befalleth the sons of men befalleth beasts; even one thing befalleth them: as the one dieth, so dieth the other; yea, they have all one breath; so that a man hath no preeminence above a beast: for all is vanity. All go unto one place; all are of the dust, and all turn to dust again" (Ecclesiastes 3:19–20). No!

Death will prevail at last, the ancient ghost will ultimately strike every man. All do not go to the same place. But in Solomon's life under the sun, in his rebellion to the living Lord God, he cannot see any good at all in life or the ghost of death. Vanity. Emptiness. Futility. Such is the result of wealth without health to Solomon.

10. The Problem of Life Without Length (6:7–12)
a) The Desire for Food Described (6:7a)

One last problem Solomon has seen. It occurs in the life of virtually every one of his age. It is the problem of life without length. His days are numbered! No more runs in the park. No more swims in the stream, ascents of the stairs, or tracks up the mountains. No more building projects, long trips, or dances in the parlor. He has been relegated to his chair, his bed, and he realizes, *"All the labour of man is for his mouth, . . ."* (6:7a). Every day his desire focuses on food, and it is all he can handle. Eating breakfast is a chore. It just did not hit the spot.

b) The Depths of Folly Described (6:7b–9)

Rather, it is his shallow excuse when he says, *". . . and yet the appetite is not filled"* (6:7b). You must understand that the problem is never the problem! His lack of appetite for food is rarely, if ever, the real problem. Down deep in Solomon's soul rest two issues that rob him of his appetite. If Solomon had not had a change of heart before he began this sermon, he would have most likely here considered this treatise concerning the problem of life without length. But he could not! He knows the reality. He has figured out that the lack of a satisfied appetite is just a physical symptom of an emotional catastrophe deep within. Two characters most often are the culprits. Their names, Despair and Disgust.

(1) A Word of Despair (6:8)
(a) Regarding Wisdom (6:8a)

Solomon gives a word about despair in regard to two things, wisdom and wealth. In regard to wisdom, Solomon says, *"For what hath the wise more than the fool?"* (6:8a). Both are apt to lose their appetite when despair engulfs their souls. Neither the wise nor the fool is any different when despair takes over. Every person is just as susceptible to despair as another. The standing of the wise is no better than that of the fool. Neither is the fool in any better standing than that of the wise.

What, pray tell, is despair? It is hopelessness! The absence of hope. What is hope? It is a feeling of trust that some certain thing will happen. Solomon, at the end of his long life, without a promise of many more days, cannot rely on his God-granted wisdom to find any points of sure trust in his life and despair had taken over. He might as well have been a fool all his life under the sun because the outcome would have been no different—he thinks.

(b) Regarding Wealth (6:8b)

In regard to wealth, Solomon says, *"what hath the poor, that knoweth to walk before the living?"* (6:8b). The one who has everything knows how to walk among the living, but the poor man does the same. He eats one meal at a time just like every other man. His appetite can be filled or unfilled one meal at a time. Solomon, with all his wealth, ranks no better than the poorest man on earth. Both experience the same hopelessness under the sun—true despair. Solomon has met the one named Despair.

(2) A Word of Disgust (6:9)

(a) Staying Desires (6:9a)

Solomon gives a word about his disgust in regard to two things, desires and dreams. In regard to desires Solomon says, *"Better is the sight of the eyes than the wandering of the desire"* (6:9a). Poor old Solomon must settle. No doubt he had spent most of his reign carried by servants here and there on his ornate litter. Surefooted and agile, he could leap from his perch to play at will. But now, at his advanced stage of life, he reveals his disgust. No longer can he leap at this desire or that. Rather, he must settle for what his eyes can still see more than "the wandering of the desire." The Hebrew is *mehaloch nephesh* which literally means *traveling soul*. Solomon has not surrendered his momentary impulses but the deepest desires of his soul. During most of his reign he was carried as a royal. As an old man he was carried as an invalid. His mind still works. His eyes still work. But the rest of his body fails to cooperate. Solomon has met the one named Disgust!

(b) Stupid Dreams (6:9b)

Solomon had reached the point in life where he was consumed by ridiculous dreams. *"This is also vanity and vexation of spirit"* (6:9b). Empty and exasperated of spirit, he soaks in his disgust.

Solomon was no different from Ol' King Saul, his father's predecessor. Poor old Saul, vexed in his spirit, spent a quarter of a century trying to kill the young man anointed to take his place one day, David. All across the hill country of Canaan, he had chased David in vain. It began on that fateful day when David slew the giant, and the people chanted, "Saul hath slain his thousands, and David his ten thousands" (1 Samuel 18:7). A pill not too easy to swallow for the king. Yet he tried until his spirit got the best of him.

One day in deep despair and disgust, King Saul found himself in trouble in battle up on Mount Gilboa. He needed help. His nation needed help. His army needed help. Saul knew that the only man in the kingdom and on earth who could help him was David, but he would not dare call upon David for help. He had tried to kill him no fewer than twenty-four times.

Saul was in a pickle. He could not call upon Samuel because Samuel was dead. He could not call upon heaven because God would not speak to him. It is a horror of eternal magnitude when God remains silent. Even the new puppet high priest could not get an answer from God when he sought the Lord. Saul decided to don a disguise, take a five-mile trip to the little village of Endor, and knock on hell's door.

Down in Endor lived a witch. She was not supposed to be there. By his own command, Saul had decreed that all witches must leave the land. Nevertheless, she remained there in secret, but not so secretly that Saul's men could not find her. The witch was supposed to be able to communicate with the dead; the law of God strictly forbade such attempts (Exodus 22:18; Deuteronomy 18:9–12).

She was leery of Saul from the start. He did not look like the king but there was something about him that made her nervous. He demanded her to do something that she could not really do—collaborate with the dead. People who tamper with spiritism imagine that they are talking with loved ones who have gone on before but in fact they are communicating with fakes (1 Samuel 28:6–25). Instead of calling upon the Lord for answers, these witches call upon the demons. But the demons have no authority or ability to actually do what Saul has asked this witch to do.

There in her abode, King Saul commanded the witch to summon Samuel up from the dead. No doubt, she had accomplices hiding in the shadows to assist in the charade. She had a reputation that made her stand out and made her the target of Saul's desperation. Today witches such as these are called psychics, and their little houses of business can be seen in almost every town and city in the world. The Bible expressly forbids any communication with that kind.

The witch of Endor began her customary mumbo-jumbo and hocus-pocus. Someone in the shadows would impersonate and speak from the shadows. It would be just an audible encounter; she could never conjure up a visual because no witch ever could. It was all a sham! But this witch was terrified by what actually happened. She said, "An old man cometh up; and he is covered with a mantle." The Holy Spirit adds, "And Saul perceived that it was Samuel" (1 Samuel 28:14). Saul saw Samuel with some kind of a body, one which could be described, one recognized. Her particular demon, which may have been her assistant behind the curtain, could not produce this miracle. The same Spirit who would one day raise our Lord Jesus Christ from the dead materialized Samuel at that moment. The seemingly impossible had happened. The interaction between Saul and Samuel went like this.

> And Samuel said to Saul, Why hast thou disquieted me, to bring me up? And Saul answered, I am sore distressed; for the Philistines make war against me, and God is departed from me, and answereth me no more, neither by prophets, nor by dreams: therefore I have called thee, that thou mayest make known unto me what I shall do. Then said Samuel, Wherefore then dost thou ask of me, seeing the Lord is departed from thee, and is become thine enemy? And the Lord hath done to him, as he spake by me: for the Lord hath rent the kingdom out of thine hand, and given it to thy neighbour, even to David: because thou obeyedst not the voice of the Lord, nor executedst his fierce wrath upon Amalek, therefore hath the Lord done this thing unto thee this day. Moreover the Lord will also deliver Israel with thee into the hand of the Philistines: and to morrow shalt thou and thy sons be with me: the Lord also shall deliver the host of Israel into the hand of the Philistines. (1 Samuel 28:15–19)

Saul fell on his face in fear! The witch sought to bring him comfort with a meal, but he refused and would not eat (1 Samuel 28:23). She killed the fatted calf and made the unleavened bread anyway. By the time it was done, he and his servants ate a little. That night, under the cover of darkness, Saul and his men returned to Mount Gilboa. The next day he died in his despair and disgust by his own hands with his own sword. In order to kill himself he had to fall on his sword in disgrace.

Solomon had spent his forty years as king on a similar path as Saul had spent his forty years as king: on terms of rebellion against the Lord. In this sermon, Solomon has not given a clue yet if he will change his direction. From here, he develops a fatal doctrine instead.

c) The Doctrine of Fatalism Described (6:10–12)
(1) You Cannot Change Your Fate (6:10a)

And so Solomon developed a doctrine of fatalism. He had determined that you cannot change your fate. *"That which hath been is named already, and it is known that it is man"* (6:10a). In other words, Solomon had subjugated everything that occurs in a man's life to destiny and that man is powerless to change any part of it.

(2) You Cannot Challenge Your Fate (6:10b)

He had determined that you cannot challenge your fate. *"Neither may he contend with him that is mightier than he"* (6:10b). Somewhere in the vast universe the playbook had been written, the plot had been set, the script had been sealed, the stage had been designed. Moreover, the actors had rehearsed, the audience had arrived in their seats, the tickets had been punched, and the lights had been focused. The curtain was pulled—and there Solomon stood on a stage that he had no control over in a seventy-year play and a role that was tailor-made for this king who must recite every word. His destiny had been designed by someone else greater than he.

(3) You Cannot Choose Your Fate (6:11–12)
(a) Life Is Very Shallow at Best (6:11)

He had also determined that you cannot choose your fate. Solomon sees that life is very shallow at best. *"Seeing there be many things that increase vanity, what is man the better?"* (6:11). Perhaps along the saga of Solomon's life this or that came along that might change the path, it might add to the performance just a tad. What would be the result? Will it change the ending? Absolutely not! Life is shallow for Solomon the actor. The play is the story, and the actor is paid to follow the script. No depth, no difference. No better, no worse. What is written is what must be performed. The end is the same with or without embellishment. The fate cannot be chosen by the actor—man.

(b) Life Is Very Short at Best (6:12)

Solomon saw in this problem of life without length under the sun that life is very short at best. *"For who knoweth what is good for man in this life, all the days of his vain life which he spendeth as a shadow? for who can tell a man what shall be after him under the sun?"* (6:12). Decrepit and sickly, Solomon could not see past his last breath with his doctrine of fatalism. Is there something after this life for him? Is there anything after this life for any man? Is the fate of all men the same as all beasts of the field? After the last breath—nothing? Vanity! In the span of all eternity, Solomon's life filled but a speck of time. No one on earth had heard of him before he was born. Seventy years later Solomon wonders if anyone will remember him when he is gone. What could he have done better? What could he have done differently? One more building? One more ceremony? One less tax? One less wife? One exciting trip? One exciting gift? One profound proverb? One profound song? One nothing? Nothing will change his destiny. He found himself no different from many at the sunset of life, filled with despair, filled with disgust in a predetermined life where his days were numbered and the last one was soon to arrive.

    C. Things He Had Studied (7:1–10:20)
        1. Life's Frustrations (7:1–29)
            a) Cynicism About the Better Things of Life (7:1–14)
               (1) Character Values (7:1a)

How is it that Solomon knew about all the problems about which he had just preached? He knew because he had studied. Oh, how he had studied this thing he calls life under the sun. You and I know that life can be lived in the joy and blessing of the Lord with His hand gently and lovingly guiding by clearing the way, straightening the paths, raising the valleys, lowering the hills. Or, on the other hand, life can be lived in rebellion to the Lord, without His help, without His guidance, without His Spirit. That's exactly where Solomon has lived for the past forty years as king of Israel.

    Oh, how he had studied life. His life in reckless rebellion to the Lord God Almighty foreordained him to be king long before the crack of creation. What had he seen? Life's frustrations for one thing. Life's fallacies for another. Then life's finalities soon to be his; life's falseness in his past and life's fickleness at every turn. For each, Solomon had developed pitiful little concrete sayings, each with at least two contrasting points. We might call them proverbs. Proverbs they are! Many of these are found also in the book of Proverbs, although with a twist of cynicism included.

    So in Solomon's continued lament over the meaninglessness of life under the sun, he begins with life's frustrations, and he will use proverbs to prove up his point. To this place in his sermon he has laid out his case as in a court of law, but now he must lay out the proof. Proof of what? Proof that in his cynical opinion the better things of life are true. At the core, Solomon does not believe there are better things in life. He begins his pitiful case with two statements that call upon the emotion of people and their staunch character values. *"A good name is better than precious ointment"* (7:1a), he says. In general, both man and God will agree with that character value, at least for those people who have an ounce of character within them. Thankfully, it seems that the majority of people do.

Do not be fooled by Solomon's words that we find here. This well-known proverb of Solomon has been altered for this sermon. We find the original in Proverbs 22:1, "A good name is rather to be chosen than great riches." Let us look at some of the examples of a good name from the Exploring Series commentary for that verse.

> This verse reminds me of the old French count who, because of the spendthrift ways of his ancestors, was reduced to living in a common lodging house in the Paris slums. When his neighbors invited him to join in their lawless expeditions, he pulled himself up to his full height and said, "Thank you, but no! You see, I am a French count, *Noblesse Oblige*. Privilege has its responsibilities. If I were to do as you suggest I should bring dishonor upon the noble name I bear. I pray you, have me excused."
>
> Then there is the story of the little southern boy who, when asked his name, replied, "Ah is George Washington."
>
> The man who had asked his name said, "My! That is a great name. You will have to be careful that you *live* like George Washington."
>
> The little fellow responded: "Of course ah behave like George Washington. Ah *is* George Washington!'
>
> A soldier in the army of Alexander the Great was a habitual offender and a malingerer. When he was brought before the general for punishment, the commander-in-chief looked at the soldier and asked his name. "Alexander," the man replied.
>
> "Look here, soldier," said the conqueror, "you either change your behavior or you change your name." . . .
>
> Writers of fiction know the value of names. Think of Bunyan's characters: Mr. Worldly Wiseman and Madam Bubble, for example. Then there was Mr. Brisk, who made an attempt to court Mercy, but Bunyan had his number—Mr. Brisk was "a man of some breeding, and that pretended to religion, but a man that stuck very close to the world." Mercy soon sent him about his business. And what a collection of wretches comprised the jury in the town of Vanity Fair when Faithful was put on trial for

his life: Mr. High-mind, Mr. Enmity, Mr. Liar, Mr. Cruelty, Mr. Hate-light, Mr. Implacable, Mr. Blind-man, Mr. No-good, Mr. Malice, Mr. Love-lust, Mr. Live-loose, and Mr. Heady.

Dickens was just as good as Bunyan at naming characters. Who can forget his artful Dodger, or Mr. Fang the magistrate, or Mr. Bumble, or Mr. Grimwig, who offered to eat his head if Oliver did not abscond with the money? And who can forget the terrible Mr. Murdstone, the bane of David Copperfield's early life? Or the execrable Uriah Heep? Or Mr. Stryver, the pushy up-and-coming lawyer? Or Magwitch the convict? How appropriate for a discontented young man to be Pip, and a mean old miser to be Scrooge! Then there was Pecksniff, the arch-hypocrite; Mrs. Gamp, the disreputable old nurse with an indispensable large umbrella; Quilp, "an uglier dwarf than could be found anywhere for a penny" and Gradgrind, the ruthless utilitarian. The names alert us to what we can expect from the characters.

Solomon, a keener observer than either Dickens or Bunyan, said, "A good name is rather to be chosen than great riches." And have not we who love the Lord been given a good name? There is a whole bevy of good names by which we are known in the New Testament: believers, brethren, saints, disciples. We should be proud of all these names and strive to live up to them. But there is a touch of special genius in the perceptiveness of the pagan people of Antioch who coined the name *Christians*. They chose it for the disciples in the first century and it has stayed with us from that day to this.[36]

But there is a grave difference between a good name being better and a good name being chosen. The first is just happenstance, the second requires an action. In this sermon a good name is not chosen, it is fate for Solomon! In Solomon's doctrine, if you are lucky enough to have a good name in your life there was nothing you did to bring that name to yourself. You either have it or you do not. To confuse the matter more, your inherited good name does not guarantee that you are good! Many a soul in this world has had a good name in the public realm but deep, hidden, dark, evil secrets in the private. For proof, just look at all the highly esteemed actors and politicians whose names are revered for decades in the public life until their private secret life is revealed and their careers are destroyed.

Solomon preaches that a good name is better, but better than what? "A good name is better than precious ointment"? Here and in Proverbs 22:1, the focus is often on the good name, but what about the good ointment? Not everyone would agree with Solomon's statement. Do you remember the last days of our Lord on this earth? He was in Bethany and he entered the home of Simon the leper for a visit. They were not there by themselves. The Apostles were there. A woman was there too, a sinner she was. Matthew tells us that the woman had an alabaster flask of very expensive oil. She poured it on our Lord's head. An Apostle rebuked her and said the oil could have been sold for a great deal of money which could be given to the poor (Matthew 26:7–12). The Apostle John tells us that the woman was Mary, the sister of Lazarus, whom the Lord had raised from the dead (John 11:2). Six days later our Lord was in Lazarus' home there in Bethany too. Mary was there. That was her home. Martha, their sister, was in the kitchen trying to scrounge up a meal. The Apostles were nearby. Mary had another expensive flask of oil, about a pound in weight, and she poured it all on the Lord. This time we know the name of the Apostle who rebuked her; this time we know for sure that it was Judas Iscariot. His complaint was the same as it was the week before. This time John tells us how much Judas thought it was worth.

"Why was not this ointment sold for three hundred pence, and given to the poor?" (John 12:5). But John continued to explain the true character value of Judas' life, telling us, "This he said, not that he cared for the poor; but because he was a thief, and had the bag, and bare what was put therein" (John 12:6). Judas was a thief. Judas Iscariot, the son of Simon the leper, of the town of Bethany (John 12:4)! Twice in a week's time Mary anointed the Lord with good expensive oil and twice Judas complained and showed his true colors, first in his father's house and then in Mary's. Such an extravagant gift to the Lord was a waste in the mind of Judas. Three hundred pence was the price he thought he could get for that good ointment, the price of spikenard, that is, the price of an alabaster flask of the aromatic oil from the East Indian plant called the *Nardoshachys jatamansi*. Now a man in Bible times would work all day for a pence. The Greek word for pence is *denarion*, from which we get the word denarii or denarius, and most other translations of Judas' complaint say, "Why was not this ointment sold for three hundred denarii?" It was a Roman coin often called a penny. A denarii was the common daily wage for most jobs in the Bible, and it is the currency most frequently mentioned in all of Scripture. Three hundred pence would be three hundred days' work. To Judas, the spikenard of good oil was worth much more than a years' wages and it was wasted on the Lord, twice in a week—two years wages, if you catch the drift. No wonder Judas, the thief, threw a fit.

You know the rest of the story. Judas Iscariot was not concerned about a good name; he was concerned about the money. In just days he would slip over to the high priests and make a deal for himself that involved thirty pieces of silver for the positive identification of the good man with a good name, Jesus. The silver shekel of the Temple amounted to almost four pence each and it was the highest price the priest would pay; therefore, the life of the Lord was worth about 120 days' wages, the market value of a slave or the retribution for an ox goring a slave. That's the price of Judas' loyalty to the Lord, the price for which He could be purchased.

I dare say, Solomon knew too many stories like that of Jesus and Judas which had occurred in his business dealings and that is the reason he was not willing to quote the proverb in this sermon the way he quoted it in the book of Proverbs. He was cynical about both, the good name and the good ointment. Is Solomon really sure about one being better than the other?

(2) Conventional Values (7:1b–6)
(a) Life's Sum (7:1b)

Solomon cannot be sure about the character values of a good name versus a good ointment. Why? Because he has looked at the conventional values of life and summed it up somehow. He says, *". . . and the day of death than the day of one's birth"* (7:1b). Both man and God disagree with this statement. The day of a person's birth is the day of his beginning in this world. The life he lives is a blessed opportunity from the Lord to choose Him. It is also a blessed chance to do something good for someone who needs to see the Lord. Solomon has already established that, in his mind, there is nothing after death, so how can the day of one's death be better than his birth? Why does this proverb speed to the grave? Is it because of life's sorrows?

(b) Life's Sorrows (7:2–4)
(i) The House of Mourning (7:2)

Solomon must also face the conventional values of life's sorrows. He does not focus on the future and a glorious eternity. He focuses on a house full of depressed and tearful souls here on earth. *"It is better to go to the house of mourning, than to go to the house of feasting: for that is the end of all men; and the living will lay it to his heart"* (7:2).

The thoughts of the worldly man make no sense at all. Repeatedly in his sermon,

Solomon has concluded that man should eat, drink, and be merry for after this life there is nothing left but rotting in the grave. Yet, in this proverb, he states that it is better to go to the funeral of someone than to a party. Is death better than life in man's heart? Because death is the ultimate destiny of all men, is attending a funeral better than attending a party?

True, a countdown begins with the birth of every child. With that child a living soul comes with a built-in fuse. Some fuses burn quickly; some burn slowly. With every birth there will come a death when the fuse burns out. Between birth and death there is a one-way, dead-end street. Every day four or five people are born every second, about four hundred thousand every twenty-four hours. But every day, hundreds of thousands leave this earth bound for eternity, their time when their fuse has burned out. We do not know the length of our fuse. It is no wonder that God urges each of us to number our days and apply our hearts unto wisdom.

I cannot help but remember the story of that sad night in the cold Atlantic. The *Titanic* had hit an iceberg and begun to plunge slowly into the icy sea. On board there were many souls, and the stark reality of the countdown of their lives had begun; the burning out of the fuses of their souls was imminent. Some decided to drink to their death. Reports say that some argued, others were in great despair. This world is like that, too, but on a much grander scale. Daily, it carries an enormous passenger list to the chilly waters of the grave.

We know that we should look to God, but it is not Solomon's purpose to make that point yet in his sermon. He still must prove the insanity of his cynicism concerning life without a God under the sun. To Solomon, ending the toil and struggle of life and going into obscurity is better than living on earth. It is a sad commentary on the sum of his search for wisdom. Death is at his door and ever present on his mind. Why does Solomon speed from the party to the funeral? Is the funeral a reality check on the meaninglessness of life? Is it because of the heart of man?

(ii) The Heart of Man (7:3–4)
(a) Things We Laugh About (7:3)

People of this frustrated world, living without God, do not want a person to be happy. Solomon had studied this and determined in his cynicism that in the heart of man there are things that we laugh about. He says, *"Sorrow is better than laughter: for by the sadness of the countenance the heart is made better"* (7:3). This way of thinking about life is warped. Solomon has said it on purpose. In

Proverbs 14:13 the reverse is spoken: "Even in laughter the heart is sorrowful; and the end of that mirth is heaviness." There, Solomon knows that laughter is a good medicine to ease the pain of deep sorrow, momentarily at least. It is the heavy heart briefly lightened by a joyful song or thought. But many cultures and many religions teach that man can find happiness only through sorrow. A man must experience how bad life is before he can appreciate the few good things that come along from time to time. "For when a face is sad a heart may be happy," he says. Once again, this belief is fostered in life without God.

The world without the Lord will never make us happy. It is filled with our sins. We are filled with guilt because of our sins. We are miserable. Sorrow latches on and points us directly to the path of hell's gate. Where is the happy heart in that? It is nowhere to be found. Solomon did not say, "when the face is sad" the heart *will* be happy. He said it *"may* be happy." There is a world of difference between the word *will* and the word *may*. The first is a fact. The last is a hope. In this sermon, Solomon has taken hold of only one end of the stick. He needs to grab the other end where he will find the Lord.

Thanks to God, the Lord offers joy. That is not happiness! Happiness all too often depends on circumstances and outcomes, but joy, real joy in life, unspeakable joy that is full of glory, can come only in a relationship with the Lord (Psalm 16:11; 1 Peter 1:8). Solomon may have found a happy heart behind a sad face, and he may have found that true in the godless world he lived in, but the Lord came to make laughter better than sorrow and joy better than a sad face.

(b) Things We Learn About (7:4)

Solomon finds himself bogged down in sorrow and he cannot let go of the idea of death. He ties sorrow to the plight of wisdom, and pleasure to the plight of the simpleminded fool. He says, *"The heart of the wise is in the house of mourning; but the heart of fools is in the house of mirth"* (7:4). Is the wise mind found in the house of mourning and the fool's mind found in the house of pleasure? Is that what Solomon has really learned with all his wisdom? In truth, it should be the other way around, but not in Solomon's frustrated mind. For him, the fool accepts death as part of life, celebrating the life of the dead person and continuing to live life in celebration of each day given to him. For him, the mind of the wise, stymied by the grave, questions every aspect of the event that causes mourning and, therefore, dreads every part of life. Frustrated, he says, "This life is not going to end well, so why bother?"

> (c) Life's Seriousness (7:5–6)
>> (i) The Rebuking Comment of the Farsighted Man (7:5)

It is serious business, this thing called life! What is a man to do with the life he has been given? Solomon continues to be frustrated with his life and his cynicism bursts forth in this proverb. He was granted wisdom from the Lord and it has brought him nothing but pain. He speaks, *"It is better to hear the rebuke of the wise, than for a man to hear the song of fools"* (7:5).

Solomon has searched everything under the sun within his limits and he has calculated the results of each. It is thought that the farsighted man has gathered wisdom from the ends of the earth. But which is easier to swallow, the rebuke of the wise or the serenade of the fool? The rebuke settles uneasily on the last nerve of a man. The song of the fool is much easier to accept. It soothes for the moment. It does not warn of the future. But the wise man will take every opportunity to give direction so mistakes will not be repeated. Could it be that in all that he has studied he has found frustration in the actions of those who have sought his wisdom and evidently failed to heed his counsel? After all, for forty years, "All the earth sought to Solomon, to hear his wisdom, which God had put in his heart" (1 Kings 10:24). But do they take his counsel to heart? One of Solomon's favorite themes can be found in his words, "A wise son heareth his father's instruction: but a scorner heareth not rebuke" (Proverbs 13:1). Rehoboam, the king's son, has spent much time in the palace of his father. He has heard each of his father's proverbs ad nauseam. In solid stupidity he has rejected most, if not all, of them. See him there in your mind's eye in the court of Solomon. Sullen faced. Closed-minded. Bored by the dusty and dry. He'd rather be out and about. Solomon was not that way with his father and the dealings in the court of King David. At the end of every case, he wanted to know how his father made the decision and, perhaps, why a penalty was not imposed according to the maximum allowed by law.

Rebuke? Solomon knew about rebuke. But the classic example in his life was not from David, but from God! Remember in 1 Kings 11. Don't you remember the judgment of God on the throne of Solomon? It was because of how he had wasted his wisdom. There, God made it clear to Solomon that after his death his kingdom would be divided into two independent monarchies. The successor of the newly established crown, the head of ten of the tribes, had already been selected and the prophet Ahijah was about to announce his kingship and protect him from Solomon. Solomon did not repent. He failed to learn that lesson from his father. Had David heard the same words from God, he would have written a psalm of penitence to the Lord immediately. Not so with Solomon; he dug in his heels and sought the life of Jeroboam. Needless to say, Solomon's son had learned the wrong lessons from his father! Rehoboam would prove the point when he declares that his little finger is mightier than the waist of his father. He would not listen to the counselors of his father but leaned on the counsel of his young foolish friends. It was easier to swallow and more pleasurable to spew out his rage before the elders of the ten northern tribes. It will not be the only mistake made by Solomon's son, for he was a fool.

Solomon firmly believed that the one who listened to the song of the fool would continue to make the same mistakes over and over until the hard reality of the mistakes reared their ugly heads. Then it would be far too late for a fellow to correct his course because the damage was done, all the while he was enjoying the melody of the fool. It is serious, and as Solomon looked back on his life, he must have known he was guilty.

(ii) The Ribald Cackling of the Foolish Man (7:6)

Frustrated by his life, Solomon associates his actions with a sound he has heard all his life. His proverb says, *"For as the crackling of thorns under a pot, so is the laughter of the fool: this also is vanity"* (7:6). The trunks of the Texas mesquite tree rarely grow larger than an inch or so in diameter. The branches of this tree seldom grow larger than the thickness of a pencil. When placed in the fire, they quickly pop and burn away while creating a hot fire that lasts for only a few minutes. So, too, is the laughter of the fool. It is alive like the fire of the thorn bush under the pot, but it lasts only a few minutes. Without fuel, the fire soon dies out, and so it is with the song of the fool. It will die unless more fuel is added. The fire is meaningless. Although it burns hot for a moment, it will not last long enough to heat the pot of stew or roast the skewer of meat. Wood must be added to continue the fire but that too will burn quickly. So is the laughter of the fool. It lasts for only a few minutes. Without additional fuel, the laughter soon dies out. And so is the cackling of the foolish man! A serious thing among the conventional values of life!

(3) Contemptible Values (7:7)

Solomon casts his eyes on another facet of life, that of its contemptible values. Cynically, he says, *"Surely oppression maketh a wise man mad; and a gift destroyeth the heart"* (7:7). His frustration abounds. Oppression exists everywhere. Does it make a wise man mad? Surely! The wise man knows and understands when true injustice oppresses the soul of a man and he hates it. He hates every aspect of oppression. Just what kind of oppression has Solomon experienced? Where can we find oppression in Solomon's life? He's had it all. Done it all. Controlled it all. Manipulated it all. Is there one shred of oppression for Solomon recorded in the Holy Writ?

When was Solomon persecuted, abused, maltreated mentally, physically or spiritually? Surely no one on earth dared do such to him, the mighty king of Israel. Had Solomon observed the oppression of men that he considered wise? Did their oppression lead to insanity? The Authorized Version (KJV) translates the Hebrew word *halal* as "mad." *Halal* means to be boastful or arrogant, perhaps even to act insanely in that arrogance. Solomon's intent must mean that oppression makes a wise man do things he would never do under normal circumstances. He becomes contemptible, disgraceful, despicable, and distasteful, his values compromised. Did Solomon allow such oppression in his kingdom? Why would he? Nay, we must say! That was not the motive of the king. He is not speaking of others; he is speaking of his own life. His age has oppressed him, his health has oppressed him, and his reprobate life has oppressed him. It is a serious thing for this king; he has been his own oppressor, and it has affected him mentally!

The second contemptible value hangs on Solomon's words, "and a gift destroyeth the heart." I wonder why the English translated the Hebrew words *mattana abad* as "gift destroyeth" when the negative sense of the context would be *bribe corrupts*. We might find a way to construe a gift to "destroy the heart." Money lavished on a child, the one with the golden spoon in his mouth, often destroys the life of that child, at least in the minds of many of the adult onlookers, but that is not Solomon's point. He is talking about that which destroys the heart of a man, not a child. He is talking about a bribe. Bribes can turn the heart of a man. They can redirect the integrity of a man. They can corrupt a man thought to be incorruptible in his morals, decisions, basically his faithfulness and fairness to others. Solomon understands this! Many a good man has found himself chasing the allurement of a bribe. A person who is not satisfied with the provisions of God in his life can therefore be tempted by the lure of position, money, notoriety, gifts, or whatever else someone uses to bribe him into a decision he would not normally make. It is another one of Solomon's frustrations with the better things of life. Compare the opposite; the fool is not made insane by oppression. It is a curse for only the wise man. Two contemptible values of frustration for old Solomon!

(4) Conclusive Values (7:8a)

The contemptible values lead Solomon to a thought about conclusive values. He speaks, *"Better is the end of a thing than the beginning thereof"* (7:8a). Do you see the two values? They are bookends. Every project has them, and every life has them too! They are conclusive, definite, irrefutable. The end! The beginning! But which is really better? Out of context, Solomon's statement seems true. The end of a matter is better than its beginning. To build a beautiful cabinet all begins with a thought, an idea which leads to a draftsman who draws the design. The wood is selected, dried, cut to a rough size, finished with a joiner, and a planer, readied for the craftsman to do his work. Finally, the cabinet arrives at the home and it brings great joy to the owner who began the process. In that case the end is better than the beginning.

But a good dose of reality should set in at this point. In real life, for those of us who love living, the opposite is usually true, the beginning is better than the end. For those of us who struggle with living, hiccups in life continually throw a curve. Think of how many marriages start great but end badly. Most of us are great at starting, yet we sometimes grow weary and seldom finish. Most of us barrel down a road until we hit a snag. When we do not know what to do, we abandon that road and take a detour, repeating the process again and again. Here we find Solomon! In his frustration with his own reprobate life, Solomon determines that the end is better than the beginning because it all ends in emptiness and death which is better than life. Our writer of this message believes that life is hopeless. Why not just die and be done with it? After all, Solomon has already made the case that after this there is nothing. Remember his words, "For that which befalleth the sons of men befalleth beasts; even one thing befalleth them: as the one dieth, so dieth the other; yea, they have all one breath; so that a man hath no preeminence above a beast: for all is vanity" (Ecclesiastes 3:19). Solomon is ready to get it over with.

(5) Crucial Values (7:8b–9)
(a) The Principle Expressed (7:8b)

Then we see that in light of Solomon's desire for life to be over, the principle of certain crucial values still exists. He recognizes those values when he says, *"and the patient in spirit is better than the proud in spirit"* (7:8b). Solomon has not lost his wisdom; he still understands the difference between these two crucial values, that of the patient and the proud. Surely, the patient is always better than the proud.

Here, Solomon is trying to express a principle. Everyone can understand the concept of patience. Most struggle with it. But the concept of being proud may not make plain common sense in this passage. No one should find fault with pride. We should take pride in our families, our works, our lives. A healthy pride cannot be argued; such pride shows the character of a person's life and accomplishments. Here, we must switch gears and grasp a different definition for the word "proud." The Hebrew is *gabeah*; the Authorized Version (KJV) translates it as "proud"; the New American Standard Version translates it as "haughty"; but the best translation for today's reader would be the word "arrogant." That word hits the spot. That word tells the tale, for there is a crucial difference between the patient and the arrogant. Solomon says patience is better than arrogance, but the context of this passage is about patience to wait for the end to finally come so the good and the bad will be over. Arrogance considers the future, longing for the meaninglessness of life to be over under the sun. Both are crucial to Solomon. The first will wait; the second will make haste into a spirit of folly.

We must admit, nine times out of ten, arrogance, leading to a spirit of hasty folly, is no asset to anyone. For an example we can look a little more than eighty-six years past the life of Solomon and see Israel's King Jehoram. As the son of wicked King Ahab, he did not take the throne directly after his father's death. His brother Azariah took the throne for two years first. Although Jehoram destroyed the images of Baal erected by his father, he continued to be a worshiper of the calf instituted by Jeroboam some eighty-odd years before. Although the Northern Kingdom may have been a godless country, it was not without the presence of God. His prophet Elisha was there to speak and act on behalf of the Almighty. As for Jehoram's attitude about Elisha, it ranged from ambivalence to dislike.

As king, Jehoram was under constant threat from Ben-hadad, the king of Syria. Ben-hadad's general was Naaman who won a decisive victory against King Ahab about three years before. Many hold that it was Naaman who drew his bow to fling the arrow that killed Ahab (1 Kings 22:34). Back in Syria, Naaman learned from a slave girl that he might find healing for his leprosy in Jehoram's kingdom. Naaman approached Ben-hadad and asked for aid in going to the Northern Kingdom to seek healing. A letter was written questioning the words of the maid about the prophet in Samaria (2 Kings 5:3–6).

Upon the arrival of Naaman, with his letter from Ben-hadad, arrogant Jehoram flew into an episode of foolish rage. Jehoram screamed, "Am I God, to kill and to make alive, that this man doth send unto me to recover a man of his leprosy? wherefore consider, I pray you, and see how he seeketh a quarrel against me" (2 Kings 5:7). Jehoram had a short fuse. But lest we forget, Naaman was known for his short fuse. The meeting of the two was a tedious moment. No doubt an explosion was about to take the Northern Kingdom into war with Syria over Naaman's request for healing. Nothing but Elisha's timely message and intervention averted the angry words from both sides.

Solomon, in his own investigation, understood the difference between the spirit of the patient and the spirit of arrogant pride. He knew, in principle, the importance of kindness and the patience of others as intervention to save the arrogant fool of his folly!

(b) The Principle Expanded (7:9)

Solomon not just expressed the principle of the crucial values of the patient in spirit versus the spirit of the proud, he expanded the principle. *"Be not hasty in thy spirit to be angry: for anger resteth in the bosom of fools"* (7:9). In Proverbs 14:17, Solomon covered this topic in his words, "He that is soon angry dealeth foolishly." In John Phillips' *Exploring Proverbs* we find the following example of an arrogant and prideful fool.

> One man whose life illustrates this proverb is England's powerful Plantagenet king, Henry II. Sixteen words he uttered in a fit of temper undid a lifetime of striving and planning for the good of England and the power of the throne. . . .
>
> In their youth Henry and Thomas Becket became firm friends. The son of a commoner, Becket was trained by Theobald, the archbishop of Canterbury, and became a polished man of the world. He was a brilliant talker and thinker and possessed great charm and diplomacy. Henry made his friend chancellor of England and Becket turned the position into one of far-reaching influence. Soon Becket was the power behind the throne and everyone knew it. His loyalty to the king was absolute. . . .
>
> Meanwhile the papacy under Alexander III was asserting itself throughout Europe. The church in England, Roman Catholic to the core, was at the height of its influence and power. Rome ruled with an iron hand. People worshiped God, His Son, and the virgin and bowed to pope, cardinal, bishop, and priest with simple unquestioning faith. The

church was immensely rich and powerful because when rich men died they often left their lands and money to the church to pay for prayers to be said for the good of their souls. Churchmen were as arrogant as barons. Henry was determined to curb the power of the papacy in England and his closest ally was his chancellor. . . .

Then Theobald died leaving vacant the post of archbishop of Canterbury, which was second in power only to the throne itself. Henry had a brilliant idea: *Why not make Becket archbishop of Canterbury? If I put such a loyal subject as Thomas in this all-powerful ecclesiastical post, I will have a leader in the church who has never failed to support me in my secular desires and designs.* From the standpoint of the throne the idea seemed perfect—a marriage of church and state designed to strengthen the throne. . . .

"If you do as you say," Becket declared, "you will soon hate me, my lord king, as much as you love me now." But Henry was not to be denied. . . .

However, Henry's hopes of combining the offices of archbishop and chancellor were soon dashed. The new archbishop at once resigned his post as chancellor and a remarkable change took place. The ostentatious, flamboyant, and worldly Becket disappeared. In his place appeared an austere ascetic, a zealot determined to uphold all the privileges and power of the Roman church in England. Henry was stunned. War was declared between these two resolute and powerful men. . . .

The fierce battle went on for years. Becket threatened to excommunicate Henry. (People thrust out of the church were believed to be damned and were boycotted, ostracized, and treated as lepers.) Henry retaliated by having his son Henry crowned as coregent by the archbishop of York, Becket's rival. And so, it went on. . . .

The fateful words were spoken when Henry was in France. Aggravated by the archbishop's latest move, Henry raised his fist above his head and cried in a towering rage, "What cowards have I about me that no one will deliver me from this lowborn priest!" He regretted the words at once, but it was too late. Four knights had already gone on their way to rid the king of his enemy. They arrived at Canterbury and followed Becket into the sanctuary. They exchanged bitter words with the archbishop and killed him. . . .

Becket was considered a martyr, and the pope made him a saint. Then the pope brought out his big guns and threatened to excommunicate

Henry and put England under interdict. No bells would be rung, no masses would be said, no marriages would be performed, no confessions would be heard, and nobody would be shriven before dying.

The threat was all an elaborate Roman farce but almost everyone believed it.

Henry capitulated. Rome's power and authority, against which Henry had been struggling for years, was fully reimposed in England. Other costly exactions were required. The king had to walk barefoot through Canterbury and humble himself before Becket's tomb. He had to make confession and beg forgiveness. Meekly this powerful king bared his back to receive stripes laid on him by the officers and monks of Canterbury. His back was cut open to the bone. He sat in silence and pain the whole night in front of the tomb of his baseborn priest.

The king had played dice with Rome and lost. He had lost his temper and dealt foolishly. A few words spoken in anger had given crafty Rome its opportunity, and Rome played as usual with loaded dice.[37]

Being eager to be angry is part of the heart of the fool and resides in his bosom. There is no sense in anger. It is worthless. Anger is fleeting, and so it is in the heart of fools. Anger frustrates Solomon.

(6) Comparative Values (7:10)

Solomon has not lost the last bit of his common sense and wisdom, even in his frustrated and cynical state of mind. He speaks, *"Say not thou, What is the cause that the former days were better than these? for thou dost not enquire wisely concerning this"* (7:10). He understands that comparisons of values of the past and present do not entirely line up.

We often hear someone speaking of the "good old days." All have lived through experiences that cause us to cherish them as the "good old days." Yet, were they the good days? They were part of our past and belong to no one else. Were they the good days when bathing occurred once a week and the wash was hung on the line in the backyard? Were they the good days when the water had to be heated on the stove for the bath and the wash? Were they the good days when soap was made in a fifty-five-gallon drum over a fire in the backyard? Were they the good days when schools were air-conditioned by opening a window and running a fan? Were they the good days when firewood had to be cut in order to warm the house? Were they good days when beds were passed down from generation to generation regardless of their condition? Perhaps the memories of the better days of the past have overtaken the memories of the bitter days of the past. With every generation through time, innovations have made things better for the present. It is true that the innovations of the last two hundred years have come at a much more rapid pace than all the time before; nevertheless, with every generation came inventions that made life easier and better than the days before, as slow as they may have been to arrive.

(7) Concrete Values (7:11–12)
(a) Wisdom in the Daily Things of Life (7:11)

In the midst of Solomon's frustration with the better things of life, he still sees two concrete values. For the first he says, *"Wisdom is good with an inheritance: and by it there is profit to them that see the sun"* (7:11).

Notice the two parts to Solomon's first thought. One is inheritance, the other is profit. Both are good for the man living "under the sun." But what inheritance? What profit? Does the absence of either negate the goodness of wisdom? At first glance, Solomon's statement seems true, but it is encased in a context of false, negative, worldly thought. Is he saying wisdom and money provide protection? How false can that be? Wisdom does not keep us from making the same mistakes over and over again. If you cannot manage your money before an inheritance, you will surely mismanage any inheritance you will receive. Money can make the road a little easier to navigate for a while but, in the end, it will not last, it surely does not guarantee protection from harm. To say that wisdom, coupled with an inheritance, preserves the life of its possessor is compelling. But in the context of this passage, it is a false statement. Solomon has not used his wisdom or inheritance correctly and he will prove it to himself in the last two chapters of the sermon.

We must pause to look at the word "inheritance." When the first English translations used that word, it did not mean to receive something when someone dies. Rather, it meant to be the one who set up the gift for the heir. If Wycliff, Tyndale, Coverdale, and Matthew used the word correctly, Solomon was looking for a glimmer of hope in his heir. Therefore, Solomon was hoping that what he had prepared for Rehoboam would be of a great profit to him during his days of life under the sun. This application makes plain sense for Solomon to think of himself as the grantor to the heir. David left Solomon a nice inheritance when he died, but it was a pittance compared to all that Solomon would leave to Rehoboam. With that interpretation, we can understand how Solomon could see the wisdom in caring for the daily things in life to leave an inheritance to the next generation. Just to clear the air, in the etymology of the word "inheritance," it will be a hundred years after the death of Tyndale before the meaning of the word will shift to mean "the one receiving the inheritance" instead of "the one giving it."

(b) Wisdom in the Deeper Things of Life (7:12)

Solomon's thoughts of the daily things of life led him to consider the deeper things of life. He speaks, *"For wisdom is a defence, and money is a defence: but the excellency of knowledge is, that wisdom giveth life to them that have it"* (7:12). Ah, we might say, there is a difference between wisdom and knowledge. Solomon knew that too! It takes knowledge to have wisdom, but it takes wisdom to use knowledge correctly. Knowledge can be thought of as a gathering of lists, details, and facts about anything of interest. Speaking of wisdom, Solomon says, wisdom "is a tree of life to them that lay hold upon her; and happy is every one that retaineth her" (Proverbs 3:18). Old man Solomon is no fool. He has caught hold of the daily and deeper things of life when he looked at the concrete values surrounding him.

(8) Considered Values (7:13–14)
(a) The Works of God (7:13)

The concrete values of life cannot be ignored by Solomon. He had seen far too much designed by the God of all creation. He must stop to think about His work. He says, *"Consider the work of God: for who can make that straight, which he hath made crooked?"* (7:13). Could we pause to say that wisdom does not help when it comes to God? Do you see Solomon's frustration continued in this verse? When he asks if anyone can straighten out what God has bent, the obvious conclusion brings a "no" answer. Is it correct in the context of Solomon's meaningless disparity? In his mind, the future is set, and he can do nothing about it. Therefore, it makes no sense to try for a better life and work. Just be happy where you are, especially when it comes to the things of God.

It is amazing that Solomon registers his complaints in ways that raise questions to which he fails to attempt to give answers. We must back up and look at the larger picture. Solomon's focus deals not with mountains, rivers, or valleys. Neither does it deal with the shape of trees, bushes, or plants. It has nothing to do with a leg, arm, or back. We must take a deeper look, deep into the very soul of mankind. Deep into the heart. Deep into the thought of the heart, of the soul. The works of the mind, not God's, but man's. Should we blame the workings of the mind of man on God? Should the evil crookedness of man be rightly placed on the work of God in His creation process? Look again at his words. "Consider the work of God: for who can make that straight, which he hath made crooked?" Philosophically, Solomon places the blame of the crookedness of mankind squarely on the shoulders of God. Albeit, God can surely shoulder that blame if need be, but it is not His to shoulder, yet Solomon will not admit the truth. He knows the blame of all blames lies on the vile nature of humanity, misdirected by the vile character of mortality, guided by the vile course of the enemy, God's enemy, the devil. The Hebrew word "straight" in this verse is *taqan* and it means "to put in order" or "to put right." Here we see a paradox of mammoth proportions. That which Solomon complained about being "crooked" by God and needing to be put right was not of God's doing at all. No wonder Solomon is frustrated with life. No wonder Solomon is cynical about the better things of life.

(b) The Ways of God (7:14)

Neither does Solomon understand the ways of God. He speaks, *"In the day of prosperity be joyful, but in the day of adversity consider: God also hath set the one over against the other, to the end that man should find nothing after him"* (7:14). Does God really pit prosperity against adversity? Does not the Holy Writ proclaim that we should be joyful in both prosperity and adversity (James 1:2–4)? Solomon did not have that revelation available to him, but God had surely provided several sources of truth. Solomon was without excuse. Had Solomon erred in forsaking the text of the story of Job? Had Solomon forgotten the outcome of that story? Had Solomon fallen into the same trap as the three so-called friends of Job? Let us, pray tell, add to that lot the theology of Job's wife. Yes, indeed he had.

Poor old Solomon, his frustration and despair as he aged caused him to forfeit almost all the wisdom he had gained. Had he remembered his Scripture, these words would not have come from his lips. Had he remembered Job's reply to his wife when, in his adversity, she urged him to curse God and die. No, no! He would not do that. "What?" Job said. "Shall we receive good at the hand of God, and shall we not receive evil?" (Job 2:10). Then there was that man, Eliphaz, Job's Temanite friend. We might think that he had been jealous because of Job's popularity in earlier days. Job was the wise man of his time, living there in the

Arabian Peninsula. He was the source of counsel by those who would come from near or far, the trail worn bare by the countless multitudes on their journey to the threshold of his door. Sarcastically, Eliphaz asked the wisest man of that time, "Should a wise man utter vain knowledge, and fill his belly with the east wind? Should he reason with unprofitable talk? or with speeches wherewith he can do no good? Yea, thou castest off fear, and restrainest prayer before God. For thy mouth uttereth thine iniquity, and thou choosest the tongue of the crafty" (Job 15:2–5). Was not Solomon in this ecclesiastical utterance guilty of the same sin as that lamebrained so-called friend of Job?

Not to beleaguer the point, but had Solomon forgotten Job's outcome with God? Did not God turn upon Eliphaz the Temanite in response to all the torment with which he had abused Job? "My wrath is kindled against thee, and against thy two friends: for ye have not spoken of me the thing that is right, as my servant Job hath" (Job 42:7). Solomon, too, stands on shaky ground with his portrayal of the ways of God.

"Oh," you say, "Solomon probably had not read the story of Job in a long time. After all, Job's story occurred shortly after Jacob and his family joined Joseph in Egypt." We will take that one on the chin, but we will answer it with the words of Solomon's father, whom God said was "a man after [my] own heart" (1 Samuel 13:14). It might have been almost forty years since his father's death, but Solomon could not have forgotten his father's words, at least not without thinking about it. Those words were written in songs that were sung regularly, and songs are hard to forget! To take the position that, in the end, after prosperity and adversity, "man should find nothing after him" does not find grounds of support in David's songs. We find a problem in Solomon's theology when David sang, "Many are the afflictions of the righteous: but the LORD delivereth him out of them all" (Psalm 34:19). But that was the end of it. David sang in another song, "I called upon the LORD in distress: the LORD answered me, and set me in a large place. The LORD is on my side; I will not fear: what can man do unto me?" (Psalm 118:5–6).

Truly, Solomon's theology does not even stand against the muster of his own wisdom. Did not earlier in his life he say, "So shalt thou find favour and good understanding in the sight of God and man. Trust in the LORD with all thine heart; and lean not unto thine own understanding. In all thy ways acknowledge him, and he shall direct thy paths" (Proverbs 3:4–6)? And then, dare we miss his words, "If thou faint in the day of adversity, thy strength is small" (Proverbs 24:10). What has happened to Solomon in his old age? How is it that he has so boldly misinterpreted the ways of God? Question that! He has! It is a classic sign of many in this world who live a life without God. It is the classic example of a hell-bound soul, rebellious to God and ignorant of the true work and ways of the Supreme Ancient of Days. Solomon did a poor job of considering the values of God. No wonder he criticizes the better things of the Lord.

> b) Cynicism About the Bitter Things of Life (7:15–29)
>> (1) Cynicism About the Well Doing (7:15–19)
>>> (a) What Solomon Saw (7:15)
>>>> (i) Good Behavior Does Not Guarantee a Prolonged Life (7:15a)

Solomon cannot help but move from that which is better to that which is bitter in the things of life. Being cynical about the better, he cannot help being cynical about the bitter. In his almost seventy years of life, he had seen many things, perhaps many things the average person would never see. Anything that could be summed up as good behavior does not guarantee a prolonged life. *"All things have I seen in the days of my vanity: there is a just man that perisheth in his righteousness, . . ."* (7:15a).

A classic example, for instance, was offered in the life of Uzzah. Surely Solomon could remember poor man Uzzah from the record of his father's life found in 2 Samuel 6:1–11? Why did the Lord kill him? In Solomon's younger years, King David was bringing the ark to Jerusalem. He had it placed on a cart that was being pulled by an ox. At the threshing floor of Nachon, the ox stumbled and the ark nearly fell off the cart. Poor Uzzah, with all the best intentions in the world, reached out to steady the ark, to keep it from falling to the ground. He was struck dead. Why? Because he was not authorized by the Lord to touch the ark. He broke the requirements of the Mosaic law. Had the Kohaths had hold of the poles that lifted the ark on their shoulders, had they been carrying it according to the prescribed instruction of the Lord, Uzzah would have had no reason to try to help the Lord protect the ark. Yes, Uzzah died because of the sin of David and the Kohaths. Sinners bring heartache on those who surround them. The punishment may be severe. Was Uzzah sinless? No. He was an Israelite, but he was not a Levite. He also knew the law and the penalty. His action may have been in haste, but his death startled the nation, especially King David. It was a case of trying to do the right thing in the wrong way. Trying to be righteous, he died. Being righteous, he died. Intending righteousness, he died. Offering righteousness, he died. In his frail humanity, sinner he may be, still a man in pursuit of righteousness—he died. A life cut short, "perisheth in his righteousness."

(ii) Bad Behavior Does Not Guarantee a Premature Death (7:15b)

The converse of pursuing righteousness is the pursuit of wickedness. Righteousness does not guarantee a long life, and wickedness does not guarantee a short life. Solomon has seen both and says about the latter, *". . . and there is a wicked man that prolongeth his life in his wickedness"* (7:15b). Scripture does not provide an example of this from the time of Solomon's life, but we only need to step back to his father's predecessor for a classic application. King Saul was forty years old when he was selected to be the first king of the nation of Israel. Samuel the prophet had been the default leader of the nation for many years when the people began to clamor for a king. Samuel was disturbed but the Lord assured him that the people had not rejected him as their prophet, they had rejected the Lord as their God. It is good that God does not fret over the thoughts of man. It is good that He rises far above the desires of man. It is good that He remains unchangeable in His plan. It is good that He keeps His promises in spite of being rejected and despised.

They asked for a king and the Lord gave them Saul. He never promised that Saul would be a good king. Try as he may, Saul did not have the ability to be a good king. The story reveals that even with Samuel's involvement with Saul's anointing, the majority of the Israelites did not trust him at first. The cry for a king was evidently from a relatively small group among the tribes. After Saul had the opportunity to prove his leadership, all the tribes came on board. About three weeks later, the Lord commanded Saul to move on the Amalekites and totally destroy them, including all men, women, children, infants, and animals. Saul made the decision to spare the king and keep the best of the animals. A problem occurred; he had to return home with the spoils. What would he tell Samuel when he arrived? Instead of taking the straightest route home, he took the long way around the mountain. He could run from Samuel, but he could not run from the eyes of the Lord. He sent Samuel to find him in the valley on the far side of the mountain. No doubt, Saul was surprised to see the faint view of Samuel's form as he made his way up the trail. Wouldn't we love to have been a birdie in the tree to hear the bantering of Saul when Samuel arrived. It did not matter. Saul knew Samuel well enough to know that Samuel did not put up with nonsense. "Saul, what is that bleating I hear in my ears?" Samuel asked.

Saul was caught! He could tell the truth, or he could tell a lie. He chose the lie. "The people wanted to keep the spoils," he said. Just remember this, anything that is in rebellion to the will of God is wickedness! We can sugarcoat all we want. We can put wickedness into various classifications of sin. Some terrible, some not so bad! Man seeks to categorize sin. Man seeks to justify sin. Man seeks to diminish sin. Man seeks to explain away a personal sin and expose the sins of someone else. Sin is sin is sin is sin in God's eyes. Any and all sin is wickedness. In his wickedness Saul lied to Samuel, "The people wanted to keep the spoils. They wanted to offer them to the Lord." It was their fault, not Saul's. They made him do it.

Samuel was ready with his reply. "Because you have rejected the word of the Lord, the Lord has rejected you from being king." It was too late. Plead and beg, the Lord would not pardon Saul, and neither would Samuel. Samuel called for the Amalekite king, who came cheerfully. Little did he know that Samuel would not deny the word of the Lord. Then the prophet hewed the Amalekite king into pieces in front of Saul. As Samuel left, in his desperation, Saul grabbed his robe and ripped it. Samuel turned and said, "So has the Lord ripped the kingdom from you." Saul was nothing short of a wicked king for about four decades (1 Samuel 15). He would soon make the death of his anointed successor his wicked life goal. Tormented as he was in his spirit, evil as he was in his relationships, godless as he was in his last search for an answer with the witch of Endor, forty years of rule were filled with wickedness. But his behavior did not shorten his life. Eighty years of his life led him to take his own life by falling on his own sword. No wonder Solomon was cynical about life.

(b) What Solomon Suggested (7:16–17)
(i) Be Moderately Religious (7:16)

Thus, Solomon has some suggestions. Worldly-minded suggestions. Half-baked suggestions. Ungodly suggestions. By comparing Solomon's suggestions to the rest of God's Word, one might just doubt his ability to be wise. Perhaps the spoon from his place setting had dropped to the floor. Perhaps his pencil had become dull. Perhaps his knife needed sharpening. Rather, perhaps he had worshiped too many false gods with his one thousand wives. Perhaps he had a drink of wine with too many leaders and foreign dignitaries. Perhaps he had made too many deals with neighboring nations. Perhaps he had taken his eyes off the Lord and set his sights on the things of a world without God. We need to just stop using the word "perhaps" because he had. Wasted, that's what he had done, wasted his life, wasted his rule, and wasted his wisdom.

Now, he has some suggestions for all the rest of mankind who know little about the true God. You might ask, "Why would the Lord allow these words of Solomon's to be recorded in the Holy Scriptures?" Simply, the living God wanted a written record that demonstrated the thoughts of a godless man. From the get-go of the first words in Genesis, the Lord began laying out His divine will. He revealed that which is good and that which is evil in His eyes. The righteous take notice and focus on God; the wicked take notice and focus on the world. What does the world say? It says, use God when you need Him, call upon the Lord when you need Him, do without the Savior until you need Him. Use Him in your negotiating and maneuvering among humanity, only when it is to your advantage, but not too much. Solomon was worldly-minded at this point of desperation in his life. Here we will see his thoughts. Here we will see the hogwash of his suggestions for others living in the same gutter without God. No disrespect to the hog, but it was not kosher, and neither were Solomon's suggestions.

The preacher speaks, *"Be not righteous over much; neither make thyself over wise: why shouldest thou destroy thyself?"* (7:16). Does not the Lord declare through the Apostle Paul to "put on the whole armor of God," or are we to put on just a little, just a tad, not too much, we would not want to offend others with our full-blown declaration of our undying trust and relationships with the King of Kings, Lord of Lords, and Savior of our souls. The God of Solomon should have been the same God of the Christian—the God who never changes. What He expects from the Israelite He expects from the Christian! His plan for the two may have different paths but both were for the purpose of entering into the same relationship with Him. The Israelites rejected Him, at least for a season, but He will not forget His promise to them. He will gather them back. In the meantime, the Church operates on His plan with the same purpose, to lead the lost to an undying relationship with God.

> When a person becomes a Christian, he enters into a new relationship with God and into a new relationship with God's people. Both these new relationships call for major adjustments in the new believer's thinking and attitudes. His relationship to God is adjusted by the believer's consecration of his own body to God. His relationship to other believers is adjusted by the believer's consideration for the new body (the mystical

body, the church) into which he has been introduced. His relationship to the body of believers is to be both intelligent and intimate.[38]

Here a warning must be recorded. Here the alarm must sound loud and clear. Run from this suggestion! We must be hot in our pursuit of Godliness and cold in our rejection of the world's viewpoint. Solomon's suggestion is to be lukewarm—a dangerous place to be with God. In the end, He will spew the lukewarm from His mouth!

(ii) Be Moderately Rebellious (7:17)

Solomon could not stand to just address the problem with being overly righteous. He had to counter the balance of thought with the opposite reaction. Almost all Hebrew writing does this. The proverbs of Solomon show how he perfected this technique, the good versus the bad, the high versus the low, the sinner versus the saint, and on and on we could go. Here, Solomon keeps his thought form by balancing the wickedness against the righteousness he had just introduced. Solomon says, *"Be not over much wicked, neither be thou foolish: why shouldest thou die before thy time?"* (7:17). Buried at the end of this verse is the true problem that Solomon is dealing with—death. He knows his time is near. He had seen the penalty that extreme wickedness and foolishness had dealt on individuals, and he was right. But saying a little wickedness and foolishness is tolerable is wrong. His real point was his frustration with where he was in his stage of life—facing death very soon. Solomon dealt correctly in his proverbs about this subject; surely at this point in his life he has chosen to ignore his former theology. I cannot address this topic any better than it has already been explained in the Exploring Series. Thus, we find the following.

> Raising a side issue, Solomon dealt with the question, how long will a man live? Proverbs 10:27 gives the answer: "The fear of the LORD prolongeth days: but the years of the wicked shall be shortened." This proverb states a general rule that is not without exceptions. In this sinful world godly people may die young. Certainly, though, those who fear the Lord have a better quality of life and often a longer span of life than those who are wicked.
>
> The obvious biblical illustration of this proverb is the longevity of the antediluvians. We do not know of course what special climatic or

other conditions prevailed in the age before the flood. There is however an almost studied contrast between the godless line of Cain (Genesis 4) and the godly line of Seth (Genesis 5).

The godless line of Cain was marked by its preoccupation with this world. The Cainites built great cities and filled them with the fruits of art, science, and industry. They generated an industrial revolution that changed the face of society. They developed a feminist, pleasure-loving, materialistic, godless, and humanistic society dedicated to "the good life." They were interested in the occult and in exploring the deep things of Satan. How long did each of the Cainites live? Nobody knows. God ignores the issue. The Holy Spirit simply records their occupations. Whether the lives of the Cainites were short or long, their horizons were dominated by the things of time and sense.

In contrast to the Cainites, the godly line of Seth lived for the world to come. The Sethites simply lived for God and died. The death of each one is lovingly and tenderly recorded.

Genesis 5 reads like Heaven's register of births and deaths. We are told when each of the godly was born, how long he lived, and when he died. From one generation to the next we are told the name of the son who carried on the testimony for God in this world. And that is about all. The Sethites contributed little or nothing to the materialistic culture of the Cainites' world. While evil men and seducers were waxing worse and worse in Cainite society, the Sethites were renowned for their devotion to God.

And the godly all lived to a ripe old age! Indeed, the ages of these patriarchs astonish us. Adam lived until he was 930, Seth until he was 912, Enos until he was 905, Cainan until he was 910, and Mahalaleel until he was 895. Jared lived until he was 962 and Methuselah lived to be 969. Lamech, the father of Noah, was 777 when he died. Enoch escaped death altogether.

The two people who lived longest were Jared and Methuselah. One was Enoch's father; the other was Enoch's son. This fact suggests the influence an especially godly man can have on his immediate family. There can be no doubt that in those days that godliness and longevity went hand in hand.

Solomon also dealt with the question, how long will a man laugh? The ungodly man often thinks he has the last laugh. However, Solomon wrote, "The hope of the righteous shall be gladness: but the expectation of the wicked shall perish" (Proverbs 10:28).

What hope does the godless person have? He can hope for the best, as the world says. But what is "the best"? Is it health and strength, peace and prosperity, honor and respect, a rewarding occupation, promotion and applause, a loving family, congenial friends? These are the ingredients in what the world calls "the good life." The worldly man can hope for these things. But even if he attains them, death still lurks in the shadows. Death will not be denied. The godless man may laugh himself into Hell, but he'll never laugh himself out of it. "The expectation of the wicked shall perish," Solomon said. How right he was. Even the wicked acknowledge that "you can't take it with you."

The contrasting truth is that "the hope of the righteous shall be gladness." Only those who love the Lord have what the New Testament calls a "blessed hope" (Titus 2:13). Whether or not we receive our "good things" (Luke 16:25) in this life, we certainly have something to look forward to. Jesus is coming again! Heaven and home are ahead. We have ". . . an inheritance incorruptible, and undefiled, and that fadeth not away, reserved in heaven" (1 Peter 1:4). "At the appearing of Jesus Christ: Whom having not seen, [we] love; [we will] rejoice with joy unspeakable and full of glory" (1 Peter 1:7–8). Obviously, it is the righteous person, not the wicked person, who has hope—and that hope is far beyond anything envisioned by Solomon.[39]

And so, we can conclude that Solomon's suggestion strayed far from the plan of the Lord, far from the desire of God, far from the leading of the Spirit.

(c) What Solomon Sensed (7:18–19)
(i) The Support of Wisdom Recommended (7:18)

Solomon has just presented his suggestions about life and now he must defend his thoughts. Notice the support he recommends. Notice the trap he sets for the man of little wisdom. It is the same ploy used by false teachers to lure the innocent into their lair of man-made theology. Solomon speaks, *"It is good that thou shouldest take hold of this; yea, also from this withdraw not thine hand: for he that feareth God shall come forth of them all"* (7:18).

First Solomon speaks of the good it will do if his suggestions are accepted.

". . . take hold . . . withdraw not thine hand." Why is that good? Because second, Solomon invokes the name of "God." If you will grab hold of his suggestions, "he that feareth God shall come forth of them all." Nothing good will ever come from Solomon's suggestions because they lead to lukewarmness in a relationship with Almighty God. The words God, Scripture, Lord, Bible, and Jesus are used by all false teachers to give support to their godless theology and teaching. For the most part, everyone loves God, the Scriptures, the Lord, the Bible, and especially Jesus. Who doesn't love them? Everyone loves God. Right! Invoking any of these names or sources never guarantees the message is truly from God.

The classic example of invoking the name of the Lord to give credence and authority to a lie from the pit of hell is found in the prophecy made by Hananiah. It was about 390 years after the death of Solomon. Nebuchadnezzar had already taken control of Jerusalem, looted the Temple, and carried back to Babylon all the sacred items that were made at the foot of Mount Sinai within two years after Moses had led the Israelites out of Egypt. The people were frantic. King Jeconiah had been carried off with the Temple items, and Nebuchadnezzar had made Zedekiah king. He was a puppet king with no real power. Early in Zedekiah's reign, the Lord instructed Jeremiah to take a message to the people. We can only imagine how Jeremiah delivered the message, how he acquired their attention. Maybe he said something like, "People of Israel, listen to me, 'Thus says the Lord.'" Here is a paraphrase of the message. "People, false prophets, conjurers, soothsayers, and teachers are about to tell you that the Temple treasury will be brought back to Jerusalem soon. Do not believe them!" Within a few days, Hananiah had gathered a crowd of elders and proclaimed, "Thus speaketh the Lord of hosts, the God of Israel, saying, I have broken the yoke of the king of Babylon. Within two full years will I bring again into this place all the vessels of the Lord's house, that Nebuchadnezzar king of Babylon took away from this place, and carried them to Babylon" (Jeremiah 28:2–3). Hananiah carried on and promised that Jeconiah, the exiled king of Judah, would also return when the vessels returned. To that Jeremiah said, "Amen: the Lord do so" (Jeremiah 28:6).

Now in Hananiah's prophecy he invoked the name of the Lord as if he was a divine spokesman for God. Jeremiah knew better! He was not fooled by the lie of Hananiah. You see, the Lord must have known that Hananiah was going to make that blunder. That is why He instructed Jeremiah to warn the people of the Lord about that very prophecy. We can imagine in our mind's eye the posture, the tone, the intent, the voice of Jeremiah as he said to Hananiah, "Hear now, Hananiah; The Lord hath not sent thee; and thou makest this people to trust in a lie. Therefore thus saith the Lord; Behold, I will cast thee from the face of the earth: this year thou shalt die, because thou has taught rebellion against the Lord." Nebuchadnezzar destroyed the Temple and carried off the vessels on Av 9th, the fifth month of the year. Hananiah died in the seventh month of that same year. He lived less than ninety days (Jeremiah 28:1–17).

All cults love the Scriptures, the Bible, the names of God and Jesus. They love to use them as hooks to trick the young, innocent, unlearned. Children love Jesus. Naturally they love Jesus. They love the name of Jesus. They love when a person speaks of Jesus. When the head of the Integral Yoga Institute, Swami Satchidananda, said, "Blessed are the pure in heart, Jesus said, for they shall see God," he then invoked that Scripture in a twisted way to press his personal theology on the listener. He then said, "Yes, blessed are those who purify their consciousness, for they shall see themselves as God."[40] Heresy! Neither you nor he will ever be God. Why did he do this? He knew what Hananiah knew. In the days of Hananiah, everyone loved the Lord. In our day, everyone loves the Lord Jesus! Right? He quoted Jesus; therefore, the Yoga interpretation must be right! Right? Wrong! Dead wrong! Both are false teachers and both will feel the punishment of the Lord for leading the innocent astray. Solomon's support, as wise as he was thought to be, was no wisdom at all. That wisdom did not support his suggestions.

(ii) The Superiority of Wisdom Recorded (7:19)

Surely Solomon knew that his support statement fell short of its intended goal. Now he must support his support statement by pulling the proverbial "wisdom" card. He speaks, *"Wisdom strengtheneth the wise more than ten mighty men which are in the city"* (7:19). After all, wisdom trumps all other arguments. Right? Wrong! Wisdom comes with a plethora of knowledge. We must think of knowledge as the building blocks that lead to wisdom. The building blocks are details that have been gathered through life's experiences and education. Details must be sorted, categorized, prioritized, and synthesized. Then the magic of wisdom can begin to grow by applying all the details into theories, hypotheses, and most of all reproducible actions. Now wisdom is built on knowledge, but knowledge does not guarantee wisdom; a pile of false facts and details will lead to false conclusions. Then the two most important facets must be added, righteousness and wickedness. This world that we live in is filled with the wicked wise. Their wisdom is built on worldly truths that edify their wickedness and lead to worldly profit. Relatively few can be found in this world who are righteous wise. Their wisdom is built on Godly truths that edify their righteousness and lead to heavenly profit. The worldly man is drawn to the wicked wise; the Godly man is drawn to the righteous wise. Which wisdom card is Solomon playing in this sermon? Remember his suggestion! "Be moderately righteous and moderately rebellious." Is Solomon offering wisdom to be righteous or wisdom to be rebellious?

"Wisdom strengtheneth the wise more than ten mighty men which are in the city" for either good or bad. Which one is it? No wonder Solomon is cynical about the bitter things of life and concerned with the well doing of the things he has seen, suggested, and sensed. His path has led to wickedness. His path of wisdom took him away from the Lord.

(2) Cynicism About Wickedness (7:20)

From a cynicism about "well doing," Solomon turns to a cynicism about wickedness. He preaches, *"For there is not a just man upon earth, that doeth good, and sinneth not"* (7:20). Taking what Solomon says at face value, no just man exists! Every man must be wicked! No man does good, and every man is a sinner! Let us focus on the first part of this dreary verse—"there is no just man upon earth." Focus on the word "just." What exactly does that mean? As Christians, we have heard that word. "The just shall live by faith," declared the prophet Habakkuk, but he was three hundred years after Solomon, so that is not a good example. Paul said the same in Romans and Galatians, but that was nine hundred years after Solomon, so that is not a good example. But wait! Didn't the writer of Hebrews recognize Abel, Enoch, Noah, Abraham, Sarah, Isaac, Jacob, Moses, and David as being just in the faith? Did not all of these come before Solomon (Hebrews 11)? Yes, all of them were sinners, yet they all did good in some ways in the eyes of the Lord. Good enough that because of their faith their sins were not counted against them. In other words, they were "just" in the eyes of the Lord. Solomon could not see past his sin to accept his own wickedness and lay that sin at the feet of the Lord. Here Solomon has tried to justify himself as a "just man" but with little good evidence. What vanity of vanities under the sun!

(3) Cynicism About Wordiness (7:21–22)
(a) A Word of Advice (7:21)

Solomon's cynicism now turns to the use of words. No doubt he has heard his name mentioned within the palace. No doubt the words heard were not uplifting, encouraging, or comforting to Solomon. What can he do? He is old. He is decrepit. He is unhealthy. He is dependent on his servants. Who else can he trust? Will his thousand wives care for him? Will his blubbering foolish son take care of him, the one who can't wait to take his place? Absolutely not! Even the care of the old king was the work of servants, not the family. With that, Solomon says, *"Also take no heed unto all words that are spoken; lest thou hear thy servant curse thee"* (7:21). In today's vernacular, he would have said, "Ignore the servants and mind your own business." What was Solomon going to do? He lived in a glass house. His servants had no doubt been with him a long time. Even though he was hard to live with and his words were rather sharp at times, to the servants, he was better than his son who would take his place. They knew that a change was coming. They knew their jobs were in jeopardy. They knew that when he died they would be subject to the whims of Rehoboam. They were not alone in their fears; the country had the same consternation. Solomon was not stupid. After all, he had asked the Lord for wisdom and then wasted most of the rest of his life as a reprobate—living without God in the center of his life. We must keep in mind that the troubles of the Israelite nation that followed the days of Solomon were caused by Solomon. Had it not been for the Lord's love of David, the kingdom would have been ripped from Solomon during his life. So, Solomon has a word of advice in his crotchety old age. "Don't listen to what the staff is saying about you. It won't make you happy." Besides, the Solomon they knew was better than the Rehoboam in the wings. Surely, they wanted to keep Solomon alive as long as they could.

(b) A Word of Admonition (7:22)

Guilt had gripped Solomon. Evidently, he had heard a cursed word from one of his staff, but he was not without blame. He had a word of admonition. *"For oftentimes also thine own heart knoweth that thou thyself likewise hast cursed others"* (7:22). Picture Solomon in his palace bedchamber. He has heard the voice of a servant. "The king will not do this. The king will not do that. The king is stubborn. The king will not do what is best for his health. For all the wisdom the king has, he is the dumbest person I know." These are words that one would not dare say to a king in fear of one's life. Nevertheless, words like this are said in royal circles by the servants. Such circles develop code words and slang to say what they want in undetected language. The insiders know the meaning, the outsiders do not. Solomon was smart enough to decipher anything said by his servants. He had heard their talking far too long. He could piece the puzzle together by the picture they were painting with words. Surely, he knew. Surely! But what was he to do? He could not walk without help. He could not eat without help. He could not ride in the countryside without help. He could not call for a wife without help. With each day he has become more helpless. See him sitting on his couch. His feet are hung over. His head is down. His hands are on his thighs. He has just been washed and dressed by his servants. He has heard their words about him around the corner and all he can do is sit, wait, and ponder until they return to help him to his chair. What does he ponder? Perhaps he ponders all the curses he has hurled at those same servants over the past forty years.

(4) Cynicism About Wisdom (7:23–25)
(a) A Resolve (7:23)
(i) What He Desired (7:23a)

What good has it all been? He had asked the Lord for wisdom and where had it gotten him? And so, our old king Solomon is cynical about wisdom. He must, in some way, resolve his dilemma. He must settle this blessing that has in many ways cursed him. He speaks, *"All this have I proved by wisdom: I said, I will be wise"* (7:23a). Solomon had desired to know everything about everything. He had traveled the world, researched its history, entertained its royalty, built mighty structures upon it, recorded its pithy sayings in proverbs and plays. Where did it get him? He knew about the world, he indulged in the world, he collected the treasure of the world both in created objects and human lives; yet, where had it gotten him? He knew about man, how he thinks, what he desires, his lusts, his sins, his traits, his ills. Where did it get him? The one most important thing he had not studied—God! Where did it get him?

(ii) What He Discovered (7:23b)

From what Solomon desired to what he discovered, we hear him speak, *". . . but it was far from me"* (7:23b). He had missed it all! If he had just remembered the words of Psalm 2:1–4 he would have been on track from the get-go!

Why do the heathen rage, and the people imagine a vain thing? The kings of the earth set themselves, and the rulers take counsel together, against the LORD, and against his anointed, saying, Let us break their bands asunder, and cast away their cords from us. He that sitteth in the heavens shall laugh: the Lord shall have them in derision.

Solomon should have known that song; he should have used it as a guide in his search for wisdom. Perhaps he did. But perhaps he lost his way. He started searching out the "heathen rage" and the "vain thing" that "the people imagine." He also searched the doings of the kings and rulers of the earth, but he lost his way. He joined them in rebelling against the Lord; he married their daughters and they brought their idolatry with them. Had he kept searching past the gutter of this trash-filled earth he would have turned his eyes upward toward the heavens and learned the same things that Isaiah and Paul had learned.

For my thoughts are not your thoughts, neither are your ways my ways, saith the Lord. For as the heavens are higher than the earth, so are my ways higher than your ways, and my thoughts than your thoughts. (Isaiah 55:8–9)

O the depth of the riches both of the wisdom and knowledge of God! how unsearchable are his judgments, and his ways past finding out! For who hath known the mind of the Lord? or who hath been his counsellor? Or who hath first given to him, and it shall be recompensed unto him again? (Romans 11:33–35)

(b) A Realization (7:24–25)
(i) The Failure of His Research (7:24)

Solomon has come to a stark realization. His research has failed. Rather, his method of research has failed. His direction of research has failed. His focus of research has failed. He speaks, *"That which is far off, and exceeding deep, who can find it out?"* (7:24). According to the opening chapter, Solomon was going to seek wisdom and discover all he could about it. Here he is now judging everything according to his wisdom. In his wisdom, he was seeking to become wise, but he could not achieve it. Why? He could not discover the answers he wanted. He had rejected the answers from the Lord. Solomon had spent just about his entire reign attempting to hold an image of who he was in the public eye, but he didn't even know who he was in his own eyes. He could not find the answers he wanted, that matched his thoughts, that matched his dreams, that matched his desires, that matched his theology, that matched his theories, because he was looking in the wrong places.

(ii) The Fervor of His Research (7:25a)

Oh, how Solomon had sought for answers. There was a fervor in his research. He says, *"I applied mine heart to know, and to search, and to seek out wisdom, and the reason of things, . . ."* (7:25a). One would think that Solomon had all the tools he needed to find wisdom and the reason it existed. But did he? Dare we tiptoe back to the beginning of his reign to find the answer? Dare we start with the genesis of his wisdom to find the answer? Dare we rethink the purpose of his wisdom to find the answer? Did Solomon have the "heart to know, and to search, and to seek out wisdom, and the reason of things"? Perhaps not as has always been assumed!

In the beginning of 1 Kings, King David was still alive. He was ill, very near to death. Moreover, he had not left the kingdom in a sound and solid position for an easy and smooth transition to the next king. Quite frankly, the kingdom did not know which of his sons would take his place, if any. In the midst of the indecisiveness of David's last days, Adonijah, David's fourth son, assumed that he would be the king. The first three of the king's sons were dead. The oldest had fallen in lust with David's daughter Tamar and lured her to his bed. After defiling her, Amnon, the oldest son, did not want Tamar any longer. David did nothing to punish Amnon. Absalom, David's third son, became impatient with his father and took things into his own hands. He sliced the throat of Amnon to avenge the wrong his brother had done. Amnon was dead. David's second son did not live to reach his teen years. He was dead. Absalom continued to be frustrated with his father and tried to take the kingdom away from him. Several years into the ordeal, Absalom was riding through the oak trees, and his hair became caught in the branches and pulled him from his horse. Dangling in the air, men, faithful to his father, pierced him with their spears. Absalom was dead. That left Adonijah as the next living heir in line to David's family.

Before David died, Adonijah threw a crowning party and invited Zadok, the priest, to anoint him king in his father's place. None of David's influential family and friends were invited. Nathan, the prophet closest to David, heard of the party, and while it was still in process, told Bathsheba. Evidently, Nathan and Bathsheba had confirmed word from David that the king wanted Solomon to take his place. In a rush, David instructed that Nathan was to anoint Solomon as king. The deed was done. Adonijah found out. Adonijah acquiesced to Solomon.

David called Solomon to his bedside. The dying king had some enemies that he had not taken care of when he was healthier. Zadok, the high priest, was not faithful to the king and would not be faithful to Solomon. Joab had joined forces against David and wouldn't be good for Solomon's reign. Shimei had cursed David, and his angry mouth might do the same to Solomon. David made Solomon promise to take care of them as soon as he was dead. David died. Solomon took care of the enemies of his father. Then, to make things worse, Solomon broke the law, he abandoned the faith, he went against the Lord, he flaunted his kingship and authority in the face of the nation, he married the Egyptian Pharaoh's daughter and moved her to Jerusalem! How dare he! He needed help, and he needed it quickly. Furthermore, he played like he loved and worshiped the Lord by offering his worship on the high places in Israel, the same places the false gods were adored and worshiped.

The brutality of Solomon in his first days as king did not bring confidence to the people of the nation. Solomon was struggling. Finally, in the first of three times recorded in the Bible, the Lord spoke to Solomon personally and directly. That first meeting was in a dream. Don't think that that was strange. Throughout Scripture, from the Garden of Eden to the end of the book of Revelation, the Lord spoke to His earthly representatives in dreams, visions, and oracles (revelations). In dreams, the Lord would play out a whole scene in living color to tell the person what was about to happen, or He simply spoke to them word for word. Visions are the same as dreams except that the person is awake. We call those *daydreams*. They could be a whole scene played out or a word-for-word conversation. Finally, the oracle was a direct word-for-word conversation with no ifs, ands, or buts. You have seen them in Scripture, "thus saith the Lord," tell the people this or that! In the dream the Lord said to Solomon, "Ask what I shall give thee." Solomon admitted to the Lord at that moment that he was too inexperienced to know how to dispense justice for the multitude of people in his kingdom. Here is what Solomon asked for and what the Lord granted. "Give therefore thy servant an understanding heart to judge thy people, that I may discern between good and bad: for who is able to judge this thy so great a people?" (1 Kings 3:9).

And the Lord answered Solomon with the following promise: "Because thou hast asked this thing, and hast not asked for thyself long life; neither hast asked riches for thyself, nor hast asked the life of thine enemies; but hast asked for thyself understanding to discern judgment; behold, I have done according to thy words: lo, I have given thee a wise and an understanding heart; so that there was none like thee before thee, neither after thee shall any arise like unto thee" (1 Kings 3:11–12).

But the Lord did not stop there, he gave Solomon something else that he did not ask for. "And I have also given thee that which thou hast not asked, both riches, and honour: so that there shall not be any among the kings like unto thee all thy days. And if thou wilt walk in my ways, to keep my statutes and my commandments, as thy father David did walk, then I will lengthen thy days" (1 Kings 3:13–14).

What is "a wise and an understanding heart"? The Lord uses the word *chakam*, and although it came to mean *wise*, it is more commonly translated *skillful*, as in a skillful craftsman or the skill of an artisan.

(iii) The Focus of His Research (7:25b)

From Solomon's realization about the fervor of his research, he turns to the realization of the focus of his research when he says, "*. . . and to know the wickedness of folly, even of foolishness and madness*" (7:25b). In his search for wisdom, Solomon found that which he did not expect and did not want, wickedness. His focus found the wickedness of folly, foolishness, and madness. He studied it too much, too long, too deeply. He squandered his time in the gutter of life seeking to find the wisdom in life. In the darkness of evil, he could not find the light of good. No wonder he was cynical about wisdom. All he learned brought heartache. All he learned brought a desire for more. All he learned brought him to the place in his life where he was preaching the message of a man without hope in the last days of his life's frustrations. One thing brought him more frustration than anything else in this world and every conversation in all of Solomon's writings include it—women!

(5) Cynicism About Women (7:26–28)
(a) Their Schemes (7:26)

His discovery led him to a woman who was worse than death and only God could help him escape from her. But for the sinner, God will not help him escape this woman. Is the writer changing his mind? Is God not just up in His lofty heavens watching us? Does God intervene in the lives of His creation? In the past chapters, Solomon concluded that God did not intervene. But here, he seems to change his mind. Perhaps he is growing in his wisdom about God and realizing that God will help the sinner who turns to Him to escape from the snare, nets, and chains of the wrong woman for his life. It is a bitter frustration. He says, *"And I find more bitter than death the woman, whose heart is snares and nets, and her hands as bands: whoso pleaseth God shall escape from her; but the sinner shall be taken by her"* (7:26).

In his commentary on Proverbs, Phillips says the following about a wanton woman, and it bears repeating here.

> Solomon warned against the wanton woman's smiles and *the promise they reveal*: "The lips of a strange woman drop as an honeycomb, and her mouth is smoother than oil" (Proverbs 5:3). Two Hebrew words, *nākar* and *zūr*, are used in the Bible to depict the "stranger." The word *nākar* refers to a temple prostitute. In the foul Canaanite religion, idol worship was consummated by having sexual relations with one of the priests or priestesses. *Zūr*, the word used in Proverbs 5:3, refers to a Hebrew woman who has become an apostate and has sold herself to the immoralities of one of the pagan cults. She is a professional harlot.
>
> The wanton woman baits her trap with honeyed words. She is well versed in what to say to seduce careless men. She knows how to inflame the passions of those who stop to listen to what she says. She is an old hand at enticement. She knows which words to use in her approach, how to respond to the reply, how to make the next conversational move. She has no trouble sizing up each prospective client. She knows how to choose the words that will lead him on.
>
> Solomon continued to warn against the wanton woman's smiles and *the peril they conceal*. Those inviting lips conceal the *danger* into which she is luring the unwary: "Her end is bitter as wormwood, sharp as a two-edged sword" (Proverbs 5:4). Her lips also conceal the *death* that lurks in her shadow: "Her feet go down to death; her steps take hold on hell" (Proverbs 5:5). The last thing a person thinks of when listening to the siren voice of a wanton woman is the danger and death that accompany her, so Solomon warned of the wormwood and bitterness that seize the soul and conscience of the adulterer.
>
> The Bible is blunt about sexual sins. There is nothing prudish or Victorian about the Bible. But although the Bible is quite frank, it contains

nothing prurient in its pages. It does not pander. The so-called adult novel, on the other hand, moves the reader slowly and enticingly through one torrid scene after another. Such a book titillates, excites, and stimulates, gloating over every detail and constantly stirring the filth portrayed. The Bible, however, cuts through sin like a surgeon's knife. The cut exposes to view the moral ruin, the physical wreckage, and the shameful death that result from sexual sin. The writer of pornography is a depraved sensualist; the Holy Spirit is a surgeon. . . .

Solomon, wise in the ways of women, warned against being *beguiled by her loveliness*: "Lust not after her beauty in thine heart." He also warned against being *beguiled by her look*: "Neither let her take thee with her eyelids." This kind of woman can put a world of meaning into what she says with her eyes, her eyelids, and her eyebrows. She has mastered the sudden look downward in pretended modesty; the well-known wink; the raised eyebrows; the slanting look; the sudden raising of both eyebrows in pretended surprise or horror; the drawing together of the eyebrows in a scowl of disapproval; the crafty look out of slits formed by eyelids half drawn down. Oh yes, the harlot can speak volumes with her eyes.

Ah, those eyes! They light up her face. They beckon and bewitch. Half her attraction is in her eyes and she knows how to use them. "Come," they say, "look into our depths. Read our promise." They gleam, glitter, dance, and delight. They swim with tears and sparkle with mirth. They are merry, and they mock.

"Don't be fooled by her eyes, boy," Solomon said. And who should know better than Solomon? He had been fooled many times already. There was one woman, however, whose eyes he had read correctly. "Turn away thine eyes from me, for they have overcome me," he wrote (Song of Solomon 6:5). He had read scorn in her eyes. All of a sudden, though still eminently desirable, she was "terrible as an army with banners" (Song of Solomon 6:4).[41]

No wonder Solomon was cynical about women. He had studied far too long the wickedness found in the folly, foolishness, and madness of a worldly woman. Count them! He had many by this time in his life. Seven hundred wives! Three hundred concubines! All focused on the world. All focused on scheming their way to the preeminent position in Solomon's court, heart, and bedchamber. Had Solomon met a Godly woman? Yes. Once! But will he admit it?

(b) Their Scarcity (7:27–28)
(i) His Frustration (7:27–28a)

Solomon concluded that wicked women are plentiful but Godly women are scarce. In his frustration he concluded, *"Behold, this have I found, saith the preacher, counting one by one, to find out the account: which yet my soul seeketh, but I find not: . . ."* (7:27–28a).

"Behold" is an interesting word used throughout the English Old and New Testaments. In the last one hundred years its meaning has shifted. We now think it means "to look or see," but those were not suitable synonyms for "behold" when Tyndale used it in the first English translation of the original Hebrew and Greek texts. "Behold" in 1525 meant "to hold in high regard." That's what the Hebrew *ra'a* and the Greek *idou* meant in Scripture. When John 1:29 says, "Behold the Lamb of God," Tyndale used the word *behold* to say, "Hold the Lamb of God in high regard." It was the Old English *bihaldan* which meant "to keep a hold of." When Solomon said, "Behold," he was saying something that was important, something to hold on to, something worth paying attention to! He had counted "one by one, to find out the account." He had taken a piece of parchment and prepared it with columns. His intent was to write down the name of every woman who had characteristics of life far different from every woman he had met in his life. One, two, three, and on he inquired; yet, not one name was written down. His "soul seeketh," but his soul could not find one. The parchment has no names. Thus, his frustration again.

(ii) His Finding (7:28b)

Solomon even deviated from searching for women by cataloging the names of men too. He says, *". . . one man among a thousand have I found; but a woman among all those have I not found"* (7:28b). What was Solomon doing by putting a man's name on the list? What was Solomon thinking? His finding resulted in one man and no woman who met the criteria. Who was that man? Who was the one among a thousand? How many thousands of men did he inquire about? One, two, three, or ten thousand? Did he have one name, two names, or ten names on the list? What was he saying? Were there no good Godly women on this earth in his day? With that idea, no wonder he was cynical about women.

We dare not leave this section of the commentary without turning the finger and pointing it at Solomon. He was his own worst enemy! He did not understand women! A thousand women could not satisfy his longing. Put it this way, Solomon had a problem with women! His findings were skewed. His wisdom was not so wise. In the twentieth and twenty-first centuries, it is hard to find a good Godly woman who wants anything to do with this Solomon of the Bible. May I say, *hold this in high regard*—there are ten thousand upon ten thousand good, Godly women in this world in the Church today! Surely, there were some alive in the days of Solomon; he just did not know where to look; he just did not know what to look for; he wanted to do more than just look; he wanted to acquire and at least once he sought one he could not get, a woman faithful to her beloved and not to Solomon.

It is said that Solomon composed 1,005 plays in his life. I have to wonder if that was one for every fling with a woman that he had. None have survived except the Song of Solomon, recorded in the Old Testament. It is a repulsive play to most good, Godly women in the Church today because of the way it is taught. Preachers have lustfully made it into a sex manual for the modern relationship. Preachers have handled it in a topical manner from the male position of a relationship with a woman. Preachers have forgone the female side of the relationships. Preachers have misrepresented the evil in the Song for good and dangled it in front of congregations all over the globe. But did Solomon mention that woman here? No! His attempt to lure her had happened at a time when he only had sixty wives and eighty concubines, long before this Ecclesiastes was preached.

In Solomon's Song that survived, he met a woman betrothed to her beloved, another man. Her beloved had gone off to the far country and would one day return to take her as his bride. Solomon portrayed himself in the Song as the king. He disregarded the engagement and took the woman into his palace, into his private banquet room, and had the table spread with all sorts of quality foods that a common woman would most likely never see in her life. He offered that which only the rich could afford; yet she looked out the window, hoping to see her beloved coming over the hill to take her away. Solomon decided that if she was going to stare out the window, he would give her something to look at. He organized a parade of all the wealth in his kingdom and he was the center of attention. There, tagging along were the sixty queens and the eighty concubines. It was a glorious parade of Israel's finest, wealthiest, prestigious, and admired. Surely, any reasonable woman would want to join Solomon's train, but not this one, not this beauty, not this devoted bride-to-be; she was going to wait for her beloved and Solomon would not change her mind. Even Solomon knew that it would be wrong to force himself on her. After all, he had a half brother who did that, and it did not turn out so well for him. Solomon knew what his other brother thought about that. Solomon knew what his father thought about that. Solomon could not take her until she approved, but she was not budging.

Back in the palace, Solomon would try another tactic in his lustful arsenal. He would be blatantly lustful to her. While she dreamed, she thought of her beloved coming to the door, knocking, putting his hand through the door for her to join him and go away to the place that he had prepared for them. While she was awake, Solomon lustfully spoke to her about her hills and valleys, her clusters and mountains and pray tell, her teeth, as if that would entice a woman to succumb to the ungodly intent of a godless king. Every word was nastier than the last. She would not succumb, she would not budge. On to another tactic Solomon went. Five times he had all his other women, the "daughters of Jerusalem," as they were called, put female pressure on her. They said to her, "Come be one of us! Join us in a great life with Solomon!" But each time, the Godly woman said, "I charge you, O daughters of Jerusalem, that ye stir not up, nor awake my love, until he pleases." She was not going to let her love loose until it was at the right time with the right person. Solomon was not that person! Solomon did not have the power to force her into his harem; therefore, he would put her in bondage. A field was given to her to work, and one for her brothers too. When she failed to bring in the crop, she would be indebted to Solomon and have to agree to his demands and abandon her willingness to wait for her beloved to come. But that she would not do! She worked hard in the field. She became darker from the sun. Swarthy she was. As for Solomon, each field was to bring in a thousand pieces of silver when the crop was sold. But this woman needed twelve hundred pieces to pay her debt. Solomon had her cornered. Her brothers wondered what they would do with her. They needed to put pressure on her to bow and bend to Solomon's ways, but she would not. When the crop came in, she paid her debt to the king, she also paid the debt of her brothers. She was free of the king. She turned to the hills and said, "Make haste my beloved, and be thou like a roe or a young hart upon the mountains of spices." She was ready to patiently wait for her beloved to arrive. She had been tested by the most powerful of the world and won. Now that's a story that women of every century can get behind. That's the story in the Bible. It is a story that tells all just how much Solomon misunderstood women. All he did was tell the truth of the story. The story revealed his ignorance.

So, Solomon had not found one woman to put on his list, but he found one man. Now we ask the question again. Who was that one man in a thousand? By placing precept upon precept to find the answer to all his questions, Solomon failed. Yet he found one man among a thousand. Who was this man? Who was he who helped with Solomon's discoveries and knowledge? We do not know who he was. Yet there had not been one woman to help him in his search. He had learned nothing from his encounter with the woman in his Song.

(6) Cynicism About Worldliness (7:29)
(a) God's Intention (7:29a)

Could the whole world be as Solomon thought? Could the whole world be wicked? Could Solomon find any good in anything in this world! What did he find? He says, *"Lo, this only have I found, that God hath made man upright, . . ."* (7:29a). With all said and done, Solomon can only conclude that God made man to stand on his two legs for some reason. It was God's intention from the beginning and that caused Solomon to be cynical about the worldliness he had discovered. Why would God do that to man? Why would God allow the world to be the way he discovered it to be?

(b) Man's Inventions (7:29b)

But Solomon saw more in his cynicism about worldliness than in God's intentions; he also saw it in man when he says, *". . . but they have sought out many inventions"* (7:29b). Man had sought his own devices. He had constructed an engine that could allow him to manufacture his own intentions and schemes. It was another bitter frustration in Solomon's attempt to seek wisdom.

Wisdom led Solomon down a terrible path of cynicism first about well doing, then wickedness, then wordiness, on to wisdom, then women, and finally worldliness. All were part of life's frustrations for Solomon in the things he had studied.

2. Life's Fallacies (8:1–17)
a) The Fiction About Being Great (8:1–9)
(1) King Solomon and His Wisdom (8:1)
(a) The Challenge (8:1a)

With the turn of the eighth chapter, Solomon switched directions in his message concerning the things he had studied. From life's frustrations he began to focus on life's fallacies. In the frustrations, he looked at the world. In the fallacies, he looked at himself. In his studies of the world as king he faced the fiction about being great. He had to look at himself and his wisdom. First, he spoke of the challenge: *"Who is as the wise man? and who knoweth the interpretation of a thing?"* (8:1a). Solomon used the word *perher* for "interpretation." It is an unusual word for him to use. It is Chaldean, pure Chaldean, and found in no other part of the Bible except the Chaldean section of the book of Daniel. It means more than just our understanding of the word "interpretation" in our English. The word means "to find a solution." The interpretation is the action of explaining the meaning of something but, when it is tied to the thought of a solution, it is also the action of solving a problem or dealing with a difficult situation. But in the day of Tyndale's 1525 translation from Hebrew to English, it meant "to translate for understanding." Thus, King Solomon was the best in the world at listening to a problem and finding the answer to give the proper direction to a people and their needs.

Solomon was the wise man of the world at that time. Sought by all! The trail of seekers arrived from the miles of roads from every country in the world and they would wait for days to hear his interpretation of this, that, or the other. Yet, Solomon, in his old age, doubted his wisdom and interpretation of things. Was there a person wiser than he? That was the challenge. Who would it be? Solomon could not find one. He illuminated himself but not humanity in general. He was looking inward, not outward. But Solomon knew where he was going in his homily and the two questions were simply leading to his next statement.

(b) The Change (8:1b)

Who was the wise man? Who knew the interpretation of a thing? It was Solomon speaking about himself when he says, *". . . a man's wisdom maketh his face to shine, and the boldness of his face shall be changed"* (8:1b). Surely the people of the world were amazed at the responses given by Solomon, but no one was amused more than Solomon himself. He could feel the change in his countenance with each decision he made. See him there on his throne as his stern face would begin to beam. He was thrilled with his counsel that surprised him more than others. In fact, with each decision Solomon became bolder in his ability to exhibit his skill in judging the people. Not only did the change occur on his face but it also occurred within his countenance. But all of that was a fallacy. He may have been great in the eyes of the people of the world, he was not great in his own eyes, at least in retrospect when his health was failing and his days were nearing the end. Nevertheless, during the prime of his life, to keep up the charade, he would have to keep up the talk. To keep up the talk, he would have to keep up the commands.

(2) King Solomon and His Word (8:2–5)
(a) A Word of Counsel (8:2)

As the great king, Solomon had been worried about his wisdom, but now he was worried about his words. What had he counseled? What had he cautioned? What had he commanded? With his counsel Solomon says, *"I counsel thee to keep the king's commandment, and that in regard of the oath of God"* (8:2).

Throughout the book of Ecclesiastes, Solomon used the word "I" 87 times in 215 verses. The first time he used it was in 1:12 when he said, "I the Preacher was king over Israel in Jerusalem." Then, every time he used it after that, the "I" was followed by an action word of some kind: I communed, I came, I said, I proved, I sought, I made, I gathered, and many more. The only exception to Solomon's style of writing is found in this verse. Notice that the Authorized Version says (KJV), "I *counsel thee.*" The italicized words that are in the text were placed there by the committee that put this version before King James for his approval in 1611. None of the other action words that followed the "I" in any of Ecclesiastes were placed in italics save this one alone. Why?

Our first task to answer that question is to look into the preface of the Authorized Version (KJV) to discover what italicized words mean in the text. In the "Notes of the Translator to the Reader," we find that all italicized words were inserted by the committee to help the reader understand in English the intent of the Hebrew or Greek text. Furthermore, italicized words were included when the committee felt that something was omitted from the original that should have been included. In other words, the committee was interpreting the Word of God for the reader by including these extra words. But we must ask the question, "Did the translation committee make this decision or was it made by a previous translator?" The Authorized Version (KJV), by the committee's own admission, relied heavily on the works of Wycliffe, Tyndale, Matthews, and Coverdale. The works of these men have been published in the various versions by their names and other names such as the Geneva Bible, the Great Bible, and the Bishops' Bible.

Leaving the Authorized Version (KJV) and picking up John Wycliffe's original 1362 English translation of the Latin text of Jerome, we find the following: "I keep the mouth of the king, and the commandments and swearings of God." Wycliffe made that English translation from the Latin that said, *ego os regis observe et praecepta iuramenti Dei.* The Latin literally translated by Wycliffe should have read, "I observe the mouth of the king and the commandments of the swearings of God." We might wonder why Wycliffe chose to use the word "keep" instead of "observe." Here is a major pitfall in the study of some Bible students! What is the pitfall? Today, the word "keep" means to "have or retain possessions" and is the major snag in many modern Bible studies. It leads to many cults!

Of the approximately 42,000 cults in the world today, most of them are English and birthed by this same issue! What is the problem? Using today's definitions for words that have evolved from their original definitions! Bible students must look into the etymology of the English words being used, their origins, their original meanings. It is not enough to look up the Hebrew or the Greek and find out what the English word is! The student must find out what that English word meant when that dictionary or lexicon was published. For instance, if the Thayer's Greek-English Lexicon of 1889 is being used, the student must have an English Dictionary of 1889 in hand to understand why Thayer chose those words to define the Greek. A 2004 Webster's Dictionary will never do! You will never find a definition old enough to properly interpret Scripture. A good etymology dictionary is well worth the exorbitant price you will have to pay to find out why our English versions of God's Word use the words they do. In Wycliffe's case, we find that in the thirteenth century, the word "keep" meant "to care or heed in watching." Thus, when he used the word "keep," it was the best word of his day to translate the Latin word "observe." With that as the groundwork, we still have not answered the question of why the Authorized Version (KJV) italicizes the words "counsel thee" in this passage.

Wycliffe was the first to provide an English translation in 1362 from the Latin translation, the Vulgate, but William Tyndale was the first to provide one from the original Hebrew and Greek in 1525. He did not live long enough to complete the whole Bible. After finishing the New Testament, the first five books of the Old Testament, and that of Jonah, he was captured, imprisoned, judged, and executed by strangling. Then his body was burnt at the stake on October 6, 1536, in the Duchy of Brabant for his heresy in making an English translation. John Rogers (who wrote under the name Thomas Matthews), Joseph Johnson, and Miles Coverdale completed Tyndale's work in peril of their own lives. In 1537, the Old and New Testaments in English were published in what was called the Matthew's Version, a completion of Tyndale's work. The fifty-four men who served on the 1611 Authorized Version (KJV) committee used Tyndale's and Matthew's work as the basis for their version, basically updating words whose meanings had changed in the preceding seventy-five years.

The Matthew Bible translates our passage as follows: "Kepe the kynges commaundemente (I warne the) and the that thou haste vnto god." Yes, that is the English found in the 1549 Matthew Bible. This Bible version agrees with Wycliffe and used the word "Kepe" or "keep." But notice that Thomas Matthew includes "(I warne the)" in parentheses. What is he telling us? He is telling us that "(I warne the)" is not in the original Hebrew manuscripts that they were using to make the translation. The Hebrew transliteration is *"ani phi mlk shmur uol dbrth shbuoth aleim"* or in our English today, *"I command king observe regard oath of Elohim."* As you can see, "I warne the" or as the Authorized Version says, "I counsel thee," is not anywhere in the Hebrew. It is not in the Greek Septuagint. It is not in the Latin Vulgate. But it is in the English translations.

Where did they get it? They got it from the absence of Solomon's style of writing in Ecclesiastes. They got it by noticing that something was missing. On average, every two and a half verses Solomon used the word "I" followed by a verb, and this time the verb is missing. By including "(I warne the)" Matthew told us that something was missing. He knew it. Wycliffe, 150 years before, knew it. Jerome, eleven hundred years before, knew it; and the Jews, who translated the Hebrew into Koine Greek eighteen hundred years before, knew it! They all concluded that a word had been dropped from the copy of the Hebrew they were using somewhere along the way, and that error continued to be copied into all subsequent copies. Whether going to the Greek, Latin, or English, each translator had to make a decision for his manuscript. One used the word "warn," another "keep," or, as in our Authorized Version (KJV), "counsel thee." When they were used, they all meant the same thing to the committee completing the thought as best they could.

Now we return to the words of Solomon and, as we can, avoid what he may or may not have meant but was interpreted by King James' committee as "I counsel thee." We must move to understand that the truly wise man will "keep the king's commandment." Solomon knew the fallacies of these words. He knew that the king was not always right. He knew the king was not always forthright, forthcoming, or just. Solomon, in his last days, could look back and see the evil he had done in the sight of God under the oath he made to God. Solomon may be preaching to the congregation of Israel in this sermon but here he is preaching to himself. Solomon knew that an Israelite might have an understanding in a matter but if it contradicted one of his orders, Solomon had the power to inflict immediate punishment upon that person. He may have had a right to his thoughts, but if they were not in perfect harmony with his oath to God and had God's approval on those thoughts, he, the king, would be the final authority in the matter. The fallacy in Solomon's mind must have been that he had come to realize that he had not been the best king for the people. God did not think so either! By this time Jeroboam was waiting in the wings, hidden in Egypt from Solomon's wrath. Solomon was taunted by the prophet's word that warned him that the kingdom would be divided after his death. Solomon knew his death was near, and he could do nothing about it! In some kingdoms, the people must flee because of the wrath of a king, and in Solomon's kingdom so did Jeroboam under the direction and oath of God Almighty!

(b) A Word of Caution (8:3–4)
(i)   The King's Presence (8:3a)

Could Solomon change the course of history with this word of caution? Here we find the fiction of being great again. For example, could Solomon, with all his greatness, lure Jeroboam back into the king's presence with the words of this sermon, *"Be not hasty to go out of his sight"* (8:3a)? Today, the king would say, "Son, don't leave my palace too quickly!"

Jeroboam came along fairly late in Solomon's reign. He was an Ephrathite from the town of Zereda to the north of Jerusalem. His father died when he was young, and he was raised by his widowed mother. He was industrious and brave and that caught the eye of Solomon, who enlisted him into the king's service. The door to Solomon was always open to Jeroboam. He was put in charge of the men of the forced labor of his own tribe and his cousins in the tribe of Manasseh. Their job was to fortify Jerusalem. Due to Solomon's poor financial decisions to build more and more buildings, the taxes on the people were extremely heavy, and work in the king's projects was not optional.

One day Jeroboam ran into the prophet Ahijah at the sanctuary in Shiloh. The prophet took off his coat and tore it into twelve pieces and gave ten to Jeroboam. He then explained that God was going to give Jeroboam ten pieces of the kingdom and leave two to the descendants of King David, specifically David's grandson, Rehoboam. Solomon heard of the prophecy and condemned Jeroboam to death. As soon as Solomon's plan reached the ears of young Jeroboam, he ran from the king's presence. Pharaoh Shishak gave him a place of safety in Egypt until the death of Solomon. "Be not hasty to go out of his sight," Solomon said. We might want to look at it from Jeroboam's position, for he was a young man who intended to remain faithful to the king. When he realized that the king was truly up to no good, he left. And he did so quickly!

(ii) The King's Perception (8:3b)

Jeroboam was already safely in Egypt when Solomon preached this message. With all he could muster, Solomon knew that he was wrong. He wanted Jeroboam dead because he thought the young man should *"stand not in an evil thing"* (8:3b). Jeroboam was not evil, at least not at this point in his life; Solomon was! From the king's perception, he meant his words; he thought Jeroboam was evil. It was his word of caution. But why?

(iii) The King's Prerogative (8:3c)

Solomon gave the word of caution because he knew about the king's prerogative. He speaks, *". . . for he doeth whatsoever pleaseth him"* (8:3c).

The king can do what he wishes when he wishes, and, frankly, people who live under a king might need to flee his presence (or kingdom) to keep from being forced to commit an evil act. To Solomon, wisdom was good only for self and not for others. We cannot find this to be a true statement in the rest of Scripture. Remember Joseph in Egypt? Each new ruler saw the wisdom of Joseph and put him in charge of most of his kingdom. Remember that Daniel also found favor in each new ruler's eye and was given authority not only over his people, but also over the Babylonians, the Medes, and the Persians. Different rulers from different dynasties with different languages, yet they all saw the wisdom of Daniel. True wisdom not only illuminates an individual; it also illuminates those around him. True wisdom spreads like wildfire through the forest to the masses. Even evil kings can see the need for a truly wise man. But Solomon, in all his wisdom, knew that a king did not have to be fair, just, honest, good, or righteous. A thumbs up or a thumbs down could determine the life of a paltry soul. Solomon had brought the end of life to many souls because he had the right to do "whatsoever pleaseth him." Solomon would have been afraid of himself had he not been the king. Why?

(iv) The King's Power (8:4)

Solomon fully understood the power of the king. In this sermon he speaks, *"Where the word of a king is, there is power: and who may say unto him, What doest thou?"* (8:4).

In Solomon's day, no one could question the actions of the king; his rule was absolute. As king, Solomon knew this well. He had the power over the life and death of every soul in his kingdom in his hand. With one flick of his finger, a man could lose his life that day. Solomon also knew well that there was a proper time and a proper way for subjects to approach the king. Before Solomon was born, his father was approached by Nathan. It was done carefully and at the proper time—according to strict protocol. I am sure the sin of David weighed heavily on Nathan when the Lord sent him to face the king.

We, too, face all kinds of stress and heavy burdens today because of governmental pressures. Solomon's conclusion was a good one. We should do things in the proper order and at the proper time, especially when it comes to dealing with the king. However, the king was not God. He may control a man's fate on earth but not in eternity, and that shows the fallacy of the fiction of Solomon's thoughts.

(c) A Word of Command (8:5)
(i) Protection Available (8:5a)

Solomon stirred his soul with the words of counsel and caution. It seems he had motivated something within to return to be the king he once was when he felt better. In his fiction about being great, he spoke a word of command as if he still had it within him to offer protection. *"Whoso keepeth the commandment shall feel no evil thing"* (8:5a). To explore his thought, we need to return to the issue of Solomon's last foe, Jeroboam, the one who would take ten parts of his kingdom under his control when Solomon died, and Solomon knew it. He attempted to offer Jeroboam protection from evil if he would just return and keep the commandment of the king, if he would just be faithful to the king, if he would just do away with any idea of one day ruling ten parts of the kingdom. Jeroboam had already tried to deal with Solomon. It was Solomon who put the death penalty upon his head. It was Solomon who was not faithful. Because of Solomon's order, Jeroboam had to seek protection, but it was not the hands of the King of Israel; it was the protection found in the hands of the King of heaven! Solomon could not be trusted. Try as he might, Solomon could not change this course of history and anything he might try to do was just part of life's fallacies and the fiction about his being great. The Lord had sealed Solomon's fate too. His reign was coming to an end and had it not been for the Lord's love for his father, David, Jeroboam would have already been in control of ten parts of his kingdom.

(ii) Prudence Advisable (8:5b)

Solomon spoke one last word about his ability to make a command as a fictitious great king, "*. . . and a wise man's heart discerneth both time and judgment*" (8:5b). Whose prudent heart was wise? Was it Solomon's or was it Jeroboam's? Whose prudent heart discerned both the "time and judgment"? Perhaps both! A little explanation is needed and advisable at this point.

Surely Solomon had not forgotten his words found earlier in this sermon. Back in chapter 3, Solomon listed beautifully and poetically the reality of time on human life. Solomon had experienced just about everything covered in that list. All that awaited him from the list was death. He was near that point of transition from here to there, from temporal to eternal, from death to life. His days of prudent decisions and discernments were almost past. In the last days of his breath he could try to make a last-ditch effort to save what he had accomplished. He could try to make a last-ditch effort to control that which he knew before he faced the future which he could not know. It is the same fate of every aged king, queen, grandfather, grandmother, father, or mother. The opportunity to affect the lives of those given, led, and guided by the Lord but almost gone. What was left to change? Nothing could be done to correct all the wrongs. Solomon was nearly done. The most prudent thing he could do in his life was to make amends and wait for God's timing to fulfill all the final things in Solomon's life.

On the other hand, Jeroboam's day was on the way. He did not know the pressure of being a king, but he would. He did not know the fate of decisions he would make, but he would. He did not know if he would have the discernment needed to lead his people, but he would. He did not know if he would have the wisdom to lead his kingdoms, but he would. He did not know if the people would follow him, but he would.

What is the difference between the lives and discernment of Solomon and Jeroboam? One old; one young. One with his life behind him; one with his life ahead of him. One had made his decisions in life; one still had decisions to make in life. One intended to kill the other; one intended to survive the other. One must come to the end of his life as king; one must begin his life as king. Solomon could not see past his end; Jeroboam could not see past his beginning. In the plan of the eternal God Almighty, one generation comes to an end, another takes its place; no one can stop this plan put in place by God. At this point in the lives of Solomon and Jeroboam, both were using "a wise man's heart" to discern "both time and judgment." Solomon was exactly where God wanted him and so was Jeroboam! Both were prudent! But for Solomon it was a fictitious greatness because his command meant nothing at his age and circumstance.

(3) King Solomon and His Weakness (8:6–9)
(a) His Logic (8:6)

Solomon must face his weakness. He must rely on the same logic he relied on earlier in his sermon. He must revert to the dreaded issues of man and the effects upon him. He says, *"Because to every purpose there is time and judgment, therefore the misery of man is great upon him"* (8:6). Solomon may have been the great king, but he had to admit that the misery of "time and judgment" were far greater. Forty years earlier, in his mind, nothing and no one was greater than he. Now, two great eternal creations of the Lord God Almighty had taken over! Time and judgment! They had always been there! They were greater than Adam, Noah, Abraham, Isaac, Jacob, Moses, Joshua, Deborah, Gideon, Samson, Samuel, Saul, David, and Solomon. All humanity humbles before "time and judgment." The logic of the great Solomon, the wisest man in the world, was just a fallacy. It was real to Solomon alone; in God's creation, it was fiction.

(b) His Limitations (8:7–8)
(i) A Future He Cannot Discern (8:7)

In his weakness, the force of Solomon's sermon began to crack as his logic degraded. *"For he knoweth not that which shall be: for who can tell him when it shall be?"* (8:7). Solomon stopped describing the fallacies of the king and the plight of man because no one could discern the future. Today we would say that no one has the ability to see the future, and we cannot know the events of tomorrow. Man is limited. Solomon was limited. Solomon could plan his calendar for the next day, but he could not be assured that he would live to see that day! A man without God has no clue about the future. Solomon was so focused on himself that he could not see God; he could not see what God had already promised in his future; he could not see what his father, David, had written about the glorious eternity awaiting those who put their trust in the God of all! Solomon could not, at least to this point in his sermon, see past the dreadful state of the last days of his life. However, he could see the sight of a funeral!

(ii) A Funeral He Cannot Defy (8:8)

"There is no man that hath power over the spirit to retain the spirit; neither hath he power in the day of death: and there is no discharge in that war; neither shall wickedness deliver those that are given to it" (8:8). There it is! Solomon's profession of his ultimate limitations. Death he cannot defy! His death he cannot defy! His destiny he cannot defy! It all leads to one day, a day set for all born on this earth, a day of calling, a day of purpose, a day of intention—a funeral. There it is! Selah! What do you think of that? All the wickedness Solomon engaged in during the last forty years of his life could not defy the day of his funeral. All the power Solomon could muster in the last forty years of his life could not defy the day of his funeral. All the gifts of the Spirit which had animated the body of Solomon for the last forty years of his life could not defy the day of his funeral. The day was coming. Nothing could deliver him from the judgment and power of the grave.

(c) His Lesson (8:9)

Solomon, great in his own eyes, spoke of his wisdom, his word, and his weakness. He presented his logic, limitations, and lesson. His apologetics must force Solomon to admit what he had finally learned in his weakness. *"All this have I seen, and applied my heart unto every work that is done under the sun: there is a time wherein one man ruleth over another to his own hurt"* (8:9). How shallow was Solomon's greatness under the sun. Nothing he had done could stop his death and the coming of a new king to take his place. Nothing could extend his power. Nothing could extend his authority. Nothing could extend his breath. Nothing could extend the days of his work. Nothing could extend the days of his beating heart. Nothing could extend his days under the sun. Nothing could; nothing would. Lesson earned. Lesson learned. His greatness was turned to weakness. His reality was turned to fiction. His fact was turned to fallacy. Why? Because he had lived a godless life which led to a hopeless fate!

b) The Folly with Being Godless (8:10–13)
(1) The Fate of the Wicked Man (8:10)
(a) His Funeral: The Burial of the Man (8:10a)

We find it common throughout all of human existence for a person to speak of the fate of another when actually speaking about himself. Solomon did this in his sermon when he says, *"And so I saw the wicked buried, who had come and gone from the place of the holy"* (8:10a). He had attended enough funerals that he could imagine his own. Therein he imagined the folly of being godless. Therein he imagined the fate of the wicked man. Therein he imagined the funeral procession from the "place of the holy." Think of that as the sacred place. Yes, in death, the wicked seek religion, too, but they use it for ill purposes. It is the fallacy of being godless in God's realm. The wicked want to continue in their sin and do as they wish and yet they still have a desire for their eternal souls to be safe. And if it is not their desire then their family attempts to cover their evil ways with a Godly funeral for a godless soul.

Consider two brothers, one eighty-three and the other eighty. The older was nothing; the younger, a denier of God's existence. The older would not accept the Lord because the younger would not accept the Lord. Why could they not accept the Lord? Because the younger did not believe in any possibility of a resurrection from the dead. "Impossible," he said. Finally, just months before dying, the older, who always believed in a Creator, awoke in the middle of the night to the enlightenment that if the Creator could make all the world in just six days, raising Jesus from the dead ought not be too difficult. He told his children that he became a believer in the Lord of Glory. At the funeral, the younger, decrepit, wheelchair-bound man listened closely to a grand proclamation of God and the salvation given through the Lord Jesus and all the dearly departed had already experienced in heaven. At the end of the graveside ceremony, he had the nurse roll him to the head of the casket. He put his hand on the casket and said to the preacher, "I want this." Years before he made arrangements with the preacher to do his funeral too. "I want this!" The preacher said to him, "I promised I will do your funeral. If the Lord grants me life, I will be there to do your funeral." "No!" he said. "You don't understand. I want the same funeral as my brother." The preacher said to him, "I am so sorry, you cannot have the same funeral because your brother believed in the Lord and you do not." "I know, I want this." When it comes to death, even the wicked want a Godly funeral.

Solomon cannot be speaking of a commoner in this passage. Funerals for the regular folks were swift in his day. The hole was dug, the body washed, rubbed with spices, wrapped in a sheet, lowered in the grave, and covered in the dirt as soon as possible and definitely before the setting of the sun. If it wasn't in a hole, it was in a cave of some sort. To begin with, burial was the only permissible way to dispose of the body (Genesis 23:19; 25:9; 35:8–9). Stones would be heaped up over the site to keep the carnivorous animals from enjoying a meal on the remains.

Burning the body or leaving it exposed to the animals was strictly done for the purpose of condemnation. To counter that condemnation, the beheaded bodies of King Saul and his sons were quickly burned after they had hung on a wall near Mount Gilboa. This was done by the Jabesh-Gileads, whom Saul had helped and befriended years earlier. They cremated the lot and carried the bones back to their hometown and buried them under an oak tree in their own custom. But they were not Jewish. They were Canaanites. The law did not apply to them. They honored Saul and his sons according to their customs, in the best way they could—but not God's way for his people. King David corrected the mess by having the bones dug up and buried properly in the tomb of Kish, Saul's father, in Zela in the tribal area of Benjamin (2 Samuel 21). In those days the family carried the body to the grave (Genesis 35:29) but toward the end of the days of the Southern Kingdom, professional pallbearers were enlisted to do the job (Amos 6:16). Professional mourners were there too. Weeping, wailing, flailing! After the burial the family met for a funeral meal (2 Samuel 3:35; Hosea 9:4). But the ceremony was not over. In the Jewish customs, the tomb would be revisited on the third and seventh days and then at the end of the month as well as at the anniversary of each year. We can only imagine the dynamics of Solomon's funeral when he really died, with all those wives! But at this point in Solomon's sermon he was expressing the fate, folly, and funeral of the wicked man. No doubt he had witnessed such funerals and the condemnation expressed by the mode of the handling of that wicked one's body. Solomon knew his godlessness. Solomon could only wonder, "Would he be handled the same way?"

(b) His Fame: The Burial of His Memory (8:10b)

As king, Solomon had a different perspective about the death and burial of the godless wicked than most subjects in his kingdom when he said, *". . . and they were forgotten in the city where they had so done: this is also vanity"* (8:10b). But humans are human! They are all the way they are. They think the way they think. They cluster together in groups joined by the way they think. Those in control think one way; their subjects think another way. Humans have not changed in their thinking processes since the beginning of time. Solomon, in his plush palace in Jerusalem with his thousand women at his beck and call with servants and subjects beyond number, did not think like the common people. As king, he may have forgotten about the fame of a wicked person once dead but that was not the way of everyday folk. Solomon had been a ruthless taskmaster in his rule because he forced his subjects to build his projects when he wanted, where he wanted, and how he wanted with little consideration for their family. As such, he was no different from any other evil king throughout history.

The fame of good and evil kings rests on the people. The faults of the kings are on display because everything they do is so public. In reality, all of us have been guilty of similar sins, but ours are not so public. A wicked and evil king is not soon forgotten as the text implies. What was Solomon's time frame for this forgetfulness to occur? Was it over a month or a year, a decade or a century? In the span of eternity, Solomon may be correct, but for the few generations that follow, a wicked king's dealings and death are not forgotten. They will be remembered and retold as stories of the pain placed on them and their families by such rulers. We have not forgotten the evils of the tyrant of World War 2, and we will not soon forget the evils of the tyrants who masterminded the Twin Towers' destruction in New York, nor the flight into the Pentagon. Generations to come will remember. So, too, Solomon concluded that this knowledge was meaningless in man's view—and it was! Vanity, he says! That too! Emptiness is the better word! That too! Those who put their trust in God remember the sins of the past and dare not become like the evil men who do as they please. But even the godless remember. Solomon remembers. If he did not remember, he would not have spoken about it in this sermon. Solomon was haunted by his past. Solomon may be preaching this sermon to the world and recording it for all generations, but he was the target audience of the message.

(2) The Foolishness of the Wicked Man (8:11)
(a) The Reason for His Folly (8:11a)

In Solomon's study of life's fallacies, he has noticed the foolishness of the wicked man and the reason he continues to be and do wicked things. It was *"because sentence against an evil work is not executed speedily"* (8:11a). In his family alone, Solomon knew of the delayed penalty of his wicked siblings. His brother's lustful and wicked sin against his sister lingered for days and months. His father, the king of Israel, did nothing. The wicked brother showed no remorse for the shame he brought on the family. His ways did not change. No doubt he continued in wickedness in other ways. He was a wicked brother and wickedness begets wickedness. Finally, another brother, distraught with the unchecked wickedness, took things into his own hands and sliced the throat of his father's son. He did not have the authority to do that! He, too, was now wicked in the sight of God.

His wickedness begat wickedness and he sought to take the kingdom from his father. The king had no choice but to run from his wicked son. The king left behind ten of his secondary wives; concubines, they were called. When his evil son stormed the palace, he took those ten wives to the roof and defiled them! His sin was, in fact, ten times worse than that of the brother whose neck he had sliced. Unchecked, the sin of the son continued against his father for several years it seems, and the sentence of punishment was never delivered by his kingly father. Finally, the Lord intervened. The son was flying through the woods on his horse when his hair caught in the tree. While he was dangling there, the report of his dilemma reached the patriots of his father who quickly took matters into their own hands and ran him through with their swords. His folly had continued too long in their minds. But when the report reached Solomon's father of the demise of his wicked brother, his father grieved. Wickedness begets wickedness. Then the king would need to handle the patriots who had become the next in the wicked line.

(b) The Result of His Folly (8:11b)

And what is the result of the folly of the wicked? Solomon speaks, *". . . therefore the heart of the sons of men is fully set in them to do evil"* (8:11b). Solomon saw nothing but wickedness in the "sons of men." Evil was their lot in life. Solomon was just a child when his evil brother tried to take the kingdom from his father, but he was already king when another evil brother sought something forbidden, something he wanted as a gift, something Solomon did not have the authority to give, something sought in a backhanded way that could have tripped up Solomon in the first days of his kingship. His brother, who had had himself anointed as king prior to his father's pronouncement and anointing of Solomon as king, asked for the wife of his father as a bride. Surely, she was young, fair, and beautiful! Surely, she was a virgin and drew the attraction of men who saw her caring for the ailing king on his deathbed. Surely, she would have made a wonderful wife for any young man. But! And there always seems to be a "but" in these stories. She had become the wife of King David for the purpose of being his nurse in his last days.

As such, the marriage was never consummated. She and David had every right to consummate the marriage; they were wed, but David, in his ill and aged condition, could not complete the marriage union. As the wife, she washed and dressed the king. She cleaned him up when soiled, changed the linens, and fed him his meals. At his death, she washed his body for the last time, wrapped his fingers and toes in bandages, then his hands and feet. In the process she anointed every portion of his skin with the most costly of the perfumer's oils. She wrapped his face in a handkerchief and then his head. She wrapped his legs and his waist, his chest and shoulders, and then his arms. One last wrap encased the whole and he was ready for the litter to be carried away. She knew the king intimately! She was his wife. But in the Jewish custom, because the marriage had never been consummated, she did not fall under the laws of marriage after the death of a spouse. She did not have the privilege of a kinsman-redeemer as was the case with Solomon's ancestor-mother Ruth, who was able to marry Boaz. This wife was not allowed to marry under the custom. When she signed on to be David's wife, she knew she was signing on to be celibate forever. She would never marry again. She would never have children or grandchildren. She did not belong to the new king and Solomon could not give her to his brother even though Bathsheba, Solomon's mother, had asked for her to be given to the brother. To do so would have been a wicked, evil act on Solomon's part. To fix the problem, what did Solomon do? He had his brother executed. The result of the wicked man's folly begets wickedness.

(3) The Future of the Wicked Man (8:12–13)

(a) His Continual Wickedness (8:12a)

Solomon has already made his point—judgment comes slowly for sinners. He speaks, *"Though a sinner do evil an hundred times, and his days be prolonged, . . ."* (8:12a). No matter how many hundreds and hundreds of times a wicked sinner commits his evil deeds and it seems that he is never caught, finally, when judgment comes, it seems "too little, too late." Once again, Solomon contradicts his own theology by stating that the evil person can extend his life with his evil acts, but it is not so. In our earthly thinking, we often feel that judgment comes too late. To think that we can extend our lives by doing evil or we can shorten our lives by doing good is a godless theology. Solomon had lived a godless life and he knew that lesson well. Continual wickedness continues with more wickedness.

(b) His Constant Warning (8:12b–13)

(i) The Shallowness of His Life Revealed (8:12b)

And so, in his constant warning, Solomon begins by bringing God back into the picture to reveal the shallowness of his life when he says, *". . . yet surely I know that it shall be well with them that fear God, which fear before him"* (8:12b). It seems that Solomon was trying to get somewhere in his sermon. It seems he was trying to get back to a place he once knew. It seems that he expected the lesson to lead him into a healthy walk with God. It also seems that he had departed from the path that would lead him through the deep blessing of God many years before. In exchange, he had skipped through the shallow allurement of the trinkets of a godless world for nearly forty years. Solomon looked for a shelter of safety in God, whom he had avoided for four decades. He needed a structure strong enough to protect him in the storm of life he was about to endure. He was so shallow in his life, but he saw the depth present in others' lives who had a true relationship with God, who feared God, who worshiped God! Solomon's fear and worship of God was as thick as a thin film of olive oil on his skin. For all the wisdom bestowed on Solomon, he wasted it. Think of this, the historical story of David's life takes 3 books of the Bible (Ruth 4, 1 Samuel 16–31, 2 Samuel 1, 1 Kings 1:1–2:12), 42 chapters, 1,228 verses, or 38,139 words.

On the contrary, the whole historical story of Solomon can be found in 1 book (1 Kings), 11 chapters, 448 verses, or 10,968 words. Across the historical pages for the lives of David and Solomon, David has on average a four to one lead over Solomon in books, chapters, verses, and words. At least 73 of David's songs made it into the Hebrew hymnbook (Psalms), but only 1 of Solomon's songs made it into the Bible (Song of Solomon). David did not write a proverb that we know of; Solomon was said to have written 3,000 proverbs and 1,005 songs, but most did not make it into the Word of God (1 Kings 4:32). It seemed that with all of Solomon's activity in the Bible, it would have recorded many more details in his life, but it couldn't! As can be seen in this very commentary, Solomon may have been a charmer of women, but he was not a charmer of God. He may have had authority over hundreds of thousands of forced laborers in Israel and surrounding nations, but he did not have the authority over God. Why? Because he was far away from God for most of his reign as king! His wives had brought their gods into the marriage and Solomon was not grounded enough in the theology of his father to deflect the effects of idol worship in his own enormous family. Early on, Solomon must have forgotten the words of one of his father's songs, Psalm 91.

> He that dwelleth in the secret place of the most High
> shall abide under the shadow of the Almighty.

> I will say of the LORD, He is my refuge and my fortress:
> my God; in him will I trust.

Surely he shall deliver thee from the snare of the fowler,
And from the noisome pestilence.
He shall cover thee with his feathers,
and under his wings shalt thou trust:
his truth shall be thy shield and buckler.
Thou shalt not be afraid for the terror by night;
nor for the arrow that flieth by day;
nor for the pestilence that walketh in darkness;
nor for the destruction that wasteth at noonday.
A thousand shall fall at thy side,
and ten thousand at thy right hand;
but it shall not come nigh thee.

Only with thine eyes shalt thou behold
and see the reward of the wicked.
Because thou hast made the LORD, which is my refuge,
even the most High, thy habitation;
there shall no evil befall thee,
neither shall any plague come nigh thy dwelling.
For he shall give his angels charge over thee,
to keep thee in all thy ways.
They shall bear thee up in their hands,
lest thou dash thy foot against a stone.
Thou shalt tread upon the lion and adder:
the young lion and the dragon shalt thou trample under feet.

Because he hath set his love upon me, therefore will I deliver him:
I will set him on high, because he hath known my name.
He shall call upon me, and I will answer him:
I will be with him in trouble;
I will deliver him, and honour him.
With long life will I satisfy him,
and shew him my salvation.

Solomon's life was so shallow that when the storms of life were staring him in the face, he needed to look for a place of refuge. He had seen it in his father's life and more than likely his mother's too. Surely, he had seen it in the lives of others because he says he did in this verse. Yet he did not have the assurance of a secret place with God. He could not be assured that God would fight the lions, adders, and dragons of his life. Why? He did not have that kind of relationship with God and therefore he saw the great folly of being godless and the fatal future of the wicked man. Solomon was scared; he should have been. He was that wicked man. Why did Solomon bring up God at this point in his sermon? He realized that the person who had a relationship with God did well whether it was in this life or the next. Eternal life for the Godly was secure and blessed—that's God's message, not man's. Solomon had been following man's way far too long and he did not know the way to the secret place of God because he did not seek to dwell there during his life.

(ii) The Shortness of His Life Revealed (8:13)

The days of Solomon's life were nearing their conclusion and he knew it. He made one last stab. He speaks, *". . . but it shall not be well with the wicked, neither shall he prolong his days, which are as a shadow; because he feareth not before God"* (8:13). Seventy years was not enough for Solomon. His father lived eighty years. Why the decade difference? His father did reign for forty years and Solomon chalked up the same, but if he had just ten more years of life like his father, he could be the king for fifty years, but his health will not permit it. No matter what he did, he could not extend his life for one moment past his earthly expiration date. The future of this wicked man was set and the shortness of the rest of his life was revealed. Solomon was in a pickle of a situation.

c) The Fantasy of Being Good (8:14–15)
(1) The Good Man Gets a Guilty Man's Reward (8:14a)

Solomon must have slipped off into some fantasy world. Wicked as he had been, he thought about the philosophy of opposites. Perhaps the good are really the bad, and the bad are really the good. Insane as it sounds, humans down through the ages have bought into this same philosophy. Solomon speaks, *"There is a vanity which is done upon the earth; that there be just men, unto whom it happeneth according to the work of the wicked"* (8:14a). Could Solomon actually imagine that the good man would receive the guilty man's reward? If so, what good is it for being good? Where does living good get you?

(2) The Guilty Man Gets a Good Man's Reward (8:14b)

Conversely, Solomon speaks, *". . . again, there be wicked men, to whom it hap-peneth according to the work of the righteous: I said that this also is vanity"* (8:14b). So, could Solomon actually think that the wicked man would receive the good man's reward?

Why do bad things happen to good people? Why do good things seem to happen to bad people? Solomon sees this dilemma and uses it to show the futility of life. The answer to the two questions usually deals with choices. Some wicked people make wise and calculated choices that allow good things to come to them here on earth. The problem is that things on earth are only temporary. Eternity will deal them the final blow. On the other hand, good people often make poor choices. Thus, their temporal blessings are few, but their eternal blessing will be great. Nevertheless, bad and good things happen that are not related to choices. People get sick. Today, we know about cancer. In Solomon's day, it was not even a consideration. They did not know about kidney failure, heart attacks, blocked arteries, liver disease, or a ruptured appendix. They had ointments for boils and herbal concoctions for fever and other ailments, but they did not have the knowledge of what happened internally. Today, we can prove that a person's brain is misfiring. In Solomon's day, they just thought they had lost their minds. Whatever they thought then and no matter what we know about it now, noth-ing changes the fact that a person can have a medical brain problem. We do not know the answers to these medical mysteries, but God knows!

(3) The Worldly Man's Materialism (8:15a)

Solomon was guilty of being a worldly man in every fiber of his body, soul, and spirit. When nothing else made sense to him, he had a pat answer. *"Then I commended mirth, because a man hath no better thing under the sun, than to eat, and to drink, and to be merry"* (8:15a). For the fourth and final time, Solomon shows his materialism as a worldly man. All of Solomon's earthly thinking had only led him back to his same conclusion: "Boys, when the chips are down, go enjoy yourself, go eat, drink, and be merry, for nothing in this life has eternal everlasting meaning. Good happens to the bad, bad happens to the good, and it cannot be changed. Nevertheless, food, drink, and merriment can get us through it all." For Solomon, man cannot understand or know the ways of God, so why bother? Life is meaningless to Solomon, a fallacy in his long study of wisdom under the sun.

(4) The Worldly Man's Memory (8:15b)

Solomon continues to speak, *". . . for that shall abide with him of his labour the days of his life, which God giveth him under the sun"* (8:15b). Make no mistake. Man can discover the ways of God. God has revealed His ways to man; therefore, man is without excuse. God is communicating with man through the words of the Bible, the creation in which he lives, and testimonies of the changed lives of people who belong to God. It is man who does not want to communicate with God except when he has no other place to turn. The worldly man's memory is short. He forgets God's goodness. He forgets God's judgments. He forgets God's penalties; he forgets God's wrath. Plainly, he forgets God, until he needs Him! Short memories show the frivolity of being gleeful in the face of the seriousness of life under the sun without God.

d) The Fault with Being Gifted (8:16–17)
(1) The Weary Man Misses the Mark (8:16a)

What is it in humanity that causes the gifted of this world to be so ignorant about eternity? Where does the fault lie? What causes the gifted man to be so weary in the tasks of each day? Driven in many ways to do the unimportant for the unnecessary? Then Solomon speaks, *"When I applied mine heart to know wisdom, . . ."* (8:16a). Where did it get him? He studied life's frustration, its fallacies. He saw the fiction of being great, the folly of being godless, the fantasy of being good, the frivolity of being gleeful, and then he studied the fault of being gifted. Oh, this old Solomon may have been gifted in the eyes of the people, but he was no match for the giftedness of God Almighty! Keeping up with God is a weary task. Who in the world could ever compare? Solomon's problem was deep. He missed the mark by missing a relationship with God. The gifted do that! They do it often. The brains of this world deny God. They think they are smarter than God. They find a reason why there can be no God. They influence the world to believe God does not exist. They seek to explain why man is not really man and woman is not really woman. They counter the creation of God by stating that man can be what he thinks he is and woman can do the same. They proclaim, "If you think you are, that you shall be!" They look into the heavens and speculate on how it all started. They pick a number with no real basis and declare it to be the age of all creation. They gather the few facts that they can and fill in the gaps with speculation. They weary themselves with findings that miss the mark. They deny the written Word of God that explains it all. They say, "It is not so!" 'Tis the fault of being gifted, and Solomon was among the best of them.

(2) The Working Man Misses the Mark (8:16b)

Not all are weary from trying to apply their wisdom and therefore missing the mark. Some are working so hard that they are missing the mark. Solomon says, *". . . and to see the business that is done upon the earth: (for also there is that neither day nor night seeth sleep with his eyes:)"* (8:16b). I find it so amazing that some people are so busy being busy that they miss the most important things that they should be doing in life. The classic story, for instance, to express this problem is not found in the Old Testament; it is found in the Gospels with the anointing of Jesus in the home of Mary, Martha, and Lazarus in Bethany, just a short distance from the Mount of Olives. The time of Jesus' crucifixion was near at hand. Six days before in the home of Simon, Mary had broken a vase of perfume and anointed Jesus. Then, in the home of Mary, Martha, and Lazarus, Mary broke another expensive vase worth a year's wages for the common man to anoint Jesus again. Martha was in the kitchen preparing the meal and she was up to her chin in anger about what Mary was doing with Jesus in the other room.

Judas was there too! He had also been at Simon's home, his father's home. In both places he had protested the cost of the oil being wasted on Jesus. Nevertheless, the Lord allowed Mary to anoint Him. Jesus said it was for His own burial. From out of the kitchen Martha demanded that Mary stop the unnecessary ceremony and get on with woman's work in the kitchen. Jesus put that attitude to a stop too. Martha was so busy being busy that she missed the whole important moment with the Lord. She missed the mark!

Missing the mark in this same way has not changed since the time of Solomon or Jesus. Our churches are filled with people who are so busy being at church that they forget what it means to be the Church, to spread the Gospel, to share the good news, to lead sinners to the foot of the cross where they can be cleansed of their earthly sin and on to the glorious relationship of eternal life with the Lord. Jesus charged the Church with that job. Yet, doing the work of the church for some is more important than fulfilling the great charge of the Lord to go and make disciples, baptizing them in the name of the Father, Son, and Holy Spirit.

They miss the mark. They miss the joy. They miss the blessing. They miss the high calling. They miss the reward. It is their fault in being gifted at working too much in the wrong way for the wrong reasons and the wrong outcomes.

(3) The Wise Man Misses the Mark (8:17)

Finally, Solomon admits that in the studying of life's fallacies, the wise can miss the mark. He speaks, *"Then I beheld all the work of God, that a man cannot find out the work that is done under the sun: because though a man labour to seek it out, yet he shall not find it; yea further; though a wise man think to know it, yet shall he not be able to find it"* (8:17). All the wisdom of Solomon was really no wisdom at all. In all his labor under the sun, at his old age, he had missed the mark. He had failed to find what he was looking for. He had studied that which was unnecessary. He had judged the people, forced them into labor, taxed them to the point of poverty, lavished himself with the best, collected a thousand women, and where did it all take him? He had arrived at the age of seventy no different from every other person that old. More days were behind him than were in front of him, and what did it get him? He did not dwell in the shelter of the Almighty! He dwelt in the palace of his own making. He had failed God. God had not failed him. God gave him the wisdom he needed. Solomon misused that wisdom for godless purposes. As the wisest of all humans who have ever lived, he unwisely left his Creator out of his life for far too long. It was time for him to admit what he had studied about life's finalities.

3. Life's Finalities (9:1–10)
a) A Common Destination (9:1–3)
(1) The Omnipotence of God (9:1)
(a) His Power (9:1a)

"For all this I considered in my heart even to declare all this, that the righteous, and the wise, and their works, are in the hand of God" (9:1a). Once again, we must remind ourselves that Solomon was still preaching this sermon under the inspiration of the Almighty God. That point alone does not make the words of Solomon Godly! Mentioning God's purpose in this message was not to expose the Godly man but the godless man under the sun. Far too many preachers have made the worst of this by twisting the godless topic of these passages thus far into that which is Godly to the detriment of righteous theology and behavior. So, Solomon transfers

the finalities of life by directing his attention to the omnipotence of God and His power over death for "the righteous, and the wise, and their works." Why did Solomon place those restrictions on his statement? Why did he mention only the works of the wise and the righteous? Why did he not mention the wicked, and the ignorant, and their works? Does the Lord not have power over them as well? Even if Solomon had mentioned the wicked and the ignorant, the common destination of them would still be "in the hand of God," but that is not a promise of a good result and an eternal blessing. The same God who has the power to take the Godly one to glory to be with Him can send the godless to the eternal fire. Yes, indeed. Truth can be found in Solomon's words, but they do not assure a soul alive here on earth of the direction he will go when the final day of his life arrives! But surely the destination will be in the power of God's hand to say, "For you, it is time! Your stay on earth has ended." But then, what does Solomon say?

(b) His Presence (9:1b)

". . . no man knoweth either love or hatred by all that is before them" (9:1b). This statement shows just how distraught Solomon was at that point in his life. The finality of his life was "in the hand of God," yet Solomon did not know whether his future would be filled with love or hate when he entered into the presence of the Lord. Can you see the hopelessness? Can you see the struggle? Can you see the distress of this so-called righteous and wise man named Solomon? He did not have one work that he could rely on that promised his future. What was he saying? Maybe he knew the love of God would take him to heaven and the hatred of God would take him to eternal flames? For the one who has been faithful to God, God will love, and entering into His presence will be glorious as He says, "Well done my good and faithful servant. Enter into the joy of your salvation." But for the one who has been unfaithful to God, God will hate, and entering into His presence will be disastrous as He says, "Why should I let you into My heaven? Go and serve the one you served while on earth." What can man do about it? Nothing, in Solomon's determination. It was all in the hands of the omnipotent God.

(2) The Impotence of Man (9:2–3)
(a) The Inevitability of Death (9:2a)

If the finalities of life are in the hands of the omnipotent God, where does that put man in the equation? Solomon speaks, *"All things come alike to all"* (9:2a). In other words, man is impotent in the grand scheme of life and death. Death will come, and it is inevitable! Man cannot do one thing about it. Man can wait out his days and wither away in sickness and then he sees death. Man can fight in a war and be killed by the enemy and then he sees death. Man can cut short his life by his own hand and then he sees death. Solomon had figured it from every angle: man is incapable, man is powerless, man is impotent to change anything about the inevitability of death. It will come "alike to all."

(b) The Injustice of Death (9:2b–e)

It awaits:

(i) The Righteous Man and the Lawless Man (9:2b)

Solomon's mind drifted into a warped reality of the injustice of death. He could not see one quarter of an inch past his own nose. He could see only his state of being and not God's. He was so self-focused that he could not see the true justice in the plan of God. He had lived long enough to see that *"there is one event to the righteous, and to the wicked"* (9:2b), and that was death. How can it be that the righteous and the lawless end up alike? Dead? Unfair! Yes! In Solomon's mind. He cannot see past the last day of his life. All he can see is the death. True, both the righteous and the wicked pass into eternity through the portal of death, and true, that is the one event in front of both, but Solomon does not mention here that death of a man actually opens to a pathway of eternity and eternal home, but still he cannot see it at this point in his life.

(ii) The Respectable Man and the Licentious Man (9:2c)

Solomon was not through. He continued to see more injustice, *". . . to the good and to the clean, and to the unclean"* (9:2c). The one event, death, was not for just the righteous and the wicked, it was also for the good, clean, and unclean, meaning the respectable and licentious man. In other words, Solomon addresses those who were ritually clean, who had kept the law, made the offerings, prayed the prayers, jumped through the hoops, and were without blame in all areas of their lives as well as those who lived in the world, in the streets, in the depths of evil. How could that be fair? How could both have the same reward called death?

(iii) The Religious Man and the Lost Man (9:2d)

Then Solomon's mind dissects what he has just said, and he says, "*. . . to him that sacrificeth, and to him that sacrificeth not*" (9:2d). That has to do with keeping the law of God! All the gifts given to the Lord that will classify a man as religious versus how much wealthier a man could have been if he had not given to the Lord. That's the thing that will classify a man as lost. Hmm, Solomon thought. In the end, what is the difference? One does a lot to please God, the other does nothing. But in the end, both arrive in the same place. Dead!

(iv) The Resolute Man and the Lackadaisical Man (9:2e)

Solomon then thought about what he had just said and dissected it even more when he said, "*. . . as is the good, so is the sinner; and he that sweareth, as he that feareth an oath*" (9:2e). Can you see Solomon sink in his despair? Can you see him hopeless? Picture him on his throne, arms to the sides, palms up, head leaning back, staring toward the roof, just thinking, perhaps talking to himself. I, too, have been there at some time in my life. So have you! I've thought, and so have you, "Where is the fairness in this world? Why does injustice exist in this world? How can anyone overcome the inequality in this world? When will the disparity end in this world? Who will heal the discrepancies in this world?" If the mighty wise King Solomon of Israel did not have an in with God here, who does? He lorded with a heavy hand over all but to no avail in the end! He saw his demise will be the same as those whom he lorded over. As resolute, as firm, as unbending as he was in his rule, he will lie horizontal at the same level with the lackadaisical, apathetic, half-hearted, lazy man in the end. Dead! No higher, no lower. Add it all up and Solomon says, it is all up to the omnipotence of God, the impotent man cannot escape the injustice of death, but more than that, Solomon must accept the inescapabilty of dying.

(3) The Inescapability of Death (9:3)
(a) The Ghost That Haunts Us All (9:3a)

The thought is there. The thought would not leave Solomon. Death looms. Death haunts. Solomon says, "*This is an evil among all things that are done under the sun, that there is one event unto all*" (9:3a). He saw that death is an evil thing. It is a ghost to him, hanging out on his every thought. To be honest, at some point in all our lives, the ghost of death haunts us all. But what does death look like to one who belongs to the Lord and has confidence in his eternity?

Just six weeks ago, I found it quite difficult to write a Bible study on Ecclesiastes 9. Something was missing. I could have plowed through the material but, it would not have the same spirit, the same zing, the same power, the same flow. Death I know about. Hardly a week in forty-four years of ministry have I not dealt with death. In the 21,000-member church I serve, it is common to have a dozen deaths each week. It is common to get that call in the middle of the night and I must go to hold the hand of the spouse until the funeral director arrives. It is common to sit at the funeral home and carefully help explain the options and how things work. It is common to carve out the time in the week to meet with the family to listen to their memories to incorporate in the funeral sermon. I have spoken about those last few minutes of life. I have spoken about crossing the metaphorical chilly Jordan and how it is only chilly for those left behind. I have spoken about the entry into heaven, the steps to the city, the gate that you enter through, the golden streets, the river leading to the throne, and the conversation that the Lord has with God the Father. I have covered the "well done good and faithful servant" words as well as the "enter into the joy of your salvation" invitation. I have spoken about the meeting of loved ones, what they then learned in that first instance of moving from this life to the next. I have spoken about how they know about you as well as what they are thinking about you now. But, death did not haunt me. I was ready. My ticket was purchased on March 10, 1967. My bags were packed. I knew my mansion had been prepared. My name has been engraved in the Book of Life, never to be blotted out! I had learned many years ago to never leave something unsaid. I never need to tell someone I love him or her, I do that every day. I never need to ask for forgiveness, nothing is left undone, nothing will be found hidden away that I would be embarrassed about if someone found it. Yes, there are some old cars that I am working on, but someone can be paid to finish them or there are a whole host of crazy car folks that we could give them to and they would be blessed, but every day when I close my eyes, everything that truly matters in this life is done. But, in sixty-two years of life, death has not haunted me. I have never thought that I have lived past my human expiration date. It is not stamped anywhere on my body. It is not written in any earthly book yet. Only the Lord knows that date.

But that is not the way it is for many. I have sat at the doctors of many when the news came that it was cancer. They heard the aggressive cancer would give them no more than four months to live. The exact moment is not known, neither is the exact day. Neither are doctors God, but He has provided doctors with many tools, and their experience and knowledge are rarely wrong these days. I have been there when the four months turned out to be three. The healthy one with no aches or pains, gone in ninety days. I knew it, but I did not know what it felt like, emotionally or spiritually. I paused writing with the start of chapter 9. I wondered, "How do I handle what I do not truly understand? How do I convey the finalities of life when I have never faced the same moment and emotion that Solomon was facing? How do I write about the same future that Dr. Phillips was facing too, in this his last commentary of his life's work?"

A little bump came up in the corner of my eye. Just a bump. The first doctor said, "Let's just watch it." A week later it was bigger. Another doctor said, "Let's get an MRI." A week later that doctor says, "I think it needs to come out." But his schedule will take five weeks to get in surgery. A second doctor and the second opinion says the same, "We need to take it out." When can we do it? In three days. Let's do it! One week and the pathology. It is not good. Another big test is needed. Where else is it in the body? How much has it already spread? Word is that the eye is the last place it usually shows up. It's cancer.

My first reaction is I will give glory to God in all. I am going to walk this road to glory with my Lord. I am not afraid of death, but that is not the problem. The staff I have served with since October 1990 will want to know the results of the surgery. I do not know what to tell them. We do not have the whole story. How do I tell them? I do not dare tell them the kind of cancer in this modern age that we live because if they do a computer search all they are going to see is the worst-case scenario. Less than a year. If that! My trust is firmly in the Lord and my resolution is strong. As Job says, "I know that my Redeemer liveth!" It's another week until the big test, head to toe. After the test I ask for a copy of the disk to take to the doctor and amazingly, the radiologist has already made his report. They include it. I read it and cannot believe my eyes. Even though this cancer is a whole-body disease, its first sign was next to my eye where all the world could see. It wasn't hiding away in the organs as it usually is, growing in this one or that one. Most people find this cancer when something else is being treated; it is a surprise, a deadly one, an irreversible one. For those in my same case, a regular scan and preventative treatment each year gives a 99.7 percent essential cure. Yes, it is there. Yes, untreated, it will bring death. Yes, I have cancer. But, chances are, the Lord will use something else to usher me into eternity with him.

Nevertheless, in my experiences, for almost three weeks I had to stare at the possibility of less than a year to live. That experience haunted my wife every moment. In some ways, its ghost haunted me too. What kind of funeral? What kind of grave? What kind of gravestone? What can I do to make my departing easier for all? I understood! I had preached the glories of going on! I had taught about the glories of going on! I had written about the glories of going on! Faced with it, did I believe it? For me, yes. For my wife, yes. For my daughter, all I can say is, "I hope so." I want her to see my faith in the Lord. I do not want her to see my doubts because I have no doubts. I want her ready. I want her prepared. I want to leave her with a blessing. I want her to trust in the Lord with all her heart too and lean not on her own understanding. I want her to see that big picture that her mother and I have seen in almost forty years of marriage. I want her to say, "Well done, dad! Thank you for everything and I will be seeing you in glory in another six or seven decades! If you have any pull, could my mansion be next door to yours? By the way, make room because the whole family will be headed there one day too!" I understand the inescapability of death, but I also understand, because I belong to the Lord and He belongs to me, that Solomon was wrong when he said, "This is an evil among all things that are done under the sun, that there is one event unto all." Death for me will be a new beginning. I have the hope of glory. I am not looking at myself. I am looking to the One to whom I belong! I have assurance, Solomon did not. He could not see past the end of his life, I can! Death is not an evil thing.[42]

(b) The Grave That Hunts Us All (9:3b–c)
(i) The Follies of Life (9:3b)

Solomon just cannot get out from under the sun. He cannot look ahead. He can only look behind at the follies of life and how the grave hunts us all down. "... *yea, also the heart of the sons of men is full of evil, and madness is in their heart while they live, . . ."* (9:3b). What kind of world was Solomon living in? Had it turned upside down? What had happened to God in their lives? His father had left the kingdom to Solomon in pretty good shape! God was the God of all. The people were faithful in their worship! In general, they were all true worshipers. In the last forty years, what had happened to the people under Solomon's rule? Where had they placed their faith? Where had they focused their worship? Where had they bowed? Why is there evil in their hearts? What kind of madness has engulfed their hearts? Who had led them astray? Solomon, hold out your hand. Solomon, make a fist. Solomon, point one finger. Solomon, you can blame one quarter of their faithlessness and evil on everyone else. They should have known better. They had heard the law. They knew what you knew. They had seen the faithfulness and devoted worship of their parents under David. Surely, 25 percent was their fault.

But Solomon, three of your fingers are pointing back at you! Three quarters of the problem can be laid on your shoulders, your leadership, your actions, your demands, your worship, your devotion, your obedience, your defiance. You married all those women who worshiped other gods. You brought their idols into the Temple. You sacrificed on the high places. Your example became the custom of the day. Your example became the law of the day. Your example became the folly of the day. Solomon, to your people, everyday life was just that. You had made it permissible. You had made it the norm. You had made it the road of evil and madness to the grave.

Solomon was looking back on what he had designed and created in his kingdom and realized it was folly, all of it. It was not Godly, and it was too late for him to change any of it! The grave was haunting him, death was inescapable, he was going to leave things undone. He was going to leave things in a mess. He was going to leave with words that needed to be said and this sermon would have to do because it was all the time he had left and the strength to do so. What was left for Solomon to face?

(ii) The Finality of Death (9:3c)

Solomon must have wondered how many more breaths he had within him. He saw it. He saw the finality of death. The preacher says, *". . . and after that they go to the dead"* (9:3c). After all the folly of life, after all the taunting of the ghost of the grave, after all the injustice of death, impotence of man, where does it get him? Only one place. Solomon lived most of his life as the king in defiant rebellion to

God inside his palace, breaking the rules, bending the laws, blending the proverbs, breaching the boundaries, buttressing the evil, and beginning the madness
of life under the sun without God. It was now time to bow to the omnipotence
of the God he defied. The God who would have taken his kingdom away from
him had he not been the son of David. Oh death, where is thy sting? Oh grave,
where is thy victory? Solomon can see the sting of death creeping up on him,
but unlike me, he could not see the victory beyond the grave and beyond death.
Emboldened, Solomon made his callous declaration about life and death that was
in total opposition to the theology of God found in the rest of the Holy Writ!

> b) A Callous Declaration (9:4–6)
>> (1) A Fatalistic Statement (9:4–5a)
>>> (a) A Cynical Comparison (9:4)

Heartless, unfeeling, coldhearted, insensitive, callous words Solomon conjures
up. A fatalistic statement. A cynical comparison. *"For to him that is joined to all
the living there is hope: for a living dog is better than a dead lion"* (9:4). A living
dog versus a dead lion? Those of us who live in the west do not understand the
severity of this cynical comparison. We love our dogs, we adore our dogs, we
often give our dogs better health care than we provide for ourselves. Our dogs
have a special place in the house, in the car, in the yard. We spend thousands of
dollars each year on their bedding, grooming, feeding, and tending. We spend
more time with them and train them from birth better than we pay attention to
and train our own children. More than that, every few years we get another one
and start the whole process over. They become part of our families and often
hold rank above that of our human family members. For some, they become the
best friend and in a whole host of cases, the only friend. When we say, "such is a
dog's life," it holds highest regard for the animal, the hero of the family pampered
at the salon, the boutique, the photo shoots, the all about town. That's how we
Westerners feel about our dogs in this modern age.

But even in the Western world we are beginning to get a taste of some of the
world's view about dogs as Middle Easterners come to America, those who have
lived their whole lives in a culture embedded deep in essentially the same setting
of Solomon's day. Put your home up for sale and let a Muslim come to look at
it. In many cases, the first question about the house has nothing to do with the
color, floor plan, roof, foundation, storage, backyard, or neighborhood. The first
question is about dogs. "Has a dog ever lived in this house?" Nothing about cats,

rats, raccoons, cockatoos, hamsters, monkeys, ferrets, skunks, and the bunch! Only dogs! Why?

From the earliest records, dogs were used for herding and security, trained for specific jobs (Job 30:1; Psalm 22:17–21; Isaiah 56:10). But they were outside animals. By the time of the prophet Samuel, the dog was a term of complete distain for another. The Philistine asked David, "Am I a dog, that thou comest to me with staves?" (1 Samuel 17:43). Later, David asked the question of King Saul, "After whom is the king of Israel come out? after whom dost thou pursue? after a dead dog, after a flea" (1 Samuel 24:14). Back in the last days of Moses in the wilderness journey, the wages paid for the work of a dog or that of a prostitute were of such disrepute that they were not to be accepted as an offering in the sanctuary (Deuteronomy 23:19). Many years after Solomon, Isaiah will complain about the degradation of the priesthood by saying, ". . . he that sacrificeth a lamb, as if he cut off a dog's neck; he that offereth an oblation, as if he offered swine's blood; he that burneth incense, as if he blessed an idol. Yea, they have chosen their own ways, and their soul delighteth in their abominations" (Isaiah 66:3). Dogs, swine, and idols were three Jewish ingredients in their pot of abominations. Jesus warned the people not to listen to the theological teaching of the dogs (Matthew 7:6). "Give not that which is holy unto the dogs, neither cast ye your pearls before swine, lest they trample them under their feet, and turn again and rend you." Even Jesus associated dogs with swine! Paul agreed with Jesus and said, "Beware of dogs, beware of evil workers, beware of the concision" (Philippians 3:2).

Oh, but the lion—that's a whole other animal of a glorious sort! Lions were admired, kept as pets, revered, respected, valued, esteemed, treasured, and cherished. More than a hundred times the Old Testament speaks of the strength, power, and daring of this animal. Remember its roar? Why, even the Lord is called the Lion of Judah! What a picture! Much different from the characteristics of the dog.

Solomon's cynical comparison that "a living dog is better than a dead lion" once again shows how debased he has become. The mighty carnivorous and most feared and ferocious animal meant absolutely nothing once it was dead! It would have been better for the lion to have been a detested live dog. At least a live dog had the chance of living another day. The dead lion had no hope!

(b) A Cynical Comment (9:5a)

Solomon could not help himself. He had to follow his previous statement with this, *"For the living know that they shall die: but the dead know not any thing, . . ."*

(9:5a). A cynical comment! The trouble comes in the last part. No one will argue one moment about the first part. Truly the living know that one day they, too, will face death, but to say that the "dead know not any thing" shows Solomon's lack of knowledge. And let us make sure that we are clear about whom Solomon is speaking! He is not talking about dogs and lions. Those are just examples used to make his point. Not one animal in this world besides humans looks into the future and thinks about death! Only humans. Furthermore, not one animal in this world besides humans knows anything after death! Only humans. Here Solomon has gone back to the disparity of death and specifically, life after death! Remember in that famous third chapter of this sermon where Solomon spouts off all the times for this and the times for that and the seasons for this and the seasons for that, each point, by the way, in conflict with the rest of the completed Word of God in some way.

Do you remember? Funerals abound where those words have been used as if they might bring some sort of comfort. They always agitate me when I hear them and perhaps they should agitate you too! Why? The readers always stop short of Solomon's conclusion about those times and seasons. Reading on would agitate the listeners. Solomon's words were agitating to him there too! What was his conclusion to the times and the seasons? Let us take a moment to remember his words because Solomon has not changed his mind thus far in all that he has studied under the sun. Here is what he said then and what he means by this cynical comment.

> For that which befalleth the sons of men befalleth beasts; even one thing befalleth them: as the one dieth, so dieth the other; yea, they have all one breath; so that a man hath no preeminence above a beast: for all is vanity. All go unto one place; all are of the dust, and all turn to dust again. (Ecclesiastes 3:19–20)

No hope can be found in Solomon's thoughts. But he was and is not alone. The world, the people of the world that is, who have not listened to the Word of the Lord, know nothing about the sure fact of eternity after the last breath of life is taken on this earth. Never should Solomon have said that "all go unto one place." Yes, the vessels of clay that we live in return to the dust but the persons within will go on to an eternal home. Now you see why I say, "Solomon cannot see past his last breath." Not so with his father! David knew about eternity. Did not David try to impress on Solomon the following?

And thou, Solomon my son, know thou the God of thy father, and serve him with a perfect heart and with a willing mind: for the LORD searcheth all hearts, and understandeth all the imaginations of the thoughts: if thou seek him, he will be found of thee; but if thou forsake him, he will cast thee off for ever. Take heed now; for the LORD hath chosen thee to build an house for the sanctuary: be strong, and do it. (1 Chronicles 28:9–10)

Yes, that is a warning to Solomon! But David knew about the hereafter and this warning included his words, "but if thou forsake him, he will cast thee off for ever." Forever! Have you ever stopped to think about that? David must have known that forever has two possibilities, two destinations, two eternities. All the same! Which would Solomon select? Would he take the road to forever with the Lord or would he take the road to forever without Him? Did Solomon not know? If he didn't, he should have! The psalmist says:

So foolish was I, and ignorant: I was as a beast before thee. Nevertheless I am continually with thee: thou hast holden me by my right hand. Thou shalt guide me with thy counsel, and afterward receive me to glory. Whom have I in heaven but thee? and there is none upon earth that I desire beside thee. My flesh and my heart faileth: but God is the strength of my heart, and my portion for ever. (Psalm 73:22–26)

(2) A False Statement (9:5b)

From Solomon's cynical comment, he makes a false statement. "*. . . neither have they any more a reward; for the memory of them is forgotten*" (9:5b). We might want to step back and look at this sentence from both sides, but it doesn't really matter which side you select because both are false. Some will look at this and say, "People will soon forget the departed and remember them no more." That is not a true statement because people are connected to people in this world. Let's just look at me, for example! I have siblings, parents, grandparents all the way back to Noah. When I look at my parents, it took 2 to make me, 4 to make them, 8 to make them, 16 to make them, and the math continues. Looking just ten generations back it took 1,024 grandparents, half male and half female, to make me. But with just one more generation, the eleventh line of my ancestors, it took twice as many grandparents to make the following generation. Astounding! Therefore, the math shows that 2,048 people from my past eleven generations were involved in making me. Go to the twelfth generation and it has taken 4,096 people to make me. There were the same number on my wife's side! And yours too! We are all alike. From an earthly position, to say that the "reward for the memory" of those who are now dead is forgotten is simply not so. Part of all our ancestors back to Noah and then back to Adam are within us as their reward passed on through each generation. The Hebrew word for "memory" is *zayker*, and it means a "memento." It means to remember, recollect, or to bear in mind a little part, just a *memento*. In that sense of the word, we have a little memory of all our past ancestors within us; therefore, they are not forgotten because they live on through us.

Now from the other position we must look at our reward and memory from beyond this life, in the state of death, and, in Solomon's day, all the dead resided in the graves. Could it be that once death has occurred that the memory of this life in this world is forgotten, wiped away? Could it be that there is no reward in the afterlife based on what was done here on earth? Could it be that the dead cannot see that which is continuing in life on earth? Could it be? Could it be that Solomon had misconstrued his father's words in Psalm 6:4–5? "Return, O LORD, deliver my soul: oh save me for thy mercies' sake. For in death there is no remembrance of thee: in the grave who shall give thee thanks?" David was in trouble when he wrote this. He needed health restored for "mercies' sake" which means the loving-kindness of the Lord. David was basically saying to the Lord, "If You want praise from me, heal me while I am still alive and kicking. Once my body is in the grave, it can never give praise again to You." That was David's excuse. It, too, was a false statement. One day even his body will rise in glorification to be with his soul and live in the presence of the Lord forever. But then, for both David and Solomon, all they could see was the temporal use of the body and not its eternal use. True, all the wonderful blessings of life beyond the grave were not privy to those two or anyone else before them, but that does not mean that the revelation of the promises about life beyond the grave will not be theirs too! They will. But in the next breath, Solomon actually tripped over two thoughts that are factual statements in his callous declaration.

(3) A Factual Statement (9:6)
(a) Their Passions Have Faded Away (9:6a)

The physical, emotional, and cognitive passions of those who have gone on through the portal of death will no longer be heard by those left behind, not at least in the way they did when the person was alive. When Solomon says, *"Also their love, and their hatred, and their envy, is now perished . . ."* (9:6a), he is speaking of the things that the departed did while he was alive. Here Solomon's statements are factual. A young man once gave this testimony:

> I can no longer hear my father and mother tell me how much they love me, at least not while I am still here on earth. That is not to say that I am not reminded often, as I am at this moment, of those times I heard them say, "I love you." In my mind I can still see them there, their eyes, their lips moving, even the embarrassment in my young teen years of their arms around me. Somehow it is all very real even though Dad went to be with the Lord in 1967 and Mom in 2002. The memory of the teaching they gave me is ever present even though they are gone. The same can be said by me of those who have gone on that clearly said hateful things to me as well as those who were envious of what the Lord was doing in my life versus what was going on in theirs. I can still remember them, but they can harm me no longer. They cannot add one more word to what has been said since they crossed the portal of death. The ability of their passions that caused them to love, hate, or envy in this earthly life has surely faded away but my memory has not.[43]

(b) Their Persons Have Faded Away (9:6b)

Solomon correctly stumbled over another truth, although we cannot be sure if it was intentional on his part in his depressed state of mind. *". . . neither have they any more a portion for ever in any thing that is done under the sun"* (9:6b). In other words, the persons have faded away from this world, never to influence it again by their personal presence. Let's clarify that just a tad by adding *as they did while they were on earth before seeing death.* Why would I say that? We have the full Word of God now. We know that all who belong to the Lord will return with Him to this earth when He sets up His kingdom here. We, in our glorified spiritual bodies, will have jobs to do that will direct and influence those on earth still in their human temporal bodies. But then, we will be under the divine direction of the Lord and will not err in our decisions. Then, we will guide exactly as the Lord's will directs. Then, we will act exactly as the Lord's will demands. We will be part of the holy band of heaven, an army dressed for battle, prepared by the Lord, mounted on white horses, dressed in the purest white linen, totally devoted to the Lord of Lords and the King of Kings. But Solomon was not privy to that information from the Lord. He was talking about the body being in the grave, dead, rotting, turning to dust, gone from this world in the human flesh, gone from the family unit still here, gone from the enemies of this life, out of view, faded away from all the activities under the sun. How true!

  c) A Carnal Decision (9:7–10)
    (1) Enjoy Your Wine While You Can (9:7)

In a snap, Solomon turned his mind from the grave and returned to the vanity of his life under the sun and made a carnal decision; in other words, he offered four statements in his decision that are held by the unconverted man and an enemy of God. *"Go thy way, eat thy bread with joy, and drink thy wine with a merry heart; for God now accepteth thy works"* (9:7). There it is! Enjoy your bread and wine while you can! There it is! Don't worry about God, He will accept all that you have done in the past. There it is! Get drunk and have a merry heart! Nothing to worry about! Nothing to fear! Nothing to vex! Nothing to perplex! Nothing after death so nothing to worry about in eternity! The high priests were not allowed to drink wine ever because it would interfere with their duties (Leviticus 10:9). Even Solomon had said of the use of wine, "Let him drink, and forget his poverty, and remember his misery no more" (Proverbs 31:7). Even in that passage we see Solomon admit that it dulls the thinking process to forget the misery of poverty, in this case, but it will have the same effect on sinful actions. Under the influence of wine, sins and misery will be forgotten, at least until the mind awakens from the stupor. Then what? The sin and misery returns. So Solomon says, "Get drunk and be happy to forget the misery of your actions in life before you die." Solomon had one large heap of misery to drink away from his forty years of rebellion during his reign as king. One last thing. The carnal minded are always making excuses as to why God will accept what they have done in life. Accept it He will! They were your actions and you are responsible for them, not Him. At some point, each carnal man must realize that he is a sinner and turn to the Lord and accept His offer of salvation. Sadly, for most carnal people, that moment of silence in the pew at Christmas and Easter is all they need. Sadly, that is not enough for the Lord. A moment will not do. He wants every moment of every day in devotion to Him. It would have seemed that Solomon would have done that because of what he saw in his father's relationship with the Lord, but he did not follow in his father's faith and walk. To that Solomon said, "Drink enough wine to make you happy!"

(2) Enjoy Your Wealth While You Can (9:8)

Solomon's second carnal statement is, *"Let thy garments be always white; and let thy head lack no ointment"* (9:8). We would interpret Solomon's words like this, "Enjoy your wealth while you can!" It took money to purchase white clothing. Such clothing was kept for special days, feasts, and festivities. Rarely were they spotless but that is the intent of Solomon's words here; no stains were to be on the garments. That was expensive. See him mention the ointment for the head too! No lack, he says. He is speaking of anointing oil. This would have been olive oil mixed with incense. One pound of the mixture used on Jesus by Mary in the home in Bethany was worth more than a year's wages for the common man. A pound of ointment used every day was just sixteen ounces. That would last a little while if used just once a day, but say it was applied three times a day. Several years' wages could have been used up in just a month. You cannot spend your wealth once you die, Solomon was thinking, so spend it now on your dress and smell!

(3) Enjoy Your Wife While You Can (9:9)

Solomon's third carnal thought is, *"Live joyfully with the wife whom thou lovest all the days of the life of thy vanity, which he hath given thee under the sun, all the days of thy vanity: for that is thy portion in this life, and in thy labour which thou takest under the sun"* (9:9). I cannot help but ask of Solomon, which wife is he speaking of in this passage? Let's see, by the end of his life he had seven hundred wives and three hundred concubines. Those concubines were considered secondary wives, so we must consider them too. Was one out of the thousand his favorite? Or perhaps was he still mourning over the one that he could not get, about whom he wrote in the Song of Solomon? Which wife did he mean when this sermon came from his lips? Oh yes, and all the days under the sun are nothing more than "vanity," emptiness: they mean nothing in the whole scheme of things in eternity! Because you cannot take her with you, because you cannot enjoy her company after death, make up for it while you are alive and enjoy your wife while you can. I must wonder, did it matter or not to the wife if she enjoyed him? Probably not. After all, he was the collector of wives, they were not collectors of husbands. They had only one husband and he was not satisfied by just one of them enough to love and adore her beyond all others and devote himself only to the one in joyful living. In Solomon's world, his wives had to wait on his whim and desire.

(4) Enjoy Your Work While You Can (9:10)

Solomon's fourth carnal thought was, *"Whatsoever thy hand findeth to do, do it with thy might; for there is no work, nor device, nor knowledge, nor wisdom, in the grave, whither thou goest"* (9:10). I clearly understand what old Solomon was thinking. When even the thought of death lingers, even while the body is still healthy, the carnal mind strays to think of all the things that still need to be done, the unfinished projects, the messes that need to be cleaned up, the files that need to be arranged, the places to go, the things to do, and the list of to-dos goes on and on. Hurry up and get everything done that you want to do, is Solomon's carnal thought. But for a child of God, even a diagnosis of cancer does not need to send one scrambling with many "to do's." God's priorities become quite clear.

> When I was faced with revelation of cancer, a deadly one at that, I, too, thought of all the "to do's" left in my life, but my reaction was different from Solomon's. When I thought of the antique cars I have been lovingly restoring for more than forty years, my first thought was not to get out in the garage and finish them; my thought was, "I can pay someone to finish them!" Those cars were for my personal enjoyment and not for any sense of pride or show. They truly mean nothing in the huge scale of my life and eternity. There were dozens of thoughts about other things and the answer was the same with them all, I can pay to have them finished, I can give them away finished or unfinished, I can downsize my stuff so my family does not have that task, I can lift that burden with a phone call and an offer to those who would gladly take them and, most likely, sell them for a sizable profit! Perfect in my mind!
>
> My time in doing special things is much more important. What are those things? For more than fifty-one years I have loved the Lord and worked to tell the world about Him and His plan. For more than forty-four years I have served him in full-time ministry and He has never forsaken me at one moment. He has always provided for me and my family every day and in every need. I have been on the straight path, I have preached about Him, I have taught about Him, I have written about

Him, I have lived for Him in my work life and my family life. With the bad news came the good news in my heart, I will not change one thing I am doing even until I take my last breath and He comes to receive me and take me to my heavenly home to be with Him forever and ever (John 14).

I will not take the position posted by Solomon in this passage. Even after this life, I still have work to do, praises to give, family to reunite with, and family as well as future descendants to watch on their earthly journey. Solomon had it wrong. The Apostle Paul had it right. "For now we see through a glass, darkly; but then face to face: now I know in part; but then shall I know even as also I am known" (1 Corinthians 13:12). Here on earth we *partially know* about things, but when we take our last breath we will *fully know* even as we have been *fully known* by the Lord from before creation. Here on earth we understand the concept of *partial knowledge*; there are many things we just do not know, and we accept it.

But here on earth we cannot understand the concept of *full knowledge*. Full means full and that means everything. It means that in an instant, in the twinkling of an eye, once we take our last breath, we will know everything about everything fully, all the past and all the future, the reasons why and the reasons why not. You cannot tell me that such full knowledge is limited to the heavenly things of God because all of that is integrated with the earthly things of this world. We speak of the family of God, with whom we will be in heaven, but the nucleus of the biological family is the foundation set forth with Adam and Eve and continues to this day. How can it be that when we leave this world in death, the earthly family becomes of no use any longer in heaven? That makes absolutely no sense at all! Truly, there is no giving and taking in marriage in heaven and that concerns the sexual relationship between the husband and wife, but that does not negate the eternal biological relationships built here on earth that will be shared with joy in heaven with those of our families who have loved the Lord their God with all their hearts and put their trust in Him. Why would the Lord do away with that? Nonsense!

But more than that, it is ever so comforting to know that when a loved one dies and is with the Lord and has full knowledge, *when we think of him or her, he or she knows we are thinking of them.* No, they cannot reply. No, we should not pray to them. No, we should not worship them. No, we should not seek to contact them. Contacting them will come soon enough when the Lord comes to take us to be with Him in the heavenly realms, but the relationship with family and friends does not end at death. It just begins! From this side of glory, nothing will be better than being in eternity with the Lord and all our loved ones worshiping and serving Him for all time! Solomon was wrong with his carnal thoughts about life's finalities in the things that he had studied under the sun.[44]

4. Life's Falseness (9:11–10:15)
   a) The Triumph of Fate (9:11–12)
      (1) The Unattainable (9:11)
         (a) Choice: The Great Inequity of Life (9:11a)

We cannot begin to imagine that Solomon was actually thinking about all he had studied but one thing we do know, he was taken aback at this point in his sermon about life's falseness. For almost seventy years life seemed real to him, but now, it seemed unreal. As he considered his past he settled on the triumph of fate. He was lucky enough to be the chosen son of the king. Yet, he was doomed to be the chosen son of the king. We might call that the good news and the bad news. Fate put Solomon where he was, but fate did not allow him to live the normal life like all those under his authority. His life was privileged, the lives of his patrons were not. Under his leadership, many of them were prescribed to forced labor under the sun for his personal projects. But at this point in his life, fate was taking him where he did not want to go. Longer life was unattainable. The only choice he had was to accept the great inequity of life. Solomon speaks, *"I returned, and saw under the sun, that the race is not to the swift, nor the battle to the strong, neither yet bread to the wise, nor yet riches to men of understanding, nor yet favour to men of skill"* (9:11a). What has he said here? Simply, he has admitted that nothing he did in his life had given him any advantage over the peasants in his kingdom. Surely, he should have had an advantage over this thing called life, at least in his own mind. But it did not matter; he was headed to the same destination as all who had gone on before him.

(b) Chance: The Great Inevitability of Death (9:11b)

Fate was involved in Solomon's first point; chance was involved in the second. Fate was the choice that set in motion the great inequity of life, chance set in motion the great inevitably of death. *". . . but time and chance happeneth to them all"* (9:11b). Just as with fate, Solomon cannot shake chance away. With time, chance becomes real and death is on the way.

> (2) The Unavoidable (9:12)
>> (a) Life's Limitations (9:12a–b)
>>> (i) Indicated (9:12a)

When death arrives, it will be unavoidable. Life has its limitations. Life has its borders, restrictions, and boundaries. Life comes to an end. When? Solomon says, *"For man also knoweth not his time"* (9:12a). The end is not indicated on the earthly calendar of life. Only the Lord knows, yet death knows and is unavoidable.

>>> (ii) Illustrated (9:12b)

To illustrate his thought to address his dilemma, Solomon said, *". . . as the fishes that are taken in an evil net, and as the birds that are caught in the snare . . ."* (9:12b). The fish cannot avoid the evil net in its path and the bird cannot avoid the snare in its nest. Solomon's point is not the net or the snare; his point is the quickness for which its fate occurs. Neither the fish nor the bird can know that it is caught until it is caught! Fish swim freely at will; birds fly freely at will. Only when either is suddenly trapped does its freedom end.

>> (b) Life's Liabilities (9:12c)

After his illustration of the fish and birds, Solomon concludes, *". . . so are the sons of men snared in an evil time, when it falleth suddenly upon them"* (9:12c). For Solomon, man's life is not any different from the freedom of the fish and birds. Death traps the man in the same way that the net and snare trap the animal.

> b) The Triumph of Forgetfulness (9:13–18)
>> (1) The City (9:13–15)
>>> (a) The Size of the City (9:13–14b)
>>>> (i) No Outward Significance (9:13–14a)

Solomon's mind moved on from the triumph of fate to the triumph of forgetfulness over life because of death. He was reminded of a city. He was reminded of the size of the city. He was reminded that the city had no outward sign of significance.

He speaks, *"This wisdom have I seen also under the sun, and it seemed great unto me: there was a little city, . . ."* (9:13–14a). Why, pray tell, was Solomon studying a "little city" under the sun? He did so because this story illustrates just how easy it is to forget the most important person in any city. In a large city a person might accidentally be forgotten, but in a small city, surely not! At least not from any onlooker viewing it from the city's outer limits. That's the way it is with life. By just looking at the living life of a human, no one truly knows what is inside.

(ii) No Inward Strength (9:14b)

When Solomon studied the interior of the city, he found a major problem because it had no inward strength. Why? He said, *". . . and few men within it; . . ."* (9:14b). Solomon could not look within a human life, but he could see the symptoms. To him, it seems that little life remains within.

(b) The Siege of the City (9:14c)

Continuing his allegory, Solomon says, *". . . and there came a great king against it, and besieged it, and built great bulwarks against it"* (9:14c). Within this story, Solomon spoke of the great enemy that comes upon the city, but for him, he was alluding to the enemy, death, that builds its bulwark against life.

(c) The Savior of the City (9:15)
(i) Their Ignorance of Him (9:15a)

Although there were few men in the city, Solomon saw something important. He says, *". . . now there was found in it a poor wise man, and he by his wisdom delivered the city"* (9:15a). He saw a savior of the city and yet, the few men within it did not know about him. They were the ignorant; the poor man was not. Something he did saved the city. For Solomon, something within him saved his life for another day; something kept him from his day of death; something he knew nothing about protected him.

(ii) Their Ignoring of Him (9:15b)

"Yippee!" The city's people surely said, in Solomon's imagination. The city was saved. It did not matter who did the saving. However, had it been a dignitary, a parade would have been planned. Horses without number, dressed and adorned in gold, silver, and plumes of purple and red. A carriage would have held the savior and men would have lifted it high as it wound around the streets of the city. But the savior was not a dignitary; he was just a poor man. Therefore, the city rejoiced, *". . . yet no man remembered that same poor man"* (9:15b). The people of the city ignored him.

(2) The Cynic of the City (9:16–18)
  (a) And the Despised Man (9:16)

Solomon was the cynic of the city in his story. He says, *"Then said I, Wisdom is better than strength: nevertheless the poor man's wisdom is despised, and his words are not heard"* (9:16). Do you notice how the savior of the city was despised? Solomon must have been thinking about himself as the savior of the city. He was wise enough to keep it from all dangers, but no one cared. To him he was the despised man. What did it get him in his life? Nothing! Death still stared him in the face despite what he had done for himself in life. Little strength remained within him and wisdom could not help him now.

(b) And the Deluded Man (9:17)

Solomon had become the deluded man. He was mistaken. He was misled. He was fooled by the wisest fool of them all. *"The words of wise men are heard in quiet more than the cry of him that ruleth among fools"* (9:17). In Adam Clarke's commentary, the great Methodist theologian says the following: "I cannot help pursuing this illustration a little farther. The soldier who found Archimedes busily employed in drawing figures upon the sand, put to him some impertinent question, withal rudely obtruding himself on his operations. To whom this wonderful mathematician replied, 'Stand off, soldier, and do not spoil my diagram;' on which the bloody savage struck him dead! In the tumult of war the words of Archimedes were not heard; and his life was lost."[45]

With all his wisdom, death was about to strike Solomon down too, regardless of how busy he was in divining his proverbs, scribbling his plays, and "dispensing with" wisdom and justice within his realm. Not all he did was justice. Not all he did was wise. At the end of his life, his breath was not strong enough to proclaim his wise and noble words for all the nation to hear. Relegated to a whisper, most of his nation was not listening to him anymore. They were looking forward to his death and the new king Jeroboam who would take over, at least among the ten northern tribes. Fools they all were and that's what Solomon thought of them! He was the cynic of the city, deluded and soon to be forgotten by ten parts of his kingdom.

(c) And the Dangerous Man (9:18)

What did that make Solomon? It made him the dangerous man. He spoke, *"Wisdom is better than weapons of war: but one sinner destroyeth much good"* (9:18). Perhaps Solomon could have used his wisdom to thwart death. Perhaps not. Perhaps Solomon had sinned too much to change the direction of his life and his kingdom. Perhaps not. Perhaps he was the wise sinner that the people of his city wanted to forget. Perhaps he was just being cynical. Perhaps not. It would do him no good. It would not change death's triumph of fate and its triumphs of forgetfulness. Solomon, the screaming sinner and the fool, destroyed all the good that he had done in life.

c) The Triumph of Folly (10:1–7)
(1) Over All That Is Reasonable (10:1–3)
(a) The Parable of the Dead Fly (10:1)

The chapter break at this point senselessly divides the flow of Solomon's thoughts. Although he begins to speak in parables, a favorite method of communication for him through his life, they are not to be separated from the message to stand alone as those found in his book of Proverbs. All of these sayings are used for a purpose to continue his thoughts from his story about the poor man who saved the city and was quickly forgotten. He quickly surmised that he was in fact the poor wise man, despised by the people, deluded in his thoughts, a danger to the health of his nation because of his actions.

With these proverbs, Solomon's mind began to drift in folly. His desperation led him in the same direction as the thoughts of most men who are hopeless in their lives and their eyes refuse to look at God and their ears refuse to listen to His Word. With a parable we find Solomon looking for a permanent solution to his temporary problem. In his sermon he voices his first thought of a solution—a deadly but virtually painless solution. *"Dead flies cause the ointment of the apothecary to send forth a stinking savour: so doth a little folly him that is in reputation for wisdom and honour"* (10:1).

After perusing some fifty or so commentaries of the great theologians of the past, I found almost all agree that the words "dead flies" should be better rendered *death flies* or *flies of death*. Then, most of the writers would agree, these flies would land in the oil used as ointment, die, and turn the oil rancid, which would cause the oil to stink and be useless for its original purpose. That is a fine way of looking at this passage, but it is a parable, a saying, which always has a meaning just under the surface that is the intended message. I sought to scratch away the surface and dig a little deeper. Why? Something just did not make plain common sense about that whole interpretation even though I highly respected the works of the great theologians I studied.

The Hebrew word for "dead" is *mawveth* and 128 times it is translated *death*, 22 times it is translated *die*, but only 8 times is it translated *dead*. Therefore, because of such a great use of the word *death*, I, too, conclude that *flies of death* or *death flies* was the proper interpretation.

Then there is the word "ointment." An ointment was nothing more than an oil. Whether extracted from an animal, mineral, or vegetable, it really does not make a difference for this example. In one case, oil was thickened by an inert powder to make a salve of some sort that our English translators would call an ointment for moisturizing the skin. But because Solomon mentions the "apothecary," a whole new direction must be explored. Anyone could gather oil from any of the sources and make his own moisturizing concoctions, but the apothecary used the oil to mix the medicines. The oil was a carrying agent for the application of some healing mixture of some extraction or herb. Frankincense was mixed with oil to apply to warts as well as cracked and rough skin. The extract of lavender was added to oil and applied to bruised skin to cause the body to quickly break down and reabsorb the collection of blood. Eucalyptus and/or peppermint were mixed with oils and applied under the nose or rubbed on the chest to open up the bronchial tubes for breathing. Spearmint with oil was placed on the temples to stimulate the mind. Thyme and/or clove with oil were used to kill disease. Rosemary with oil stimulated the healthy scalp. Myrrh with oil was used to clean the mouth and throat. The apothecary would make other mixtures with oil for skin application to keep away bugs that bite and sting. That leads us back to Solomon's parable. How many flies of death would it take to make a vase of oil go bad?

When I turned eleven I took a job working with honeybees. For eight years that was my job every Saturday. We had three five-hundred-gallon vats that were always covered with dead bees. Once a week it was my job to collect the dead bees. I wondered if there was that much difference between the potency of a dead bee versus a dead fly? How many flies would it take to make a pint of oil go bad? Then how long would it take before the oil began to stink?[46]

Off to Israel and the African continent I went in my books and found the most unexpected thing. In that part of the world a fly exists that is called the tsetse fly. Ashby, my dear friend from that part of the world, came into my office while I had the books open, and I asked him, "Have you ever heard of the tsetse fly?"

"Oh, my friend," he said. "That is the fly of death! If several of them bite you, you will die."

A little more reading and I learn that this fly brought death to almost every living thing it landed on. It would attack animals, thrust its tube into the skin, and drain the blood from the animal, leaving behind parasites which causes a disease we know today as African sleeping sickness. It is not an easy death. This disease starts with a high fever, aches, and itching. All the organs are attacked before the parasites reach the nervous system. Then comes the coma. Then comes death. Although it may seem like a long time of agony and suffering, the week or so would be quite short compared to waiting on the natural things of life to kill you. The symptoms of this attack on the body were not uncommon. Even Solomon's generation had to battle various viruses as we do today. Who would know if the illness one had was secretly induced by the tsetse fly? And what does all that have to do with the ointment having a "stinking savor"?

The parable uses the words "stinking savor" for the effect of the oil mixed by the apothecary. The Hebrew uses one word for our two words, and it is *bawash*. It can mean to stink but it also means "abhor, abomination, or loathsome." Solomon was at the place in his life after he had studied everything, mostly the things he had done personally, and in his great despair he was thinking about a mixture that could be ordered by doctors from the local apothecary that could hasten his death. He was the king! He could order a potion himself, a potion made from oil infested with the parasites deposited by the tsetse flies. No one would know. The death would be fairly sudden. It would look like a natural death! But, it would not be natural. It would be suicide. In the Jewish culture, it would be an abomination. If the apothecary let the word out that Solomon had ordered a special potion, all of the king's wisdom, life, and work would be abhorred. The people would think of Solomon with loathsome thoughts after he was dead and buried. What would they write on his tombstone? His son, Rehoboam, would surely write something exalting! That's fair to think. We often lie about our dearly departed, you know. Families often try to get the preacher to preach the ungodly into the Godly realm. But what would the people say? A personal testimony from an old preacher is appropriate as an example!

> Forty-four years ago, I preached my first funeral in a church I had been at for only a week. I did not know the people or the local lore on everyone. I met with the family and they told me all about the dead one. I repeated their thoughts in the message. At the end of the service, I stood at the head of the casket to greet everyone as they passed by for their final goodbye, before the lid was shut for the final time.
>
> Four friends of the dead man said to me as they shook my hand. "You did not know him, did you?"
>
> "No sir, I did not."
>
> "I thought so." The last man said, "Had you known him for even one moment, you would have never said one thing you said today."
>
> Wow! What had I done? Come to find out, the man was the local personification of evil in the community. The few that were there, besides the family, were attending in joy and celebration for his passing. One later told me, "The moment I heard he had died I rejoiced, I felt a comfort, finally, the turmoil of my life was over."[47]

Solomon's proverb addresses that point in reverse in its conclusion. The proverb had ended with "so doth a little folly him that is in reputation for wisdom and honour." The dead man that I buried was known for the folly of his evil. Everyone expected it. Everyone would have been shocked if he ever treated anyone with kindness. Even more, had he turned his life over to the Lord, most would have had to watch him for decades, for he had much in his background to overcome. But Solomon was trying to think of himself in a different way. He wanted to think of himself as the wise person he attempted to be in the sight of all the people of his nation and the nations into which he had married. What would they think if, in his despair, he took his life with an apothecary's potion? What if he ended his internal pain with that external oily substance tainted by the poison of the tsetse flies? What would the world think of him? He had a reputation to uphold. He had a standard of honor to keep. Even in his death, he had to be presented to the world as the king in all his glories! If he used the potion, if he fell into that one folly in his distress, the stain would taint his entire life. Listen here!

We have all put on our best of the best clothing. For me, it is always one of my beautiful ties, of which I have hundreds in my closet going back to the first tie that I ever bought with my own money in 1967, earned working honeybees, by the way. It is about an inch and a half wide. Silk. Black. Long. The threads are now rotten, but the memory of that purchase is still there in my heart. It was the style and I was so proud of it. I put it on for the first time, grabbed a soda pop, and ran to the car. Feeling good about myself, I popped the cap on the drink and it spewed on my new black silk tie. At church I tried to wash it off, but I couldn't. From afar the tie looked OK, but up close, it was dreadful. Stained. Stained forever. Stained even today. I looked at it this morning, knowing that I would be in this passage today. It has the same effect on me now that it had then. The same message. The same eternal truth. One silly, unintentional folly, a shake of the soda, ruined the whole thing forever. It is only in one spot about a half of an inch by an inch, but it's right in the middle of the tie where it shows to the world. Ninety-nine percent of the tie is still beautiful, but that which matters is not.[48]

So it is with the folly of sin and evil. One folly can ruin an entire life. Solomon did not want to take that chance.

How many flies would it take to make a pint of oil go bad? Then how long would it take before the oil began to stink? It does not matter how many flies were in the ointment. The flies were simply the means by which the parasites were introduced into the oil. One or a thousand made no difference. Once the parasites were in the oil, the oil was deadly. Surely Solomon's generation knew nothing about parasites. It knew only that when the "death flies" were found in the oil, the ointment was to be abhorred because it was poisonous.

Solomon must have caught himself because he turned to another parable to try to correct his thoughts.

(b) The Parade of the Deluded Fool (10:2–3)
(i) His Left-Handed Heart (10:2)

Solomon already knew that he was a deluded fool. He had come to that conclusion in his example at the end of chapter nine. His first attempt to soothe his aching heart was with a medical suicide that he had rejected. Now a parable came forth to correct him. *"A wise man's heart is at his right hand; but a fool's heart at his left"* (10:2). By the time Solomon spoke these words, the Scriptures available to him had already established the importance and difference between the right and left hands. Looking back to the last days of Jacob's life in Egypt, we see that Joseph brought his sons to Jacob for a blessing. Manasseh was put at Jacob's right hand because that was the place of prominence and importance for the oldest son. It was a sign from Joseph to Jacob that Manasseh was to be Joseph's heir apparent. Ephraim, Joseph's youngest son, was placed at Jacob's left hand. He, too, would be blessed but not with the same esteem as the oldest brother. We also see the same thought brought out in the whole Bible concerning the privilege of being at the right hand of God.

In the culture, the right hand did all the business. Transactions were confirmed with the right hand. It was a pledge of fidelity, given in submission to victors and lifted when taking an oath (Genesis 14:22; 2 Kings 10:15; Psalm 45:9; 60:5; Isaiah 28:2).

The left hand was to be avoided. Even across at least one-fourth of the population of the world today, the left hand is never to be extended to another. Why? As in Solomon's day and before, the left hand was the filthy hand because it was reserved for personal hygiene. Scratching under the surface of this proverb, we see that Solomon was saying that the heart of the wise man was always focused on that which was healthy, powerful, and wholesome, like the actions done in the culture with the right hand. In contrast, the heart of the fool was always on the filthy, the mucky, the soiled side. That is where Solomon felt he belonged, but that was not where he wanted to be. He was considered wise, therefore he needed to do that which was right and not turn to the desires of a left-handed heart.

(ii) His Loud-Voiced Herald (10:3)

Solomon has more to say about the fool and the left-handed heart. He speaks, *"Yea also, when he that is a fool walketh by the way, his wisdom faileth him, and he saith to every one that he is a fool"* (10:3). This proverb Solomon conjures up to further prove that he would not dare do something that would look or sound foolish to his patrons. No doubt he had seen fools in his kingdom and abroad. The proverb means that a fool walks like one, speaks like one, and acts like one at all times. Even when a fool tries to say or do something smart, his words and actions show his ignorance. As Shakespeare said, "The fool doth think he is wise, but the wise man knows himself to be a fool." The loud voice of the fool is most often ignored by the crowd.

Within congregational churches, the staff of ministers conducts business, but the power of the vote is held within the voice of the congregation. Such was the case back in 1969 in a little church in Texas.

> Growing up in a congregational church, I dreaded the first Wednesday night of each month. I jokingly called it *The Monthly Wednesday Night World Fighting Match*. Even at the age of eleven I was readily appalled at the things that were said on the floor of the monthly church business meeting. I remember the first absurd meeting I witnessed. The new item of business turned to the offer of a brand-new free forty-five-passenger bus that would be a gift to the church. The only miles on it would be the ones driven from the factory to our parking lot. The donation value of the commercial bus in 1969 was almost $50,000, a fortune in that day! The offer had actually come before the church the month before, and a committee had been selected to study the gift and bring back a recommendation to the congregation.
>
> The committee brought back the recommendation that we accept the gift. Then, for three hours people from the audience criticized the recommendation and verbally abused each of the committee members personally. One man specifically spoke often, way too often. As an eleven-year-old I had just about had it with that man and his yelling fits. I even thought to myself, "He's a fool." I wanted to say something, but I dared not.
>
> Finally, a man of small stature stood to say the following. "It is clear that the church cannot financially afford the insurance and upkeep of the bus; however, I would like to amend the motion that we accept the bus as a gift and immediately put the unit for sale on my car lot." He further stated that the unit could be sold at as much as a 50 percent discount of its original value and every penny would be brought to the church to pay the entirety of the church debt in full.
>
> The congregation was silent. No one else stood to say anything. Finally, the pastor called for the vote. The bus was accepted. The bus was sold before the next monthly *fight down at the church*. The church was debt free. The loud voice of the fool only stirred the congregation

into a lather. The quiet voice of the wisest and most respected voice of the congregation was the voice of the Lord for that moment.

That night, even though it was late, Benton Cain, a wonderful man of God, asked me if I would come sit with him in the adult choir rehearsal. He had asked before, but I had refused. I thought eleven was a little young for that opportunity of service, but I was big for my age. The next Sunday, I was in a robe and sitting by him in the choir loft during the Sunday morning service. There I would be every week, as best I could, until I took my first position on a staff at a church when I went to college.

Within a few weeks, I began to notice something interesting. I remember thinking, "Those fools who show up every business meeting to cause a fight never attend church." Gently I asked the pastor one day, "Those people who give you grief at every business meeting, are they faithful members of the church?"

"No, not in any way," was his answer.

I did not understand the meaning of what he said until one of my positions on a church staff involved the administration of the finances and attendance of the church. It was then that I understood the loudness of the fools. On one occasion, after a terrible meeting, the pastor and the deacons came to me and asked me to research the books and write a check for every penny the loud fool of the church had given since he joined.

I was shocked by the research. I was amazed. I reported that I had the total for his thirty-two years of membership. I gave them the check. They visited him at his home with his membership card, and they delivered to him a check for twenty dollars and invited him to find another place to worship.

You see, the day he joined the church he gave a gift of twenty dollars and not a cent after. It was a clear example to me of the parade of the deluded fool. I have seen so many now that I can pick them out of the crowd by their behavior and words. I can almost foretell those who will be the fools when they join. Rarely am I wrong. Solomon was the same. His standard for the fool was, of course, himself. Oh, he had seen the fools in the crowd many times. That's part of being a king and a leader. But Solomon was struggling with his own foolishness in his sermon. He had mishandled his power and that was worse than the examples of the fools in the congregation.[49]

(2) Over All That Is Right (10:4–7)
    (a) When Power Is Mishandled (10:4–5)
        (i) The Proper Reaction (10:4)

The triumph of folly greatly affects all that is right in this world. *"If the spirit of the ruler rise up against thee, leave not thy place; for yielding pacifieth great offences"* (10:4). Solomon sees the problem when power is mishandled, and he offers a proper reaction. Do you see it? It is contrary to the teaching of today in the Western world. We have the right of the First Amendment in America. We have the right of the freedom of speech. We have the right to say what we think, when we think, about what we think, without government reprisal, especially when we are abused verbally and physically! Not so in the world of Solomon. One moment you could be laughing and drinking at the right hand of the king in the place of honor. You were drunk, the king was drunk. In the next moment, because you said one word that offended the king, you were down in the dungeon where the executioner has been ordered to swing his ax to sever your head from your body. What could you say then to make amends? Nothing.

When the king awoke from his drunken stupor in the morning and called for his favorite friend to join him for lunch, what a surprise he would have when he found that he had mishandled his power the night before and you were the one on the sharp edge of his anger. Do you see Solomon's counsel? He knew the problem. He was the king! He knew what should be said to the king when the king was out of bounds. Here is his suggestion in modern terms. Stay still. Stay quiet. Stay compliant. It will save you a world of trouble. Solomon was preaching to the choir; his message was for himself; he was the one who let his folly overrule that which was right.

(ii) The Probable Reason (10:5)

Carrying on, Solomon expresses why folly overrides what is right with a probable reason. *"There is an evil which I have seen under the sun, as an error which proceedeth from the ruler"* (10:5). Rulers mishandle things. We all do, for that fact. But with rulers, they have an extra punch to their mishandling of things. We common people can be unhappy, speak our mind, complain why things aren't done, but when the ruler is unhappy, speaks his mind, and complains why things aren't done, punishment usually follows. In Solomon's day, a bystander could be accused and punished with death, then the trial would occur to see if he was guilty or not! It was a great error that proceeded from the rulers of many nations over many years.

(b) When Pride Is Misplaced (10:6–7)
(i) The Dignified Fool (10:6)

Solomon had also recognized that folly often overrides that which is right when pride is misplaced. He had seen the dignified fool and said, *". . . folly is set in great dignity, and the rich sit in low place"* (10:6). Surely, Solomon was looking to the time when his son would take over the kingdom after his death. Rehoboam was the only bloodline heir that Solomon had birthed, and he was the king-in-waiting. We would like to call him the dignified fool but "dignified" might just be too good a word to truly express how foolish he was. In Solomon's life, he never knew just how foolish his son would be. We know because the history records his foolishness. It would have broken Solomon's heart. It would have angered him to the point of changing who would take the throne on his death, had he known. It is the first classic example of the misplaced pride of a dignified foolish ruler. In 1 Kings chapter 12, the Israelites gathered at Shechem to crown Rehoboam as king after Solomon's death. Solomon had made things extremely difficult with his regulations and he had not changed them before his death. The Israelites asked Rehoboam to remove the heavy yoke of regulations from their necks. His evil reply was this:

> My little finger shall be thicker than my father's loins. And now whereas my father did lade you with a heavy yoke, I will add to your yoke: my father hath chastised you with whips, but I will chastise you with scorpions. (1 Kings 12:10b–11)

What a fool! Jeroboam would soon lead the northern ten tribes away from the kingdom in a new nation.

But Solomon had also seen "the rich sit in low place." Let's just be blunt about this. Solomon had done enough dancing around the difference between the wise man and the fool for one sermon. He had more to say than we will cover. Here, he had brought up the idea of wealth. The rich are rich, and the poor are poor. The rich are rich because the rich people do what rich people do. The poor people are poor because the poor people do what poor people do. Even if a poor person inherits the wealth of a rich person, that wealth will soon be gone. Why? Because the poor person will still continue to make the same poor choices and waste the wealth acquired in the same way he has with all the cash flow he has acquired in the past. It is amazing to me, in my business at the Church, that I see hundreds of poor people come through my office seeking financial counseling because they cannot pay their bills as a result of the choices they have made on how they spend the money they earn. Then I am flabbergasted as the meek and mild little couple come to seek counseling on how to prepare what they are leaving behind for their children and grandchildren. They are wealthy beyond imagination. I never would have thought they would be worth so much. I thought the poor person was worth a lot, but he was worth nothing. I thought the wealthy person did not have a dime to his name. Soon I learned to watch the signs of wealth and poverty. The poor flaunted their cash flow, the rich kept their money silent. The money in a poor person's pocket burned a hole in it and had to be spent. The money in a rich person's pocket was safe. The poor loved to spend money; the rich loved to save money. They both loved money but for different reasons and purposes. Misplaced purposes.

Solomon compared what he said was an "evil" to an "error" that he had seen in the world. For some reason, the fool ended up in the place of prestige and the rich man ended up in the place of abasement. But the prestige was misplaced, and the abasement was not. The rich man does not normally want to be out in front with the job of jobs, the position of positions, the esteem of esteems. Rather, he takes his place quietly with the wise and allows the fools to do what they do, be fools with their money.

(ii) The Dandified Flunky (10:7)

Solomon had also seen the dandified flunky when he said, *"I have seen servants upon horses, and princes walking as servants upon the earth"* (10:7). Slaves carried! Rulers walked. He believed this to be an error in societies and unfair. It's part of the misplaced pride that goes along with the folly of that which overrides right.

In one church a new pastor had come on board just as another staff member was leaving for another position. They served together about a month before the staff member left. In just a week or so, an older couple had wormed their way into the new pastor's heart. They would arrive at church and make their way to the front. The new pastor would ask others already in seats to move so this couple could have the front-row view and the front-row experience. Somehow, they were mentioned in every message for some trivial thing. The congregation knew about them, but no one wanted to fill the pastor in on the problem. They were dandified flunkies, both of them.

On the day the staff member was packing up his office, the pastor came in, shut the door, and sat down.

"I need to ask you something."

"What is that?"

"Have I been played the fool?"

"Yes, you have."

"Why did you not tell me?"

"For your own edification."

"What does that mean?"

"It means that you are fortunate that you are at a loving church that will look past your inexperience with people and look to the great potential you have as the Lord's chief under-shepherd with this congregation."

"You told me to keep tabs of the congregation by keeping tabs on their giving. Did you do that on purpose?"

"Yes, I did."

"Why?"

"I learned a long time ago that people speak and vote with their tithes a long time before you will hear them utter a word in private or public or cast a nasty vote in a meeting. As pastor, you need to keep tabs on the giving. Those faithful to the Lord will be faithful to the pastor. They will be your greatest supporters because they will most often be in the center of His will."

"Why did you not tell me about the couple?"

"You mean that they both had been married four times? Both were alcoholics? Both were hypocrites in the faith, users of those in power, and in general like the Judaizers in the Bible?"

"Pretty much! And you left out that they do not trust the Lord with their tithes and offering."

"Yep, pretty much!"

The new preacher was experiencing what the old Solomon had learned in his study of folly and trouble that comes with pride misplaced in the dandified flunky, the one concerned about looks, place, appearance, and social acceptance—a flunky, that is, who is living vainly under the sun.

d) The Triumph of Futility (10:8–15)
  (1) Over the Lawless Man (10:8–9)
    (a) Preparing Evil (10:8)
      (i) Digging: A Great Fall Awaits (10:8a)

It was natural for Solomon to set aside this sermon to present his findings. He had spent his adult life studying humanity from every angle possible. Over the years we have separated the study of human life into categories. Since his day, thousands of people have attempted to do the same: study people. The big areas of study we all recognize quickly—anthropology, psychology, and sociology—but there are many more studies of human life such as philosophy, art history, ethics, biology, chemistry, language studies, kinesiology, human growth and development, anatomy and physiology, history, humanities, and human geography. Thus far in Solomon's sermon, it is clear that he touched on each of these areas even though he did not divide his findings into specific categories as we do today.

When we interact with the individuals who study one of the categories of disciplines we have listed, two things become readily evident. First, the person will generally believe that the area of his study is the "all in all" answer to man's problems. Second, he usually has a hidden personal interest in the field of study and wants to help others avoid the pitfalls he has experienced. What does that mean? Think of the counselor you might hire to help you get through some difficult times. That counselor became interested in sociology or psychology because of personal experience. He became a counselor to offer help to those ailing in the futilities of this life with which he has had to deal. As such, in general, each person who enters a field of study of human life has a vested interest in it. He seems to be trying to find a way to fix himself to overcome the potholes he had dug in his life. To mask his true intent, he presents his research as a desire to help people get through the devastation of the triumph of futility in their own lives. There is nothing wrong with that! God uses people for that purpose in magnificent ways. But the opposite is true, too! Some use the study of human life for evil purposes and bring great struggle to those who need to draw closer to God rather than further away. The tragedy in all the studies of human life today is that they lead away from God, lead to evil, and lead to lawlessness.

Today, we can put highfalutin names on everything that happens. We tend to do that! Everything needs a name, a label, an excuse. Solomon was not that advanced. He just boiled everything down into a few words, a parable. He looked at how people prepare to commit evil and said, *"He that diggeth a pit shall fall into it"* (10:8a). How true that is! Metaphorically, every evil act begins by digging a hole. Deeper and deeper a person digs. Many a person has dug a hole in the yard to plant a tree or shrub then accidently backed into that hole. That was not for evil purposes, but it is a perfect example of just how often a person falls into the hole he dug.

Back in 1965 a young man and his father built a platform in the backyard and permanently mounted on it a dark green two-man, army style, pup tent. For about three years, almost every weekend and most of the nights in the summers the young man would be found sleeping in that tent—rain, sleet, shine or hot, cold, pleasant. Different buddies from the street would often join him. One weekend they noticed that one of the boards was loose. They made it a secret compartment to hide their good stuff. After a while, they decided they wanted to dig a tunnel to China. For weeks they dug! They spread the dirt out on the big yard and dug some more! Down, down, down they dug. It was a grand adventure. The time finally came when the tent was no good—down it came. After a while the uncovered platform rotted, and they took it apart. There was the hole, about a foot deep. The dad had died by that time, so it was the son's job to mow that big yard every week. They had scattered the dirt, so there was nothing available to fill the hole. It seemed like every week for eight years the son fell into that hole when he mowed. He should have known and expected that a great fall awaited.

The same was the case for Solomon. Remember, we said that people who study human life usually have a vested interest in the topic. Solomon did too. He had made a mess of his time as king. Metaphorically, he had dug a huge hole into which he could not avoid falling. Looking back, Solomon wanted to express his problem in a simple way, not profound, because he wanted even the ignorant fool to understand. "He that diggeth a pit shall fall into it," is pretty simple, to the point, experienced by most, understood by all.

Lawless men dig holes for themselves. Those who worshiped the golden calf at the foot of Mount Sinai had gone too far, proverbially dug a hole for themselves in the eyes of the Lord. The earth opened and swallowed them at the height of their evil worship. Dathan and Abiram had led their Reubenite relatives to rebel in evil against the authority of Moses because he did not take them on into the Promised Land after they had voted not to go. When Moses called them to come to the Tabernacle, they refused to heed his word. Moses marched to their tents . . .

> And he spake unto the congregation, saying, Depart, I pray you, from
> the tents of these wicked men, and touch nothing of theirs, lest ye

be consumed in all their sins. So they gat up from the tabernacle of Korah, Dathan, and Abiram, on every side: and Dathan and Abiram came out, and stood in the door of their tents, and their wives, and their sons, and their little children. . . . And the earth opened her mouth, and swallowed them up, and their houses, and all the men that appertained unto Korah, and all their goods. They, and all that appertained to them, went down alive into the pit, and the earth closed upon them: and they perished from among the congregation. (Numbers 16:26–27, 32–33)

The Reubenites had gone too far in their evil. The hole was too deep with the Lord. He opened the earth and swallowed them up. What a picture of sin and its penalty! Solomon has found nothing new in his study—just the natural and logical consequences of evil.

(ii) Destroying: A Great Foe Awaits (10:8b)

But Solomon saw something else in his study and put it in plain simple terms. *". . . and whoso breaketh an hedge, a serpent shall bite him"* (10:8b). The Hebrew word for "hedge" is *gawdare*, and it means an "enclosure," something that surrounds something such as a wall, a hedge, or a fence. In the translation, any of those words would do nicely. The most important word in the first part of the proverb is the word "breaketh," and it means to "tear down, tear apart, or destroy." Evil people do not seek to build something good for humanity; rather, they seek to destroy good for personal reasons. Solomon was a builder. That was one of the reasons he employed Jeroboam earlier in his reign, a move he would later regret. Solomon selected him for his skills of leadership to lord heavily over the forced labor needed to build his self-glorifying projects.

In February of 1999, Dr. John Morgan, the founding pastor of Sagemont Church in Houston, Texas, called one of his staff members and told him he was outside the door and he wanted to take him for a ride to look at a project. They traveled forty miles south to a private fishing club where the owner had just signed over a gift of eighty-seven acres to the church to build a retreat center. Literally, the ink on the documents was less than an hour old.

They had to wind their way through the lakes and down a dirt road by a deep culvert on one side and a thick forest on the other. They stepped out of the truck and were immediately attacked by thousands of vicious mosquitoes.

The preacher looked at the thick forest and said, "I want you to build a lodge right there!"

"Where?"

"Right there! There are three huge two-hundred-year oak trees back in there, and I want you to place the lodge between those three trees."

The staff member paused, stunned in amazement, and took a big swallow. He stuck his hand into the brush, and it was so thick he could not see it just twelve inches in. He retrieved his hand, swatted the mosquitoes, and said, "OK, preacher. What is the budget?"

"I will let you know that later. Get at it!"

"Hmm . . ."

No plans, no money, no time line, no help, no idea what God was going to do. With 105 lakes on the property with every kind of freshwater fish imaginable, snakes were everywhere. On the next Saturday he took a crew of guys and planned to use chainsaws to drop all the trees in the building area. That was most certainly a mistake. Snakes on the ground, snakes in the trees, big snakes, little snakes, poisonous snakes, and more! They were there less than thirty minutes when they decided they needed big, big, big equipment to do the job, and they were right.

Solomon did not have the luxury of bringing in big earthmoving equipment; everything he did was by hand. At any moment a great foe awaited as brush was removed or a wall was broken down to make room for Solomon's project. As with every building project, something had to be destroyed in order to erect something new. He and his men knew about the dangers of snakes. It was a perfect metaphorical example of how evil was alive and active, and all the people understood his intent in an instance. Solomon had a vested interest in the project, he had devised the plan, forced the labor, and, as the first book of Kings tells us, took the nation to the brink of bankruptcy. For one of his projects he had to pay the debt he owed the king of Tyre for the supplies he provided by taking land from some of the northern tribes and giving it to the king. Evil! That land belonged to the heirs of those sons of Israel, not Solomon. It was their perpetual inheritance, not Solomon's. Behind every dirty deal, a proverbial snake awaits. The heirs of the sons of Israel had no idea that when Solomon was forcing them to build his grand complex, they would be forced by him to pay for his dealings with their own land. He was the snake who hid in the wall to bite them when they were through! A lawless man he was. He took what was not his and paid his own debt with it with indifference to the true owners.

(b) Prosecuting Evil (10:9)
(i) Deception Practiced: Hurt Lurks Unseen (10:9a)

But the lawless man does not just start the evil process, he pursues it with deceptive practices. That is what Solomon did with his building projects. He did not care what they cost. As a prosecutor prosecutes the lawless man, so the lawless man prosecutes evil. He waits with his deceptive practices to attack, just as Solomon waited to reveal how he would pay for his building projects. Just like snakes that lurk unseen to attack, so do the inanimate objects, and Solomon speaks, *"Whoso removeth stones shall be hurt therewith"* (10:9a). The people understood this too. Stones cannot do evil. They have no will. They cannot jump out to hurt someone. They cannot plan and lie in wait. Rather, nature must be involved with stones.

In Solomon's day, the biggest problem with moving stones was gravity. The beautiful Temple Solomon began constructing in his fourth year as king had huge stones. The stones were cut at the quarry where workmen used chisels and hammers to fashion the heavy blocks. At Zedekiah's Cave, often referred to as Solomon's Quarry, piles and piles of chipped rocks can be seen even today. More material was chipped away and left behind than all the material of the completed stones carried away. On the walls, the edges and ledges can still be seen where the stones were hewn. No doubt flying stones from the chipping process injured the workmen. The completed stones had to be carried out of the quarry and up to the Temple Mount. All by hand, tied with ropes, hung from poles, placed on the shoulders of the forced laborers, dangerous by all imagination.

Solomon understood the way he had gone about his evil and all those who were hurt by his actions, innocent bystanders who had tried to help Solomon move his stones, but gravity forced the stones upon some of them and hurt them severely! Why was it deceptive in Solomon's mind? Because no one ever knew when the stone would fall. Solomon had made this a physical problem and surely it is! But it also addresses the emotional problem too. Every day when a worker was forced to go to the stone quarry, his family was left behind to wonder, "Will he come home safely? Will he come home unhurt? Will he come home at all?" Such is the deceptive hurt that lurks when an evil, lawless man is in charge.

(ii) Destruction Practiced: Harm Lurks Unseen (10:9b)

Splitting wood was just as dangerous, a simple job where harm lurks unseen with every blow. Solomon says, *". . . and he that cleaveth wood shall be endangered thereby"* (10:9b). Sooner or later, when splitting wood with an ax, an injury will occur. It is not so much a case of "if" but rather "when." The evil man wakes every morning with a plan that could hurt someone, splitting logs was just one of those cases. Solomon did not care how many people were hurt, he wanted the building built. Construction of the building versus destruction of the flesh. One will last much longer than the other, at least in earthly terms, the shortsighted terms of Solomon. The opposite is actually true. Solomon had it wrong. The construction projects were temporary in God's timing, but the humans were eternal!

Nevertheless, swinging the ax was a dangerous business. Solomon had swung the ax throughout his reign, not literally but metaphorically. Looking back, he could see the destruction he had practiced and the harm he had caused unintentionally. As Solomon was speaking this sermon, those he had hurt were bothering him greatly. Their unintentional hurts were just accidents in his mind because he had not intended to place them in harm's way, in the way of his ax, his project, his goal, his plan. But now, all those hurt by his unintentional yet intentional plans were haunting Solomon. It caused him to stop and consider the harm he had done but it also caused him to pause to wonder why the laborers worked so hard on his futile projects.

(2) Over the Laboring Man (10:10)
(a) Why He Works So Hard (10:10a)

Solomon must have wondered about those who worked for him with all his projects. The men labored daily, taking only the Sabbath as a break in the week. Why did they work so hard? The preacher saw something that could not be denied about the workers. *"If the iron be blunt, and he do not whet the edge, then must he put to more strength"* (10:10a). Solomon was speaking about the iron ax in this passage. If the edge of the iron was dull, it took more work to get the job done. If the worker "whet" the edge of the iron, then each cut would do the job faster. "Whet" is an Old English word that means "to sharpen." Interesting enough in the Old English, it was used literally, as in this example, but also figuratively. The Old English, Proto-Germanic, and Middle Dutch used the word figuratively to mean "to incite or encourage." Both physically and figuratively, the meaning was similar: it meant to put an edge on something to get the job done! Solomon had to have wondered, with all his blunders, why the men worked so hard, why they were so encouraged to get the job done for the king, why he would see them "whetting" the edges of their axes to make the work easier and to keep up the pace. Why?

(b) Who He Wants to Heed (10:10b)

Why were the laborers working so hard? Who were they wanting to heed? Was it the king's attention they wanted? When Solomon spoke of the need to "whet" the edge of the iron to make the work easier, he also concluded the thought with *". . . but wisdom is profitable to direct"* (10:10b). The wise laboring man knew when it was the right time to take the ax to the "whetstone" and put an edge on the tool. The dull ax slowed the work, exhausted the muscles, and wasted time. The sharp ax sped the work, spared the muscles, and saved time.

A young child would work with his father in the garage on wood building projects. They started off making cages for small animals such as hamsters, rabbits, and birds. The construction was very rough but easy for a youngster. From that they progressed to picnic tables and backyard furniture, which needed to be a little nicer than the cages, so they were a little more careful about the quality of the cuts. Then when the child was about ten years of age, they started building coffee tables, end tables, a desk, and rocking chair. It was then he learned about grades of sandpaper and hand planers. Everything was done by hand. Few power tools existed for the home back in the 1960s. They used a brace and bit for holes, hand planners for smooth edges with different designs, and hand screwdrivers for assembly. They had a crosscut hand saw, a rip saw, a coping saw, and a hole saw—all manual. Even their lathe for turning spindles was manual with a foot pedal like the old sewing machines. It seemed that every tool always needed an edge to keep it sharp. The "whetstone" was always near and a bottle of oil close by. The file was at hand too. Every time they picked up a tool, they checked the sharpness of the edge before they put it to work. If it was not razor sharp, they sharpened it before they started.

At first, the child thought it was silly. He would work with tools that were dull, and it took him much longer to complete his project than it did his father. He thought it was just because his father was older and more experienced. The father would watch as the child struggled. He would say, "Do you need to put a little edge on that knife?" The child wouldn't want to, so the father would let him struggle. Finally, the child would give up and sharpen the tool. Amazingly, the work would speed up until the tool became dull again. He was learning. But in the process, he always wanted his project to look as good as his dad's. When he followed his lead, cut like he cut, sharpened like he sharpened, routed like he routed, his work would be almost as good as his father's. The child wanted to please him. He is the one the child wanted to heed. No doubt, the workmen in Solomon's force wanted to heed him too. With Solomon, the chances of garnering his attention were slim with hundreds of thousands of men in the force—futile we might say and rarely if ever remunerated.

(3) Over the Loquacious Man (10:11)

Solomon noticed the futility of the loquacious man and said, *"Surely the serpent will bite without enchantment; and a babbler is no better"* (10:11). The word "enchantment" is the Hebrew word *belo lachash*, and it means *without hissing*. A rattlesnake may shake its tail to tell you to get away, but most snakes strike without any warning at all. Even a hissing snake will try to leave when it is afraid and fearful for its life. The point of Solomon's verse is actually easier to understand when turned around to say a talkative talker who slanders you is just as dangerous as a biting serpent! The slanderer will attack you without your knowledge that the bite is coming. Therefore, it is futile for you to think you can do anything to stop it.

(4) Over the Learned Man (10:12–15)
(a) His Words Described (10:12a)

Solomon had also learned that the words of a learned man were futile in this world. He describes the words of the learned man by saying, *"The words of a wise man's mouth are gracious"* (10:12a). Solomon considered himself to be a learned man in the way he used his words. At least the way he attempted to record his proverbs and sayings for posterity was "gracious." His words showed favor toward all, but that was most likely not the norm for Solomon in his daily life and that is the futility he was dealing with in this part of the sermon. But as a learned man, Solomon also noticed something else about words and how they are received.

(b) His Words Disregarded (10:12b–15)
(i) The Words of the Fool (10:12b–14)
(a) They Are Self-Destructive (10:12b–13)
####### (i) Who They Devour (10:12b)

Sometimes words are disregarded by people, especially when they are the words of a fool. Solomon speaks, *". . . but the lips of a fool will swallow up himself"* (10:12b).

A wise man speaks "gracious" words, but a fool cannot stop talking. His words are self-destructive, his words devour him.

(ii) How They Develop (10:13)

Solomon focused on the words of the fool and how his message is developed. *"The beginning of the words of his mouth is foolishness: and the end of his talk is mischievous madness"* (10:13). The fool begins his talk with "foolishness" and he ends with "mischevious madness." The Authorized Version (KJV) uses the English word "mischievous"; it is the Hebrew word *rah*, and the majority of the time this word is translated as "evil" or "wicked" in that version. The word "madness" is the Hebrew word *holelut* and it means "folly." This is the only place that this word is translated as "madness" throughout the Authorized Version (KJV).

(b) They Are Self-Deceptive (10:14)
(i) The Fool's Talkativeness (10:14a)

The fool's words are self-deceptive, and he is talkative. *"A fool also is full of words: a man cannot tell what shall be"* (10:14a). In the fool's "mischevious madness" his words are unpredictable, and he wears people down so that they do not know where to turn.

(ii) The Fool's Thickheadedness (10:14b)

The foolish man is thickheaded. He is unintelligent. He is stupid. He makes thickheaded decisions at every turn and they get him nowhere. Solomon says about the fool, *". . . and what shall be after him, who can tell him?"* (10:14b). Solomon may be speaking in proverbs, but he well understood the tragedy of the meanings behind his sayings. Solomon, as a learned man, had been the fool, he had been the thickheaded one, he had been the one who had come to the end, and where was he? What could be done to change anything he has wrongfully said? How many times had he told the same thing over and over again until even he believed the lie? As a fool he had denied significance, relevance, and evidence by convincing himself of his version of the truth in order to hide the eternal truth! That's the place of the fool's mouth. But what about his work?

(ii) The Works of the Fool (10:15)
(a) The Weariness of His Works (10:15a)

Solomon saw that the works of the fool brought weariness. He said, *"The labour of the foolish wearieth every one of them, . . ."* (10:15a). I must confess, I know this truth all too well. For four decades as a minister I have watched people like this, working in futility and never getting anywhere. Along the way I had to change my mind and heart about them. Why? Someone had to! No one else was going to change the way they felt about the fools we deal with in the ministry and the community. Instead of telling you a story about two or three, let me tell you the characteristics that cause people to be wearied by them. First, they are single focused on some topic of their life. It is all they talk about and think about. It is in essence their job that earns them no money and gets in the way of earning money.

Second, they are never wrong about anything, know-it-alls we might call them. Normal two-way conversations cannot be held with them in any way, any time, for any purpose. They know everything about everything and they are going to instruct and inform you in the right way to get something done or how something should be done or how you should think about something. It, for all practical purposes, is their way or the highway.

Third, they have a mission, a futile mission, and they will use everyone in their path to accomplish that mission. They are relentless in their pursuit of their mission. When normal people see these kinds of people, their guts will drop inside them, and they will do anything to get away from them. I have tried to embrace them, help them, guide them over the past decades, just to be nice, just to be Godly, just to provide a place where they know they can come when they finally hit the wall of reality and seek help.

In all my years, and I have seen hundreds of people every day, I have never seen a fool change in his ways and that wears people out! I have, however, seen a fool change from one futile mission to another futile mission. I often wonder how successful such a person could be if he selected a mission that met the needs of thousands of people, but no, their missions are always self-serving—foolish. And the worst part of it all, they try to enlist others to join their foolish mission.

(b) The Waywardness of His Works (10:15b)

Solomon goes on to define the works of the fool more when he says, *". . . because he knoweth not how to go to the city"* (10:15b). How true! I was very careful in the first part of this verse to describe the characteristics of the weariness of the work of the fool; I must now be extremely careful in discussing the waywardness of the work of the fool. Fools are rarely stupid. The fact is, most of them are extremely intelligent in some facet of knowledge. There are the mathematicians who can work any problem in the world but cannot put a one-hundred-piece tabletop puzzle together. There are the electronic architects who can draw the most detailed schematics but cannot take the actual components and solder them together according to the schematic. There are the musical geniuses who can draft the most beautiful scores but not play a lick. And while those examples apply to Solomon's description of the fool, that may not be the undertone of his intent. Solomon's message truly dealt with common sense. The commonsense person learns how to get around in life, to remember to lock the doors, take out the trash, function in a grocery store, get home from school, clean themselves, clothe themselves. These folks abound in the world. But there is the doctor who can replace a heart valve but does not know how to attach a water hose to an outside faucet. Cannot figure it out! But more than that—he thinks he knows everything about everything and he is the expert. Vanity! Futility!

5. Life's Fickleness (10:16–20)
    a) Something to Watch Out For (10:16–17)
       (1) A Key to Bad Government (10:16)
            (a) An Immature Sovereign (10:16a)

Solomon was thirty years old when he became king. Rehoboam, Solomon's son, who will take his place at his death, was an adult, too, when he took Solomon's place on the throne. Therefore, it is difficult to determine the reason Solomon turned his message to this line of thought. *"Woe to thee, O land, when thy king is a child, . . ."* (10:16a). Why did Solomon give this warning, "Woe to thee . . . when thy king is a child"? This is a topic under the sun that Solomon had to have studied during his life. More than likely this is a topic Solomon had to deal with during his life. More than likely this is a topic that Solomon was worried about concerning his foolish son, Rehoboam. The word "child" is the Hebrew word *na'ar*, and it does not specifically mean a child in chronological age. For example, Solomon called himself a child when he took over the kingdom at the age of thirty (1 Kings 3:7). Joseph was called a child when he was sixteen years of age (Genesis 37:3). Rehoboam was almost forty-one years of age when he took the throne, but he acted like a much younger boy in the way he ruled. As such, he ruled only for seventeen years, not nearly what his three predecessors did (1 Kings 14:21).

Solomon saw just how fickle life could be. Life was uncertain! With all those wives, Solomon surely thought he would have more children from which to choose his successor, but he was stuck with the only child he had. Life was unpredictable! With only one son Solomon surely thought the kingdom needed to be warned to watch out because a bad government was about to be in place when an immature sovereign would take the throne. Life is inconsistent! With all that Solomon had done, he could have surely changed the course of history had he governed differently, but it was too late for him to do anything about it. Rehoboam may have been about forty-one when he took Solomon's throne, but he did not have the maturity to hold the kingdom together.

(b) An Immoderate Senate (10:16b)

Solomon must have known the friends of Rehoboam and he must have had a sneaking suspicion they would become his son's counselors. Solomon speaks, *". . . and thy princes eat in the morning!"* (10:16b). Rehoboam's friends must have been over-the-top as young counselors to the new king. For all practical purposes, they were his senate. When questioned about how Rehoboam would run the country, his young immoderate senate gave him terrible counsel and within days the kingdom was divided with only two tribes remaining under his control. These "princes" of Rehoboam would "eat in the morning." Rather, Solomon was speaking of how these princes devour their food when they awoke! They gorged themselves like at a banquet. Their whole day was upside down, and that was what they wanted to do with the kingdom, change it in every way, and that was the key to a bad government!

(2) A Key to Better Government (10:17)
(a) A Truly Royal Prince (10:17a)

But as fickle as life was, maybe Solomon was wrong about Rehoboam—the more he thought about him, that is! *"Blessed art thou, O land, when thy king is the son of nobles, . . ."* (10:17a). Rehoboam was the son of a noble, and Solomon was a noble in every way, at least in his mind and the minds of all the surrounding nations. He was feared by all. Maybe some of that rubbed off on Rehoboam. Maybe the foolish son at age forty-one would sprout his wings, show his true colors, and rise to the occasion. Maybe he would become a true royal prince on the throne of his father. Maybe if his father was still alive, he would say, "Well done, my son!"

(b) A Truly Responsible Prince (10:17b)

Could Rehoboam turn into that truly responsible prince Solomon wanted him to be? Solomon must have been wishing that when he said, *". . . and thy princes eat in due season, for strength, and not for drunkenness!"* (10:17b). If Rehoboam was going to be responsible, if he was going to bring in a new crop of counselors for his senate, if he was going to be respected by the nation of Israel, he would have to get with the program and make some drastic changes, redirect his counselors, and take the helm of the kingdom in hand and steer that ship into calm waters. Solomon would not be leaving the kingdom in such condition. Jeroboam was waiting in the wings in the west, waiting for Solomon's death. Trouble was bubbling. Could Rehoboam do it? Solomon could only hope! But it was not to be. Rehoboam was the key to the better government for Israel, but he would fail.

b) Something to Wake Up To (10:18–20)
(1) A Warning About Laziness (10:18)

Without a doubt, Solomon was wise enough to see the handwriting on the wall for his kingdom. Much to his chagrin, upon his death, the kingdom would wake up to a new leader with different qualities and characteristics than it was used to. He speaks, *"By much slothfulness the building decayeth; and through idleness of the hands the house droppeth through"* (10:18). Oh, how he knew Rehoboam was lazy. Oh, how he knew that Rehoboam was guilty of idleness. Oh, how he knew that Rehoboam was slothful. Oh, how he knew that his kingdom was about to fall apart. Rehoboam would not do a thing to maintain the house of Israel until it was about to collapse around him—and so it did. Solomon was worried and rightfully so. He had not built the house of his kingdom correctly; the rafters were sagging, the roof was leaking, and the floors were rotten.

(2) A Word About Life (10:19–20)
(a) As to One's Mirth (10:19a)

Oh, the fickleness of life under the sun. Nothing was new! Solomon had seen it all his life. He could not change its path. He could not direct its will. He could not straighten its futility. Vanity of vanities, emptiness of emptiness! When it was all said and done, and he was afraid that his last breath was about to be gone, Solomon could only look back and pick up some of his favorite words about life. First, as to one's mirth he says, *"A feast is made for laughter, and wine maketh merry"* (10:19a). A feast and wine! Food and drink! Gorging and inebriation! Throw away all cares and concerns about life and join the Epicureans and the drunkards. That's where the happiness of life is found! Nothing else really matters.

(b) As to One's Money (10:19b)

But if you have a real problem, Solomon has another word about life for you. A word about life in regard to one's money, *". . . but money answereth all things"* (10:19b). There it is! The fix-all of fix-alls. Money can solve your problems. Money can change your circumstances. Money can bring you happiness. Money can wipe away all pain, agony, heartbreak, distress, hardships. Sure! That's right! That's what money can do! If for no other reason, everyone who reads Solomon's sermons and comes to this point should say, "Stop! That is not true!" This whole message is about how a man without God in his life thinks and nothing thus far truly represents the rest of God's Word. "But money answereth all things" is in direct conflict with the words of the Scripture: "For the love of money is the root of all evil: which while some coveted after, they have erred from the faith, and pierced themselves through with many sorrows" (1 Timothy 6:10).

(c) As to One's Mouth (10:20a)

But beyond money, Solomon has another word about life—one's mouth. *"Curse not the king, no not in thy thought; and curse not the rich in thy bedchamber"* (10:20a). Some things just should never be said anywhere at any time to anyone. Surely do not say it to a ruler, don't even let the thought pass through your brain. Most definitely, never say it even in the privacy of your own bed with the person you love. If it is heard, now or later, there will be consequences to pay. That is the way the ungodly world is.

(d) As to One's Matter (10:20b)

Solomon has one final word about life—one's matter, *". . . for a bird of the air shall carry the voice, and that which hath wings shall tell the matter"* (10:20b). Shhhh! The walls have ears. Shhhh! A little bird will repeat what you have said. Many parents have been embarrassed when their little child repeated their words in the wrong place at the wrong time. Many a prisoner has been convicted by telling his true story to the snitch in the cell. Many jobs have been lost by things said about the boss in jest. Solomon had learned the lessons of this sinful world well. His words were not safe even behind the closed doors of his bedroom. Someone will hear what has been said and retaliate. The rich man will also hear and make things difficult for the average person who has a complaint. It is not fair. To Solomon, food was prepared for enjoyment. Wine was used to make people happy. Money fixes everything. We must be careful about what we say. A little birdie may tell someone what you said, and the bird does not care whom he tells!

The Preacher's Summary

Ecclesiastes 11:1–12:14

a) Remember Your Creator (12:1a)
b) Remember Your Condition (12:1b)
2. Man and His Mortality (12:2–8)
   a) The Outward Permanence of the Heavenly Order of Things (12:2)
   b) The Obvious Impermanence of the Human Order of Things (12:3–8)
      (1) The Increasing Feebleness of the Aged (12:3–4)
          (a) The Arms (12:3a)
          (b) The Legs (12:3b)
          (c) The Teeth (12:3c)
          (d) The Eyes (12:3d)
          (e) The Lips (12:4a)
          (f) The Ears (12:4b)
      (2) The Involuntary Fears of the Aged (12:5a–b)
          (a) Fear of the Heights (12:5a)
          (b) Fear of the Highway (12:5b)
      (3) The Incurable Failings of the Aged (12:5c–e)
          (a) Loss of Dominance—Hair (12:5c)
          (b) Loss of Drive—Strength (12:5d)
          (c) Loss of Desire—Life (12:5e)
      (4) The Inescapable Fate of the Aged (12:6)
          (a) The Spine (12:6a)
          (b) The Skull (12:6b)
          (c) The Blood (12:6c)
          (d) The Heart (12:6d)
      (5) The Inevitable Funeral of the Aged (12:7–8)
          (a) Doom Triumphs (12:7)
          (b) Gloom Triumphs (12:8)
3. Man and His Mind (12:9–12)
   a) The Preacher's Wisdom (12:9)
      (1) His Mission (12:9a)
      (2) His Method (12:9b)
   b) The Preacher's Words (12:10)
   c) The Preacher's Worth (12:11)
   d) The Preacher's Work (12:12)
4. Man and His Mission (12:13–14)
   a) Man's Supreme Duty (12:13)

(1) To Stand in Awe of God's Purpose (12:13a)
(2) To Stand in Agreement with God's Precepts (12:13b)
b) Man's Sobering Destiny (12:14)
(1) Our Outward Behavior Judged (12:14a)
(2) Our Innermost Being Judged (12:14b)

PART 3: THE PREACHER'S SUMMARY (11:1–12:14)
A. He Repeats His Complaints About Life (11:1–10)
1. Look Well to Life's Future Prospects (11:1–6)

Form those prospects, if you can:

a) Be Prudent (11:1–2)
(1) Sow Bountifully (11:1)

Solomon was near the end of his sermon, just a mere few minutes of thoughts left to deliver. He must make the most of them. He must deliver a suitable summary of all that he has said. He must present his point one more time before he draws his conclusion and ends the sermon. He must repeat his complaints found in his discovery of his study of life under the sun. However, he knows he needs to put a new spin on all the dreadful things he has presented in order for his listener to have some sort of hope. He needs to give his listener some sort of direction in order to look well to life's future prospects. He wants his listener to form healthy prospects, if he can, from all that he has to say in this sermon. First, he wants those listening to him to be prudent. With all that Solomon has said, dim, bleak, half-truths, one might think, "What is the use in doing anything in this life at all?" But that is not the conclusion Solomon wishes his listeners to take away from this sermon. He has advice. He wants everyone to sow bountifully in future endeavors. Solomon says, *"Cast thy bread upon the waters: for thou shalt find it after many days"* (11:1).

Based on Solomon's message—his focus on the vanity of life, its emptiness, its senseless future, its direction that when all else fails, "eat, drink, and be merry" for this life is nothing more, so make the best of it now because there is nothing after death—it would be easy to take this verse to imply that Solomon was recommending that a person should cast all sense to the wind, live a carefree life, and take chances with everything! Everything will work out! Don't worry about anything. But is that what Solomon meant in this verse? Let us take a moment to look at three words—cast, bread, waters.

When Wycliffe and Tyndale made their first English translations, they did not use the word "cast," rather, they used the word "send." We are indebted to the men who helped them translate the Hebrew, Greek, and Latin texts into English. They were the first to hammer out the best words that matched what was being said. Neither Wycliffe nor Tyndale dared used the word "cast" in this verse because it was tightly tied to the hurling of dice and figuratively used to take a chance on fortune or fate. Just as the dice were thrown away with no guarantee of a desired outcome, so too, life's events should never be thrown away with no guarantee of anything in return. That might nicely fit Solomon's sermon thus far, but they used the word "send" purposefully. The definition of "send" in their day was to "go as on a journey, to transport to a new place." In other words, control was in place, no random pitch, no careless toss, no thoughtless action.

The word "bread" carries many great and varied meanings in the Word of God. Prior to the work of Wycliffe and Tyndale, a different word was used for what we commonly think of for bread, it was "loaf." Soon, the word "bread" began to appear as the name for the crumbs that fell from the loaf. Through a series of changes in Proto-Germanic and Old English, the word "bread" began to appear to mean "cooked food" or "a piece of food." The reason for this transition of the use of the crumbs to bread applied to certain foods such as baked meat pies and dumplings. By the twelfth century and the time of the translators, it meant "food or sustenance in general." It would be a while before the word "bread" would replace the word "loaf" as we use it today. When the translators were doing their work, they used the word "bread" because it meant food in general and nothing else. Even when the Lord says, "Man shall not live by bread alone, but by every word that proceedeth out of the mouth of God," it means food in general (Matthew 4:4).

The word "waters" should not surprise anyone. It has a breadth of use in Scripture starting with the "waters that covered the earth" in the first chapter of Genesis, to the "voice of many waters" in Revelation 19. We find the waters of the Red Sea in Exodus, the waters of bitterness, and the waters of living creatures in Leviticus, the cedar trees beside the waters in Numbers and the waters beneath the earth in Deuteronomy. And so, you will find such references to "the waters" in almost every book of the Bible. There are the mighty waters, the flooding waters, the multitude of waters, the waters that cover the seas, the heap of great waters, the living waters, the perils of waters, and the fountains of waters. There are the waters of the Euphrates, Tigris, Nile, Jordan, the Great Sea, and more. Suffice it to say, unless Scripture is specific, whatever we call the waters, such as the seas, oceans, rivers, streams, lakes, or springs, the Bible may simply refer to them as "waters." We cannot assume that Solomon is using the word waters for some other purpose such as a parcel of land, a group of people, or some nation. It must mean water of some sort.

Surely Solomon was not suggesting that actual bread should be cast into the water. Bread was too important to life and death. Grain grew only in certain seasons of the year, had to be stored, had to be rationed, and had to be guarded. Casting bread into the water may feed the fish and grow them larger to catch later, but that would be silly advice to give everyone in the world. The fish would like it but the people might starve. It would be better to pull all our understanding of these three words to form a solid theological thought.

Some commentators try to make Solomon's proverb apply to charity toward the poor. But with all the emptiness Solomon has addressed in life, with all the focus he has placed on himself, with the hopelessness he has found in his study of life, specifically his life from his perspective, his eyes were not on charity. His eyes were making a suggestion of how he would do things differently in this short life on earth, how he would brighten his prospects if he had another chance. Instead of importing the essentials of life and paying for them out of the resources of his people, he would send the resources of his people out across the waters of the earth bountifully and after many days, the reward, the profit would return and benefit his nation. To take this to the lowest common denominator, the family, it is virtually impossible for a single family to provide everything it needs to survive on its own without bartering or buying from others. The successful family would focus on one or two products in large quantities to be produced every year and sold for a profit. Specifically, these would be products that everyone needed. That thinking agrees with the virtuous woman found in Proverbs 31.

> Who can find a virtuous woman?
> for her price is far above rubies. . . .
> She seeketh wool, and flax,
> and worketh willingly with her hands.
> She is like the merchants' ships;
> she bringeth her food from afar. . . .

> She considereth a field, and buyeth it:
> with the fruit of her hands she planteth a vineyard. . . .
> She perceiveth that her merchandise is good:
> her candle goeth not out by night.
> She layeth her hands to the spindle,
> and her hands hold the distaff. . . .
> She maketh fine linen, and selleth it;
> and delivereth girdles unto the merchant.
> (Proverbs 31:10–24)

As the virtuous woman sold what she had, what she made, and what she owned, so Solomon suggests in this proverb to "cast thy bread." Not someone else's. Not something stolen. Not something borrowed. Not something that does not exist. Solomon wanted the person to cast what he had to cast, to send it forth across the seas, down the rivers, across the lake, or wherever ships could take it to be sold for a profit. Solomon wished he had done such! This verse is about commerce and what he would have done differently. As with all who have a vested interest, Solomon is trying to help others not to make the same mistakes he did during his life. He may have lived a glorious life as king, but his people suffered greatly because of it and for all practical purposes he took his nation to the brink of bankruptcy. Focus not on the salary he made; instead, focus from where the salary came and the heavy burden he laid on his people. Solomon could have lessened that burden had he exported more than he imported.

(2) Sow Beneficially (11:2)

A second suggestion for Solomon's prudent listener would be to sow beneficially. In other words, in order to look well to life's future prospects, people should *"Give a portion to seven, and also to eight; for thou knowest not what evil shall be upon the earth"* (11:2). All sorts of speculations have been given to this verse through the years. Some have tried to make this apply to giving charity to the poor. Others have tried to make this apply to giving gifts to the Lord. Because the Sabbath is the seventh day, and Sunday is the eighth day that follows the Sabbath and starts a new week, some try to apply this to the faiths of Jews and Christians. We call that "twisting Scripture," and it is common in topical preaching. But because Solomon has just given commercial advice for making a profit (11:1), it only seems logical that in the next breath he would give all the financial advice he could. If Solomon was speaking today, he would say something like, "Men and women, don't ever put your eggs in one basket. Diversify between seven or maybe even eight products that can provide you with a living. You never know when something you are selling will go out of vogue and you have nothing else to offer."

Over the last one hundred years we have seen companies come and go because in some way they did not diversify enough in the market, such as Kodak, Comp-USA, Blockbuster, Radio Shack, Woolco, S. H. Kress, Bombay Company, Sam Goody, and FAO Schwarz. Those are the national names that many will recognize from television ads of the past two decades. But of the mom-and-pop businesses in the small communities across the world, stories abound with companies that have always done what they have always done, and when the market changes, they keep trying to sell the same old product and end up going bankrupt in the process.

To the person with a retirement fund, Solomon would say, "Split that money into seven or even eight different funds." To the sole proprietor or individual, Solomon would say, "Become an expert in seven or even eight areas of business." To the corporation, Solomon would say, "Open seven or even eight different kinds of businesses in your portfolio." Why? Solomon gave the answer, "For thou knowest not what evil shall be upon the earth." Let's put that in modern English: "You never know what bad thing will happen with what you are trying to do tomorrow!" Therefore, be prudent—show care and thought about the future.

      b) Be Practical (11:3–4)
           (1) Things We Cannot Help (11:3)
                (a) The Falling of the Rain (11:3a)

In order to look well to life's future prospects, Solomon needed to tell the people to be prudent, but they also needed to be practical because not all things were going to work out right in all cases. Following up on his thought of "for thou knowest not what evil shall be upon the earth," Solomon names some things that just cannot be helped. He speaks, *"If the clouds be full of rain, they empty themselves upon the earth"* (11:3a). Sometimes that's the best thing that happened for the farmer, which most of the people in Solomon's day were. When the rain came, they were blessed, and they could not stop it. Sometimes that's the worst thing that happened for the farmer when the rain came, they were cursed, and they could not stop it.

Just south of Dallas, Texas, was a farming community in Ellis County. An old Presbyterian farmed all his life on the same land and was looking forward to retirement after that year's crop of cotton was in the gin. The year was great! As things were going forward it looked like he would end his career with a larger profit than he had ever made in his life, one greater than what he had made in the last twenty years. Prices were up, weather was great, labor was cheap, equipment was in good shape. Sure enough, he was overjoyed with prospects. A new process was in vogue for harvesting the cotton. A combine would cut the plants and separate the cotton from the stocks and begin packing the cotton into modules forty feet long, seven feet high, and seven feet wide. One day the cotton was still standing in the fields and the next day the modules were standing in the fields with perfectly formed blue tarps on each unit. After one day's work all the cotton was picked and ready to be taken to the gin. The man had no fear for the future; he and his wife could retire and live out their lives as they had never lived before.

The next process was for large trucks to come and scoop the modules off the ground and take them to the gin. Then, the unthinkable, the unexpected, the horrible happened. It began to rain. You would think that because the cotton had the tarps on it, everything would be fine and that was the case with just a little rain here and there. However, it rained for three weeks straight. The trucks were idle everywhere! They could not get into the fields. The fields were so soaked that literally three inches of water was standing on them. The problem was that the cotton was sitting right on the ground. The protection on the top and sides did nothing to help the bottom. At the bottom, the cotton began to act like a wick and the water soaked all the way to the top of each module. All the cotton was ruined. The farmer's hopes were dashed. Good or bad, if the clouds have rain, it is going to rain! It is one example of something that no one can stop or help.

(b) The Falling of a Tree (11:3b)

As a practical matter, Solomon gives the example of the fallen tree when he says, "*. . . and if the tree fall toward the south, or toward the north, in the place where the tree falleth, there it shall be*" (11:3b). Whether the tree points to the north or to the south, what matter does it make? The tree is on the ground, and that is where it is going to stay. Solomon's two examples make an important point: some things just cannot be helped, some things are not worth fighting, some things are not worth trying to fix, adjust, alter, or lose sleep over. Be practical, Solomon is saying, and roll with the flow of life and nature.

(2) Things We Can Help (11:4)

But Solomon was wise enough to realize that there were things that could make life's future prospects go well! There are some practical things that everyone can do. He says, *"He that observeth the wind shall not sow; and he that regardeth the clouds shall not reap"* (11:4). He's saying, "Look at the signs. Learn the signs. Make your plans according to the signs." Modern-day planting and reaping is different in the last fifty years than it has been for all the centuries since the time of Adam and Eve. We plant with machines that place the seed in the ground and cover it with just the right amount of soil. As long as the ground is still solid enough to get the machine's tires in the rows where the plants do not grow, harvesting can be done under less than ideal circumstances. But for most of history, that was not the case. Planting was literally done by throwing the seed with the hand across the soil. Farmers would not scatter those seeds when the wind blew because it was hard to control where the seed was going and keep it in the prepared soil. When harvesting occurs, rain threatens the harvest. As long as the wheat is still on the stalk, harvest can be postponed. But the moment the stalk of wheat is cut, it must be processed. Even though it can be cut in the field, if it cannot be carried out of the field, the weather will destroy it while it lies on the ground. Watch the signs, is Solomon's message. Be practical! Do the work when it is time to do the work. Do it when you can, not when you can't.

c) Be Perceptive (11:5)
(1) God's Ways Are Beyond Our Knowledge (11:5a–b)
(a) The Way of the Holy Spirit (11:5a)

Continuing with his complaints about life and how to look well to life's future prospects, Solomon adds the idea of being perceptive to God's ways, which are beyond our knowledge. He first speaks of the Holy Spirit and says, *"As thou knowest not what is the way of the spirit, . . ."* (11:5a). Solomon did not have all the Scripture that we have in our complete Word of God. At his fingers he only had the history we have from Genesis to 1 Kings 10, most of the Psalms, his Proverbs, and the Song of Solomon. So much more remained to be revealed through the work of the Spirit of God. We are without excuse. We know what the Spirit's job is and how He goes about His work. Solomon and his generation were still struggling with the things of the Lord and the Spirit. But quite frankly, Solomon did not understand the Spirit because he had not studied Scripture; if he had it would have told him about the Spirit.

We would like to think that Solomon was a mature follower of the Lord, but he was not. He had studied more of the world than he had studied God. God never changes, not the Father, not the Son, not the Holy Spirit. God is the same today as He was before creation occurred. Had Solomon studied God more than man under the sun, and may I add candidly, as it pertained to him personally, he would have understood the way of the Spirit. Nevertheless, this proverb is not without merit. His people needed to be reminded to learn about the Spirit just as everyone today needs to be reminded to learn about the Spirit. It is part of learning the signs, just as we learn when to sow and reap by watching the clouds, so we can learn to live and prosper by watching the work of the Spirit.

(b) The Way of the Human Sperm (11:5b)

We are fortunate today with all our medical technology to be able to look into the womb and watch the growth of the child. That was not the case with Solomon and that is why he says, *". . . nor how the bones do grow in the womb of her that is with child"* (11:5b). Truthfully, nothing has changed. We think we know how the bones of a child grow in the womb, but when we get down to the pure facts, we can only tell you what is happening and why it is happening after the fact; we really cannot tell you how it comes to be. We can tell you how it works, but we really cannot tell you why it works. Why? Because it is about life, and all life begins with God. No one can reproduce it, no one can create it, no one can copy it, no one can make it happen—only God. We can best look well to life's future prospects by perceiving that we will never know or fully understand God's ways until we take our last breath and join Him in glory.

(2) God's Works Are Beyond Our Knowledge (11:5c)

Study as you will. Consume the books. Interview the masses. Vote your convictions. Spout your theology from the moon or Mars if you wish, *". . . even so thou knowest not the works of God who maketh all"* (11:5c). You will be happiest when you finally submit to the fact that the works of God are His works, not yours. Give all the glory to God; it is not about you. Accept the works of God; it is not about you. Enjoy the works of God; it is not about you. Lift your praises to God for all He has done; it is not about you. Share God with others; it is not about you. Use what He has provided in Godly ways; it is not about you. You cannot create what He has created; you can only use what He has created. Use it for good and not for evil; it is not about you. Solomon could not explain the works of God because he had not studied the works of God. Solomon was all about Solomon and he knew it. That is why in this sermon he is finally telling his listeners to accept God's ways, be prudent, be practical, be perceptive, and, finally, be provident!

      d) Be Provident (11:6)
         (1) The Choice We Make (11:6a)

Before leaving the subject of helping his listeners look well to life's future prospects, Solomon says to be provident—that is, make timely preparation for the future. For him, that has to do with the choices we make. He says, *"In the morning sow thy seed, and in the evening withhold not thine hand"* (11:6a). In this world where we do not know the works of God who has made it all, there are things we do not know about, but we do know how to use what He has given us to use. In this case, because most of the world's men were farmers in Solomon's day, we know how to use the land.

Let's back up and follow the progression of Solomon's summary in this chapter. He starts by encouraging everyone to sow bountifully, and then to sow beneficially because that is the prudent thing to do. Then he addressed the practical by telling everyone about the things you cannot help and the things that you can. From there, Solomon attempted to put life in perspective by separating the things of God that we know nothing about, and that leads us to this point in his message where he handles the few things we do know about. In those things, we must be provident, we must be prudent, we must make the right choices. Life is about choices, no matter how you look at it. Every day, every moment, we must make choices. One little hiccup with a poor choice and years of a life's work can be destroyed. The one thing Solomon has to say in this verse as he continues with the context of his summary could be stated like this: "Boys, when the weather is good, and the season is right, get out there early and sow those seeds. Oh, and by the way, keep working through the evening and don't be lazy."

We should pause here to talk about the word "evening." In our Western world we call "evening" any time after 6:00 p.m.—after the normal workday is over. But that is not what the word "evening" means anywhere in the Bible. From the very beginning in Genesis we remember the Lord saying, ". . . and there was morning and evening the first day" or ". . . morning and evening the second day," and so on through the week. Later in the Bible man developed the different watches of the day and night but that had nothing to do with the words morning and evening. Originally, the day was split into two parts by the Lord. Morning lasted from sunrise, or about 6:00 a.m., until noon. At 12:00 noon or what we call *high noon*, when the sun reaches its highest peak and begins its descent, that is the start of evening in Scripture. We call it afternoon in the Western world, but in the biblical account it is called *evening*. When 6:00 p.m., we prefer to call that evening, but in the biblical account it is called *night*. With that understanding, when Solomon suggests that we make the choice to "in the morning sow thy seed, and in the evening withhold not thine hand," he is telling us to work all day and not be lazy. It is the right choice for everyone!

(2) The Choice We Take (11:6b)

Why does Solomon preach that we should be provident and make the right choice? He speaks, ". . . *for thou knowest not whether shall prosper, either this or that, or whether they both shall be alike good*" (11:6b). Solomon has rightly made the most logical, linear progression possible. If he were to say this in plain English today, he would say, "Work hard all day because you do not know what is going to happen in the future. If you work hard, make the right choices, plant your seed, cultivate your fields, chances are, more than not, that your land will provide for your needs." Well, that's a fact. In his day, if you wanted something to eat tomorrow, you'd better have planted it five or six months ago. We are fortunate in America that we have grocery stores that import food from all over the world that is grown as the seasons change from the northern hemisphere to the southern hemisphere and back. By doing that, there is no produce of the ground that we cannot have on our shelves year-round. In Solomon's day, that was impossible. Even the ships in the great Mediterranean Sea took safety in ports and harbors from October until March. No one would risk the cost of a vessel in the winter months to deliver goods. Choices had to be made. Good choices. We really know very little about planning for the winter, storing food, and rationing our resources like our ancestors had to do even up until the mid-1900s. Solomon's words were right. If you wanted to eat, if you wanted to feed your family, you had to work the land from daylight to dusk.

2. Look Well to Life's Fleeting Present (11:7–8)

Fill that present . . . if you can:

a) Light Is An Enjoyable Thing (11:7)

Solomon makes the natural and logical transition to the thought of working under the sun during the daylight hours. He says, *"Truly the light is sweet, and a pleasant thing it is for the eyes to behold the sun"* (11:7). Truly, there is only so much daylight in the day, and the sun constantly moves across the sky. It is a fleeting presence. In general, we have twelve hours of daylight and twelve hours of dark. Twelve hours to work in the field and twelve hours to be with the family and rest. If we can, we should fill the daylight hours with work. The light of the day is an enjoyable thing that should not be disdained. Those who plan evil, do so at night. Those who do evil, in general do so at night. Evil lurks in the night but the righteous work in the day. Enjoy the sun while you have it; make the most of it, and it will make the most of your labor for you.

b) Life Is An Enjoyable Thing (11:8)
  (1) Oh, Happy Day (11:8a)

The light is an enjoyable thing and life is an enjoyable thing. We should think "Oh, happy day!" Every day should be a happy day. Solomon speaks, *". . . but if a man live many years, and rejoice in them all . . ."* (11:8a). This one is easy to apply because we all know the Scripture that says, "This is the day that the LORD has made, I will rejoice and be glad in it." Every day, in every way, in every circumstance, in every trial and tribulation, in every moment of worship, in every song of praise, in every word and deed, rejoice in all of them and be glad.

  (2) Oh, Hateful Darkness (11:8b–c)
    (a) How Endless It Will Be (11:8b)

But we are not promised every day to be happy. Solomon knew that dark days would come, and he said, *". . . yet let him remember the days of darkness; for they shall be many"* (11:8b). In the midst of the dark days, they will seem endless. How endless will they be? Solomon had many dark days and he should have—he rightfully earned every one of them with his ungodly decisions. For those of us who did not follow the path of Solomon, to chase the wind, to study evil, to attempt to learn everything about everything except God, we must admit that we have had our dark days also, but not to the extent that Solomon did. We who have studied God and all His glories instead of the world and all its ill repute look at dark days from a different direction. We see the troubles as opportunities to let the glory of the Lord shine through us to our family, friends, neighbors, and the world. Our attitude is more about God than self. We want people to see our faith in Him so that they will want Him as much as we do. When we accept the Lord as our Savior, our ticket that guarantees our safe passage to be with the Lord for all eternity is punched. The transaction is complete. We are ready to board. Our bags are packed. The itinerary is set. We are heaven bound. We are ready for the Lord to come and receive us unto Himself and take us to the throne of God the Father. In between our accepting the Lord and His coming to take us away from this graveyard called earth, we are all on the sales team of life, living the Godly life, the righteous life. We strive to walk the path that is straight and narrow. Then, when the hiccup comes, we live what we have preached, sung, and testified.

Do you really believe what you sing at the top of your lungs? When the dark days come, do you sing the uplifting lyrics to "I'll Fly Away" and "This World Is Not My Home," or do you turn to the hopeless message of "Day Is Dying in the West"? A preacher said,

Recently, terrible health news came to my door. For most it would have shaken them to their core. It was not good. The stats were not good. The prognosis was not good. I did not flinch one bit. I stood firm in the theology of my life's work, in my relationship with my Lord, and in knowledge that I have been ready for my departure for fifty-one years. When others heard the news, they wanted to pray and beg the Lord for my healing. I let them. I was overjoyed with the first one who asked the Lord to grant me the ultimate healing. He meant a full physical recovery in this earthly life. To me the ultimate healing is the transition from this life on earth to be with the Lord for all eternity.

Soon I realized it was time to talk about God with the folks who wanted to pray for me. "This is not about me," I said. "This is about my Lord." "This is not about praying for my will or your will; this is about praying for His will." "I want you to pray that the Lord will use me in an incredible way every day for the rest of my life. When the Lord brings victories, I want to shout those victories to the world. I want to continue to do what I have been doing since I made Him my Savior fifty-one years ago. I want the world to know who I belong to and I want the world to want Him too."

That calls for a different kind of prayer. How dare we tell the Lord that we want healing in the name of Jesus! He is Jesus. He knows the beginning from the end. He knows me and my time, as well as my value for Him in this world. He also brought a thing called cancer into my life, not to slow me down or lessen my life and ministry but to enhance it, take it to a new level, a new dynamic, a new urgency, a new focus on Him revealed to the lost, hopeless, and dying world. Oh, when the hateful darkness comes, and the days seem to go on and on, they are but a moment in this life, in the whole spectrum of time, just a speck on the calendar of eternity. It is my time to shine for the Lord when the dark days come![1]

(b) How Empty It Will Be (11:8c)

Solomon had not lived the same life that I have had the opportunity to live. He took forty of his years and wasted them on women, songs, projects, and study of all the evil the world had to offer that led him only to emptiness. How empty will it be? He said, *"All that cometh is vanity"* (11:8c). All! That's how much—all! It's all vanity, which means it is all emptiness. Nothing . . . at all! When all has been said and done, when the done is over and life is no more, all is done! Remember Solomon, throughout this entire book, could not see past his death into eternity. He could only look at his past and see his empty failures.

3. Look Well to Life's Frivolous Past (11:9–10)

Forget that past . . . if you can:

> a) A Call to Rejoice (11:9)
>> (1) The Young and Their Good Cheer (11:9a)

And so Solomon looked well to life's frivolous past. His positive suggestions about how to live life led him through his past that he could not forget. Forget the past he should, if he could, but he could not. So he focused on a youth and says, *"Rejoice, O young man, in thy youth; and let thy heart cheer thee in the days of thy youth, . . ."* (11:9a). He called the youth to rejoice. He called the young to live life with good cheer. Live a life of merriment, joyfulness, and optimism. Those are things that you never have to forget if they are in your past. Surely Solomon had some of each, but not enough. That was his fault. That was because of his own grave choices.

(2) The Young and Their Grave Choices (11:9b–c)
(a) What the Young Decide (11:9b)

Solomon remembers his past that he cannot forget. When he was young he made some grave choices that he most certainly wished he had not made. He speaks, *". . . and walk in the ways of thine heart, and in the sight of thine eyes"* (11:9b). He had fallen back to the old theme in his sermon; he had fallen back into the cynical mood that he had left for just a few minutes before when he gave some good suggestions about life. When he was young, he had decided to follow his own heart and to go after the things he had seen that he wanted. It was all about Solomon. He had decided to disregard all others and focus on himself, not God—himself. Such a grave choice led him for forty years—forty years with no spiritual growth. At the end of his life, Solomon was where he was spiritually, a virtual baby in the Lord. Yes, he was king of Israel, but he had blundered in almost every way. Oh, the dire message in this sermon; that of an immature preacher who knows only half-truths and causes more harm than good. No wonder every ungodly cult in the world quotes from this sermon. Even Voltaire, the most godless of the godless French "enlightenment" writers, so they say, quoted from Solomon's sermon (11:1) in his *Precis de l'Ecclesiaste*:

> Wouldst thou too narrowly inquire
> Whither thy kindness goes!
> Thy cake upon the water cast;
> Whom it may feed who knows?

Solomon may have been addressing the youth in his message but, as with the rest of this sermon, he no doubt had been preaching to himself. And no doubt, all preachers do the same. Solomon clearly regretted that he did his own thing, his own way, in his own timing without regard to any consequences. That led him to his next point.

(b) What the Young Dismiss (11:9c)

A self-centered life always leads to a dead end. In his youth, Solomon dismissed
the consequences of his choices. At the end of his life, he could look back and
say, *". . . but know thou, that for all these things God will bring thee into judgment"*
(11:9c). This warning to the youth is actually a confession of the stark reality that
Solomon was about to experience upon his death. Finally, at the end of his life he
had gotten with the program. He had finally come to the finish line unprepared.
He had sinful baggage that he could not shed, that had not been forgiven, that
had damaged his life, his kingdom, and his people. As a youth he had dismissed
that there would be a judgment one day. He had dismissed that he would have
to give an account for everything that was given to him to manage. He had dismissed the fact that he had neglected the Lord's service to serve his own desires.
He had dismissed the fact that he had used his time, talent, gifts, and wisdom in
judgment for carnal purposes. He had dismissed eternal pleasures for the sensual,
the Godly for the godless. Count his many transgressions and name them one by
one. We cannot do that because we were not in Solomon's head, but he could and
in his old age he had remembered them all, and he was about to appear before
the God of all Creation and give an account as to why he had wasted his youth
and his life on worldly gain, worldly extravagance, and worldly exorbitance at the
expense of the nation he had almost bankrupted and people who had to pay for
his debauchery. No wonder we see signs of a despondent preacher in this homily.

b) A Call to Despond (11:10)
(1) The Cynical Challenge of the Sage (11:10a)

Wise he may have been and in his despondent mood he gave a cynical challenge:
"Therefore remove sorrow from thy heart, and put away evil from thy flesh" (11:10a).
We must ask, "Did he really believe the words he had just spoken?" Sure, he does.
He was talking to the youth, or at least all those who were listening to his sermon
who were younger than he was at the time. "Stop worrying about things that
make your heart sorrowful and by all means stop doing evil things with your
flesh!" In other words, Solomon was preaching to the youth and saying, "Don't
be like me. Don't do as I have continued to do all my life. Do as I say, not as I
do!" Was Solomon so despondent that he really thought the youth would listen
to him? Well, he was the king! Maybe they would listen. Today you can just
forget it. Old men are old fogies, and youth may act like they are listening, but

they are not. They are going to be exactly like Solomon in their ways and desires until they have an eternal encounter with the Lord. That will change their lives, not the cynical challenge of an old king who can barely stand up!

(2) The Cynical Chime of the Sermon (11:10b)

Solomon knew better than to think that the youth of the world would listen to him. He knew they would not because he said, *". . . for childhood and youth are vanity"* (11:10b). He knew that the youth in his kingdom were going to follow the impulses of their hearts and respond to the desires of their eyes. Why? Because this life is short! They would not be stopped by their hearts or pain. After all, youth comes only once and will last for only a short period. They have to make the most of it while they can. Soon they will be expected to put away childish things and act like an adult.

Frankly, I don't know why Solomon thought that because he never grew up, not in the Lord at least. The cynical chime of the sermon rings the same from start to finish whether for the child, the youth, or the adult—life is nothing but vanity! Nothing but emptiness. What is here is here and there is nothing after this. Solomon may have studied everything under the sun and his complaints may have been many, but he had never studied the One who made the sun and lived above it. He should have. His father did, but not Solomon. As he looked back, all his life was frivolous! At least that is the way he presented his sermon thus far through eleven chapters. We must remember one more time, the Holy Spirit allowed Solomon to live the life he did and record this sermon for God's glory, not Solomon's. This message was placed in the Holy Writ for one purpose, to show in detail how a godless man thinks. It is a divine book breathed by the Holy Spirit through Solomon's life and word and pen for the purpose of presenting the dark side of life lived without a relationship with the Lord of creation. That is a place no one should be but many choose it. But Solomon is not through. He must end his sermon with a conclusion. What a conclusion it will be about man and his Maker!

<blockquote>
B. He Relates His Conclusions About Life (12:1–14)
  1. Man and His Maker (12:1)
    a) Remember Your Creator (12:1a)
</blockquote>

Solomon's sermon will be through in just a minute or two—only nine sentences remain. But we find them to be packed with a whole plethora of theology about

Solomon's conclusion concerning life. His previous words about one's youth took him to the place he departed from over forty years before. His memories rolled in like thunderclouds. He flashed back to the day he met his Lord, his Creator. Down in the very essence he remembered the most important thing about life. When it all boils down to what matters, what matters boils down to man and his Maker. Here, Solomon spouts his recommendation to the youth of his generation, the recommendation to which he did not adhere: *"Remember now thy Creator in the days of thy youth"* (12:1a).

Our modern translators used the word "remember." It came in the English language in the fourteenth century from the Latin. Its definition included the idea of "recalling something from the past when you needed it." But that was not the intent or meaning of the Hebrew word *zakar*. Although both Wycliffe and Tyndale had the word "remember" at their disposal to use in their translations of the Hebrew, Greek, and Latin into the first English translations, they both rejected it because it did not convey the meaning needed for the original word. Their choices led them to say in their translations, "Have thou mind on." That, we might say, differs vastly from having a memory that can be pulled to mind when needed. "Have thou mind on" means exactly what it says: "Have thou mind on thy Creator." Solomon's recommendation was not wishy-washy in any way. He did not mean that the youth should meet the Lord, tuck Him away in their memory, and pull Him out when they needed Him. Solomon did that, and it did not work out well for him; rather, Solomon's intent in this first word instructs the youth to meet the Lord and never take their mind off of Him! We might say it better like this: "Get Him while you're young children and never let Him go. Keep Him in the forefront of every thought, every whim, every desire, every decision, everything in every way."

b) Remember Your Condition (12:1b)

Solomon goes on to state why the youth need to get their Creator in their minds and keep Him there by saying, *". . . while the evil days come not, nor the years draw nigh, when thou shalt say, I have no pleasure in them"* (12:1b). One's condition in life makes all the difference in the world even as a youth. Those who come to the Lord early in life and make it a point to live for Him get a front-row seat to the blessings of living a good and holy life with what we call *pure living.* The traps of this world rarely capture these people, traps that carnal youth engage in that lead to handcuffs, jail, and detention. The traps of the carnal youth all lead to damage of the brain—mentally, emotionally, spiritually. We all sin, but intentional, major, carnal sins scare a person for a lifetime and affect relationships in the family, community, and workplace. For those who do not come to the Lord early in life may have fun for a season, but that fun comes with a price of brokenness. The tragedy comes when a youth meets his Creator and then neatly tucks Him away until he needs Him. Great trouble awaits that strategy. The Lord abides in a person's life to guide him away from troubles, struggles, and heartache. He protects, directs, and instructs. But when the rebellious believer strikes out on his own, ends in trouble's trap, and then calls on the Lord, He will arrive and help him through the rest of his struggles involved in the process of settling the trouble he found himself in. That does not mean, however, that the Lord will pardon him from his earthly penalty, even though He will pardon him from the eternal penalty.

Many years ago, at a church in Houston, a woman began visiting the fellowship. Every service she attended faithfully without fail. She sat in the balcony, in about the same place every time. As time progressed a great controversy arose over a person on death row, soon to be executed at the state prison in Huntsville, Texas. The story of that life could have been the example Solomon rose to warn about in this passage.

As a child, the prisoner picked up smoking, drinking, and drugs no later than the age of eight. Sexual relationships started at age twelve, and the prisoner left school at age fourteen to follow a rock band as a groupie. Married at eighteen and then divorced. Married again at twenty-one and then divorced. She began to live with a person after that. At age twenty-two the prisoner attempted a robbery and killed two people. Caught, tried, convicted, and sent to death row. During the stay there, the prisoner met the Lord, became a changed person, led many to the Lord, and turned out to be a force for right and the cause of Christ. Churches garnered support and sought unsuccessfully to change the death penalty to life without parole. The battle raged, the headlines roared. The death penalty opponents joined forces with the Christians, thinking this would be the case that would do away with the death penalty in Texas.

But it did not. In February 1998, the prisoner breathed her last breath. That week we found out that the woman who found her way to the balcony so faithfully knew the prisoner—personally. Her child! Her life without the Lord had much to do with the rocky path and struggles of her child. As for the prisoner, to the last breath the testimony hailed, "I am guilty for what I did and for the earthly penalty death awaits, but secure in my future awaits the heavenly reward of forgiveness and eternity with my Lord." Had that person had the Creator in mind early on, even before the age of eight, the path of life and the outcome could have been different. No pleasure can be found in the penalties of this world when the penalties of this world are just. But worldly carnal penalties can be avoided with the guidance and direction of the Lord and Creator if a person allows Him to be a part of every decision every day of one's life. It is important to remember one's own condition of life and make the appropriate choices to live a mortal life with the Lord of Creation.

   2. Man and His Mortality (12:2–8)
      a) The Outward Permanence of the Heavenly Order of Things (12:2)

Man must accept his mortality and the earlier in life the better! But he must also accept that the Lord created an outward permanence of the heavenly order of things. Solomon's words, *". . . while the sun, or the light, or the moon, or the stars, be not darkened, nor the clouds return after the rain . . ."* (12:2), bring to mind an interesting point about mortality—the heavenly order of God's creation far outlasts the days of a man's mortal life. Think of it: we see the sun rise and set every day without fail, whether or not we want it to do its designed business. We cannot stop it if we tried. The moon circles the earth in its required job description and faithfully makes its cycle every twenty-nine and a half days. It never changes and never alters its course in any way. We cannot stop it if we tried. The stars stand in the universe in their set patterns. We can see them at night, but they are there, faithfully in place, even during the daylight hours. We cannot stop them if we tried. We cannot stop the sun from hiding in the night on the other side of the earth or the moon from reflecting the light of the sun when all things are right according to the monthly schedule designed by the Creator. We cannot stop the stars from shining above because they are there, fixed in places, with the sun and the moon to help mortal man. Furthermore, even after the clouds empty themselves with all the rain they can shed, we cannot stop them from forming again and again and again. Mortal man must accept these things as the heavenly order put in place by the Creator.

   We do not really know if they have an expiration date metaphorically stamped on them. After all, the Lord of Creation promised their melting away, but when all of that takes place, we must wait to see. However, with the soul that lives within mortal man, that, my friends, bends to a different time line because the soul of mortal man never dies—its date stamp says "eternal."

b) The Obvious Impermanence of the Human Order of Things
(12:3–8)
(1) The Increasing Feebleness of the Aged (12:3–4)
(a) The Arms (12:3a)

But the eternal soul of mortal man takes its first steps in life in the obvious impermanence of the human order of things, the body of clay, its home or house here on earth. That body or house of clay contains many members, each with an important function involved with the processes of life on this earth. With each day of life, an increasing feebleness begins to show as years begin to pass. Solomon speaks about that too in a series of phrases that describe the state of a person in the last days of life in the mortal house of clay. The first goes like this, *". . . in the day when the keepers of the house shall tremble, . . ."* (12:3a). The "keepers of the house" are the arms. Oh, yes, you will find the hands adjoined to the arms as a vital part in productivity, but the arms do all the muscle work to take care of the house. Think of it this way: the hands cannot get where they want to go unless the arms help them get there.

An interesting background story exists in this verse. With the making of the first English translations, the translators could have used the term "arms of the house." Had they translated the term that way, today we would have readily recognized that Solomon was talking about the upper limbs of the human body, but not so for the readers of the first English translations. In the fourteenth through the sixteenth centuries, the first definition of the word "arm" meant "a weapon." The second definition identified the upper limb as an extension of the arm when it was being used as a weapon. The "coat of arms" was the term used for the armored protection for the body used in war and really had nothing to do with the upper limbs. Our first translators did not use the term "arms of the house" in this verse because it did not properly translate the meaning and because it had nothing to do with warfare. They used the word "keeper."

Here we have another interesting story. In the time of the first translations, the word "keeper" meant "to carry," as in an object in the course of doing work. The housekeepers used their upper limbs to carry out the business of cleaning and managing the home. People used their keepers to saddle the horses, clothe and wash themselves, swing the tools, and haul the supplies. The hands at the ends of the keepers acted like vise grips that latched onto the item, but the keepers did the moving and the hauling, the lifting and the shoving, the pushing and the hugging. Therefore, the word "keepers" was the right word for the original English translations, although our modern translations should make the change to the word *arms* for a clear understanding. Starting here with the "keepers" and continuing through verse eight, we are going to be dealing with the fourteenth through the sixteenth centuries' terms for body parts attached to this house of clay we live in.

As we live each day in these houses of clay, age takes its toll. Feebleness occurs. The arms cannot lift what they did as a youth—they tremble, which causes the hands to shake from side to side. Solomon's sermon attempts to take the young listener to a picture of the end of life so that the youth will not waste his days by following Solomon's life choices and examples. He started with the most obvious, the arms, which are the most important limbs on our bodies for most of the things we must do in life.

(b) The Legs (12:3b)

From the upper limbs, Solomon moves to the lower limbs and says, "*. . . and the strong men shall bow themselves, . . .*" (12:3b). Today, we have difficulty thinking about the "strong men" meaning the legs, but just four hundred years ago, it made perfectly good sense to the churchgoers. The Hebrew word for "strong" is *chayil* and it means "force, strength, or power." The strongest part of a man is his legs. However, as the English translations were taking form, the word "leg," taken from the Norse word *leggr*, still held its Norse definition of the jointed bone of either the upper or lower limb. That would never do for the common man's English translation. Therefore, the translators chose the strict word-for-word translation for *chayil ish* as "strong man" to identify the strongest limbs of the man, the legs. Solomon's words showed the great extent of his understanding of the actions of the human body. As people get feeble, they begin to lean over, to bend. We see the upper body in the unnatural forward position. The trunk of our feeble body does not bend much; what we see bending is the joint that connects the lower limbs to the trunk and we bend at the hips, yet, we do not always notice that association. Furthermore, the knees begin to bend also, and the whole process makes the feeble person look like he is bowing, but actually, the legs are failing in the frailty of old age. Solomon was right to call the legs the strong men of this house of clay.

(c) The Teeth (12:3c)

Solomon continues by speaking about the teeth and says, "*. . . and the grinders cease because they are few, . . .*" (12:3c). The word "grinders" was a common word for the molar teeth, the large teeth at the back of the mouth used to chew food. Our word "molar" comes from the Latin *molaris dens*, which means "grinding teeth." We have to wonder how many teeth Solomon was missing in his old age. More than that, we have to wonder about the pain experienced in getting those grinders out when they were bad. But, perhaps we must understand that the grinders were not removed when they were bad, they were just left to rot in the mouth down to the gum line, virtually gone and no good for chewing food.

(d) The Eyes (12:3d)

The eyes take Solomon's next attention. He speaks, *". . . and those that look out of the windows be darkened, . . ."* (12:3d). "Those that look" out of the house of clay are the eyes, the windows are the eye sockets. So it is that Solomon is expressing how, in the feebleness of life, the eyes can see only a portion of what they saw as a youth.

(e) The Lips (12:4a)

Getting old was difficult enough in the home, being stooped over, shaking hands, and dimming eyes, but when an old person ventured out into the world, one thing would embarrass him just as it does today—the condition of the teeth. Solomon says, *". . . and the doors shall be shut in the streets, when the sound of the grinding is low"* (12:4a). For Solomon, these "doors" were the lips that the old person would keep closed when out and about in the streets in order to hide the "grinders," the teeth that had rotted off at the gums where they no longer made a sound as the food was chewed. It was just part of getting old in the past when dental care was not as much a concern as it is today.

(f) The Ears (12:4b)

Continuing with the things that happen when a person gets old, Solomon says, *". . . and he shall rise up at the voice of the bird, and all the daughters of musick shall be brought low"* (12:4b). For some reason, many old people have traditionally taken great pride in rising from their beds early in the morning when the birds are chirping and rejoicing as the sun rises. In the last two or three decades, this habit has changed greatly. Before that, for most of the world, there were chores that had to be done just to hold the family together before the actual work began that paid the bills. That was the same in Solomon's day. The eggs had to be collected. The cows had to be milked. The livestock had to be fed. The stalls had to be cleaned. The water had to be drawn. Breakfast had to be made, and much more had to be done before the work in the fields or factories began. Getting up early in the morning was the only way to get everything done on time and in time for the health of the family. As people reached the senior adult age, the habit of rising early in the morning was ingrained in the system of the house of clay, and some sort of internal clock would wake the person up even when he was no longer doing those chores. But even though the old folks are getting up with the "voice of the bird," it does not mean that the bird's singing can be heard, because the hearing begins to fade as the years drag on. Solomon, who at one time loved to hear the music of the daughters of Jerusalem, can barely make out the sound of their beautiful voices anymore. You know these daughters. Solomon made them famous in the Song of Solomon. They were the ones who put the pressure on the Shulamite woman to give in to Solomon's advances and become one of them, one of Solomon's wives or concubines. She had the same reply to them no matter how much they pressured her. She was not in love with Solomon; she was in love with another man, her beloved. She would say to those daughters, "I charge you, O ye daughters of Jerusalem, by the roes, and by the hinds of the field, that ye stir not up, nor awake *my* love, till he please" (Song of Solomon 2:7; 3:5). The daughters had no doubt put the pressure on many women for Solomon in the past. They were probably an important part of his luring plan that led him to have seven hundred wives and three hundred concubines. He had heard their voices many times loudly and clearly, but no longer. Oh, what the increasing feebleness of age brings to the body.

(2) The Involuntary Fears of the Aged (12:5a–b)
(a) Fear of the Heights (12:5a)

But more than the physical effects aging has on the body, there are mental effects associated with aging such as a fear of heights. Solomon speaks, *". . . also when they shall be afraid of that which is high, . . ."* (12:5a). It would be natural and quite religious to interpret these words of Solomon to mean the fear of the high places of worship. That would be logical. People who have not entered into a relationship with the Lord should be afraid of the high places of worship of the Creator. The Creator should be feared, but that is over thinking, over spiritualizing, over rationalizing Solomon's words. The preacher has been talking about the effects of aging, and he is going to continue that topic through the next verses. Why would we change the direction of his message to obtain a spiritual outcome? When a person gets to the same health position as Solomon, arms shaking, legs weak, back bent, teeth bad, not seeing, and not hearing, just standing and trying to walk could be considered a great peril. The distance between standing and the ground is a great height. Too many in Solomon's situation have taken that fall and suffered greatly. We use canes, walkers, and wheelchairs now to avoid the falls, but that was not the mind-set in Solomon's day.

(b) Fear of the Highway (12:5b)

When the whole body becomes out of balance physically, the mental abilities do not always catch up with reality. "Why, I have climbed that ladder for years!" "I used to run marathons." "I have climbed Mount Everest, my son!" Yes, the aged people have done extraordinary things in their younger lives, but with age comes feebleness and with feebleness comes inabilities. With inabilities come a sense of wanting to keep your life as it was years before, but that is an impossibility. Even trying to walk on level ground brings a constant fear of the height between standing and the ground. But there are still other obstacles on life's highway for the aged. Solomon says, *". . . and fears shall be in the way, . . ."* (12:5b). The highway of life has many fears caused by bumps in the road, hurdles that must be jumped, and potholes that must be avoided. Think of what you do every day on your highway! You bathe, dress, cook, drive, clean, shop, haul, communicate, plan, and do it all without help. But with age you slowly can do fewer of those things on your own. At first you need help to help you! Then comes the day when you need help to get it done because you cannot do a thing. You cannot even feed yourself much less anything else. Solomon was near that place in his life, and it brought great fear to him. Why?

(3) The Incurable Failings of the Aged (12:5c–e)
(a) Loss of Dominance—Hair (12:5c)

Solomon's great fear of getting old had to do with the incurable failings of the aged. The first sign was the loss of dominance. Solomon speaks, *". . . and the almond tree shall flourish, . . ."* (12:5c). Here Solomon was talking about the hair on the head turning gray. In its season, the almond tree flourishes with pink blossoms. Once in full blossom, it dominates the landscape of Israel with its beauty.

But as the season continues, the beautiful pink blossoms turn to a faded white. The tree shows the age of the season; so, too, the white head shows the age of the aged. But then, with the almond tree, the white blossoms fall from the tree. With age comes esteem in many cases; however, there seems to be a point with all aged people when esteem disappears, and others must take the lead and do for the aged what they can no longer do for themselves. When the independence is gone, the dominance is gone.

(b) Loss of Drive—Strength (12:5d)

There are those who have been serving on the staff of a large church for years. One such church I know of averages eleven deaths every week. Its ministers have walked the path with the aged so many times right to the last breath. They have seen when the loss of drive arrives, when the silent thrust of strength is lost forever. Yesterday the elderly one was feeding himself; today he cannot lift the spoon. Solomon said it like this, *". . . and the grasshopper shall be a burden, and desire shall fail"* (12:5d). How much does a grasshopper weigh? It does not matter; one day the grasshopper will weigh more than the old one can lift. When that day arrives, the desire to fight for life will fail.

In some translations you will find the wording "and the caper tree shall be destroyed." The Authorized Version (kjv) does not translate the passage that way. It simply says "and desire shall fail." Even though the King James Version does not use the caper tree illustration, an explanation is in order. The caper berries from the caper tree or bush had an extremely pungent smell. The berries were carried by those in charge of giving medical care to the sick and dying in war and in peace. When someone lost consciousness, the caper berries were quickly crushed and placed under the nose of the patient. Think of it as an ancient type of smelling salts. We use ammonium carbonate today. When mixed with water, the two ingredients release ammonium gas. When placed under the nose of someone who has passed out, one sniff causes the body to take a breath.

The smell of the caper berry is not near as pungent, but it would usually do the job quite well. If the capers could not cause the mortal body to take a breath, the body was dead. The house of clay with all its intricate veins and arteries, organs and tissues, had just come to a stop. No strength without; no strength within. No strength to carry on; no strength to say goodbye. The drive and strength to live were gone.

(c) Loss of Desire—Life (12:5e)

With the loss of drive comes the loss of desire, the loss of the will to live in the house of clay under the sun. Solomon speaks, *". . . because man goeth to his long home, and the mourners go about the streets"* (12:5e). Where does he go? Where is his long home? The Hebrew for "long home" is *olam* and it means "everlasting, evermore, or perpetual." Our original English translators said it like this: "For a man shall go into the house of his everlastingness." When the mortal house of clay loses its desire, it dies. Life is gone. But even though the body dies, the man who lived within that house of clay moves on, to another home, an everlasting home.

We must stop to look at this word "man." You will recognize the word by just looking at the Hebrew or hearing it said—*adam*. Few know that it actually means *the one formed from the ground*. When Jerome made the first Latin translation from the Hebrew, he used the word *homo* which means "man or human, made from the dust." Here Solomon begins to admit that when a person dies, that person, the one living within the house of clay, leaves that body and goes to live somewhere else. That does not strike well with what he said in chapter three. There he proclaimed that when death came there was nothing else.

> For that which befalleth the sons of men befalleth beasts; even one thing befalleth them: as the one dieth, so dieth the other; yea, they have all one breath; so that a man hath no preeminence above a beast: for all is vanity. All go unto one place; all are of the dust, and all turn to dust again. Who knoweth the spirit of man that goeth upward, and the spirit of the beast that goeth downward to the earth? (Ecclesiastes 3:19–21)

Solomon seems to have changed his tune. In chapter three he was so sure. What had happened to him? Was he not so sure now? No! When he started this message, the Holy Spirit was leading him to record in the Word of God for all time the terrible way a fallen, unredeemed, and lost man thinks about this world and life. In chapter one, he began by telling how his journey of research started, what he studied, and what he discovered over his forty years as king. On that journey, Solomon did not study the Creator and all His majestic glories; rather, he studied the sinful creation and all its dreadful degradation. Every once in a while, he would mention the name of God when it was useful to his cause or when he hit a bump in the knowledge road he traveled and found no other explanation. He studied creation in order to explain life instead of studying God to explain life. Solomon was guilty of apostasy! For the majority of his life he taught half-truths. He used God when he needed Him to convey his twisted view of the realities of life. He reasoned everything according to his standards instead of God's. He questioned the questions in an endless circle of thinking until the answers were watered down to nothing, emptiness, vanity of vanities under the sun. All half-truths.

Solomon was not raised by a father who believed in half-truths about God. His father expressed the truths of God's redeeming Word in songs developed through his life's journey. His father's conclusions perfectly expressed the theology and workings of God from creation to the end of the revelation to man. But our old man Solomon had gotten off the track soon after his father's death. He had abandoned the faith of his father, not so much in word but in deed.

People have quickly, but incorrectly, concluded that Solomon was the wisest man on earth, gifted by the Lord to know how to render judgment, that he was accurate in all his words; but, to tell the truth, much of his words were heresy. His heresy was not against the orthodox thinking of man, for that he was in perfect alignment; his heresy was against the orthodox thinking of God. Just to boil it down, Solomon's basic conclusion about life was simple—what happens in this life is it, when it is over, it is over, and there is nothing after you take your last breath. Nothing has changed under the sun since the days of Solomon about that thinking in the godless world of human knowledge. And yet, with that way of thinking, it is so interesting that the man who has no hope of a life after death still seeks something beyond the something. Down deep in the hole of his hopelessness, he has the urge to keep digging for that special something. When we switch that around, the hopeless actually are hoping for something better than this life after this life. Solomon's father never had that issue, Solomon did. He could not find anyone who could tell him if the spirit of man went up and the spirit of beasts went down. His father knew the answer, but Solomon had blocked his father's faith out of his mind. Solomon searched for the answer, but he could not find it; therefore, his conclusion was that the spirit traveled neither up nor down at death.

But Solomon's message was breathed by the Holy Spirit for a purpose. It was important for the height of apostasy and heresy to be recorded in the Holy Writ and Solomon was the one selected to enter that information into the text. This sermon was a chronological message of how Solomon had experienced the life of apostasy and heresy, his thinking about the worldly and carnal aspects of the frustrating sequences and sequels of life, the fallacies of trying to find all of life's answers in studying the world, and the pessimistic results he had discovered. He retold the problems of living in the world that dealt with time, morality, prosperity, religion, wealth, and aging. He explained his studies that concluded in life's frustrations, fallacies, finalities, falseness, and fickleness. From that, he issued his list of complaints in this sermon and made a suggestion of how to live life well in the future by being prudent, practical, perceptive, and provident.

And then he gathered his gumption, swallowed deeply, and considered the short time left for him on earth and his frivolous past. It was then that he looked back to his youth, his cheers and his grave choices, before he allowed his godless wives to bring their godless theologies into his kingdom. Now he thought about all the warnings that he had for the new generation of youth, the things they should know in order to avoid the godless life he had lived. He finally arrives at the end of his sermon with the realities of life. He wanted to impress the youth to travel a different path than he had, a path of Godliness because the heavenly is eternal but the earthly is terminal. To prove that point he describes his own earthly impairments and comes to this point in the message with the true statement that conflicts with the theology of his younger days, "because man goeth to his long home, and the mourners go about the streets . . ." Solomon has made the journey from his father's theology through the depths of the world's heresy and returned to his father's theology. There is a place beyond the grave for humans that does not exist for beasts. The man, the *adam*, created from the dust, ruddy in every way, goes to his eternal home, whether to be in the presence of the Lord or to be out of His presence for all eternity. It happens in an instant with the last breath, and what does he leave behind? His heritage. Those who love him will spend several days mourning as they walk that last mile in the streets to lay all of the physical things they have left in the grave. Solomon has brought his whole apostate life into alignment with his desire of the One True and Living God of Creation—the Lord Himself!

(4) The Inescapable Fate of the Aged (12:6)
(a) The Spine (12:6a)

The fate of the house of clay of every person is inescapable! It cannot be changed. Solomon is dead-on as he speaks the following words. What caused the death which precipitated the mourners to take their positions as the lamenters of the end of a life? Today, we understand that many of the functions of life and death come through accidents and diseases. With all that Solomon had studied, even in the medical field of his day, he was limited as to what he knew about the cause of death. For all the world of that time, people died due to one of four reasons. Because of that, Solomon tells us what he knows about how a person dies. He says, *". . . or ever the silver cord be loosed, . . ."* (12:6a). We call it "breaking of the back," but more correctly we should say the breaking of the spine. When the spine is broken, the body is broken, and death will soon occur at least in their limited knowledge. The fall that breaks the spine hastens death. Without the ability to move, somehow and some way the lungs are not able to keep themselves clear and congestion develops that is associated with death. We have ways to counter that now, but in Solomon's day those means were not available. The fate of the broken spine, either by act of war or by accident, was death.

(b) The Skull (12:6b)

Solomon had seen the second cause of death due to an act of war or accident and said, *". . . or the golden bowl be broken, . . ."* (12:6b). He was speaking about the skull. Damage to the skull caused damage to the brain and the ultimate result was death.

(c) The Blood (12:6c)

For the third cause of death Solomon says, *". . . or the pitcher be broken at the fountain, . . ."* (12:6c). Solomon was not alone in this discovery; everyone had seen enough death to know that when the house of clay was broken open, and the blood began to flow, death was soon to follow. They knew that life was in the blood. They knew that from before the days of Noah. They had seen how little blood had to be spilt before death came, whether in war or accident.

(d) The Heart (12:6d)

Finally, Solomon addressed the most common of ways death came to the aged, as he says, *". . . or the wheel broken at the cistern"* (12:6d). That was the death Solomon was expecting. That was the death Solomon would get. It was the same for Adam, Noah, Abraham, Isaac, Jacob, Aaron, Moses, and David. They breathed their last breath after the "wheel broken at the cistern" stopped pumping. Of the four ways of death Solomon speaks of here, it is the only one he knew to be a natural death. We, in our advanced knowledge of the human body and its functions, know that for whatever reason, the broken spine or skull, loss of blood, or the stopping of the heart are prime reasons for death. Not so with Solomon and his generation. These four reasons made absolute common sense to his audience, and they do to us today. When the heart stops, life here on earth stops for the mortal house of clay. That leads to the next inevitable and logical step in life's journey.

(5) The Inevitable Funeral of the Aged (12:7–8)
(a) Doom Triumphs (12:7)

Men have died from one of the reasons Solomon has just explained. At death man goes to his eternal home immediately. But what else happens at that moment, besides the mourners beginning their wailing ventures in the streets? In the last part of this sermon, Solomon has correctly tied three parts of the human life together by describing how they come apart at death. The *adam* became the word to name the living soul when the Lord breathed the breath of life into him on the sixth day when his ruddy mortal body was made from the dust of the earth. At death, that part of the *adam* went to his eternal home but what happened to the other two parts, the clay that held the *adam* and the breath that animated the *adam*? Solomon speaks, *"Then shall the dust return to the earth as it was: and the spirit shall return unto God who gave it"* (12:7). Dust returns to the dust; earth returns to the earth; clay returns to the clay. However, you may want to say it like this: the mortal dirt house that holds our souls, that holds our *adam*, that holds who we are who lives in that house of clay, returns to the place from which it came, the dirt. Doom triumphs over the dust, but not over the man.

But in the second part of the verse, Solomon recorded, ". . . and the spirit shall return unto God who gave it." That's the third part of the living man that is so necessary to human life on earth but unnecessary for eternal life. Remember, Scripture repeatedly describes man as body, soul, and spirit. The body is the mortal house of clay; the soul is the man, the person who we are as we live in this body of clay; and then there is the spirit. Solomon agrees with the rest of the Word of God in this last section of his sermon. He separated them as he discussed death—man to his eternal home, body to the dirt, and the spirit to God. The Hebrew word for "spirit" is *ruah*, and it means "the animating energy or vital principle." It was well in use and understood by the mid-thirteenth century in English. Its counterpart in French, *spiritus*, meant the "animating or energy of life." It was associated with breathing or the breath of life in both English and French at the time of our first English translations of the Holy Word of God. The translators chose their words very carefully as they attempted to give an accurate rendering in English of the original Hebrew and Greek words.

From the sixth day of creation, Moses recorded the forming of man like this, "And the Lord God formed man of the dust of the ground, and breathed into his nostrils the breath of life; and man became a living soul" (Genesis 2:7). Here the parts are ordered body, spirit, soul. The order does not matter, the parts are what matter. Solomon affirms Moses' words in this passage. The spirit, the breath of life, was breathed into the *adam* at his creation. That same breath of life was passed on birth after birth through all generations. The miracle of this living clay is passed on to living clay through birth. The spirit animates the body. It is the zing that makes our hearts tick, our brains think, our lungs breathe, our arms move, our legs walk, and our eyes see. But when the body no longer needs the energy that was given from God and passed down through all generations, what happens to it? Solomon told us. It "shall return unto God who gave it." What belongs to God, belongs to God. Doomed by triumph over the dust but not over the spirit.

(b) Gloom Triumphs (12:8)

The funeral is inevitable for the aged. Almost everyone will have one of some kind. For those left behind, a gloom seems to triumph. Solomon most definitely looking ahead to his funeral says, *"Vanity of vanities, saith the preacher; all is vanity"* (12:8). The word "vanity" comes from the twelfth century and was well established in English at the time of the first English translations. It was not misunderstood then as it is now. It meant "that which is vain, futile, or worthless." Throughout his entire sermon, Solomon has reduced everything to the word "vanity." From a worldly, self-conceited position, he is right—everything is futile without God, even death. But Solomon says about the gloom of the funeral, it is the "vanity of vanities." It is the top of the heap. The emptiest of the empties! The conceited of all the conceited! The apex of futility! The most worthless of the worthless! No wonder he sees the gloom in the funeral.

3. Man and His Mind (12:9–12)
a) The Preacher's Wisdom (12:9)
(1) His Mission (12:9a)

In spite of Solomon's study, in spite of Solomon's conclusions, in spite of Solomon's sermon on the "vanity of vanities" of life, the Lord had still given him wisdom and the Lord still used him to teach words of truth. The scribe of this sermon writes, *"And moreover, because the preacher was wise, he still taught the people knowledge"* (12:9a). In other words, even though Solomon was old and death was near, he still had his mind, he still had the preacher's wisdom, and he still had his mission, initiated by the Holy Spirit. Until it was time for his soul to go to his eternal home, his body to return to the dust, and his spirit to return to God, Solomon was going to spend his last days preaching what he had finally learned about God. Knowledge!

(2) His Method (12:9b)

How was Solomon going to fulfill his final God-ordained mission of dispensing his wisdom? By his method! The scribe says, *". . . yea, he gave good heed, and sought out, and set in order many proverbs"* (12:9b). Ah, the blessed book of Proverbs. Now we know! Solomon set about to make sure all his proverbs were available. We have the ones that count, according to the inspiration of the Holy Spirit, recorded in our blessed Scripture. Quite a task for an old man, but his mind was still good, and he was full of wisdom in his aged years to be used by the Holy Spirit, as he was in this sermon where he recorded the carnal side of man's thinking. The first nine chapters of the book of Proverbs were a letter to his son, Rehoboam, as a warning about his future, the pitfalls and perils that Solomon himself had fallen into during his life. Then, the actual sayings of Solomon, the pithy little maxims, begin in chapter ten of Proverbs, words of truth, words that can steer the wayward to safety, were recorded, no doubt after the delivery of this sermon and Solomon's last effort to live a righteous life before his funeral.

b) The Preacher's Words (12:10)

But the scribe tells us about Solomon's continued preaching. He says, *"The preacher sought to find out acceptable words: and that which was written was upright, even words of truth"* (12:10). After delivering the sermon in Ecclesiastes, Solomon had more mini sermons to deliver, not along the lines of the godless man's thinking but along the lines of how to think as a Godly man. The scribe admits that not all the words of Ecclesiastes are truth, they were just the findings of a godless man; however, from that time on, after being led by the Holy Spirit to record this message so the Godly will know how to recognize and avoid the godless, he will preach messages that are righteous in every way as should always be the preacher's words.

c) The Preacher's Worth (12:11)

And so, a proverb was in order concerning Solomon's words as a preacher in his last days of life. Solomon speaks, *"The words of the wise are as goads, and as nails fastened by the masters of assemblies, which are given from one shepherd"* (12:11). The Old English "goads" was the name of a point, spearhead, arrowhead, or pointed stick that was used for driving a herd. Here the Hebrew word is *dorban*, and it means "to prod in such a way as to urge or stimulate." So should be the words of every preacher. Those goading words should land on the listener and stay there like they were attached by well-driven nails. Those who know how to put things together know how to nail them, so they will not come apart. That's the way a preacher's words should be received. That's the way to know a preacher's worth. Are his words nailed to the souls of the congregation in such a way that they cannot be shaken off or torn away? How does a preacher do that? He can only cross that line, obtain that goal, and deliver that kind of sermon when he is preaching the words of the "one shepherd" and we know Him to be the Lord God Almighty. Preach the words of the Lord and the preacher's worth will be known!

d) The Preacher's Work (12:12)

Why did the preacher preach these words? Why did the preacher record all that he had seen wrong with the world and all the world had to say about it? Solomon tells us exactly who the audience for this message was initially when he says, *"And further, by these, my son, be admonished: of making many books there is no end; and much study is a weariness of the flesh"* (12:12). The purpose of this arguably difficult book was directed originally to Solomon's son, Rehoboam, at least in Solomon's mind. It really wasn't! It was written by the Holy Spirit through the pen of Solomon for all mankind but the Holy Spirit placed Rehoboam in the pathway for Solomon to address initially.

There is nothing wrong with that! Timothy and Titus were put in the pathway of Paul by the Holy Spirit so that we could have instructions for the selection of ministers in the Church. Onesimus was in Paul's pathway to get the Word to Philemon. The Romans, Galatians, Ephesians, Corinthians, Thessalonians, Colossians, and more were all in Paul's pathway as a preacher to get the all-important message to all the Church concerning how it is to be organized, how it is to work, and how it is to believe. The Jews were in the pathway of Matthew, the Romans were in the pathway of Mark, the Church was in the pathway of John and Jude. Theophilus was in the pathway of Luke and the Hebrews were in the pathway of James and Peter. The seven preachers of the seven Churches of Asia Minor were in the pathway of John and the Revelation! Ha! Someone is always in the pathway of a message that has a greater audience than originally intended. That's the New Testament; the Old Testament is easier. The nation of Israel was in the pathway of the thirty-nine books that would have an extended audience in the Church and for everyone who has and will ever live. Ecclesiastes is no different!

This preacher's work was to warn his son of the evils of living a half-truth life in a half-truth world, and it was unnecessary. With the work of the preacher focused on the words of the One Shepherd, his son could live a full-truth life in a full-truth world. Solomon had studied all the books, he had wearied his flesh in search of the world's truth, and where did it get him? Nowhere different! As a matter of fact, it led him to a hopeless conclusion, in a hopeless world, in a hopeless life, in a hopeless palace, in a hopeless room, in a hopeless bed, but thank goodness he could still use his keepers and his strong men to raise himself up and stand before his people to preach his eternal sermon of his futile study of vanity under the sun. But his sermon does not end on a hopeless note! Not in the least!

4. Man and His Mission (12:13–14)
   a) Man's Supreme Duty (12:13)
     (1) To Stand in Awe of God's Purpose (12:13a)

Solomon was not through. Two sentences remain. They tell of the true destiny of man and his mission. They tell of man's supreme duty to stand in awe of God's purpose. Solomon says, *"Let us hear the conclusion of the whole matter"* (12:13a). When it is all said and done, there will be a "conclusion of the whole matter." You may get away with all your shenanigans here on earth, but you should not dare think that the inhabitants of this world are the only ones watching. Solomon had played all those games before, he had tried all the tricks, all the mischief, and all the monkeying around with splitting hairs and walking the line between the righteous and the unrighteous. For the most part he lived deep in the ocean of sin and came up for air only when he was desperate for a breath of God. That's how he lived. But as his health failed he became sick of living in a sin-sick world and turned his dim eyes toward God. Why? His kingdom would soon go to his idiot son and it all got to him in a flood of depression as he looked back over his life. Nothing could be done to fix that! But maybe something could be done to fix the future. Therefore, as the preacher he proclaimed to his son, "Let us hear the conclusion of the whole matter." The whole matter has to ultimately return to God because the whole matter began with God. Solomon should never have walked away from God but thank God he returned before he died.

(2) To Stand in Agreement with God's Precepts (12:13b)

Finally, Solomon understood that it was man's supreme duty to stand in agreement with God's precepts. He speaks, *"Fear God, and keep his commandments: for this is the whole duty of man"* (12:13b). Fear God and keep His commandments! That's it, nothing more, nothing less! Do it! That is "the whole duty of man." Whole means whole, it does not mean partial. It does not mean that some commandments need to be followed and some can be ignored. It does not mean that anyone can pick and choose what about God they want to accept and what they want to deny. Had Solomon held to this instruction from the get-go of his reign as king, he would not have even known about most of what he preached in this sermon because he would have run from what he discovered in a fury. He did not fear God for most of his life, but at the end, he feared God greatly as he should have, and so should we.

b) Man's Sobering Destiny (12:14)
(1) Our Outward Behavior Judged (12:14a)

Failing to fear God and keep His commandments has created a sobering destiny for man. Solomon had finally come to realize that our outward behavior would be judged, our behavior here on earth would be judged. He says, *"For God shall bring every work into judgment, . . ."* (12:14a). Now the word "judgment" can quickly shake a person deep in his bones in fear, not the fear of God, but the fear of punishment, especially eternal punishment, everlasting punishment, burning fire punishment. But Solomon's statement is not directed toward punishment, he did not use that word, he said "judgment." That word has a different meaning. It is what I call a two-edged sword, meaning it cuts both ways. Yes, if the judgment finds you guilty, the result is everlasting punishment. On the other hand, if the judgment finds you faithful, the result is everlasting blessing. The same judgment of one's outward or earthly behavior can bring about a sobering destiny of either the best of the best or the worst of the worst. But man cannot see the whole story while living here on earth. He can wonder why the Lord is slow to bring judgment and punishment on earthly things that he clearly considers evil from their outward display. But God judges from a place that man cannot see and cannot understand while he still breathes the air of this world.

(2) Our Innermost Being Judged (12:14b)

Moving from the visible, Solomon turns to the invisible, from the outward to the inward. His last and final words in this sermon concern the things he never could study, he never could grasp, he never could explain, he never could convey. Solomon speaks, *". . . with every secret thing, whether it be good, or whether it be evil"* (12:14b). The ultimate judgment rendered on each life by the Lord will not be based on our outward works, although they will be judged for the purpose of rewards, but the everlasting judgment and eternal home will be determined by the secret thing, the inner things, the way we think, the way of our hearts. Are we good or are we evil? Solomon leaves it for us to decide. If we agree with the majority of this sermon, our hearts lean to the evil side of life.

If we agree with Solomon's conclusion after all the rest has been said and the whole matter has been revealed, then our hearts lean toward the good side. But those words are spoken from an outsider who cannot see within. Neither could Solomon. But the God Almighty of Creation can see right through us. He knows our intent. He knows our heart. He already knows the destination of our soul when we take our last breath because He knows if we are good or evil. He also knows if we are about to make a change in the direction we have been living. He has already completed His part in our story because He knows the beginning from the end, but we do not. Solomon did not. Solomon was playing catch up! When he discovered that he was wrong, as late in his life as it was, he changed directions, and he made it a big deal. He had a son on the wrong path, and he wanted him to know that he needed to change direction too. Solomon had to get back to the commandments of the Lord and so did his family, his court, his city, and his nation. Was it too little, too late? Never! Solomon's presentation of the Word of God changed the hearts and direction of life for those who listened, took the admonishment, and focused on the Lord. That's all the preaching of the Gospel is meant to do. For those who refuse to hear the Word of the Lord, change their hearts and direction, the evil of their innermost secrets will land them in their everlasting place of doom. The words of any preacher, in any generation, in any church, in any town, in any nation, must be like the sword of the Lord that divides the good from the evil. The sword will cut a path for the good to enter eternal life and the evil to enter eternal separation.

I never think of Solomon and this great wail of despair that runs right through this book of Ecclesiastes, as he sits there bemoaning the fact that he made a mess of things, without thinking that the kingdom would never recover from the damage he had done. Never! And he was terrified in his secret soul about the day when he would die, stand before God, and have to look his father, David, in the face and explain to him why he had done what he had done.

Dr. Phillips began this book years ago. At this point, I believe it most fitting that we allow him to finish it in his own words with selected portions taken from the conclusion of a message he delivered to a group of ministers in 1999.[2]

I never think of Solomon, terrified of dying, having lived for the wrong world that I don't also think of the great Apostle Paul. He's sitting in prison at Rome. He's writing to his friends at Philippi. He doesn't know for sure whether he will be executed or exonerated and set free. He'd like to be set free he tells us. He would very much like to be set free and go to Spain. I imagine if you could have looked at his itinerary, you would see that after Spain he would set his heart upon the ten islands of Britain—I do not know why he wouldn't want to go there. And across the Rhine to the Germanic tribes, untold millions still could have been told if he could only be set free. But, on the other hand, he had just as soon be executed and go straight to heaven. Absent from the body, present with the Lord. He'd been there, had a taste of it, and become a heaven addict.

He said, "I have this desire to depart and be with Christ which is far better." The word translated "desire" is usually the New Testament word translated as "lust." Used thirty times, it is translated "lust." He was lusting to go to heaven, because he's been there and couldn't get it out of his blood. "I have a desire," he said. He's sitting in his prison cell, and he thinks it quite likely he might be executed.

That's great. That's fine with him. And he's thinking back over his life. And he's thinking of tens of thousands of men, women, boys, and girls who had come to know Christ because they came to know Paul. He's thinking of country after country, city after city, community after community, which he had personally evangelized. He could say to the elders at Ephesus when they came to Miletus, "I am clear of the blood of all men. There is not a man, woman, boy, or girl in Ephesus that I haven't in some way impacted with the Gospel of Jesus Christ." He could write to the Roman Church from Corinth. He could say, "Don't send any more missionaries up these parts. I have fully preached the Gospel all the way from Jerusalem to Yugoslavia." A great wide swath right across the Roman Empire, thoroughly, completely evangelized. He said, "Job's done. Job's done." He could think of hundreds of thousands of young men and women out blazing Gospel trails because they had been impacted by the life of this great Apostle. This is what he says, "For to me, to live is Christ and to die is gain."

As with Solomon, may we leave it there for you to decide your sobering destiny too. No one can do it for you. The Lord is waiting with open arms for you to purify your secret things that are good, rid yourself of your secret things that are evil, and run to Him right now. How do you want to end up? Like Solomon? Or like Paul?

Appendix

Chasing the Wind

A Summary Message of Ecclesiastes by Dr. John Phillips
Preached in 1999

Introduction

Please turn to the book of Ecclesiastes—your favorite book. Ecclesiastes chapter 1. You know Solomon wrote three books that eventually found their way into the Bible. He wrote one book when he was young and in love, a book of romance. It was really a book about the only woman he couldn't have. She turned him down stone-cold. You can hardly blame her, though, when you come to think about it. When he was proposing to her, he called her a horse. Can you imagine? You would have thought Solomon would have had more sense. How would you like this as a proposal of marriage? He said, "I've got sixty wives. I've got another eighty women that I am living with. As a matter of fact, I've got more women than I can really count, and I am just getting started on my collection. But you can be first!" She said, "Thanks for nothing." She had already given her heart to somebody else—to her beloved shepherd. And when Solomon, as the prince in this world, did everything in his power to get her to transfer her affections from her beloved to him, her answer was sublime. She said, "I am my beloved's and his desire is towards me." She did not say, "I am my beloved's and my desire is towards him." That is not near enough emotion to hold you in an hour of fierce temptation. She said, "I am my beloved's and his desire is towards me." Just imagine in heaven, ten thousand times ten thousand angels, those angels who desire to look into the things that are just part of our Christian life, they desire to look into these things. For them to know that His desire is toward us. Amazing!

So, he wrote one book, a book of romance. He wrote another book when he was at the zenith of his intellectual powers. It was a book of rules. We call it the book of Proverbs. It's the pick of his wisdom. You will notice many of the proverbs have to do with a fool. The reason for that was that Solomon had a fool for a son. His name was Rehoboam, and Solomon knew he was a fool and he could not do anything about it. He'd write all these proverbs; he tried to drill them into this young fellow's thick head and he made no progress whatsoever. I don't feel sorry for Solomon. I feel sorry for Rehoboam. Rehoboam had a fool for a father. No man played the fool more than King Solomon. When he was a young man, he asked God to make him wise. He would have been far better off if he had asked God to make him good. But he wrote this book of Proverbs, a book of rules.

Then, in his old age, looking back over the shipwreck of his life, thinking of all the damage he had done, he wrote the book of Ecclesiastes—it's a book of regrets. He tells us in this book just how the worldly person looks at life, whether an unsaved person or a backslidden believer. He says in verses 12–14, "I the Preacher was king over Israel in Jerusalem. And I gave my heart to seek and search out by wisdom concerning all things that are done under heaven: this sore travail hath God given to the sons of man to be exercised therewith. I have seen all the works that are done under the sun; and, behold, all is vanity and vexation of spirit." May the Holy Spirit add His blessing to the reading of His Word.

ILLUSTRATION—CECIL RHODES AND GENERAL BOOTH

One of Great Britain's most illustrious sons was a man called Cecil Rhodes. When he was a young fellow, he went out to South Africa to make his fortune, and he most certainly did. By the time he was twenty-seven, he founded the prestigious DeBeer's Mining Company and within five short years he controlled all the diamond mining industry of South Africa. He became prime minister of the Cape Colony by the age of thirty-six. By the time he was forty-one he not only controlled all the diamond mining industry of Africa, he controlled all the gold mining industry too. I dare say that Cecil Rhodes, in his day, was the wealthiest man in the world. His legacy to the British Empire upon his death was North and South Rhodesia, a tract of territory in Africa equal to the size of France,

Germany, and Spain all put together. It so happened that he was a personal friend of General Booth, the founder of the Salvation Army.

One day they were riding across Britain together by train, and General Booth leaned across to this multibillionaire friend Cecil Rhodes and said, "Tell me, Rhodes, are you happy?"

And Cecil Rhodes looked at General Booth for a moment and said, "Me? Happy? Good heavens, no!"

He had learned what Solomon had learned, that neither power nor prestige, popularity or anything else under the sun can make a person happy.

ILLUSTRATION—SPIDER IN THE BARN

There's an old Danish fable that tells of a spider that came down from the lofty rafters of the barn with a single thread. Down he came. Then he anchored his strand to the corner of the window of the barn. From that strand he wove his web. Well, he had chosen a very busy corner of the barn and waxed fat and prospered. In his prosperity, one day he was walking across his web and he happened to notice this long strand that reached up into the unseen and he had long since forgotten its significance. He thought it was just a stray strand of no importance and he reached up and snapped it. Instantly, his whole world caved in. That's what Solomon did. When he was a young man he established diplomatic relations with heaven. Then he waxed fat and prospered. In his prosperity he broke off his relationship with heaven. His world caved in.

ORIGIN OF SOLOMON'S TEXT

In this book Solomon looks back over the shipwreck of his life, and he preaches a sermon when he says, "I the preacher was king." It is a sermon. And since it's a sermon, of course, it has to have a text. It is not a philosophical discourse, it's a sermon. Thus he chooses his text. Do you ever wonder where Solomon found his text for this sermon? "Vanity of vanities, says the preacher; vanity of vanities, all is vanity and vexation of spirit." Well, he got it from Psalm 39. Psalm 39 says, "Behold, thou has made my days as a handbreadth and my age is as nothing before thee. Verily every man at his best state is altogether vanity. Selah!" Now when you come across that little word "Selah" in the Hebrew hymnbook, it can be translated into the American vernacular, "There, what do you think of that!" Selah.

God had come down to see him. God had become troubled up in heaven over what had been happening here on earth. He had been to see Solomon twice before

He came again. And He took a tour around the city and on every green hill he could see idols and altars to pagan gods. He could see where Solomon had made offerings to these idols. He had been down into the valley of Hinnom and seen that dreadful god Molech down there. One of the most terrible gods ever conceived in the demented mind of fallen man. The great wrath thing, hollow on the inside. They would build a fire (in its belly) until it roared like a furnace and glowed like a fierce fire. Then they would beat the drums until it would drown out any noise and they would take a little boy or a little girl and place the poor child on the red-hot lap of Molech. And Molech would tilt back, and the little child would go down into the inferno inside. To think that Solomon had put one of those things in Jerusalem! God went to see him. He didn't send a prophet, He didn't send an angel, He went to see him Himself. He said to Solomon, "If it wasn't for David's sake, I would do it right now. But for David's sake I am going to wait until you are dead. But I am going to tear your kingdom in pieces." I see a shaken Solomon sitting in his palace library, his face is white to the gills, and he is shaking in his shoes. The Divine Presence has been there and gone! He is thinking of what he has done. The damage he has done! By the time he had finished with Jerusalem, he had turned it into Babylon. I can see him as he reaches up, perhaps instinctively, to the library and pulls a book down from the shelf that must have been a copy of the Hebrew hymnbook. He starts to turn the pages, and all of a sudden these words leap right out at him from the page, what we would call Psalm 39. "Vanity! Vanity! All is vanity!" That became his text, you see!

OVERVIEW

In this book we have the preacher's subject in chapter 1, the first eleven verses. Then we have the preacher's sermon down to the end of chapter 10. Then in the last two chapters we have the preacher's summary.

PREACHER'S SUBJECT

His sermon is centered on the text, vanity. It means chasing the wind. That's what he has been doing for years. He had been chasing the wind, he had been living for the wrong world. He had sown the wind, and now he was going to reap the whirlwind. He was looking for something to salvage from the shipwreck and wreckage of his life. He decided he will preach this sermon, he will then write it down, and he will dedicate it to the young people of the land in the hope that they will have more sense than he had. "One generation passes away," he says, "another generation comes." "The sun gets up; the sun goes down. The wind blows toward the south, it turns around, it blows toward the north. Whirls about continually! All the rivers run to the sea, yet the sea is not full. The eye is not satisfied with seeing nor the ear with hearing." He says, "If you are going to live your life under the sun, if your life is to be dominated by the things of time and sin, if you are going to only live for what this world has to offer, then there is no point or purpose in anything. You just go round and round and round and you don't get anywhere, you just get older." That's his subject!

Preacher's Sermon

Now when he comes to his sermon, it has three points. He tells us about some of the things he had sought, and some of the things he had seen, and some of the things he had studied. A three-point sermon.

Things He Had Sought

He tells us about some of the things he had sought. He went in for three things. First of all, as a young man, he had decided to find the real ultimate answer to life under the sun. Maybe you could find the answer in the world of thought.

World of Thought

He decided to become an intellectual, and he became the greatest intellectual of the age. People came from the ends of the earth to sit at his feet in the university of Jerusalem of kingship. The Queen of Sheba came all the way up the long reaches of the Nile, across the sands of Sinai, and up into the hill country of Judah just to sit at his feet, listen to his wisdom, and try him with hard questions. And she said, "The half was never told me. You, sir, are the greatest." When Solomon had achieved success in the world of thought and the king's sons came from all over the world to attend his lectures, and he had all the knowledge and all the understanding and all the wisdom that was uniquely his, and he had achieved his goal of becoming an intellectual, he said, "I perceive that this is vexation of spirit. Just to become an intellectual, just to have a half dozen doctorates, cannot make you happy. It cannot even make you wise."

World of Thrills

Having tried the world of thought, he said it was obvious it was not there! "I have studied everything, I've looked at everything, I've examined everything, I know everything about everything, I'm going to try the world of thrills." And he became a playboy. He said, "I will say in my heart, I will prove you with mirth, therefore, enjoy pleasure." And he did, he abandoned himself to the lust of the flesh. Gave himself over to worldly enjoyment. Anything that the mind of man could conceive, that the mind perhaps could entertain, he went in for it! He abandoned himself to it. His harem was enormous, his resources were boundless, his rivalry was unstinted and unrestrained. If you had gone past the royal palace in Jerusalem when Solomon was living it up, going in for the world of thrills, you would have listened to the beats, the heartbeats of the music and obscene dancing on the lawns and things going on around the palace there that would have made people in Sodom blush. The world of thrills. He went in for everything. You name it, he tried it! When he had satiated himself, along that line he said, "I said of laughter, it is mad." I think that he almost went over the brink into insanity. Many a person who has gone in for the world of thrills has done that. A very slippery road indeed.

World of Things

Then he pulled himself back and said, "Obviously it is not in the world of thought, I've tried that. I've tried the world of thrills, it's not that. Maybe I think I'll try the world of things." He became a mercantile prince. He built a great commercial empire. His camel caravans went right across the Fertile Crescent, down into the exotic markets of the distant east, and his great Tarshish ships plowed the seas to bring the wealth of the world to his warehouse. And he had the Midas touch; everything he touched turned to gold, and he was extremely successful in business. He had everything that money could buy. He had ten of everything. He had a hundred of everything. He had warehouses filled with stuff. And when he succeeded in the realm of things, he said, "I hated life. I hated life." I think that you can read into that that he had actually contemplated whether or not it would be just as well he should commit suicide. These were the things that he sought.

Our educational system in this great country is dedicated to three things: to getting young people to achieve in the world of thought or in the world of thrills or in the world of things. But when you've got it all, all you've got is nothing. You've just been chasing the wind.

Things He Had Seen

After he told us some of the things he'd sought, he goes on to tell us some of the things he'd seen. "I perceived," he said. He keeps on saying, "I perceived." It occurred to Solomon, "Well, maybe I missed it and somebody else has found it." He kept his eyes open, looking to see what could be seen. Maybe he'd missed something.

Illustration—Picture of Vanity

When I first came to North America I was with a very large Canadian bank. They sent me clear across the country to British Columbia, then to the interior. And there in the interior of the great heart of the lumbering business in Canada, we met some folk who were in the lumber business. One of these men became a friend of ours, and he invited us to his home one day for a meal, and we went. He had a lovely log cabin on the edge of the bush. We went in and sat down. I was sitting on the couch, and right in front of the wall opposite to me there was a picture. It was a picture of a grinning human skull. It was a horrible thing. It didn't matter where you looked, your eye went right back to it. It just hung there and seemed to jibber at you across the room, you know. I thought to myself, *What would ever possess a man in his right mind to put a picture of a grinning human skull on his living room wall?*

By and by the man's wife said supper was ready and everyone trooped off into the dining room, and I made a detour by way of the picture. When I got up close to it, it wasn't a picture of a skull at all. It was a black-and-white pen and ink drawing done by an artist. It depicted a beautiful woman sitting in front of a vanity mirror—an old-fashioned vanity mirror, kind of a circle. In front of her she had an array of jars and bottles and things. And she'd obviously been spending her time on nature because she was admiring the end result. She had done a pretty incredible job on herself. She had piled all her hair up on top of her head somehow and she had, well, just done a nice job. She looked pretty nice.

Well, it satisfied my curiosity, and I stepped back from the picture. And as I stepped back farther and farther from the picture, all the different parts began to come together again. The round mirror became the dome of the skull, the woman's black hair and the reflection of it became the empty eye sockets, and the jars and bottles she had were the grinning teeth. So, by the time I got back across the room, all the different parts had blended back into one, and there it was, the skull grinning at you across the length of the living room. Underneath, the artist had written this one word, "Vanity." It is this concept of death writing the word vanity across everything under the sun that is the second part of Solomon's sermon.

Summary of Things He Had Seen

He tells us, for example, the vanity of time without eternity, the vanity of a new leaf without a new life, the vanity of mortality without immortality, the vanity of might without right, the vanity of prosperity without posterity, the vanity of religion without reality, of wealth without health, of life without length. Vanity.

Example—Vanity of Time Without Eternity

For example, just to take the first one, the vanity of time without eternity. Solomon decided quite young in his life that he was going to organize his life and going to have a time and place for everything. And so, he did! He became a thoroughly organized individual. He had a time for this and a time for that, a time when you did this and a time when you did that, then a time when you did something else, and his whole life was regimented and ruled and regulated so that every single passing moment of time might contribute something to his enjoyment. He wasn't going to waste a single moment of the preciousness of time. But then he said, "You made everything beautiful in its time. But, you have set eternity in our hearts." What's the use of having time when you're engineered for eternity?

Illustration—Thomas Chalmers

I suppose one of the greatest preachers ever to come from Scotland was a man named Thomas Chalmers. In his early days in the ministry he wasn't saved. He was very clever, very gifted, a decent fellow. A pastor, but not saved. In fact, he wasn't much interested in the ministry except it was just a means of making a living. What he wanted to do more than anything else was to be a professor of mathematics at the University of Edinburgh. He wrote a little pamphlet, had it published. In the pamphlet he said that he had proved by personal experience that any pastor worth his salt could discharge all his pastoral obligations in three days, leaving the rest of the week to pursue whatever avocation it was that he set his heart on. And he set his heart on being a professor of mathematics. Then came his conversion and his blessed ministry—a benediction and a blessing to multitudes of people.

Toward the end of his life he was in a meeting of the synod of his church and there was one man there who disliked him intensely and was jealous of him. And he stood up in front of all the other assembled members of the clergy and he began to read this pamphlet that Chalmers had written years ago. And he read it, underlining and emphasizing the low views of the ministry that it espoused.

And then with a sneer he turned to Chalmers and said, "Tell me, sir, did you write that?"

Chalmers, stunned to the quick, jumped to his feet and said, "Yes, sir, I wrote it. Strangely blinded as I was, I wrote it. But you see, sir, in those days I aspired to be a professor of mathematics in the University of Edinburgh. But, sir," he said, "what is mathematics? It is magnitude and the proportion of magnitude, and in those days, sir, I had forgotten two magnitudes: I had forgotten the shortness of time, and I had forgotten the length of eternity."

Solomon forgot those two magnitudes. He forgot the shortness of time; he forgot the length of eternity.

Things He Had Studied

These were some of the things that he had sought and some of the things he had seen. Now he tells us some of the things that he had studied. He becomes increasingly obsessed with the fact of death. Solomon, in the book of Ecclesiastes, was not a happy man. He was a haunted man. And in the book of Ecclesiastes, he introduces us to the ghost that haunted him. That ghost was death. It haunts every material-minded person. It is never very far away. Its shadow sometimes falls upon us and we feel its chill, it comes near then goes away for a while. But it is always there. The absolute certainty—death. Solomon becomes increasingly obsessed with death. Because death, he says, awaits everybody. It doesn't matter whether you are young or old, wise or foolish, whether you are good or bad, whether you are optimistic or pessimistic, glad or sad, gifted or lagging. What difference does it make? You are going to die. It comes creeping into your bedroom sometimes at nights, and you wake up from a terrifying dream. Thank God it was only a dream, but the ghost is still there. One day, and perhaps sooner than you think, you are going to die. "Why shouldest thou die before thy time?" Solomon says. "There is one event unto all," he said. "They go to the dead. A living dog," he said, "is better than a dead lion." "The dead," he says in a classic statement of mistruth, "know not anything." Why, that is not true! Why, that is perfectly true because that is what the worldly-minded man thinks, or would like to think, but it is not true. The dead know a whole lot. The rich man in hell woke up to be a believer too late. Believed in preaching but too late. Believed in praying but too late. He knew a whole lot, he had five brothers! He said, "Father Abraham, father Abraham, send Lazarus, he used to sit at my gate. Send him down here with a drop of water."

That was denied. No way from heaven to hell or from hell to heaven. "Impossible," he said, "request denied."

"But," he said, "I've got five brothers, send him to them."

"No," says father Abraham, "they've got the Scripture, they've got Moses and the prophets. Let them believe them."

"No, no, no, no, father Abraham, if you will send somebody from the dead they will believe."

"Oh no," says father Abraham. "If someone rose from the dead, they wouldn't believe." Have you ever noticed that the very next man that Jesus raised from the dead was a man called Lazarus? Now it wasn't the same Lazarus, but it was a man called Lazarus.

And so, Solomon is obsessed by the fact of death. "The dead," he said, "know not anything!" No, that's not true. They know everything. They can remember. That's what God said to this lost man. He said, "Son, remember, just remember." He would remember a meeting like this, he would remember exactly where he sat, and he would remember how the Spirit of God tugged at his heartstrings and how he stifled the Holy Ghost. "The dead know not anything," no the dead know everything that concerns them. But it doesn't help them. "Between you and us," Abraham said, "there is a great gulf fixed."

I was interested years ago to discover that the word "gulf" is the Greek word *casper* from which we get our English word "castle." The scholars tell us that it is one of Luke's medical words. It refers actually to an "open wound." That's what God says to the lost, "Between Me and you, there is an open wound, and I never lose sight of it, you put it there!" And He said with the redeemed in heaven, "Between you and us, we have this open wound."

God will not payment twice demand.

First at my Savior's pierced hand.

And then again at mine.

PREACHER'S SUMMARY

So, you have the preacher's sermon. In the closing chapters you have the preacher's summary. He repeats his complaints about life and he relates his conclusions about life and addresses himself to the young people of the kingdom and he urges them, and he begs them, and he prays over them that they won't do what he did—live for the wrong world. All of a sudden you know that it is all over and you can't go back, you can't change a single line of anything you have ever written, you can't change a word of anything you ever said. Can't undo anything that you have done. What a terrible thing to all of a sudden find that the sand has run out. You are going to die. You got nothing but wood, hay, and stubble to put at God's feet—the feet of His Son.

I never think of Solomon and this great wail of despair that runs right through this book of Ecclesiastes, as he sits there bemoaning the fact that he made a mess of things, that the kingdom will never recover from the damage he has done. Never! And terrified in his secret soul, of the day when he will die and stand before God and have to look his father, David, in the face and explain to him why he had done what he had done.

I never think of Solomon, terrified of dying, having lived for the wrong world, that I don't think of the great Apostle Paul. He's sitting in prison in Rome. He's writing to his friends in Philippi. He doesn't know for sure whether he will be executed or exonerated—set free. He'd like to be set free, he tells us. He would very much like to be set free and go to Spain. I imagine if you could have looked at his itinerary, after Spain he would set his heart upon the ten islands of Britain—I do not know why he wouldn't want to go there. And across the Rhine, the Germanic tribes, untold millions still untold if he could only be set free. But, on the other hand, he'd just as soon be executed and go straight to heaven. Absent from the body, present with the Lord. He'd been there, had a taste of it, and become a heaven addict. He said, "I have this desire to depart and be with Christ which is far better. This desire."

Do you know that the word translated "desire" is the usual New Testament word for "lust"? Used thirty times, translated "lust." He was lusting to go to heaven because he's been there and couldn't get it out of his blood. "I have a desire," he said. He's sitting in his prison cell and he thinks it quite likely he might be executed. That's great. That's fine with him. And he's thinking back over his life. And he's thinking of tens of thousands of men, women, boys, and girls who have come to know Christ because they came to know Paul.

He's thinking of country after country, city after city, community after community which he had personally evangelized. He could say to the elders at Ephesus when they came to Miletus, "I am clear of the blood of all man. There is not man, woman, boy, or girl in Ephesus that I haven't in some way impacted with the Gospel of Jesus Christ." He could write to the Roman church from Corinth. He could say, "Don't send any more missionaries up these parts. I have fully preached the Gospel all the way from Jerusalem to Yugoslavia." A great wide swath right across the Roman Empire, thoroughly, completely evangelized. He said, "Job's done. Job's done." He could think of hundreds of thousands of young men and women out blazing Gospel trails because they had been impacted by the life of this great Apostle. This is what he says. He says, "For to me, to live is Christ and to die is gain." How do want to end up? Like Solomon? Or like Paul?

Notes

Introduction
1. Emma Frances Bevan, "None but Christ," c. 1860.

Part 1: The Preacher's Subject
1. Lord Byron, "On This Day I Complete My Thirty-Sixth Year," 1824.
2. Isaac Watts, "Oh God, Our Help in Ages Past," 1719.
3. Alfred Edersheim, *The Bible History*, vol. 5 (Grand Rapids: Eerdmans, 1959), 70–102.
4. Wilbur M. Smith, *Therefore Stand* (Natick, MA: W. A. Wilde Co., 1945), 248–61.
5. David Brewster, *Memoirs of the Life, Writings, and Discoveries of Sir Isaac Newton*, vol. 2 (Edinburgh: T. Constable and Co., 1855), 407.
6. Charles Dickens, *Bleak House* (Cambridge: Riverside, 1869), 72.

Part 2: The Preacher's Sermon
1. Two psalms are ascribed to Solomon (72 and 127). One of them closes the second book of Psalms, and the other is the central psalm of a series of 115 psalms known collectively as "the Songs of Degrees." Some think that Psalm 72, however, was really written by David, written after Solomon's second investiture (1 Chronicles 29:23) in the year before David's death. Psalm 127 was likely selected by King Hezekiah, centuries after Solomon's time, and put by him into the collection. The childless condition of Hezekiah must have drawn him often to this old hymn.

2. Banesh Hoffman, "The Unforgettable Albert Einstein," *Reader's Digest* (Jan. 1968), 111.
3. Robert Burns, *Tam o' Shanter* (London: Marsh and Miller, 1830), 6.
4. John Bunyan, *The Pilgrim's Progress, From This World to That Which Is to Come: Delivered Under the Similitude of a Dream* (London: Samuel Bagster and Sons, 1845), 116.
5. See John Phillips, *Exploring Proverbs*, 2 vols. (Grand Rapids: Kregel, 2002).
6. Roy Gibbons, "Alcohol the Legal Drug," *National Geographic* (Feb. 1992).
7. Alfred Edersheim, *The Bible History of Judah and Israel* (London: Religious Tract Society, 1880), 100–101.
8. See John Phillips, *Exploring Genesis* (Grand Rapids: Kregel, 2001).
9. E. W. Bullinger, *Number in Scripture*, 6th ed. (London: Lamp Press, 1952), 282.
10. See John Phillips, *Exploring the Love Song of Solomon* (Grand Rapids: Kregel, 2003).
11. See Phillips, *Exploring Proverbs*, vol. 1.
12. Beryl Bainbridge, *Every Man for Himself* (New York: Carroll and Graf, 1996), 36.
13. J. J. Neave, "A Crown of Amaranth," in *A Basket of Fragments* (London: Headley Brothers, 1899), 214.
14. John Phillips, *Only One Life: The Biography of Stephen F. Olford* (New York: Loizeaux Brothers, 1995).
15. D. M. Panton, *Expiation by Blood* (London: Charles J. Thynne & Jarvis Ltd., n.d.).
16. Herbert Asbury, *A Methodist Saint* (New York: A. A. Knopf, 1927), 24.
17. W. Garden Blaikie, *Thomas Chalmers* (Edinburgh: Oliphant, 1896), 23–24.
18. Institute for Creation Research, *Evolution: Science Falsely So-Called*, 15th ed. (Toronto: International Christian Crusade, 1963), 84.
19. See John Phillips' *Exploring the Future, Exploring the World of the Jew*, and *Exploring Revelation*.
20. Bunyan, *Pilgrim's Progress*.
21. Jim Corbett, *Man-Eaters of Kumaon* (New York: Bantam Books, 1964), 27–37.
22. Graham Scroggie, *The Unfolding Drama of Redemption* (1976; repr., Grand Rapids: Kregel, 1994), 383.
23. Pearl S. Buck, *The Good Earth* (New York: Washington Square, 1931), 63.

24. H. Rider Haggard, *Colonel Quaritch, V.C.: A Tale of Country Life* (New York: Longmans, Green, and Co., 1911), 120–21.

25. Jeffery Farnol, *The Definite Object* (Boston: Little, Brown & Co., 1917), 12–21.

26. Charles Dickens, *A Christmas Carol: A Ghost Story of Christmas* (Mineola, NY: Dover, 1991), 2.

27. Maurice Herzog, *Annapurna: First Conquest of an 8000-Meter Peak*, trans. Nea Morin and Janet Adam Smith (New York: Dutton & Co., 1952).

28. See Bullinger, *Number in Scripture.*

29. Walter Martin, *The Maze of Mormonism* (Santa Ana, CA: Vision House, 1979), 26–27, 331.

30. Martin, *Maze of Mormonism*, 47.

31. See notes above on Ecclesiastes 1:15b.

32. See notes above on Ecclesiastes 5:8.

33. See John Phillips, "Chapter 18: The Law of Mention," in *Bible Explorer's Guide* (Grand Rapids: Kregel, 2002), 126–31.

34. See John Phillips, "Psalms 49—Worthless Wealth," in *Exploring Psalms*, vol. 1 (Grand Rapids: Kregel, 2002), 386–93.

35. See John Phillips, "Boasting in Our Prosperity," in *Exploring the Epistle of James* (Grand Rapids: Kregel, 2003), 163–71.

36. Phillips, *Exploring Proverbs*, 2:157–58.

37. Phillips, *Exploring Proverbs*, 1:386–87.

38. John Phillips, *Exploring Romans* (Grand Rapids: Kregel, 2002), 190.

39. Phillips, *Exploring Proverbs*, 1:255–57.

40. James Sire, *Scripture Twisting: 20 Ways the Cults Misread the Bible* (Downers Grove, IL: InterVarsity, 1980), 7.

41. Phillips, *Exploring Proverbs*, 1:126–27, 155–56.

42. This testimony from Dr. Jim Hastings was written for this commentary.

43. From Dr. Jim Hastings.

44. From Dr. Jim Hastings.

45. Adam Clarke, "Adam Clarke Commentary Ecclesiastes 9," StudyLight .org, accessed August 13, 2019, https://www.studylight.org/commentaries/acc /ecclesiastes-9.html. Originally published in 1832.

46. From Dr. Jim Hastings.

47. From Dr. Jim Hastings.

48. From Dr. Jim Hastings.

49. From Dr. Jim Hastings.

Part 3: The Preacher's Summary

1. From Dr. Jim Hastings.
2. Throughout this volume I have expounded on a sermon preached by Dr. Phillips in 1999. You can read the complete transcript of this sermon in the appendix on pages 351–61.